The Presidency of
LYNDON B.
JOHNSON

AMERICAN PRESIDENCY SERIES

The Presidency of
LYNDON B.
JOHNSON

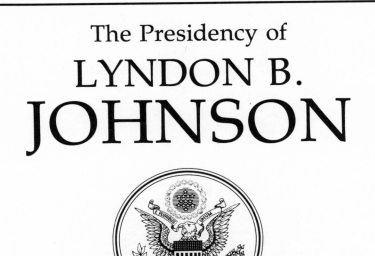

Vaughn Davis Bornet

UNIVERSITY PRESS OF KANSAS

© 1983 by the University Press of Kansas
All rights reserved

Published by the University Press of Kansas (Lawrence, Kansas 66045),
which was organized by the Kansas Board of Regents
and is operated and funded by Emporia State University, Fort Hays State
University, Kansas State University, Pittsburg State
University, the University of Kansas, and Wichita State University

Library of Congress Cataloging in Publication Data
Bornet, Vaughn Davis, 1917-
The presidency of Lyndon B. Johnson
(American presidency series)
Bibliography: p.
Includes index.
1. Johnson, Lyndon B. (Lyndon Baines), 1908-1973.
2. United States—Politics and government—1963-1969.
3. United States—Politics and government—1961-1963.
I. Title   II. Series
E847.B63   1983   973.923'092'4 [B]   83-12560
ISBN 0-7006-0237-2
ISBN 0-7006-0242-9 (pbk.)

Printed in the United States of America

Portrait of Lyndon Baines Johnson drawn by Louis Lupas
in the winter of 1965/66. Reproduced by permission
of the artist and the Lyndon Baines Johnson Library.

To librarians and archivists everywhere,
with special gratitude for the
friendly services of the librarians
of Southern Oregon State College
in Ashland, Oregon.

CONTENTS

FOREWORD

The aim of the American Presidency Series is to present historians and the general reading public with interesting, scholarly assessments of the various presidential administrations. These interpretive surveys are intended to cover the broad ground between biographies, specialized monographs, and journalistic accounts. As such, each will be a comprehensive, synthetic work which will draw upon the best in pertinent secondary literature, yet leave room for the author's own analysis and interpretation.

Volumes in the series will present the data essential to understanding the administration under consideration. Particularly, each book will treat the then current problems facing the United States and its people and how the president and his associates felt about, thought about, and worked to cope with these problems. Attention will be given to how the office developed and operated during the president's tenure. Equally important will be consideration of the vital relationships between the president, his staff, the executive officers, Congress, foreign representatives, the judiciary, state officials, the public, political parties, the press, and influential private citizens. The series will also be concerned with how this unique American institution—the presidency—was viewed by the presidents, and with what results.

All this will be set, insofar as possible, in the context not only of contemporary politics but also of economics, international relations, law, morals, public administration, religion, and thought. Such a broad approach is necessary to understanding, for a presidential administration is more than the elected and appointed officers composing it, since its work so often reflects the major problems, anxieties, and glories of the nation. In short, the authors in the series will strive to recount and evaluate the record of each administration and to identify its distinctiveness and relationships to the past, its own time, and the future.

The General Editors

PREFACE

Few presidencies will be recalled, reconsidered, and reassessed so often in future years as that of Lyndon Baines Johnson, thirty-sixth chief executive of the United States. His five years in office, from late 1963 to early 1969, were a dramatic period in which the American people were brought face-to-face with crucial questions of public policy. One was the appropriateness and feasibility of waging an undeclared war in a very distant theater for mixed and partially understood goals. Another was how far the national government should go in trying to legislate full civil rights, provide education to the extent of everyone's potential, seek at some cost to eliminate poverty, spend to control crime, fund the arts and humanities, create public radio and television services, and pursue new departures in conservation. This administration also engaged in activity designed to conquer space and to minimize the danger of thermonuclear war. Striking successes were achieved in many important areas. Yet, acutely anxious to pursue utopian goals, this presidency was not alert to the dangers inherent in making unrealizable promises. There was also excessive devotion to party well-being; overregulation; distortion of the balance between national, state, and local responsibilities; invasion of privacy by intelligence agencies; and increased federal spending that paved the way toward inflation of the currency. The most catastrophic decision, it turned out, was choosing to wage an open-ended Vietnam War for democracy and against communism without having the goal of quick military victory.

This book appears to be the pioneering effort to assess this famous presidency in all of these, and other, aspects. Its year of publication coincides with the twentieth anniversary of President Johnson's entry into office and the tenth anniversary of his death. Substantial subjects are treated here for the first time within a volume focusing on this leader and his associates. Since many of the sources of information have not been used before, only a tiny handful who lived very close to Johnson during those 1,886 days should be in a position to say they "knew all that" already. While these pages are necessarily judgmental, the effort to be fair should shine through. Readers who are familiar with some biographical accounts of this colorful man's earlier years will find that this book addresses the far more fundamental and substantial matters that occupied his maturity. From the beginning, my determined purpose was to produce a decent and balanced portrayal of this White House leader, so that readers completing the entire volume might emerge with a somewhat increased insight into their own troubled era.

I can recall reflecting, when I was chosen by the series' editors as the one to tackle this task, that some aspects of my life—probably unknown to them—might have prepared me rather well for what lay ahead. Living over the years in four different sections of the country, and in urban, suburban, and rural environments; life in the military and as a civilian; and experience teaching coursework directly related to the present assignment—all should have had a payoff. I was closely associated with a major scholar during book projects designed to appraise the leadership of Herbert Hoover and Franklin D. Roosevelt—rehearsal for this effort. Exposure many years ago to talented and diverse professors at Emory University, the University of Georgia, and Stanford University, and to editors and research personnel in four nonprofit organizations, may have provided pertinent knowledge and ideas with some relevance to this enterprise. As for archival work, it began for me in 1939/40 and has been reasonably continuous ever since.

This project has been an entirely individual effort, engaged in several thousand miles from Johnson City and Austin, Texas, and from the nation's capital. Beginning in fall, 1975, three research trips to the Johnson Library, during which my wife, Beth Bornet, and I lived comfortably with our shepherd dog, Penny, in our travel trailer in the Lake Austin City Park, enabled me to use library archives during the day and book resources during evenings and weekends. Our initial trip was partly financed by the Southern Oregon State College Foundation, the second by ourselves, and the third by a modest grant from the Lyndon Baines Johnson Foundation. Many drafts were read aloud to my wife, and an overly long semifinal draft was checked for press style by an old friend, Mrs. Lorraine Lang. Donald McCoy was my understanding liaison with the editors of the American Presidency Series.

The dedication of the book speaks for itself. It derives from years of obligation on my part. Reading-room archivists at the Johnson Library—especially supervisory archivist Tina Lawson, together with Linda Hanson, Gary Gallagher, Claudia Anderson, David C. Humphrey, and others—handled my many requests professionally. My contact with library administration was Charles Corkran, the assistant director. The friendship of Gary Yarington, museum director, meant much. The Southern Oregon State College Research Committee funded some of my xeroxing costs. Timely and expert typing was done by Mrs. Lang and by Mrs. Elizabeth Wilson and Mrs. Sandy Fisher. I will always be indebted to my physician, internist John Reynolds, M.D., whose promptness, kindliness, and skills helped me toward recovery from a heart attack remarkably similar to Senator Johnson's. My wife brought to innumerable conversations about the tone and orientation of the manuscript a lifetime of experience with people and organizations.

The frontispiece is a winter 1965/66 drawing of Lyndon Johnson, created during sittings at the White House and the LBJ Ranch, by distinguished portraitist Louis Lupas, who also sketched three other presidents. His work for the Johnson family earned him the tribute from Lyndon that "he captures me best." Reproduction here is through courtesy of the artist and the Johnson Museum.

The Presidency of Lyndon B. Johnson seeks to contribute to public understanding of an emotional period that brought improvements in life style, personal rights, and education to many, but strain, suffering, and even the supreme sacrifice to others. While this book focuses on the presidency—and is not a biography—it often displays the central figure in the Oval Office: a southwestern politician, born on the American frontier, who sought both power and the stature of a statesman. Here was a leader with a character that some have sharply criticized. His unique personality was one that all admit to have been invasive, but he won the admiration and even affection of many who served him—virtually all of whom emerged better trained and stronger from the experience. This executive's seriousness of purpose and the loftiness of his spoken goals, combined with his unparalleled ability to convince persons of substance to follow his leadership, made him an effective force for massive changes in the status quo.

It seems altogether likely that Americans in coming years will find it necessary to thank this president, even as they will still feel forced to blame him. Such thanks and blame, like oil and water, have not yet blended into a single accepted perspective. Even the passage of decades is unlikely to change this. Academic historians who were polled in the early 1980s assessed him as the tenth-best president. Experience indicates that such a view may well swing back and forth in the decades to come, with new research and writing, and with changes in national preoccupations as events dictate. I should especially like to think that my years of lonely work and thought, which have produced this volume, will help at the very least to shorten such swings in the pendulum of appraisal and thereby hasten consensus. Whatever President Lyndon B. Johnson would have thought of the portrait of the presidency in these pages, I know he would have applauded this goal.

Vaughn Davis Bornet

Ashland, Oregon

1

★ ★ ★ ★ ★

INTO THE OVAL OFFICE: 1963

The possibility that Lyndon Johnson, who for nearly twenty-four years had been a member of Congress, might someday become president of the United States increased when he took the oath as vice-president on January 20, 1961. The southwestern politician and legislator from rural Johnson City, Texas, a "hill country" town near Austin, was prepared to spend John F. Kennedy's presidential days in a subordinate but, he hoped, constructive role. What he left behind was the influential post of majority leader of the Senate, where most paths led to his powerful office and person. In his new position he soon selected the task of acting as liaison with America's space effort, served as chairman of the President's Committee on Equal Opportunity, and made short visits for the president to thirty-three countries. He would make one hundred and fifty speeches during the years of his residency at the Elms, but policy formulation remained squarely in the charismatic president's hands.

Although the vice-president advised the president behind the scenes, those years when the nation was experiencing disasters and excitement—such as the Bay of Pigs, Berlin, the Cuban Missile Crisis, the Vienna summit meeting with Khrushchev—were for Johnson a time, as he put it, of "trips around the world, chauffeurs, men saluting, people clapping, chairmanships of councils," in short, "nothing."[1] But America's most expert legislative political figure was getting to know how it felt to be in the executive branch of the government. Since 1931, with only short intermissions to direct the National Youth Administration for Texas and to serve as a navy lieutenant commander in 1941/42, he had lived in segregated Washington, D.C. There he had walked the corridors of the House: from 1931 to 1935 as a clerk; from 1937 to 1949 as a representative. Since then he had served as a senator with ever-increasing national stature.

This leader's youth had encompassed a short experience as a high-school principal and social-studies teacher and a brief stint as a lobbyist for a teachers' group. He had attended the 1928 Democratic National Convention in Houston while he was editor for the student newspaper of Southwest Texas State College. Before graduating from that San Marcos college with a B.S. and a teaching credential, he had become a talented debater, worked as student clerk in the president's office, and packed a lot of weight in campus affairs. Earlier, after high-school graduation, there had been some months of manual labor during and after a junket to Los Angeles, before he abruptly chose to attend college, thus pleasing his mother and "showing" his father.

The heritage of this man was that of small-town America in the last days of frontier conditions. His father, Sam Ealy Johnson, who had been partially successful as a farmer-rancher, a real-estate man, and briefly as a teacher, had served in the Texas legislature. His mother, Rebecca Baines Johnson, was a small-town newspaper columnist and housewife whose grandfather had founded Baylor University. The birth of Lyndon on August 17, 1908, their first-born, was a most welcome event for the parents, whose regard for him contributed to his personality and character development. His first years were spent in a small house by the Pedernales River, but during the eleven years of his elementary and secondary schooling, the family resided fairly comfortably in a white wooden house that was the equal of any adjacent to the customary dirt streets of small Johnson City. His was not normally an upbringing in abject poverty—no matter how often he would say so on the stump in later years, but there were certainly ups and downs in the family's circumstances. At home and at college he displayed leadership qualities and a strong desire to prevail whatever the obstacles—thus evoking from his companions envy, irritation, or grudging admiration.

Since what Lyndon was actually like by the early 1930s has been sharply disputed, we may do well to peruse the letter of recommendation that gave him his opportunity to become secretary to Congressman Richard M. Kleberg. Said fellow Congressman W. K. Hopkins to his colleague's influential friend Roy Miller, "I know this man to be honorable, ambitious, capable, well informed on public questions, quick minded, nimble witted, resourceful, and gifted with a very unusual ability to meet and greet the public. In fact, for a long time I have considered him the brightest and one of the best all-around young men I know and have long hoped to be able to assist him in advancing his interests."[2] There were also rough edges and traits not likely to be incorporated in such a letter. Soon the time would come when he would be aided by a loving wife and happy in possession of daughters Lynda and Luci. His love for young children would later emerge as a very well marked characteristic of his maturity.

The years to World War II and beyond were to prove fruitful not only in politics but in the amassing of influential friends. A financial competence, however, came only slowly. By the early Senate years the husband-and-wife team had accumulated a considerable fortune, chiefly through purchase of a then-unimportant radio station in Austin. They developed it, with permission from the Federal Communications Commission, into a monopoly TV outlet with network affiliations. There were also investments in real estate, ranch land, and bank stock. The marriage to Claudia Alta Taylor of Karnack, Texas, who was universally called Lady Bird, had brought under one roof his political, calculating mind and her intelligence—partially the result of training in journalism at the University of Texas at Austin. She proved to be strikingly adaptable to business matters. By the mid 1960s they would have assets that totaled from $3 million to $14 million or even more, depending on whose appraisals are accepted.

The mentors of legislator Johnson were such political figures as President Franklin D. Roosevelt, Senator Huey Long, Congressmen Maury Maverick and Sam Rayburn of Texas, and colleagues like Georgia's Senator Richard Russell—all men who were deeply involved in the legislative process. The diversity of these figures in ideology and goals suggests that young Lyndon was focusing on their style and adroit control of power. Meanwhile, Texas businessmen kept an eye on him, trading favors. The congressman probably thought he served, not oil barons, but rivals for Wall Street financial monopoly: liberators of colonial Texas. While in 1937 and for a time thereafter he had talked and voted as a New Dealer—supporting the Supreme Court packing (1937) and the minimum wage (1938), he three times voted to continue funding of the House Un-American Activities Committee and later supported Taft-Hartley's restrictive provisions regulating trade unions. The role he played in 1957 in weakening the civil-rights bill's provisions (admittedly while brilliantly guaranteeing the bill's final passage) made pure liberals of the North and East uneasy about his true ideological leanings. But the progression, irregular to be sure, was from the pure Texan of 1937 to the national figure of the 1960s.

Lyndon Johnson saw himself, by then, in the image of one who has earned the respect of others by doing exceedingly hard work during excessively long hours. His body had caved in from a heart attack in 1955, bringing a six months' absence from the Senate, as well as editorials and speeches from his colleagues that made clear his value to the presidential administration of Dwight D. Eisenhower; for Johnson had facilitated the passage of key legislation, first as minority and then as majority leader, from 1953 to 1961. He steered, during those years, a narrow course between loyalty to party and service to the executive branch, never forgetting his fervent affection for the Democratic party, which he greatly helped to unify.

Senators Johnson and Kennedy had outwardly contested as equals in the Democratic presidential race of 1960, with the older man apparently enjoying the stature of one who was clearly the senior in legislative experience. Nevertheless, the man from Massachusetts had displayed far superior political techniques in the primaries and had quickly crushed the uncertain presidential hopes of one who was now widely called "LBJ." Acceptance of the second spot, at Kennedy's invitation, surprised and disappointed many of Johnson's supporters who considered the post a political graveyard and presumed, without giving it much thought, that his vast power in the Senate would have simply continued, even with a strong Democrat in the White House. But those who hated Richard Nixon were pleased, for strength of the ticket in the South was now a certainty.

Johnson's long legislative career was not quite free of the aura of public scandal, but hard evidence never developed out of accusations. Some thought, and later charged, that he had connections with giant contractors and oil entrepreneurs who eased his financial position and compromised his independence of action, but it seems likely that these businessmen needed him more than he needed them. The manner of his exceedingly narrow election to the Senate in 1948—which was aided by lawyers and judges who shared his political leanings and was accompanied by ballot-box manipulations in tiny Alice, Texas, that shored up his vote—left many people at home and in the nation's capital wondering. There seems to be little doubt that he was helped by somebody. For a time he held a post in the Democratic party that controlled the financing of congressional campaigns, a post that some people felt made him a "conduit" for Texas money that went in cash to some grateful Democratic colleagues. Whatever he did, it seems not to have been illegal at the time, and in any case, it certainly did not very much inhibit those who tried to get him the presidential office and were disappointed when he failed. Later muckraking may be weak in irrefutable facts, although in the late 1950s his outsized consumption of hard liquor and

4

his frequent outbursts of temper were known to his intimates, if not to the public.[3]

In any event, Vice-President Johnson proved helpful to his president, just as selection of him had been essential to victory by the pair in November 1960. He became a leader in the new space effort, even to the point of advising Kennedy to undertake the "man on the moon" project. Johnson gave private counsel when asked for it, and avoided bickering when others were present. Kennedy treated him as one who had a secure and useful role in the administration. Johnson managed to stay clear of a developing scandal back in the Senate that involved a centrally located employee, one Bobby Baker, who had once served the majority leader closely in many diverse activities. And his wide-ranging knowledge of politics, government, business, and both rural and urban life well suited him to be ready in the event higher office might unexpectedly be his.

The year 1963 was, on the whole, uneventful, for it proved to be a relatively mild year in terms of disasters, scandals, economic upheavals, politics, and controversy in general. Things did not seem to be changing rapidly in fundamental respects, as they had, for example, during the two World Wars or during the transition from the 1920s to the 1930s. Many Americans felt a definite sense of euphoria as they contemplated the youthful and vibrant John and Jackie Kennedy and their children in the White House. His clarion call, in the graceful 1961 Inaugural Address, for service to humankind, no matter what the burden, had struck a spark in the media and among the public. Unrealistic and even potentially dangerous it might be when applied to defending freedom; nevertheless, the intriguing image was cherished.

In Congress, efforts to pass civil-rights legislation, tax reforms, and a tax-reduction bill all failed. The session, one of the longest since 1941, raised questions about leadership in both the executive and the legislative branch. Clearly, Senate majority leader Johnson was missed. The Democratic party controlled both branches; yet leaders watched foreign-aid and space appropriations shrink. Among citizens nationwide, stratification in ideology could not be neatly measured by party affiliation, for 28 percent of Republicans said they were "liberal" while 29 percent of Democrats said they were "conservative." Only 51 percent of people in general said they were liberal.

The nation's population stood at 189,242,000 in 1963, of whom some 20 million were Negroes and nearly 2 million were other races (572,564 were of Mexican descent). Negroes ranked below whites in life expectancy, employment, and salaries. The 5 percent unemployment figure for whites was only half of that for the other races. A third of the labor force was composed of females, two-thirds of whom were married. Inflation made little news, for the cost of living index rose less than a point during the year.

America's Negro population was much in the public eye. The year opened with incoming governor George C. Wallace exclaiming: "I say segregation now, segregation tomorrow, segregation forever." There would be a march by Negroes and reformers on Washington, which was well publicized; and demonstrations, sit-ins, and reports of victimization in housing and elsewhere were being somewhat noticed. Yet, of whites, 65 percent said they favored segregation, and 18 percent of those said they did not realize that Negroes were unhappy over their situation in life. Asked if Kennedy was pushing racial integration too fast, 46 percent agreed; only 12 percent said he was not going fast enough.[4] A presidential commission found that as to women, a constitutional amendment "need not now be sought" and saw equal-pay laws to be a responsibility of the states.

In education, the federal government had helped to fund colleges and universities after the Soviet Union had launched its satellite Sputnik; secondary education, especially in the sciences, was also being aided. But most education at every level was being financed from other sources. There were nearly six hundred junior colleges and over eight hundred public library systems. Average salaries for public-school teachers rose from $3,405 in 1953 to $5,735 in 1963. Expenditures per pupil in 1960 had been $206 in Mississippi, but $562 in New York. Spending for education in 1962/63 was about $32 billion—a threefold increase in a decade. Yet spending according to race and one's geographical location was decidedly unequal.

Medical care had improved greatly since World War II. Still, some political figures had for a long time been pushing for some kind of national health insurance for everyone; but their efforts had been deterred by inadequate public interest, lobbying, and, especially, the fact that nearly 100 million Americans had medical-care insurance, over 130 million had some form of surgical insurance, and more than 140 million had hospitalization insurance, most such policies being related to employment. The costs of medical care had escalated over 50 percent since 1950, however, and the poor and many aged people were being cared for through welfare or charity or through cancellation of charges by physicians and hospitals—a situation that had long obtained. Here was a gap in the national promise.

Conservation matters made little news during the early 1960s until, in May 1962, Rachel Carson's book *Silent Spring* created concern over pesticides. A presidential commission urged more judicious use and

new research. The expression "man's contamination of his environment" was heard. There was a small flurry of activity against cigarette
smoking. As for welfare, only 29 percent, according to one poll, thought
that the federal and state governments rather than local governments,
should regulate "relief." Meanwhile, some matters of future controversy were receiving little attention in 1963. Birth control was favored in
order to help control population growth overseas, but the issue of
abortion created hardly a ripple. Research on nuclear energy continued
quietly, with opposition only occasionally surfacing. As Vice-President
Johnson defended the space program, recent Nobel Prize winner Linus
Pauling attacked the "pitiful venture" of the nation in space, saying that
something was wrong with the American system of values.[5]

President Kennedy summed up his administration's attitude toward government on November 18, by saying that growth in the federal
establishment posed no danger to the private sector, that continuing
deficits and the mounting national debt would by no means drive the
nation into bankruptcy, and that the nation's fiscal policies would not
lead to inflation. Polls showed that he was still very popular, and he
announced publicly that he would be retaining Johnson on the 1964
ticket. Although Kennedy occasionally worried privately about reelection, his white middle-class countrymen did not seem unduly
concerned about trends that might have an impact on them.

Divisions among the population by age, educational status, military
service, or lack of it, and sexual preferences did not seem inimical to
national unity of purpose. Only the most erudite citizens realized that
the 1960s would soon see the dawn of a space- and computer-induced
revolution in science, technology, and daily life. Said one intellect on the
cutting edge of knowledge, "One senses a euphoria in the social
atmosphere scarcely compatible with the problems before us." Nothing
in the newspapers or TV in late November 1963 gave much in the way of
warning that things would not continue to be—in coming months or
even years—the way they had been, though slowly modified, of course,
by reasonable legislative change at every governmental level.[6] So things
were when, in late November, President Kennedy was hosted in Dallas,
Texas, by the vice-president, Governor John Connally, and their political allies on a fence-mending tour looking toward 1964.

At 1:23 P.M. on November 22, 1963, in a small hospital room in
Dallas, Texas, Vice-President Lyndon B. Johnson was told very simply,
"He's gone." Now there would be a new president of the United States,
due to the death of the incumbent. Mrs. John Connally has described
what happened: "We had been with the president and Mrs. Kennedy
during the tour. . . . I had just turned to him and said, 'You can't say

7

Dallas doesn't love you, Mr. President,' and that was it." The fact that John F. Kennedy had been assassinated meant that there was urgency about having a rapid and legal succession by the vice-president. He was driven to the local airport in a Ford car with Secret Service men on top of him, without "benefit of counsel" or "a moment to call in anyone to consult," he recalled. Like eight vice-presidents before him, he said, aboard Air Force One at 2:30 P.M.: "I do solemnly swear that I will faithfully execute the office of President of the United States and will, to the best of my ability, preserve, protect, and defend the Constitution of the United States, so help me God." He would later tell an audience: "I swore to myself that I would carry on. I would continue for my partner who had gone down ahead of me."[7]

From the very outset the new president was firm in voice and manner. With Mrs. Kennedy and Mrs. Johnson beside him and with Judge Sarah Hughes reading the oath, he spoke in clear and decisive tones. Some members of the Kennedy cabinet were enroute to Japan and had to be called back. Johnson phoned his condolences to Attorney General Robert Kennedy and sought his advice. The government moved forward without disruption as certain key appointments were arranged before the plane touched the ground in Washington. Waiting were scores of media people. The government officials who were present probably felt as one did: "Mr. President, we are ready to carry out any orders you have." Johnson's first public remarks were simple: "This is a sad time for all people. We have suffered a loss that cannot be weighed. For me, it is a deep personal tragedy. I know that the world shares the sorrow that Mrs. Kennedy and her family bear. I will do my best. That is all I can do. I ask for your help—and God's." Now a rural Texas accent and way of doing things abruptly replaced the Boston and Ivy League style to which the country had become accustomed.

What the public thought as a consequence of this deplorable event has been studied. Sorrow for Jackie and the children easily ranked first. Other strong reactions, in declining order, were regret that a young man had been killed at the height of his powers; shame that it could have happened in the United States; a sense of loss of someone near and dear; and anger at the terrible deed. It certainly never occurred to 85 percent that Kennedy might have brought it on himself, or to 82 percent that they ought to feel guilty. Asked if worried about how the United States would "carry on without its leader," only 16 percent worried "very deeply," and 25 percent "quite deeply"; 29 percent said it had "crossed their minds," but 30 percent said that it never had. From this, one must conclude that the general public of the day did not identify the national well-being or survival with the person of John F. Kennedy—

whatever would be conceptualized about "a thousand days" or Camelot. The researchers found that "approval of Kennedy's performance as President showed a notable climb after the assassination."[8]

Certain niceties were essential as the new president assumed leadership. Party leader Edwin L. Weisl, Jr., said he called practically every leading banker and businessman in New York, including executives at U.S. Steel, Union Carbide, Westinghouse, and other corporations. All expressed confidence in Johnson and were willing to offer appropriate support. Two aides went to see Herbert Hoover, who authorized "any statement" that was wanted. Aide Walter Jenkins talked with many leaders of the Democratic party, such as William McKeown and Edward Kostician; all thought that if the new administration could get "any" piece of legislation through, it would be good.[9] Meanwhile, Johnson avoided the Oval Office, settling in the three-room high-ceilinged vice-presidential suite—to which he brought his secretary, Marie Fehmer; his chief political agent, Cliff Carter; Bill Rogers; and his number one assistant, Walter Jenkins. Enroute from Dallas, Johnson had talked with Undersecretary of State George Ball and Secretary of Defense Robert McNamara. Now, he saw Senator J. William Fulbright, chairman of the Foreign Relations Committee, and Ambassador Averell Harriman, a senior among Democrats. Quickly the president began to phone former presidents—first Harry S. Truman; then, eight minutes later, Dwight D. Eisenhower. Leaders of Congress who called were asked emotionally for help and counsel. At 9:27 he asked Jack Valenti, his friend and aide, to accompany him home.

Now, at the Elms, came a hug for Lady Bird, a glass of orange juice, and a bite to eat. But not before delivering an introspective toast to the portrait of the late Sam Rayburn: "I salute you, Mr. Speaker, and how I wish you were here now, when I need you." There were a few words with trusted speech writer Horace Busby and the concluding of arrangements for associate Valenti to take up residence in the White House. Said the chief executive, "You know, when I went into that office tonight and they came in and started briefing me on what I have to do, do you realize that every issue that is on my desk tonight was on my desk when I came to Congress in 1937?" He named civil rights, health insurance for the elderly, federal aid to education—eight or nine topics in all. At last came the climb into bed, but not yet for sleep. With Valenti, Carter, and aide Bill Moyers seated quietly nearby, Lyndon Johnson—president of the United States—mused about his next steps, while Valenti took thirty pages of notes. The new leader seemed to be free of anxiety, worry, and hesitation. The session finally broke up in the early hours.[10]

Meanwhile, members of the Kennedy cabinet and aides of the fallen leader had problems with their emotions. They had to consider their own futures and that of the Democratic party. What of policies, ideology, and programs? Telephoned Secretary of Agriculture Orville Freeman to Jenkins: "I don't know how many deals have been made at the capitol, but I am sure that President Johnson is not bound by any of them. I am going to get together a little task force to put something on paper. May I get it to you? I went to see Sorensen to talk about this, but he was in another world. I did talk to Ken Galbraith and he feels as I do about the importance of a liberal impact at this time."[11] Much more was at stake than the personality of the late president.

A smooth transition in the presidential office is essential to the United States constitutional system. In the first moments, according to *Reporter* magazine, "everywhere there was silent unease at the inability to locate the source of government, to know even where government was." Reporters scuttled about, concentrating on the physical whereabouts of officials. But with Johnson's visibility in the capital, "the known, manageable Washington" emerged again. It was a godsend, wrote senior columnist Roscoe Drummond, that a man of presidential stature had become president. In the *New York Times*, Tom Wicker wrote that Johnson might be more closely in tune with his party and the people than was his predecessor, for Kennedy had suffered from "a sort of detachment, a form of intellectuality, a lack of ingrained, instinctive conviction." Men and nations are not led, but moved, Wicker thought; and while "LBJ" might be a flawed person, he might meet his challenges just as Truman had. About Truman, Johnson remarked wryly to Moyers, "At least his man wasn't murdered."

It was, of course, helpful that in this constitutional democracy, leaders of the opposing party would behave responsibly. Wrote Eisenhower, "If in these days of intense national concern there may be any way in which I can be helpful to you, it goes without saying that you need only to command me." Johnson replied, "Thank you for all your kindness to me at a time when your support and your presence meant a great deal to me." The public was apprised of this exchange.[12] An important element to be weighed was Wall Street's reaction. When the market finally opened, the Dow-Jones industrial average was up thirty-two points, which indicated confidence in the new president.

The media quickly tried to take the measure of the new leader. Some journalists, like William S. White, thought themselves already fully knowledgeable; others, like president-watcher Hugh Sidey of *Time*, had been on intimate terms with Kennedy's White House. That journalist rushed to tell his magazine's staff in New York that Johnson lied and deceived in small matters without being conscious of it. Sidey's editor in chief casually observed that maybe such a man might lie on big things as well; maybe character could not be divided.[13] The first Harris poll surprisingly showed Johnson with exactly the same 55 to 45 lead over Nixon that Kennedy had enjoyed a month earlier. Goldwater did two points worse than Nixon. Moreover, 72 percent of the public expected the new leader to perform from "good" to "excellent."

A spectrum of leaders wrote to convey support and advice, none more fulsomely than the famous James A. Farley, an orthodox Democrat who was now a Coca-Cola executive. He thought that Johnson had already delivered "outstanding" public utterances and that he was handling his responsibilities excellently. Such a "unique" man, who had many old friends in Congress and a vast knowledge of government, had Farley's blessing: "I express the hope that God will give you the health and strength to carry on with the great problems of your office. I am sure He will and that you will have the daily prayers of millions of Americans interested in your effort to further our cause and that of the Free World." Such letters could turn one's head, but staff members duly warned their chief that Truman had enjoyed a press honeymoon; in December, however, when Truman had used a government plane in order to visit his mother, the floodgates of criticism had quickly opened![14]

To one who was trying to hold together the Roosevelt/Truman/Kennedy coalition, reassuring letters from union and Negro leaders were meaningful, especially one from Roy Wilkins, who judged, "Good. Good." The mind of the nation in the first days was really not so much on Lyndon Johnson as on Kennedy's televised funeral, his stricken family, and the real and conceptualized memories of him. A Johnson aide asked twenty-five Texans about his boss and found that "no one opposed the new president and only one seemed lukewarm about him."[15]

Expert opinion suggests that TV held the nation together for the first four days, showing people vividly that President Johnson had taken command of the situation and that the transfer of power had taken place smoothly. But there were portentous reactions among college students, who as a group had been won over by the Kennedy charisma. Many had "an immediate reaction of resentment" toward Johnson, partly because of his Texas background, partly because he seemed ("irrationally," they acknowledged) to be somehow usurping the presidential role. One student said, "I first realized that I really had a sort of a resentment towards him as soon as he was inaugurated and they started calling him President." The *fait accompli* quieted—but may not have killed—such sentiments. Aide Bill Moyers early stressed the need to retain the enthusiasm of people under fifty; his memo said a cable to all members of the Peace Corps was indicated. Jotted the president, "Real good idea."[16] Johnson's preexisting rating was not too bad, for on October 1, a survey of 244 student Democrats had shown that 100 percent ranked Kennedy "acceptable," with Johnson at 90 percent, Stevenson at 93, and Humphrey at only 69, because 24 percent found him "unfamiliar." The *person* of a president had been killed. The *promise* of that individual and his *program* did not have to die, especially if the Johnson image—based on performance, it was hoped—could be gotten across.

Interviews with working-class people after the funeral showed that "initial feelings that Lyndon Johnson could not possibly match President Kennedy's stature give way to the idea that Johnson is different but adequate to the role." When a kitchen helper said that Johnson would "never be the man Mr. Kennedy was," a Negro friend replied that Johnson was intelligent and had been in politics for years. One of Italian extraction observed that Johnson had been all over the world; a truck driver thought he would reap the benefits of the Kennedy administration; a fireman thought he would be unable to deviate in foreign policy; and several workmen noted that the cabinet and the party would be the same. Said a cook sagely: "History is going to keep on, whether we like it or not. The government's going to keep on. . . . Things will have to fall into place as they have in the past." *Newsweek* now had Kennedy on its cover, but *Time* had Johnson. Some were looking backward; others, forward. An appraisal by Theodore H. White was that no word less than *superb* could be used to describe Johnson's transition performance: he had done much that was right; he had avoided entire areas of what could have been wrong.[17]

The new president instantly found his office a place of work and a center of global responsibilities. While no declared war was in being and the crises in Cuba and Berlin were in the past, who knew when testing from the international Communist systems in Europe, Asia, or elsewhere under Soviet or Chinese stimulus would begin? The nation had learned much about Communist expansion in the years since World War II. The new chief executive was fully aware that only with difficulty had the Soviet Union been negotiated out of Iran and Austria, and kept out of Yugoslavia, Greece, and Turkey. But Estonia, Latvia, and Lithuania had been absorbed permanently. The USSR had kept some Japanese islands and would continue to do so, even after the United States had returned Okinawa. The Iron Curtain of Soviet tanks, troops, and terror had rung down on half of Germany and on Poland, Czechoslovakia, Hungary, Rumania, and Bulgaria. Albania turned to a form of communism. In Asia, China had fallen to the Communist forces of Mao, then had intervened to preserve a Communist North Korea, had absorbed Tibet, and had made war on India. Chinese-supplied guerrillas were operating in Malaysia, Thailand, Laos, and Burma; and for a time, Chinese Communist subversion had threatened Indonesia. In Cuba, dictator Fidel Castro had become a Communist-financed pawn and a source of growing subversion in Latin America. All of this, and more—including the nature and extent of Communist infiltration in other countries all over the planet—was known to the former vice-president, just as it was familiar to informed members of the American public. New Commander in Chief Johnson had to be alert to overseas threats, for an unobtrusive man with a black briefcase had followed him onto Air Force One, carrying the secret code with which, if need be, he might order a nuclear launch. Here was a fearsome and never-ending responsibility.[18]

Matters of moment pressed at home as well as abroad. As he sat in bed that first night, the president discussed how to make the economy robust. On civil rights, he recalled how he had differed with Kennedy, believing the matter should be taken to the country over the heads of Congress as a moral crusade. (The new leader could hardly wait for his own battles to begin.) Medical aid for the aged and aid to education were headed for the top of his agenda. He resolved to effect radical changes in the social environment of the nation in order to bring balance to the chance for a quality life. The poor, the aged, the blacks, and any who were being denied an education were going to benefit from "the shattering of the political and social structure"—an essential for an equitable America.

There will be many occasions to comment on the Johnson habit of making extravagant statements. Still, one must bear in mind the tone given to the Kennedy-Johnson years from the very outset by the 1961 inaugural address. *Newsday* had then commented that here was "a summons to the American people and the world to move forward into a new era in which peace will overcome war, plenty will replace poverty, and true self-government will obliterate tyranny." At home and abroad the two administrations would share continuity in *the big promise*—whatever changes there might be as the man from Texas sat straight in the saddle. "When I took over," Johnson later recalled to the cabinet, "I often felt as if President Kennedy were sitting there in the room looking at me."[19]

That first night there had been little talk of Vietnam. Jack Valenti reflected that his leader felt that Vietnam would yield to reason and informal judgment. "LBJ really believed that if he applied his total intellect and concentration to a problem and if there was any alternative possible, he would find a way to an agreement. In all his career this reliance on reason and face-to-face challenge had never failed. He had no doubts it would succeed in Vietnam." But the very next day the president received Henry Cabot Lodge, just in from Vietnam. Incredibly, on emerging from the meeting, Lodge told an ABC reporter, on camera, that he had been authorized to say that Johnson's first substantive decision was that *American aid to Saigon would continue as at present.* One can scarcely call such haste well reasoned, much less a decision arrived at after deep consideration of alternatives. Years later, Johnson said: "I constantly had the picture in front of me that President Kennedy had selected me as his executor, his trustee, to stand in for him."[20] But it was a new administration in fact.

One early decision was to keep the files of the Kennedy and Johnson administrations separate from the outset; thus, anything that might henceforth come in that had been intended for the dead president or his staff in connection with government activities to November 22 would go to the outgoing files. A quotation from President William Howard Taft, in his book *The Chief Magistrate and His Powers,* was duly noted: "The retiring president takes with him all the correspondence, original and copies, which he carried on during his administration." Everyone then agreed that such records do not become government property. Meanwhile, the Kennedy people were desperately anxious to leave their mark on history. Understandably, the theme was set by the outgoing first lady: "Don't let it be forgot, that once there was a spot, for one brief shining moment that was known as Camelot—and it will never be that way again." So, early in 1964, an elaborate oral-history program would be orchestrated by Robert Kennedy. A bulk mailing went out on January 22, calling the program, incorrectly, "unprecedented in American history." Subjects that would probably be discussed included fifty-nine on national-security affairs and forty-seven in the domestic area. Johnson and his aides may have been adversely influenced by this early memorializing effort which was being carried on under their noses to try to guarantee that the achievements of their predecessors would be fully documented. Transfer of the Kennedy papers to the National Archives was soon arranged, although provision was made for the new president to have full access to them.[21]

Two subjects were outwardly dormant during the first weeks—namely, partisan politics and the private business affairs of the Johnson family. Yet, there were incoming letters, such as one from the mayor of New York City, who wrote to remind the president of the importance of the party's Nationalities Division, a group he thought to be "one of the most important and potentially one of the most fruitful in the political arena.'' The very day the mayor wrote, the president directed that for thirty days there would be "no partisan political speeches of any sort" by anybody in the government.[22] The public expected no less. The communications and business concerns of the Johnson family were placed in a trust to be handled by Johnson's friend Judge A. W. Moursund; and Jesse Kellam took care of the Ranch, much as he had done for some years, although the Johnsons never let control slip away for very long.

Lyndon Johnson proved to be a workers' worker in the White House. On his first day he saw twelve outside visitors and made thirty-two telephone calls, in addition to taking incoming telephone calls and handling many visits from intimates and aides. The second day he met at great length with former treasury secretary Robert B. Anderson, a Texan strongly recommended by Eisenhower. It was the first of several visits from Anderson, which had deep meaning for the formulation of policy. One piece of advice that was partially ignored was to abandon the pending tax cut; but Johnson did agree to move toward cutting the budget.

The long presidential workday, with its enormous numbers of face-to-face contacts with staff and outsiders, is nearly foreign to the vast majority of Americans. Study of the diary of the Johnson administration shows that visitors to the Oval Office came from the world of affairs—business and industry, labor, various organizations; the mass media; the nations of the world; the Congress; the executive and legislative branches of government; and governors, mayors, and officials from all over the American federal system. Cabinet members and presidential assistants came; so did Democratic party regulars. Personal friends entered and left irregularly, and one is at a loss to know how far their conversations strayed from the personal and became official in content. An examination of Friday, November 29, 1963, is illustrative. The day brought the president an exchange of telephone calls with twenty-one congressmen and a variety of cabinet members, advisers, military leaders, staff, officials, labor leaders, newsmen, foreign ministers, a state governor, and still others, from 9:25 A.M. until 10:27 P.M. One could not really say that, compared with some days, it had been a day of special crises.[23]

The new president's typical day began with awakening at 6:00 to 6:30 A.M. in his fourposter bed, with the Washington Monument visible from his south window. Mrs. Johnson usually dozed a bit longer but soon departed for her bedroom. Now came tea, toast, joshing, inquiries about what the aides had experienced the night before, and serving of breakfast to an aide or two. Then the aides would dive into the mountains of papers the president had marked up the night before. Morning newspapers—the *Washington Post*, the *Baltimore Sun*, the *New York Times*, the *Wall Street Journal*—lay all over the bed. In the evening it was the *Washington Star*, the Chicago papers, and others. The appointment schedule had to be fixed. Sometimes work began here: Rusk and McNamara were phoned, with the president expressing pride that the latter was already at his desk; the West Wing personnel would be "swept clean" of what they had learned since yesterday. "He was now satisfied." At 9:00 the full day could begin.

Lunch was often at the presidential desk. Sometimes a swim came first—where Johnson's unabashed nakedness enroute and in the pool could shock some of the male guests. He wasted little time in that he was always in motion. But he did spend much time on minor details that should have been beneath his notice. He used the luncheon table, says Valenti, "to instruct, cajole, extract, inspire with logic or hope, or whatever he deemed adequate to his objective."

Many did not realize that this dynamo of a man typically got into his pajamas at about 4:00 P.M. and climbed into bed for an hour. In this he followed and expanded on the traditional routine of the patient who has recovered from a heart infarction, but part of whose heart has died. Life is sustained by whatever remains viable or is rebuilt by nature. The second half of the Johnson day began at 5:00 P.M. with both on-the-record and off-the-record appointments. Three TV sets were conveniently located in his office. He half watched the news-feature shows of morning and evening paying strict attention when he or his office was involved. More than one associate has speculated about why Johnson later tortured himself with a medium that had become so abrasive toward him.

The president was capable of working anywhere, at any time. The Oval Office, a cramped inner office, the Military Situation Room, and the bedroom were all locales for decision making; but his mind might freeze into final focus elsewhere—in the swimming pool, in distant parts of the Ranch, or, more often than may be known, when alone with Lady Bird or close friends. Anecdotes about him are legion. His bluntness in indicating on incoming staff memorandums his desired action leads today's reader to many a smile. On one long list of future appointments forwarded by a favorite aide, he scrawled: "Why do you hate me? You must hate me else you wouldn't be trying to kill me slowly, like being nibbled to death by ducks."

Johnson has offered his own judgments on what life in the White House meant in terms of performing his duties. He once described the satisfactions of the family's living room at the end of the West Hall.

There he briefed the congressional leadership and assembled with the Joint Chiefs of Staff and the secretaries of the State and Defense departments on Tuesdays before lunch. He came there in the evening while waiting to have dinner put on the table and, later, to spend some time together with family members in their robes. "I get great strength and comfort from my family . . . although we're not together very much," he said. In the living quarters the Johnsons started the day and ended the evenings, and special friends would have coffee before calling it quits for the day.

The bedroom was really a work place for extended periods. "I awaken here every morning at 6:30 and immediately begin to review the intelligence reports from 130-odd countries of the world, the cables that have come in overnight, the reports from the commanders in the field, the engagements of our troops; I look at the losses we have suffered [in Vietnam] and the developments that have taken place during the night." And, "The last thing I do before I go to sleep is to finish the night reading. I usually get here from the office about 11:00 in the evening; have a bite of dinner; and then I get into bed and read from about two to three hours—sometimes to two, sometimes to about three in the morning." What he read came from the cabinet offices, from independent agencies, and from overseas. Each document requiring action bore a legend, such as "Approve," "Disapprove," or "Call Me." He tried to act on about a hundred a night. If too tired, he would just junk it all, though he might be penalized by losing his nap the next day.

Beginning at 8:00 A.M. or earlier, his principal assistants came to the bedroom. By then he had read the morning papers and the intelligence reports, so he would go over their problems, requests, the schedule, the appointment list, and so on. Rarely did he leave the bedroom before 10:00 A.M., "so the place where you're supposed to come to leave your cares and to rest your bones—your bedroom—is really a workroom, too, for the president." It was an odd way to conduct the people's business; but it seemed to work for him, especially in view of the multitude of his health problems. Often-repeated stories about LBJ using a bathroom with an open door or having a none-too-private enema during work periods seem less bizarre when it is recognized that those close to him were fully aware that his bodily functions would not be allowed to interrupt the flow of important daily work.

The early days as president were filled with decision making, precedent setting, concerns, worries—and sheer work. Asked at the end of two weeks what his biggest single problem had been, Johnson replied, "Being president." The big picture—that is, the foreign and domestic affairs of the United States—naturally loomed large in the

17

presidential vision. But there were other matters, too, such as arranging for the physical move on December 7 from the Elms to the White House and selecting the initial members of his presidential staff. The problems of the Kennedy family needed to be handled with all of the tact, grace, and compassion possible. All of these things, plus the special worries because the assassination had occurred in the successor's home state, still did not fill Johnson's dynamic mind close to its limits.

A matter that came naturally to the former representative, senator, and vice-president now fascinated the politician-statesman. He was determined to seize at once the full leadership of the Democratic party—a prize that was now legitimately his. The existing White House staff, left adrift by the passing of Kennedy, soon came to sense this obsession, which came as no surprise to old-timers. Now came suggestions about how the youth vote might be consolidated, about the handling of leaders of black organizations, and about what labor leaders must be phoned. His determination to talk personally at the earliest possible moment with congressional leaders, men of affairs, and persons of consequence throughout the nation—perhaps even intellectuals—shines through. Said Johnson, at the first press conference, "What I have really tried to do in the first ten days here is to establish a continuity in government . . . [and] give a sense of unity in the country and in the world." Yet the duality of his role certainly needs to be seen—his twin hats: the president as leader, unifying the nation, and the man who inevitably would be a candidate for election in 1964.

The new president's early mood was revealed during *off-the-record* remarks to a group of state governors. "We do have a good many doubts and so do foreign leaders," he said candidly. "Are we going to turn loose our weapons and start shooting up each other?" Would they please help get an appropriation bill passed; not for thirty-two years had one still been pending in November! The military and the space program wanted more money; interest on the public debt was piling up. There must be a civil-rights bill and an education bill; yet in the past ten months nothing had happened! Before him were communications from Chairman Khrushchev about a possible wheat agreement and a test-ban treaty. Off-the-cuff, he chatted about relations with the Soviet Union: We must lead from strength and not let down our guard; and "we are going to seek the road of peace." Finally, the candid peroration for their ears only: "I am not the best man in the world at this job, and I was thrown into it through circumstances, but I am in it and I am not going to run from it."[24]

From highly placed and respected persons came advice early. He was warned by Professor John Kenneth Galbraith that "the whole liberal community" would be watching civil-rights matters. Long hours would be spent on the voting-rights act, even though his lawyer friend Abe Fortas at first advised not to waste time on it because a president has just so much coinage. Said Johnson, pointedly, after a pause, "Well, what the hell's the presidency for?" Such interaction had direct bearing on his first address to the Congress. One person who wrote to Johnson at length was former Supreme Court Justice Felix Frankfurter, who referred to the "awesome burdens" of the office, which he expected would be discharged with "courage and wisdom and humaneness." He hoped that Johnson would have an ample share of one of the most important ingredients in successful statesmanship: "namely, luck—that is, right breaks at the right time."[25]

The job of chief executive had indeed come to have awesome burdens over the years. In Truman's day, the office had been enlarged with the Council of Economic Advisers, the National Security Council, and the Central Intelligence Agency. The White House staff had come to assume very meaningful functions, which involved extra burdens for an already busy executive. The cabinet had grown. Kennedy had met five times with the cabinet in his first hundred days; Johnson would match this. Kennedy had met with the National Security Council six times during that period; Johnson would need only three such meetings during his first hundred days.

Apparently, the new president also consulted his Maker. He would say, quite early, "No man can live where I live now, nor work at the desk where I work now, without needing and seeking the strength and support of earnest and frequent prayer." He would assert, to one privileged journalist, that fairly often during daylight hours he would reflect in a prayerful way. "The president carries heavier burdens than I ever envisioned. You feel little goose pimples coming up your back because it's such a frightening, terrifying responsibility," he said.[26] (And his predecessor had been *shot*.)

One obligation that could not be postponed was a study of the assassination of President John F. Kennedy. Spurred on by Washington lawyer Abe Fortas, Johnson early decided that a small commission should be led by the chief justice of the Supreme Court, Earl Warren (a former Republican governor of California). The members who acquiesced, conditional on Warren's acceptance, were Democratic Senator Richard B. Russell, Republican Congressman Gerald R. Ford, Allen W. Dulles, who had served as Eisenhower's CIA director, and John J. McCloy, a distinguished public servant. The task proved nearly impossible to force on the reluctant chief justice, who recalled unfortunate earlier departures by members of the Court from their prescribed constitutional duties.[27]

The mandate of the Warren Commission was to evaluate all available information; so, federal agencies and offices were ordered to furnish services and to cooperate fully. Congress gave the commission broad powers. Said its chairman: "I doubt if any Commission could ever have better cooperation than ours received . . . wherever we sought it. Not a single barrier was raised against us." The commission took testimony from 94 witnesses; 395 more were questioned in depositions; 61 gave sworn affidavits; 2 presented statements. Johnson's testimony was included. The printed record filled 26 volumes, and the official report of September 21, 1964, ran to 888 pages. Warren later judged that "the facts of the assassination itself are simple, so simple that many people believe it must be more complicated and conspiratorial to be true." The big job had been "running down the wild rumors." Forthrightly, he condemned those who had run about making money through lectures alleging intrigues, possibly by a "palace guard"—as happens in tiny nondemocratic states. Typically, in American assassinations and attempts, said the Warren Commission, the criminal acts alone. One can respect the 1976 opinion of a Senate intelligence committee that the FBI and CIA did not fully pursue certain leads and did not convey all relevant information to the commission. In any event, the committee did not uncover "any evidence sufficient to justify a conclusion that there was a conspiracy to assassinate President Kennedy." Allegations that mysterious Texas forces were at work to gain the throne for their hero through assassination and automatic succession seem fictional.

Some revisionist versions of the assassination may be treated briefly. Was the CIA the culprit? Says its responsible head, "The fact of the matter is that the CIA could not have had a better friend in a president than John F. Kennedy."[28] Was it Fidel Castro, dictator of Communist Cuba? Who can say? But a newsman who was with Castro at the very moment when he heard about the assassination quotes Castro as having exclaimed: "That's bad news. . . . Everything is going to change. The United States occupies such a position in the world that the death of a president of that country affects millions of persons in every corner of the globe. The cold war, relations with Russia, Latin America, Cuba, the Negro problem, all that has to be rethought. . . . Kennedy was an enemy to whom we had become accustomed. This is a grave matter, a very grave matter." But the South Vietnamese guerrilla fighters would be glad.[29] Ruminating toward the end of his life, Johnson said variously that the assassination might have been part of a conspiracy born because of our operating a "damned Murder, Inc." in the Caribbean, so that the act might have been in retaliation, but he couldn't prove it. And he even commented once that given the assassination of Diem, maybe there was a form of retribution in the move against Kennedy.[30] We need not accept the unsubstantiated judgment of one author that Johnson did not believe the conclusions reached by the Warren Commission. So-called hints that Johnson had dropped to Howard K. Smith, Walter Cronkite, and Joseph Califano—but had refused to amplify—sound to me like slips that Johnson belatedly realized could lead to charges that he was attacking Kennedy or Kennedy's policies regarding Cuba. The counsel for the Warren Commission later rejected the idea advanced by the House Assassination Committee on July 17, 1979, that there was an unseen, hidden gunman. The FBI soon agreed with the commission. This, in spite of new data about the CIA's anti-Castro plots of that day.[31] Multiple-gunmen theories would run up against reputable scientists in 1981 and be rejected. Johnson's judgment, three years after he left the presidency, ought to stand. To Warren he said, "Chief, of all the things you have done for your country, the most important was your work with the commission on the assassination of President Kennedy."

Outsized attention has been focused on the theme of the Johnsons versus the Kennedys. The reader of personal correspondence in the "Kennedy" folders in the Johnson Library will certainly wonder why the question is worth raising. There is a long, emotional, and warm handwritten letter of November 26 from Jackie to the new president that implies no untoward feelings. Johnson had been her husband's right arm, one who had taught Jack from his days as freshman senator; Johnson's actions were those of a gentleman. So "we were friends, all four of us." A year later, Lyndon took a moment to write: "Time goes by too swiftly, my dear Jackie. But the day never goes by without some tremor of a memory or some edge of a feeling that reminds me of all that you and I went through together." Later he would say: "I took his program and his family after he was fallen, and I did everything that I would want a man to do for my program or my family if the same thing happened to me." Said Jackie Kennedy Onassis later, Lyndon Johnson "was extraordinary; he did everything he could to be magnanimous and to be kind." For the new president there still was a shadow; "it was a problem for me." There were animosities and jealousies among some subordinates in both camps, but these surface chiefly in Kennedy-team memoirs. Liaison between Lady Bird and Jackie was rich with reciprocal emotion. But relief would come to the former, somehow, with the Onassis marriage: "I feel strangely freer," wrote the new first lady. "I wonder what it would have been like if we had entered this life unaccompanied by that shadow?"[32]

The president more than did his part. At Mrs. Kennedy's impetuous request he renamed Cape Canaveral the John F. Kennedy Space Center; there would be the Kennedy Center in Washington; the new Medal of Freedom would be awarded to Kennedy posthumously, with extravagant prose. But when asked if the future year-end analysis of the Democratic party's 1964 record should be "the 1-year Johnson record" or "the 4-year Johnson-Kennedy record," the president chose the former.[33] He knew Kennedy's reputation was safe in fully dedicated hands. As a beginning, more than 32,250 copies of the 890-page book of tributes and eulogies *John Fitzgerald Kennedy: Late President of the United States* were printed and distributed by the Congress. Pierre Salinger told the whole staff early in 1964, "There is no objection to releasing any public statements concerning President Kennedy but I do NOT want any background statements, off record statements, background press conferences, etc. released to ANYONE without my permission."[34] The Johnson family would be justifiably irritated at the mythmakers as they swung into action: thus, columnists Rowland Evans and Robert Novak could somehow term Johnson "the detractor of Kennedy" in private and "the keeper of Kennedy's memory" in public. Annoying were such rhapsodic books as Bruce Catton's *Four Days*, which spoke lyrically of Kennedy's maturity, of "what he was" rather than what he did, and so on.[35]

The new leader's incoming mail was filled with assurances about his own stature and his early claim to fame. Ralph Flanders, a former Republican senator, wrote: "I have long been a Lyndon Johnson fan in the Senate. There is no better man among the Democrats to succeed to the presidency."[36] In any case, the new president recognized the value of guarding and protecting, at home and abroad, the stature of America's recent leader as an enduring national asset. Power, after all, had shifted; it was now *his*! Back in 1931, when he was a clerk in the Congress, a very close fellow worker noticed that "he didn't know what he wanted to be, but he wanted to be *somebody*." Now, in late November 1963, a cosmopolitan columnist said to himself after staring mutely into Johnson's eyes (finally lowering his own): "This is somebody. This is really somebody." Recalled another newsman: "He was breathtaking."[37] It was a competent, dynamic, and ambitious President Lyndon Baines Johnson, vibrantly alive and ready to govern, who would now move himself, his family, and his close associates into the White House.

2

★ ★ ★ ★ ★

A JOHNSON TEAM IN ACTION

A new president sat in the Oval Office, but a subpresidency was already in place down the long corridors. An existing executive branch administrative team (Kennedy's) was already on duty. Clearly, there were problems to be worked out at every level. The new executive brought with him a functioning team of close subordinates, some of whose members were of long standing. Modern presidents have found it essential to be surrounded by trustworthy people who are willing, if need be, to cater to their whims, however unreasonable, and who will be just down the hall in times of crisis. Such people are extremely important, and they know it, for they have access to the mind of the president.[1] Fortunately, Lyndon Johnson would be well served by his staff. Without them, much legislation of his years would probably not have come into existence.

Johnson knew what he wanted in his assistants. Top traits were "honesty, frankness, loyalty, dedication, and diligence." From a cabinet official should come "carefully considered judgments and advice": he should not withhold information and differences of opinion, and he should display maximum ability to cooperate with other cabinet officials with a minimum of rivalry. He should be an expert in his field, a strong leader, a man of candor and honesty, possessed of "untiring devotion to his country," and he should be able to work long hours. An aide ought to give independent suggestions and advice, after carefully checking what agencies wanted. He should not just produce timely warnings on problems but should also "try to anticipate them." He "should be loyal to his president and what the president stands for." Unfortunately, "the crucible of the White House brings out the best and often brings out the worst in men." Johnson surmised that most presidents are blessed with dedicated assistants who are there because they love their country and are willing to do whatever is necessary to serve it best.[2]

One notices in this the absence of any particular requirement for specialized knowledge acquired in advance. Contrary to what some people believe, neither Johnson nor most other presidents, probably, would have agreed that staffing with intellectuals and academicians would improve the government very much. Walter Lippmann was just one writer who had long thought that putting scholars into politics was a bad combination, since the universities and government should not be blended—for the good of each. A doctoral candidate has sagely said that it is the task of the politician to make policy and the task of the academician to study policy. It is not that knowledge is downgraded in favor of ignorance; it is just that so many other characteristics are needed in White House aides. Jack Valenti emerged from the Johnson years with the conviction that assistants ought to have had some experience in grass-roots campaigning, ought to consider humility a virtue, and ought to be willing to free the president of tedium and minutiae. The president's schedule must be managed, and information must be conveyed to the Congress and to government officials. Aides need to be eyes and ears for their chief, as well as a sounding board when he speaks frankly, seeking candid advice. A president should not become identified publicly with the many abortive ideas that are expressed by aides in hundreds of memorandums. Once an aide even urged this leader to wear a cap and then be quoted as saying "Every man should wear one"; or be pictured out bowling—don't include Lady Bird—so as to get the bowling vote.[3] Certainly some such odd and impractical ideas will be expressed when a president encourages what amounts to brainstorming.

Aides were supposed to produce ideas for their leader. Valenti recalled: "The president was continually disturbed about the scarcity of ideas. . . . He was amazingly open to anyone on his staff providing him with a new idea, something that had the glint of imagination in its substance and the potential for success in its implementation." The aides, in turn, picked up ideas from their mail, their friends, and their reading. An example of how the process might work well was a suggestion made to Valenti by George Woods, president of the World Bank, that there ought to be fertilizer plants in India, desalination efforts in the Middle East, and a Mekong River project. The last idea quickly appeared in a long Valenti memorandum to Johnson, who reacted favorably in an hour and caused it to go at once to speech writer Richard Goodwin; it duly appeared in the famous speech at Johns Hopkins University delivered April 7, 1965. But John Kenneth Galbraith thinks that while Johnson was excellent in handling domestic problems over which he had personal command, he failed when he had to rely on advisers. David Halberstam thinks Johnson was poorly advised. Weighing such judgments, one thinks of the time when Adlai Stevenson indicated that he really wanted to be secretary of state rather than an errand boy, and columnist Lippmann told him, "If you are Lyndon Johnson's secretary of state, you'll be an errand boy." Speaking to journalist James Reston, the president said that he wanted to recruit good people but that his years in Washington and Texas really hadn't acquainted him with talented young people in the Northeast and in the Middle and Far West.[4]

Johnson's staff ultimately consisted of 250 workers in the White House offices and 1,350 in the executive offices. A list of his special assistants, special counsel, legislative counsel, administrative assistants, and special consultants—with dates of their service—appeared in the *Congressional Quarterly Almanac* for 1968. Study of the roster shows that of those who were appointed by President Kennedy during his first year, not including members of the cabinet, only one survived past 1966, although the Texan urged all to stay with him.

In a sense, there were three categories of Johnson's staff: those who had been with Kennedy in the White House but eventually left; those in the cabinet and administrative posts who stayed on in some post; and those who were brought in by the new president. Johnson was somewhat guarded with even the most adaptable of the Kennedy crew, but he relied on their talents and could praise them extravagantly on occasion, even at the expense of his own people. He naturally trusted his own staff, especially those who had been with him for years, and he quickly came to rely on newcomers that he himself had brought in. This is to be expected.

Inadequate attention has been given to the vexatious problem that Lyndon Johnson faced of having inherited a full Kennedy team at every level of the executive branch and of having no graceful way of weeding them out in order to make room for his own array of lifetime acquaintances in government, in the private sector, and in the vast and increasingly knowledgeable byways of Texas. In mid 1968, Lady Bird blurted into her diary: "As I look back on our four and a half years, I think it would have been better if Lyndon had appointed more of his own men to strategic positions—Cabinet positions—not too long after he assumed office and certainly a great many more after he was inaugurated in January 1965. He kept many Kennedy appointees, in some departments practically the whole flock." Respecting them, still "there is a certain quality of direct relationship between you and the people you personally have chosen and put into jobs that results in a teamwork that does not always come from someone who inherited the job from another President."[5] She was right.

Inherited members were Dean Rusk, secretary of state; Robert McNamara, secretary of defense; and Robert Kennedy, attorney general. Less in the public eye were cabinet members Douglas Dillon, treasury; Stewart Udall, interior; Orville Freeman, agriculture; Anthony Celebrezze, health, education, and welfare; Luther Hodges, commerce; Willard Wirtz, labor; and J. Edward Day, postmaster general. Holdovers from the Kennedy team were in the Bureau of the Budget, the Council of Economic Advisers, the CIA, the Office of Emergency Planning, and the Office of Science and Technology. The talented Theodore Sorensen was a special counsel; other able assistants included former Harvard dean McGeorge Bundy, historian Arthur M. Schlesinger, Jr., professional politician Lawrence O'Brien, and Kennedy's dear friend Kenneth O'Donnell. The former president's personal secretary, Evelyn Lincoln, immediately had ample holdover duties that were unrelated to Johnson's needs. The new first lady soon chose her own press secretary and other helpers.

Most of the Kennedy-appointed cabinet members simply stayed on. Among the staff, O'Brien and Bundy stuck it out longer than most, the former because he was upgraded to postmaster general. O'Donnell and Sorensen left early, for their work and their loyalties were extraordinarily personalized. Schlesinger soon envisioned a major book on the thousand days as a personal obligation. The categorized White House employees stayed, in general, although there would be adjustments when some Texas subordinates of the former vice-president arrived. The new entourage was not large enough to warrant a columnist's crack about an emerging "Texocratic capital," however.

One area of effort that Johnson inherited was a plan and a team geared up to win the coming 1964 election. On November 27 a Kennedy aide offered data on progress allegedly made by departments and agencies since 1961. He even had material arranged by states and congressional districts. There were statistics comparing the Kennedy years with previous administrations "on hundreds of programs." There were abundant human-interest stories, with pictures; motion pictures were being made, with scripts for use by elected and appointed officials. Media programs of the nation's extreme right wing had been monitored, and rebuttals had been duly prepared.[6] Such planning surely impressed the politician from Texas, who felt himself to be well served during these early months. On January 15, 1964, he even said, "One of the great legacies President Kennedy left me was the finest cabinet that any president could assemble." But it was not a unit. "Udall, Wirtz, and I sort of hold the balance of power between the tax-cutters on one side and the anti-tax cutters on the other," said Secretary Freeman. "There are some real differences and the cabinet hasn't really been consulted [by Kennedy] about policy up to this time."[7]

How some who departed felt was recorded later by Sorensen, who said generously that in late 1963 he was "not motivated by the slightest ill feeling toward the new President." He remembered many of Johnson's kindnesses to his sons and praise for his work. Nobody suggested that Sorensen resign, but the White House had become "a sad and empty place." Reading the blunt pages of Kenneth O'Donnell's memoirs, it is easy to believe that a similar exodus would have occurred if anyone else had succeeded Kennedy. Although he says that "President Johnson and I always had a pleasant relationship during the four years that I worked in the White House," O''Donnell did not stay. Said Johnson, "Maybe I made a mistake . . . maybe after January 1965 I ought to have made some changes." Valenti valiantly tried to pare the staff, but he did not succeed.[8] History could have been different if Johnson had cleaned house and, especially, if he had brought in officials who could have taken a fresh look at commitments overseas, especially in Southeast Asia.

An account of this administration must include consideration of the men of real power around the president. One thinks at once of Robert McNamara, former president of Ford Motor Company, who occupied the Defense Department slot, and his prestigious successor Clark Clifford, who was a twentieth-century Washington man with influence behind the scenes. It is said that Kennedy once thought of building up McNamara as a 1968 presidential candidate, for he thought more highly of him than of anyone else in the cabinet. McNamara may have been two persons: a bit of a dove when with outside liberal friends, but a facts-and-figures hawk in office. Henry Kissinger found him tough and ambiguous, "too narrowly focused on battlefield considerations and too ready to settle for atmospherics"; he did not seem to have his heart in his assignment. McNamara's relations with Congress were apparently quite poor by the time he left office. A snide saying in the White House corridors then was: "Giving up on Vietnam isn't at all like giving up on the Edsel. The secretary of defense didn't see the difference."[9] But nothing could take away what he did to improve the defense organization. During his years, civilians often made military decisions, as, to some extent, the Constitution had contemplated. Some five million people were working directly or indirectly under the secretary. Said one defense strategist, "Mr. McNamara was determined to understand and be sure that he understood all the various important things that went on in the Pentagon, and really to get more detailed control and understanding of the questions of logistics, of base structure, of pay scales, of logistic guidance, of a thousand and one different things." The transition to Washington insider Clifford in 1968 would be unusually smooth, bringing a greater deliberateness, consultation with many people, and caution in making recommendations. Clifford concentrated on White House relations and the most important issues. Both men deferred to the president as commander in chief.

Dean Rusk was judged by Johnson to be a deliberate, judicious, and careful man, one who didn't get on his horses "as quick as I did on some things." Johnson especially liked Rusk: "He's a damned good man. Hard-working, bright, and loyal as a beagle. You'll never catch him working at cross-purposes with his president." When challenged, the president defiantly defended the team of Rusk and McNamara to the press, saying that each had a background that gave him familiarity with civilians and the military; each man understood the other. After six years in office, both were national assets. "They have gone through a great many trials together," Johnson said on February 27, 1967. Later observers can see plainly that Rusk considered the freedom of Asia almost a personal thing, no matter what the degree of later opposition to his policies from cautious colleagues back in the foundation and university world. A biographer thought him "a better man, a wiser, more decent, humane, and moral man than either of the presidents he served," but was critical of service he gave to their causes.[10]

Walt Rostow and McGeorge Bundy, former professors, were not of cabinet level but carried more influence than most of its members. Among Bundy's tasks were handling matters of national security and coordinating NSC staff activities; maintaining liaison with the United Nations delegation, the CIA, and eight additional agencies on security matters; jurisdiction over the Situation Room in the basement of the White House, where the national defense situation could be seen in electronic exhibits; and control of the Classified Message Center. He was an admirer of Henry Stimson, the statesman-warrior cabinet member of earlier years, who, Valenti thought, was Bundy's model. Bundy's intellect and self-confidence drew Johnson to him, especially since Bundy quickly made the transition to new leadership. He had an advanced sense of public duty and commitment to service. Considering the many outward differences between him and his Texas leader, the two were remarkably in agreement on fundamentals.

Rostow came into the government as Bundy's deputy, then moved to the State Department's Policy Planning Council, and finally came to the White House. A competent optimist (as early as 1961 he had said "the kind of operation" then in Vietnam could be handled), he was a well-regarded scholar. The figure of Rostow, as a planner in foreign affairs, as a supporter, and as an advocate, must be included in any treatment of the president, for Rostow was brilliant, yet he was impatient with critics and certain-sure in his moves. Few officials rubbed so many people the wrong way.[11] The "ideologically committed Vietnam hawk" came to be a ready target. He directed liaison with the Departments of State and Defense, wrote position papers, drafted serious language intended for inclusion in presidential speeches and interviews, and generally occupied a position of trust and responsibility. Johnson remained faithful to this dedicated subordinate, ignoring most of his liabilities.

Jack Valenti is an insider who is too easily overlooked. He coordinated presidential statements, handled liaison with Senate leaders such as Republican Everett Dirksen and Democrat Mike Mansfield, planned personal appointments, came to supervise the appointments calendar, and prepared special correspondence for the president's signature. Versatile and friendly, he found Johnson's oft-repeated jokes funny, dealt directly with the president, and was often the final editor of speeches. Said the president: "Jack is really an intellectual, and people would admit it if he didn't come from the wrong side of the Mason-Dixon line"—a remark that greatly pleased the Harvard Business School graduate. He fulfilled his task of keeping the gate swinging open on easy hinges so that staff could get to the president. Sometimes Valenti handled 150 or more phone calls in a long workday. More than most, he was underrated by observers.

Valenti in action can be seen, for example, as he reminded the president early in 1964 of work to be done: talk to McNamara about a Mansfield memorandum on Vietnam; see elderly jurist Felix Frankfurter; give a pep talk to the OAS ambassadors. Also, adviser to presidents Bernard Baruch had called to warn that a wage settlement with transport workers would undo all the herculean work on the economy: "Their wages go up—and soon wages all over the country will go up. Esther Peterson [in consumerism] can do nothing to help housewives when prices go up as a result of wage increases." Baruch would make a statement if the president desired. Also, "You want to talk to at least five senators every day, . . . and you wanted to have . . .

J. Edgar Hoover [of the FBI] come in.''[12] Valenti was a man next to the center of power, and a welcome friend whose wife had formerly been a key Johnson secretary. It was easy for Valenti to say publicly in Boston, ''I sleep each night a little better, a little more confidently because Lyndon Johnson is my president.'' Ridicule from the cynical was instant (the remark did have its humorous aspects). Ignored was the rest of the judgment: ''For I know he lives and thinks and works to make sure that for all Americans, and indeed, the growing body of the free world, the morning shall always come.'' Johnson kidded his good friend: ''Do you know how few presidential aides ever utter a memorable phrase? . . . Come to think of it, not too many memorable phrases are ever uttered by presidents anymore.'' Years later it was Valenti's view that the time spent with Johnson was the ''summertime'' in the lives of those who worked beside his chief.[13]

One aide who was irreplaceable, Walter Jenkins, nevertheless had to be replaced, suddenly and in the glare of disturbing publicity. President Johnson's chief executive officer for nearly a year, Jenkins had worked his way up from a clerkship in the Austin congressional office. With little to do in policy matters, he screened memorandums and documents, mastered administrative details, and handled daily visitors. On their first night in the White House, the Johnsons dined at the Jenkins's home, and Lady Bird's birthday was spent with them. Mild, scholarly, generous to colleagues, possessed of integrity, Jenkins was a workers' worker. On October 7, 1964, the drinks at a magazine cocktail party hit him hard. The dog-tired executive wandered two blocks to the YMCA, where police picked him up on a morals charge. (Johnson suspected entrapment instigated by Republicans.) Some of the media now went to work, for the event, though personal, was also news. Prospects for many more years of service disappeared in an instant. ''My heart is aching today,'' Lady Bird told the press, ''for someone who has reached the end point of exhaustion in dedicated service to his country.'' He would get needed medical attention. She hoped the love of his wife and six fine children and his profound religious faith would sustain him through his period of anguish. Johnson preserved public silence then and later, for which some would blame him, but it was a tough call. Privately, he was devastated. A secret poll showed that the public was little interested, even in the early 1960s, in such a matter of private morality.[14] The significance for the country was the loss of an assistant who had the president's total trust and was invaluable to him.

Press secretary George Reedy had been a UPI reporter and an intelligence specialist. He joined forces with the senator in 1951, admiring the boss's powers of concentration and seeing in him a future man of power, but *not* a president. Casual and self-effacing, Reedy was deliberate in talk. He left in July 1965 for medical treatment but returned as an aide in 1968. The next press secretary, Bill Moyers, would achieve TV visibility as a commentator in the 1970s; in the 1960s he was one who enjoyed a good press and sought renown. Educated in the Baptist ministry in Texas and Edinburgh, he was first employed at the Johnsons' TV station and later served with the Peace Corps staff. Beneath a relaxed exterior was a tough invidivdual. Disenchantment with his chief came in time, so he could say casually in retrospect, "Johnson was elected and discredited."[15] Both the president's brother, Sam Houston Johnson, and Valenti resented the infighting of Moyers as he maintained personal contact with the Office of Economic Opportunity, the Peace Corps, and some congressmen, advised on appointments, drafted correspondence, and helped ghost write speeches.

A pioneer Johnson colleague was the able Horace Busby, a speech writer and press secretary during the congressional era, who now necessarily had to share his responsibilities. He was there when the president was perplexed. Harry McPherson, special counsel, was literate, cultured, humane, a talented writer of memorandums, and a person who maintained good rapport with intellectuals. He "brought a touch of class," judged an observer. One of Douglass Cater's interesting functions was to oversee the preparation of books about the president and his programs—a task that kept him in communication with the academic world. Among the agencies that Cater monitored were the Smithsonian, the National Science Foundation, and the National Academy of Sciences. Conference planning was another responsibility. His four books and his experience in the magazine world attracted White House attention in 1965. His leadership would become vital to the educational program, including work on the bill on public broadcasting; there also was liaison with HEW. Robert Hardesty was an ever-dependable assistant. Marie Fehmer, personal secretary to the president, was a keeper of secrets who did not achieve the renown of Roosevelt's Missy Lehand and Grace Tully, but she was universally regarded as a model of her profession and a gem who survived well an almost impossible assignment.

Lady Bird had several employees who ranked high in the administration, especially because of her own stature as an environmental activist, hostess to the famous, and confidante to husband Lyndon. Liz Carpenter was staff director and press secretary, one whom Valenti thought good enough to play on the president's team. Bess Abell, social secretary, was an imperturbable pro. Another person who served the

Johnson family was secretary Juanita Roberts. Dorothy Territo dutifully retained key materials for the future museum and library.

Some White House aides and assistants turned author. One of these was George Christian, press secretary after February 1967, who gave two briefings daily to the press, attended meetings of the National Security Council, and conferred frequently with members of the staff. He specialized in knowing what not to say while talking privately to newsmen without stint. He seems to have had no special instructions from the president on which to base his conduct and carry forward his work.[16] Another person who stood high was Joseph A. Califano, Jr., who would have a stormy career in the cabinet of a later Democratic president. An honors graduate from Harvard Law School, he thought like a lawyer as he took stewardship over domestic programs after converting from McNamara's staff. Quick and energetic, he was one to display publicly, because both he and Valenti had symbolic value for the Italian vote. After joining the staff in July 1965, Califano directed work on presidential messages. Richard Goodwin, a literary but overly idealistic speech writer, was almost too much for other staffers to endure, but the rumpled utopian convert from the Kennedy administration made his mark. He was the primary author of some key speeches; he provided the expression "Great Society."

The appointment of John Gardner to head HEW for a time was a Johnson coup, for the president of the Carnegie Foundation enjoyed wide acceptance with educators. His successor at HEW, Wilbur Cohen, became a permanent Johnson booster, extravagantly defending the Great Society in later years. One appointee who had a bright future in the 1980s as arms negotiator was Paul Nitze. "Not one of Mr. Johnson's boys," he says, he did not serve on task forces or commissions or travel with the president. He was deputy secretary of defense after June 1967, after getting experience as secretary of the navy. He attended all meetings of the National Security Council. William P. Bundy was the straightforward assistant secretary of state for Asian and Pacific affairs during most of these years. Leonard H. Marks, director of the United States Information Agency, was often consulted off the record by the president during social visits to the Johnsons.

W. Marvin Watson—kind, gentle, and thoughtful—was a central figure in the Johnson White House, serving variously as appointments secretary, schedule planner, and office manager. His somewhat conservative memorandums show great common sense. The former professor at Baylor University had his chief's full confidence. Well known to the scholarly fraternity, then and later, was the assistant for cultural affairs, Eric Goldman, a historian whose early book on President

Johnson as symbolic of "tragedy" would preserve Goldman's name when some central figures would be forgotten. His vague mandate was to keep sending "a continuous flow of specific proposals, general approaches and opinions from a wide range of experts outside the government," but up until he resigned in frustration in mid 1966, he was relegated to an essentially irrelevant role, although not by his choice (Lyndon Johnson simply was not much interested in Goldman's efforts to perpetuate or somehow adapt the Kennedy "style," but Lady Bird was more receptive and helpful). After he resigned, he was replaced by John P. Roche. The aging J. Edgar Hoover, director of the Federal Bureau of Investigation, had served many presidents. The time for reliable evaluation of this official's role in the Kennedy-Johnson era has not yet arrived, unfortunately, although rash judgments are common.

The line must be drawn somewhere when naming all those who served during these years. Special consultants Gen. Maxwell D. Taylor, Charles S. Murphy, and James A. Lovell, Jr., the astronaut, were among some forty-three individuals who held this title at various points. A black adviser who operated quietly was Louis Martin, a former Michigan newspaper editor. Serving with the Democratic National Committee, he maintained a close personal relationship with Johnson, smoothed relations with Martin Luther King, Jr., and helped to make the White House Conference on Civil Rights viable. Charles L. Schultze was director of the Bureau of the Budget until early 1968, when he was succeeded by his assistant Charles J. Zwick, formerly of RAND Corporation. Successive chairmen of the Council of Economic Advisers were Gardner Ackley, Merton J. Peck, and Arthur Okun. The CIA was headed by William F. Raborn, Jr., then by Richard Helms. The Office of Emergency Planning was led by Farris Bryant and then by Price Daniel. Betty Furness eventually headed Consumer Affairs. The large, powerful, and rich White House Military Office, which was responsible for presidential travel, communications, and secret funds, was nominally in the charge of competent and close-mouthed Sergeant Bill Gulley.

The White House staff under President Johnson did not develop into a "Texas Mafia" at any level. When in 1968 an article appeared about seventeen men under the age of forty who had the president's ear, only two had degrees from Texas colleges; but there were five from Harvard, three each from Yale and Columbia, and two from Princeton. Nearly all had earned academic honors. Johnson liked to brag about the Ivy League degrees in his entourage. Insider Charles Frankel observed in early 1967 that Johnson was "exercising control over appointments to an unprecedented degree" and was increasingly naming personal acquaintances to the minor offices. He guessed correctly that Johnson knew he was on the way out and was rewarding his friends while he still had the chance! Frankel thought that some appointments were first-rate: "The White House keeps surprising me—first, by the way in which it turns down people of high quality, and then by the way it comes up with people of high quality." A writer for the *Wall Street Journal* in 1965 spoke of "impressive, top-quality professionals," for Moyers was one of the more talented men to hit Washington; Califano, "topnotch"; Valenti and Busby, "extremely able and intelligent" and devoted to the boss.

Unlike Kennedy's staff, this one had few prima donnas. Staff and their wives were included in the Johnson family's social life: eating, traveling, spending weekends with them and meeting their friends. Said one Kennedy holdover, "This is a smooth-working operation." Answers could be found "bang-bang quick." Still, some thought the staff was second-rate, except for Kennedy holdovers. Intellectual Roche thought the staff first-class, saying that Califano and McPherson both talked back to the boss loudly and frequently. This is important, for it is common for presidential staffs to be loyalists from campaigns, which makes for obsequiousness. Joseph Kraft observed, "In such company, any president can almost always find support for whatever he wants to do—which is precisely the trouble."[17]

In weighing all this, it is well to remember that even presidents do not always obtain their first choices and have to use long lists. Johnson did agree fully with an early Valenti memorandum on how to get "highest-caliber men" using a recruiting committee.[18] But it was never simple to get perfect strangers to leave their positions for an uncertain situation in Washington, especially without ironclad assurances that the move would "make a difference." Such promises, when made, were, naturally, impossible to honor.

Any list of those who advised Johnson must include Lady Bird. Lyndon's brother says she was the most important influence on his life, which is a way of indicating influence on the presidency. Valenti went all out: "One has to be careful when describing Mrs. Johnson. There is the temptation to go overboard in heaping laurels on her. Yet the record is plain and untarnished. How she managed to combine several lives, wife, mother, adviser, activist, ceremonial White House partner, and retain her composure and her good humor is still not clear to me." As was the case with Eleanor Roosevelt, much of her life's work would come after the White House years.[19] Years later, Lady Bird said that her husband had bullied, shoved, pushed, and loved her into being more outgoing and an achiever.

Two others must be mentioned, because they came and went, seeing the chief executive at irregular times and having variable influence. One was Hubert Humphrey, whose flashing wit and innovative mind impressed all who knew him well. Johnson's staff considered him a favorite and made it a point to keep him, the vice-president after 1964, informed, in view of Johnson's uncertain health. Underrated by most, then and later, was the president's brother, Sam Houston Johnson. Congressman Jake Pickle, long a Johnson ally, said that everybody liked this pain-ridden man, for he understood human nature and people as did Lyndon himself. "Personally," said Pickle, " I have relied on [his] judgment and appraisal as much as anyone. He was a character, but he was an interesting and colorful character." The president was fed quantities of political information by his brother; he solicited services from him and relied on his familiar mind.

The struggle of women to improve their position under the law and within the federal establishment achieved real gains under this president. Almost at the outset, the canny politician recognized the wisdom in advice from his friend Anna Rosenberg Hoffman and embarked on a crusade to place women in policy-level positions. In his January 17, 1964, cabinet meeting, he made an emotional pitch to top-level administrators; later he leaned on the next echelon. Kennedy's Commission on the Status of Women had just reported in the early fall on how the civil service was dominated by males. While they constituted a third of the work force, women then got only a fifth of the pay. An Equal Pay Act had taken effect on June 11, 1963, but progress on salaries was slow. Determined to make a splash in areas open to the chief executive—and to appear to have done so—Johnson told a *Washington Star* reporter in January that he intended to make "stag government" a thing of the past: he would begin by appointing fifty women to key posts at the policy level. Unfortunately, because he had few vacancies to work with, there had to be some fudging, but a creditable record was soon made. His standing with women in the political arena soared. Since "the day is over when top jobs are reserved for men," he chose women to head Consumer Affairs, to serve on the Tariff Commission and the Atomic Energy Commission, and to act as an assistant secretary in HEW. Two were named ambassadors—to Norway and Denmark. He brought to Washington his friend Barbara Jordan, who later became a powerful black congresswoman. Between January 1964 and October 1965 he appointed 120 women to "key positions" while 3,500 women got jobs that paid $10,600 or more each. The practice of specifying men on civil-service examinations was abolished; classified advertising in the nation was not to carry sex preferences after November 1965. An interdepartmental committee and a citizens' advisory council furthered his goals.

During the years 1963 to 1967, Congress legislated equal opportunity for women, in conjunction with minorities, thus helping minorities to obtain their own rights. Although the president played no active role in the outcome, the House did pass a sex-discrimination amendment to the 1964 Civil Rights Act by a vote of 168 to 133, which meant much to those who had struggled for such a gesture. Meanwhile the Equal Rights Amendment remained bottled up in committee until 1970. Interest at the time was much lower than might be expected, so that Johnson never had to take a public stand on the sex-discrimination amendment to the 1964 act. But his emotionalism on using women at high levels of government was a most important plus in the history of the womens' rights movement. "Every Day Is Ladies' Day With Me" was the motto that his staff ascribed to him. When presenting the National Teacher of the Year Award on April 7, 1965, he rather tactlessly criticized the selection group for not having included at least one woman among the finalists (remarks that were deleted when the speech was printed). Although the brand new National Organization for Women (NOW) ventured to tell him in 1966 that he had done "more than any other president to focus national attention on the importance of bringing women into the mainstream of public and private employment," one who was in a position to know says that the position of women in government was "not substantially improved" during these years. His crusade faded away after the 1964 election. But promotions for women in GS grades 12–16 burgeoned for a time, and executive order 11246 of October 1967 prohibited the listing of sex on notices of federal vacancies. His own top staff remained male, and the foreign service and the courts were little affected. His order 11375 added a legal basis for guaranteeing equal employment for women in the federal service.[20]

Neither blacks nor Mexican-Americans could point with pride to percentages of appointments in these years, but then the number of members of those groups who were eligible through specialized education and concentrated experience, though growing, was still low. Thanks to Congresswoman Edith Green of Oregon (a Democrat who kept close watch on the fine print in legislation), the Women's Job Corps would become part of the anti-poverty effort. Meanwhile, the percentage of women in the military, even including nurses, never reached the numbers authorized from 1948 to 1969, averaging but 1.2 percent. As the defense establishment felt the manpower pressures of Vietnam, however, it set up a task force to reassess the role of women, thus laying the groundwork for changes. Women were made eligible for permanent grades through colonel, or captain in the navy, could be appointed as a flag or general officer, and were entitled to get standard retirement benefits. The 2 percent overall limit on women was struck.[21] So, the president's record in redressing the balance between working men and women and in opening doors that had been closed was a constructive one, certainly far surpassing that of his predecessor, but extreme activists will still be able to be critical.

Certain celebrities, particularly John Steinbeck and Gregory Peck, gained special entrée to the Johnson White House. The president felt downright comfortable with such men, who earned his esteem with actions and advice while winning the hearts of the Johnson family. When shown the 1964 film *The President*, narrated by Peck, Johnson wrote a glowing letter to the actor. They would discover a mutual interest in cattle raising. Valenti wrote Peck: "It may not seem like much to you but your telegram meant a great deal to the president for even presidents, sometimes isolated, sometimes buried under an avalanche of problems that never cease and despairs that never diminish, find the spontaneous support of a good man like yourself gratifying beyond all description." Peck was a frequent White House visitor, acting as master of ceremonies or dancing with guests—quite overwhelming the incumbent's initially unmarried daughters, Lynda and Luci. This dedicated Democrat was later selected to narrate *The Democratic Faith—The Johnson Years*, a 1968 campaign film, and he was appointed to the National Council on the Arts.[22]

Sometimes, staff members had to be released or allowed to resign. Johnson disliked the very idea of people resigning from his team, taking such actions personally; it did help a bit when the change was obviously a step up in money or presitge for the departing aide. Thus, Moyers became publisher of *Newsday*; Valenti, president of the Motion Picture Association of America; and McGeorge Bundy, head of the Ford Foundation. The president helped to arrange the naming of McNamara to head the World Bank. As for firing people, he tried to get others to do it; when one aide would not leave unless fired personally by the president, that aide ended up staying until the end![23]

President Johnson ran a decentralized operation rather than having a chief of staff. Each assistant acted on behalf of a specific area of governmental operations. Valenti says that in their memos, staff members could "importune, enlighten, incite, inform, and often oppose," but normally the president's routine actions involved adding check marks and very brief notations to their memos. Johnson was his own spokesman; staff were not to "go public." He demanded loyalty; therefore, many did not give baldly unvarnished counsel—his brother,

Sam, was one who did. Said he: "I've always said that anyone who worked for my brother for at least a month deserved the Purple Heart" because of the long hours, the high standards, and the adverse impact on his home life. "An eight-hour man ain't worth a damn to me," was LBJ's belligerent slogan. Naturally, the staff divided up into those who risked presidential wrath and those who let well enough alone. But among compensations were an abrupt change from anger to praise after an interval, and favors, gifts, remembrances, simple kindnesses. One of Johnson's pleasant characteristics was that he gave direct personal attention to the wives and children of key aides; he genuinely enjoyed making them feel totally at home. But there was an unpleasant side to Lyndon Johnson, well revealed by one subordinate, who asserts that "communications" funds were diverted by Johnson's order for debatable use at the Ranch in Texas, especially late in 1968. To the lowly worker, the president could be an awesome figure—a person to be feared because there just might be extravagance of epithet or wreaking of sudden vengeance for unforeseeable dereliction, as the president concentrated on what was convenient *for him*.[24] This darker side has fascinated biographers of Lyndon Johnson the man, that occasional authoritarian who could proclaim that the White House personnel consisted of one "elephant" with all the rest "pissants"; one who littered the air with barnyard language, though not deliberately when women were present.

Nevertheless, one of Johnson's obsessions was to teach senior staff, to improve them, and to build them beyond the way he found them. In 1965 he recalled that when he was a debate teacher, he had bragged: "If they'd take one side of a question I'd take the other. I'd just try to run 'em under ground, just almost stomp 'em, but always would make it clear that I loved them, where they'd never completely run off. I would humiliate them and embarrass 'em and make fun of 'em and everything until they got to where they could take care of themselves, which they did. Califano said that one should picture a situation where people's workday went from eight in the morning to ten or eleven at night, "every night, every day. Saturdays, Sunday afternoons."[25] Staff hung in there because they knew they were learning, improving, and certainly making history.

Some got burned out, and some got fed up, whether they displayed it or not. Dean Acheson once said to Johnson: "Let's face it, Mr. President, you just aren't a likeable man." Nevertheless, Johnson certainly had some winsome characteristics, and his alumni did well. Aide Douglass Cater and speech writer Robert Hardesty became college presidents; Joseph Califano was President Jimmy Carter's secretary of health, education, and welfare; Larry O'Brien later headed the National Basketball Association; George Reedy and others became college professors; and so on. The "students" of teacher Johnson seldom languished in subordinate positions. Says Califano, the bulk of the governmental bureaucracy "just couldn't see that Johnson had a picture of educating the world and the whole country."

Some aides and famous advisers had major functions and were close to the president daily, some even hourly; others had minor roles—or at least limited contact. Thus, the index cards in the White House Diary show that Professor Goldman's contacts numbered little more than a dozen large luncheons, while Valenti's cards total over three hundred, many simply identified as "in Oval Office" or "off record." Judge Moursund, a personal friend and business counselor, boasts about four hundred cards; for it was unrealistic to expect the Johnson Trust and the Ranch to be out of mind—they certainly were not. (While few of President George Washington's countrymen expected him to put Mount Vernon out of his daily routine of thought and action, the twentieth-century inclination was to clamp down on any public servants who tried to keep their private estates in good order.)

One task for some staff members was to furnish ideas and data to the busy executive for his use during appointments. These 5" x 8" cards, typed front and back, were duly studied and retained for a quick glance during meetings. There is ample testimony to this politician's fabulous memory for briefing information; he could reproduce it flawlessly with all of the points in exact order. Staff reveled in being influential. By each act we are contributing to our country, said Valenti enthusiastically. "The plain truth is that no ascent to high corporate levels, no coup in the market or fame in the world of art and culture or academia, can compare with the juice of this sensation."[26]

A distinction must be drawn between the aides, who were on the payroll, and highly placed friends of Lyndon Johnson who proved to be of the greatest importance in helping to make up the president's mind on vital affairs of state. Some of the latter equal or transcend even such an intimate as Valenti, so well informed a person as Rostow, so experienced an individual as Rusk, and so orderly a one as McNamara. Who were these persons? When at the administration's close the Johnsons were hosted at a small gathering in New York City given by Brooke Astor, those present included such solvent people as the Charles Engelhards, the Henry Fords, the Arthur Krims, Mary Lasker, the John Loebs, the André Meyers, the Laurence Rockefellers, and the Ed Weisls. Such names appear seldom or not at all in the indexes of books on the

Johnsons. They made history, yet history, in this context, knows them not.

One of them in particular, Arthur Krim, enjoyed quiet influence that should be revealed. In 1964 president of United Artists Corporation in New York City and active with the state President's Club (a fund-raising unit), Arthur Krim was described early in the Johnson campaign as "one of our staunchest supporters and our chief fund raiser."[27] The president first mentioned him in public on May 28, 1964, in Madison Square Garden, when Krim chaired a political gala. By 1969 he had had far more than five hundred face-to-face meetings with the president! It is instructive to trace the progression of this little-known intimacy.

"Thank you so very much for your warm letter supporting my proposals for Vietnam. I hope you can imagine how encouraging it is for me to hear from friends, and have such wholehearted support," Johnson wrote his fund-raising friend on April 14, 1965. At the time, Krim was suggesting people to be appointed to jobs and was nominating individuals to receive invitations to ceremonial White House functions. Letters of thanks for his services appear in the files repeatedly; his "succinct and incisive comments" were termed welcome. Invitations to stay at the White House or to come to the Ranch became commonplace. In reply, "It was, of course the greatest weekend of our lives," one that increased his admiration for the president and gave renewed pride in the nation, thought Krim in the fall. "I want to hear from you whenever you have an idea or view to express or suggestion to make," was the president's view. "Your wisdom and your judgment are much respected by me." By fall 1965 an "honorary Texan," Krim was arranging White House viewing of Disney films and a dozen David Wolper TV films and was being asked by the president to nominate more people for governmental positions. To Krim, the Johnsons were by now "the two most wonderful people in the world." Califano asked Krim for "any information you are in a position to give" on reducing capital expenditures, because exchanges with Krim were "extremely helpful to the president and to the cabinet."[28] It was not quite in jest that Douglass Cater acknowledged one of Krim's requests with the remark, "Your word is my command." Yet the very name of Krim is scarcely to be found anywhere, in any connection, in the literature on Johnson!

Around a hundred flattering and regardful letters were exchanged by the president and Krim during the presidential years. When a delegation was being prepared to go to Mexico City, Valenti reminded Johnson that "on all delegations like this we . . . try to include some of Arthur Krim's people"—that is, donors to the President's Club campaign chest. Krim worked to get the movie industry to help stimulate the 1966 savings-bond program. In 1966 Krim was still suggesting influential people who should receive invitations to presidential receptions, for he was now chairman of the Democratic Finance Committee as well as head of the President's Clubs. He even conferred with cabinet members about the work and aspirations of the clubs.

So much activity could not be kept totally free from rumors and some gossip. Moyers was confronted in early 1966 with a published report that "in effect, the President and the White House have been selling invitations to dinner at $10,000 a year." Moyers called the charge absurd, asking oddly, "Is there such a thing as an Elite President's Club? I don't know of one."[29] Arthur Krim and his wife, Mathilde—an Israeli by background and a brilliant physician—received so many invitations from the Johnsons that they had to turn down some of them because he was too busy on the president's political business. When Treasury Secretary Henry Fowler wondered if he should go to a Krim fund raiser, the president said to tell him, "By all means—and get all his friends to go." In the summer, Krim gave advice on whom the president should support for mayor of New York City; he suggested six persons for ambassadorships and one for the National Crime Commission; and he was asked, but declined, to nominate members of the Labor-Management Council.

In 1967 Krim was off to Henry Ford II "to discuss money." When asked about a new film for the Democratic National Committee, Johnson told Watson to "clear it with Krim." Robert Kennedy's political moves and gatherings interested Krim, who worried about seating at dinners, travel, timing, and similar matters, even about what the vice-president's role would be. Krim shunned personal publicity: for example, he referred a persistent *New York Times* reporter to the Democratic National Committee for answers. Said one aide, "Mr. Krim feels his effectiveness would be destroyed if he ever gets into major stories about his political activities." Krim's master list of "our good friends across the country" was in demand inside the White House "for use with our various commissions, conferences, etc." Revealed here in the Johnson-Krim relationship is indeed an important—though virtually unknown—mixture of Democratic money, party politics, personal friendship, and public business.

The year 1968 was a hard transition year for Krim. After Johnson's famous withdrawal speech, Krim resigned as chairman of the Democratic National Finance Committee. Johnson remarked that under Krim's leadership the party had known for the first time in many years what it meant to be solvent. By mid May, Krim was at work financing the Lyndon Johnson Library and Museum of the future; he also asked to be contacted before the delegation to the United Nations General Assembly was selected; offered a five-paragraph statement about poverty in America for the president's use; forwarded a strongly pro-Israel column by Eric Hoffer, and wrote a moving note of congratulations to his leader about apparent successes in the Vietnam negotiations.[30]

Here was a personal friend, therefore, who worked long and hard for President Johnson and the Democratic party. To an audience at the LBJ School of Public Affairs the retired chief executive later said, "We wouldn't have this auditorium and these wonderful facilities except for one man more than any other man I know—Arthur Krim of New York—who spent about four or five years of his life making it possible for us to have this opportunity we have had today, because of his love for his fellow humans." The president's memoir would call the Krimses loyal and devoted friends, with Arthur "a valued adviser on matters relating to the Democratic Party"—surely an understatement. Lady Bird's expressed gratitude was to Arthur Krim, "who has shared so much."[31] The total contribution in 1964 and later by this privileged special consultant must be weighed and pondered.

The roles of Abe Fortas and Arthur Goldberg could be traced similarly. These justices were consulted frequently on matters of state that were totally unrelated to Supreme Court business; always, the questions involved appear to have been of the utmost moment. Fortas came routinely to important meetings of the National Security Council. Others who were brought in at crucial points were university president Milton Eisenhower (especially on the Dominican Republic), New Dealer Tom Corcoran, lawyer Clark Clifford (until 1968), Robert B. Anderson, and former Secretary of State Dean Acheson. A group called "the Wise Men" consisted of Acheson, George Ball, Gen. Omar Bradley, McGeorge Bundy, Arthur Dean, Douglas Dillon, Henry Cabot Lodge, Robert Murphy, Gen. Matthew B. Ridgway, Gen. Maxwell D. Taylor, and Cyrus Vance—all of whom became well known for their services to government. The group gave advice on Vietnam policy in early 1968. For Washington lawyers, said one columnist, this administration meant "an hour had come round at last."[32] Several talented women outside of government, especially volunteers Mary Lasker of New York City and Agnes Meyer of Washington, had the Johnson ear.

While Hubert Humphrey talked to the president at length on occasion, he could not count on prevailing. Nor, indeed, could any of the array of aides, advisers, officials, friends, and intimates mentioned here expect the president to surrender to them his freedom of decision. It is a fair generalization that during his years in office, President Johnson ran the executive branch and—after listening to much advice—

made thousands of final decisions himself, while delegating masses of detail in administration to those whom he fully trusted. Together, the eager president and his ambitious team in the executive branch dominated the federal government from 1963 to 1969.

3

★ ★ ★ ★ ★

FIRST MANDATE: THE LEGACY TO CONTINUE

It is a truism that the Johnson administration proved vastly productive in framing and passing new legislation. This was possible because the man who had spent twelve years in the House, twelve in the Senate, and three as vice-president was completely familiar with the machinery of the legislative process and was determined to use it fully. He had been an interested observer of five presidents who tried to take their programs through the Congress in order to make their legislative mark. He intended to equal or exceed each one of them—maybe all of them! Lyndon Johnson as president had *two mandates*. These were invaluable to him as he proceeded. He could rely on them to carry him past many who opposed him, whether in the Congress, the media, establishment circles, or pressure groups.

The first mandate that served the new president in the years 1963 and 1964 was—as he himself put it before a nationwide audience—the *"legacy to continue"* from where John F. Kennedy could be shown to have left off. Johnson would take the reins and drive the carriage along a path inescapably identifiable with that of the fallen leader. Here was, in a sense, his inheritance. The second mandate would be gained late in 1964 through the electoral process, when, in the presidential election, the accidental incumbent administered a crushing defeat to his opponent and the Republican party at every level. That victory was so overwhelming that it could be taken as a mandate for "change." It could be interpreted pretty much as the winner chose to read it. Here was the chance of a lifetime for a master politician; and the man from Texas was

45

not one to let opportunity slip by. Had Johnson entered the Oval Office with only a narrow victory in 1961, his talents and experience would surely have brought the nation some legislative results. That he achieved what he did in 1963/64, 1965, and later, however, was very considerably due to these two extraordinary mandates, the first from the Kennedy tragedy and the second from the American electorate.

Another reason for the avalanche of legislation between 1963 and 1969 was the nature of Johnson himself. He wanted results badly enough to fight for them. A problem with some administrations in American history has been that the leader seemed to be content with things as they were or had only a very limited vision of how things might be if changed through judicious use of the full power of government. The man from Johnson City desired to change things—a great many things. Indeed, as he had lived, listened, and interacted during his lifetime, he had arrived at many beliefs on how things ought to be. He was plentifully supplied with the kind of optimism that led him to believe that the road was open to improvement in many aspects of life both at home and abroad. New laws coming from presidential initiative could make all the difference!

The first order of business with Congress after the assassination was for Johnson to present himself to them as the new leader. He must allay apprehensions, create confidence, and lay the groundwork for new enthusiasm. The vehicle to start this would be an initial address to a joint session of Congress. Johnson's first thought was for Horace Busby to draft it in "a two hour spurt," but Busby wisely decided that the speech would have to be so good "for the world" that it should be crafted to last a long time. The various drafts that then came to this aide were good, he wrote, "because it is so clear that everybody helping wants so strongly for you to succeed superbly."[1] Ted Sorensen went to work, aided initially by drafts from Busby, Charles Murphy, and John Kenneth Galbraith. Sorensen started fresh anyway. Fortunately he, or someone else, rejected his own disastrous first thought: "For the greatest leader of our time has been struck down by the foulest deed of our time—and I who cannot fill his shoes must occupy his desk." When he finished more rationally, the draft was scrutinized by Rusk, McNamara, and Fortas, who still had to change it in line with a Bundy comment that it sounded "too much like JFK." Walter Jenkins greatly simplified the resulting text.

Beginning with "All I have I would have given gladly not to be standing here today," the new president quickly turned to a list of dreams that he said had been "vitalized" by his predecessor. There followed an idealistic statement of results that the United States would work to achieve at home and abroad. Kennedy had said in 1961, "Let us begin." Johnson now said, "Let us continue." Fulfill the nation's destiny. Remember Kennedy by passing the stalled civil-rights bill and the tax-reduction bill. Act on education, youth employment, foreign aid, and appropriations bills. The address was extravagant in tone but in good taste except for an unnecessary paraphrase of Lincoln's Gettysburg Address: "So let us here highly resolve that John Fitzgerald Kennedy did not live—or die—in vain." Yet conditioned contemporaries saw nothing untoward in this. The speech stressed unity and continuity; but in the long run it would handicap Johnson's independence of action at home and abroad. He was to be thought of as Kennedy's "successor" for many long months. Senator Ralph Yarborough of Texas correctly called it a strong reaffirmation of the goals of the Kennedy administration, and Johnson exalted it by sending specially bound and embossed copies to congressmen and many government officials for Christmas.[2]

President Lyndon Johnson, new in his title and his power, came into a situation in which national policies were well established. Exactly where, governmental executives at every level wondered, did the new leader disagree with present policy? The dangers and opportunities in the situation appear clearly in a card memorandum drafted by McGeorge Bundy for the president's use at a meeting of the National Security Council on December 2: Should troops be withdrawn from Europe? was the subject. Johnson was informed that Rusk and McNamara had reached agreement on tactics and policy for the meeting; so the session would be short, yet it must be held in order to show that the government's position had been "established with your participation and approval." Rusk would speak; then McNamara; then the president should state his "own judgment." All went just as the holdovers had planned. Bundy also counseled his boss on subjects to raise with the secretary of state: "management in Vietnam"; policy in Cuba; a head for the Alliance for Progress; "a new man in Pakistan." There was more, possibly including advice on handling Rusk; but even in the 1980s this would remain classified, despite appeals made by this writer.[3]

The next day brought the first congressional leadership breakfast, where the subject was the civil-rights bill, which had been stuck since May and on which hearings were not expected until the coming year. Educational bills were in a bit better shape: a discharge petition might be necessary, though unpleasant. Johnson wanted to push for the tax bill, then civil rights; nothing could be done on education without agreement between Senator Wayne Morse and Congresswoman Edith Green, he said. From the Senate minority leader, Republican Everett Dirksen, came such remarks as "Believe me, there's not going to be a political truce," and only "financial legerdemain" would achieve all the president's goals. On December 4 came an uneasy meeting between Professor Goldman and the practical president. The historian was asked to assemble a group of "best minds" to suggest objectives, goals, and directions—a "quiet brain trust." A far more elaborate scheme than this would ultimately develop under other leadership: the task forces, which will be discussed below. Of the many activities during these late November and early December days, some were for show. Thus, there would be a meeting with the national commander of the American Legion, for which Dean Rusk urged that pictures be taken. After all, the Legion had repeatedly stood for national unity and had minimized criticism.[4]

It would be an error to visualize the nation's leader as relying entirely on the secretaries of state and defense and their aides, consulting with certain internationally oriented members of Congress, and emphasizing this advice when making decisions in foreign affairs. Sometimes he did this, of course. But he also consulted repeatedly—privately and in confidence—with persons who held no office of power in the government. Among these were the three living former presidents—Hoover, briefly, despite his very advanced age and poor health; Truman; and Eisenhower—by telephone, through their aides, and sometimes in person. He consulted a few journalists of stature; one of his early visits was to the home of Walter Lippmann. One Johnson aide believed Averell Harriman should be seen "if only to hold the liberals in line." Dean Acheson should be probed on the skills and qualities of those who were now serving in the national-security area. Bundy described Acheson as a believer in the "hard line"; Acheson and Lippmann were said to be at opposite poles.[5] The president should also ask Acheson how to handle relations between the State Department and the Congress: "Stress your desire to have Acheson call you at any time. You will be calling him." The two met at a luncheon on December 6.

Many subjects were presidential concerns in December 1963. Those who bore responsibility for existing policy in Southeast Asia—where the unexpected killing of President Diem by South Vietnamese soldiers (after he had been ousted, without any regret on the part of the Kennedy team) had brought a situation bordering on disaster—looked to Johnson uneasily. They knew that he had opposed Diem's ousting in the first place. But the fledgling president had no intention of rocking the boat unnecessarily. By December 12 Bundy could write the new leader, "Vietnam: Your determination to carry on the effort there has been made clear to all concerned."[6] This was a major decision that would lead to eventual catastrophe for the chief executive, many of his assistants, and millions of others. On December 7 the first letters of condolence to the next of kin of countrymen who had been killed since November 22 in Vietnam were placed on Lyndon Johnson's desk for his review, editing, and signature.

By mid month, aides had given much thought to the Democratic party's fund raising for the following year's campaign, although the president's ban on politics in public was still in effect. Work on the State of the Union message, required in January, began early, with the task being undertaken by a Valenti team consisting of Fortas, Reedy, Moyers, Busby, Dick Nelson, and Goldman. (The historian's elaborate and overly professional draft was deemed unsuitable.)[7]

One has to reflect on the often-heard charges about presidential isolation. Through December 19 the new president had seen 673 people individually or in small groups; some 3,062 more in large groups. His activities varied. On December 20 Johnson viewed a film that treated the recent tragic, historic assassination. Reproduced into 259 33-mm and 60 16-mm film prints, it would go to 106 countries after being dubbed into 29 languages. Emotional, propagandistic, and eulogistic, it would further the Kennedy mystique on a global scale. On a constitutional matter, Johnson and Speaker John McCormack would reach agreement on conditions for the Speaker's succession, there now being no vice-president.[8]

The period of mourning for Kennedy ended on December 22 with a nondenominational service at the Lincoln Memorial. Johnson spoke in Lincolnian terms, rooted in the Gettysburg Address and the Second Inaugural Address. It came to an awkward effort, for everyone was trying too hard. On the same day a televised Christmas-tree-lighting ceremony saw the president more at home; but again the talk did not hang together very well. Nevertheless, his actions overall spoke larger than the words put in his mouth, so that a historian from his home state could think at the end of the year that Johnson's start had combined "nobility with effectiveness." All in all, in a matter of hours, he had moved out of the relative limbo of the vice-presidency to the status of an accepted working president. His careful personal deportment had been a factor. So had the television documentaries and background stories. TV especially encouraged faith in him by emphasizing his experience and capabilities.[9]

A specialist has commented on the smoothness of the transfer of power, saying that there was almost no time during which the locus of executive power was uncertain, no major period of jockeying for power, and indeed little change in personnel or policy direction, so that the validity of the central institutional structure seems to have been taken for granted. The loyalties of the military were hardly subject to question—which might not be taken for granted in many countries. Nor was any high-level conspiracy involving Kennedy's successor a subject for hostile conjecture.[10] Johnson's own best public comment on the succession came in 1966, when he dedicated the John Fitzgerald Kennedy Memorial Park at Lewiston, Maine: ''We have tried to carry forward his program, put it on the statute books, and execute it as he would have had us do.''

The biographer of Johnson will need to take full account of the role that the Ranch played as a place of relaxation, rejuvenation, and routine work on the nation's business. There would be no less than seventy-eight trips there during the Johnson years. Then work and relaxation would blend with the making of final decisions that could be reached while watching the cattle or driving about in a Lincoln Continental convertible, beer can in hand. Showing visitors about the Ranch was an exuberant occupation for LBJ; for them, it could be a chore, made even less pleasant perhaps by an injunction to shoot a browsing deer. The Texas barbeque was a hospitable institution. Soon, he was told by Governor John Connally that the official map of Texas prominently featured the Johnson Ranch.

During the first Christmas season at the Ranch, the workload was heavy, but there was fun too. Calls were placed to Hoover and Truman ''to wish them a Merry Christmas and discuss the problems of the presidency.'' The next half hour was spent looking at cattle with a friend. Soon Eisenhower was reached, after which the Johnsons chatted together for half an hour. The dependable official photographer, Yoichi Okamoto, got a thorough workout nearly every day. Ten persons were called Christmas evening, including Lippmann and McNamara. Gift time was from 9:00 to 10:15 P.M.; supper, from 10:15 to 11:30. ''Lights out for the president and his family on this Christmas Day, 1963,'' ends the secretary's chronology. In such detail, and more, can the five years of Johnson's administration be followed by those who wish to do so.

Thus ended the initial days of trial for President Lyndon Johnson, with virtually full agreement that he had done well. He had said he would do his best, had pledged ''a new spirit of action,'' and had offered ''unswerving commitment'' to work for world peace. Power had moved smoothly from the hands of the departed leader, and there had been relatively few self-aggrandizing moves for the Irish Mafia to grouse about to friends in the press. The new occupant of the White House had done far more than his share to help build what would soon become a

Kennedy mythology. Later, when clearly bothered by this as the memoirs and appraisals of 1961 to 1963 appeared, he may well have reflected on the extravagant language about Kennedy that had been placed in his speeches by holdover speech writers, the rapid naming of so many public places for a president who had served less than three years in office, and his own instant award of the Medal of Freedom to Kennedy, complete with an extravagant evaluation.

Congress in November 1963 had been considering the appropriations bill for foreign aid. Involved with this was the possible sale of surplus wheat to the Warsaw Pact countries. A pending amendment by Republican Senator Karl Mundt would have prohibited making loans to any Communist country so that it could finance trade. Immediately on returning from Kennedy's funeral, the president called O'Brien to request a head count. What was at stake seemed to transcend the immediate issue: "If those legislators had tasted blood then, they would have run over us like a steamroller when they returned in January," Johnson recalled. On December 13 the president sent aide Bryce Harlow to Eisenhower, who quickly agreed to call Republican leader of the House, Charles Halleck, to urge a figure of $3.2 billion for foreign aid.[11] This tactic would be repeated in June, with Johnson calling Eisenhower personally—and successfully—on behalf of a request for $3.5 billion. Working far into the night, the administration won in the Senate. But a similar restriction showed up in the House, so the battle continued in conference committee as Christmas approached. When some legislators headed home, the president took the risk of having them called back. To soften the blow, Lady Bird hastily organized a reception for December 23. Says Johnson, "I took the opportunity to stand up on a chair in the State Dining Room and plead my case with our guests." At 7:00 A.M. on the twenty-fourth, in the Congress, the battle was won. "At that moment the power of the federal government began flowing back to the White House." The reins of government were in his hands; "and I believe the nation knew it too." Afterward he phoned his thanks to dozens of congressmen. One said it was the first time a president had called him, and he would not forget it!

As viewed in January, the Congress faced many bills on which action had by no means been completed; but it knew it would surely have to face items in a new Johnson program, sooner or later. Together, these would constitute "the 1964 Johnson legislative program," said a long staff memorandum.[12] Before 1964 began, legislation passed and on the books dealt with college facilities, clean air, vocational education, vocational training for Indians, and manpower training. The year 1964 would bring its own successes, measured in terms of new laws—a standard quantitative rather than qualitative method of assessing progress in this administration. The list of new legislation in 1964 was impressive: it dealt with the Inter-American Development Bank, the Kennedy Cultural Center, tax reduction, presidential transition, federal aid to airports, the farm program, the Chamizal Convention, control of pesticides, the International Development Association, the Civil Rights Act of 1964, Campobello International Park, urban mass-transit systems, research on water resources, federal highways, civil-service pay raises, the "War on Poverty," criminal justice, truth-in-securities, the Medicine Bow National Forest, the Ozark Scenic Riverway, the Administrative Conference, the Fort Bowie Historic Site, food stamps, housing, interest equalization, wilderness areas, nurse training, revenues for recreation, the Fire Island National Seashore, library services, and health benefits for federal employees. The president thought that the year had brought "a new spirit of cooperation among our people." But long before the end of the year there would be preparation for the next year's battles, especially in studying committee jurisdictions in order to avoid bottlenecks. Surely Jack Kennedy would have approved of the 1964 legislation! "That remains one of the great satisfactions of my Presidency."[13]

The Civil Rights Bill of 1964 was a major concern, as will be seen, but innovation was especially well marked in the new war on poverty, effort on which began early in the year. The Johnson administration had hardly gotten started before its leader authorized major activity against poverty: "I'm interested. I'm sympathetic. Go ahead. Give it the highest priority. Push ahead full tilt." The reply was from Johnson on the evening of his first full day in office; the question had come from Walter Heller, chairman of the council of Economic Advisers. Three days before, said the former professor of economics, he had gained approval from President Kennedy to begin planning a program to alleviate poverty in America, but he had no guidance on any specific content. Heller indicated that he had already made some inquiries of departments and agencies. How great was Johnson's interest? Should he go ahead? "We were moving into uncharted territory. Powerful forces of opposition would be stirred," Johnson later recalled. A much appreciated memorandum from aide Horace Busby offered a warning: "America's real majority is suffering a minority complex of neglect. They have become the real foes of Negro rights, foreign aid, etc., because, as much as anything, they feel forgotten, at the second table behind the tightly organized, smaller groups at either end of the U.S. spectrum."[14] So, Johnson recalled, "We foresaw clearly the problems and dangers." Wage earners might resist. An attack on poverty might prove a political land mine if based on a slogan campaign rather than on effective action.

The ensuing War on Poverty, then, actually began with acquiescence in a very tentative suggestion advanced by one of Kennedy's economists who in turn had only just obtained approval from him to study a general idea. It is unclear whether Johnson was aware of a Rockefeller Brothers Fund study report of 1958 on the economic and welfare needs of Americans. Calm, reasoned, expressing confidence in growth as a tool, it had called for doubling all expenditures for education in ten years, for a catastrophic-illness plan, and for the use of general tax revenues to pay for the medical requirements of the needy aged and those unable to afford medical care.

For "low income groups," the study recommended improving social-security payments and the categorical-aid programs (Aid to Dependent Children, Aid to the Blind, Aid to the Aged).[15] Moreover, the Ford Foundation would put some $20 million into community-action programs during the next few years, thus having a definite effect on the shape of the coming antipoverty effort. Then the Supreme Court helped to make legal resources available to the poor. A task force headed by Democratic Senator Paul Douglas had issued a report on distressed areas. Printed in eight columns of the *New York Times* only eighteen days before Kennedy's inauguration, it contained many recommendations to ameliorate unemployment. Surplus food should be better distributed, education should be aided, and chronic joblessness should be fought.

Why was Lyndon Johnson so interested? Whatever influence may possibly have been exerted on Kennedy by such books as Galbraith's *Affluent Society* (1958) or Michael Harrington's *Other America* (1962), Johnson's interest had no such origins. The existing scholarly literature did not touch him either. More his style was the report *One Third of a Nation*, which had grown out of a task force during the Kennedy years. During Johnson's first year, Daniel Patrick Moynihan would use it as he wrote an influential report on Negro family life which rested heavily on obscure government statistics. Within the race he saw a crisis in family stability whose origins went back as far as slavery. From his post in the Labor Department, he stressed the importance of jobs, housing, and the ability to leave one's surroundings. He favored birth control. Negro youths could amount to something in the armed forces. Moynihan spoke openly of instability, illegitimacy, and other areas, which perhaps made emerging black leaders think their race was being attacked. Under the circumstances, the president's brave remark made at Howard University on May 4, 1965 (in a speech drafted by Moynihan and Goodwin)—"We seek . . . equality as a fact and equality as a result," thus stressing opportunity, the law, and equity—sounded inspirational but was impossible of realization in a decade, or probably even in a century. It certainly can be assumed that the president knew that his party's platform in 1960 had pointed to "a goal that is now within reach—the final eradication in America of the age-old evil of poverty"; the elimination of slums, blight, and depressed areas; and the restoration of cities—all within just ten years. The total unreality of such a bald vote-seeking pledge would appear in due time.

Study of the life of this leader is likely to lead the fair-minded to the judgment that it was primarily what Lyndon Johnson had seen and experienced that made him accept so readily the idea of a crusade to eliminate poverty from America. He had memories of marginal rural life in southwestern Texas and had seen the slums of San Antonio and Austin. While viewing the film *The Grapes of Wrath* in the White House, he cried at length. He harbored an easily stirred feeling that his native land could do far better. (His memoirs do not even intimate that he had inherited a developed crusade or that he was much influenced by personal contact with Kennedy.) His post-presidential memory was that he had visualized a program to "strengthen the moral and economic fiber of the entire country"—not just to aid the poor to the exclusion of the middle class. Homemade proverbs came easily to him: "If you do good, you'll do well." His epitaph should be "Lyndon Johnson did his best for folks who couldn't do theirs."[16] His whirlwind stint as part of Franklin Roosevelt's National Youth Administration (NYA) team was certainly a factor.

The genesis of the new program was developed in a preliminary way at the Ranch during Christmas week 1963 in a dialogue between Heller, Kermit Gordon (director of the Bureau of the Budget), and Jesse Kellam, Johnson's deputy from his days with the NYA. "I spent many long hours with them, discussing, planning, and evolving the outlines of a poverty program." That NYA experience suggested some solutions, he thought, so that heavy emphasis should be on efforts to help improve the lives of children and youths in city and country alike. The president determined to go "big and bold" and make a real impact. There was need for a title. The idea of Point One (with an eye on Truman's Point Four) was rejected; War on Poverty was then selected, right there by the Pedernales River. The hope was "to rally the nation, to sound a call to arms which would stir people."

One who was there says that once the decision to wage war on poverty was firm, the actual preparation of the antipoverty bill became an all-consuming effort.[17] Johnson decided there was no mileage in seeking to pass existing bills; he wanted a new package. One program on which to build was the 1962 Manpower Development and Training Act, which tried to match workers to jobs that were already in existence, using counseling and training as tools. The idea, said Hubert Humphrey, was that poverty is both inhumane and a drag on the economy; an investment in people would bring in taxes, improve the economy, and cut costs of welfare and unemployment; he was not surprised when the programs did not reach all their goals. "What is surprising is how much was accomplished," even though the great beginnings had been overwhelmed by the noise of critics.[18]

The War on Poverty was declared by Lyndon Johnson only a few minutes into his first State of the Union message, on January 8, 1964; but, significantly, it was not linked in prose with the speech's earlier promise to carry forward the plans and programs of John Fitzgerald Kennedy. Because many Americans live on the outskirts of hope, "our task is to help replace their despair with opportunity." Then came the famous declaration: "This administration today, here and now, declares unconditional war on poverty in America." The struggle would not be short or easy, but "we shall not rest until that war is won." The richest nation on earth surely could afford to win it. Poverty was a national problem to be defeated from the courthouse to the White House. It would be pursued "in city slums and small towns, in sharecropper shacks or in migrant labor camps, on Indian reservations, among whites as well as Negroes, among the young as well as the aged, in the boom towns and in the depressed areas." All would surely benefit from the financing of hospital costs for the aged, the building of schools and libraries, the improving of rapid-transit systems, and the training of nurses.

So far, the plan for the war lacked details, because the task force that would study what would be done had not yet been called into session. But a beginning would be aid for Appalachia; area redevelopment; youth employment; broader food-stamp programs; a national service corps (similar to the Peace Corps); modernized unemployment insurance; a study of the effects of automation; extension of the minimum wage to some two million workers; special school aid in hardest-hit areas; more libraries, hospitals, and nursing homes; hospital insurance; aid for those displaced by slum clearance and the provision of decent housing generally; and modern rapid-transit systems inside communities, with "low-cost transportation between them."

The president returned to his War on Poverty briefly in his Economic Report twelve days later, referring to a "forgotten fifth" that needed to get above the poverty line. Johnson the master politician brazenly declared, "We know what must be done, and this nation of abundance can surely afford to do it." Neither statement, it would turn out, was even remotely true. Yet a promising direction, almost a noble one, was being established in the public mind. On January 27 came a message on housing and community development. On March 16, 1964, a special message proposed a "Nationwide War on the Sources of Poverty." The shift should be noted, for what had been announced originally to be an unconditional war on poverty itself was now directed at its "sources": a few months had made for reconsideration. The war, Johnson now said, would cost one percent of the federal budget. Here was to be a sadly limited war indeed.

Key decisions had to be made. Should administration be in the hands of a cabinet member, as urged by Secretary of Labor Wirtz and Attorney General Kennedy, or in a new agency, as favored by Galbraith, Gordon, and Heller. "Don't bury the program in the departments," said Galbraith; instead, get a new staff and a new director, "so people will know what you are doing." The president agreed, but there was a far-reaching guarantee of future executive-branch infighting. There would be the Office of Economic Opportunity (OEO). (Many would never accept this decision as final.) For director, Johnson chose Kennedy's brother-in-law Sargent Shriver, then head of the Peace Corps, a man who was talented in public interaction and was imaginative and highly regarded in Congress; he was personable and, in ideology, a practical idealist. Shriver quickly generated the fervor and excitement that was exactly what the eager president sought. The secret task force got little public attention while developing new ideas, rejecting others, and adapting many from past or existing programs.

Thus, from 1961 to 1969, the ideas, language (including some titles), and the programs in the poverty area are somewhat intertwined between the Kennedy and Johnson administrations. (Much would live on into the Nixon administration.) As a coordinated, named, and recognized effort, the War on Poverty was in fact Lyndon Johnson's. Recognition of the rhetoric and spirit and some of the staff work of the Kennedy team and of the late president himself is in order, however. In philosophy, the OEO, with its goals of social engineering and eradication of poverty, went well beyond the New Deal. Our attention to the question of "credit" is warranted, for it very much concerned Lyndon Johnson, who by late 1966 felt that he must begin to arm himself with helpful historical facts.[19]

That John F. Kennedy once had the subject of poverty in the forefront of his mind is obvious enough. Heller asked him on November 19 if work should continue with an eye to the 1964 legislative agenda. "Yes, and let me see your proposals in a couple of weeks." And, spoke the politician, "First we'll have your tax cut; then we'll have my expenditures program." More soberly, he confided to Schlesinger, "The time has come to organize a national assault on the causes of poverty, a comprehensive program, across the board," a centerpiece for 1964. If the middle class should come to feel threatened, he would have to do something for the suburbs.[20]

Words were one thing; action proved to be quite another. Socialist Michael Harrington came to the task-force discussions armed with insights into the stubbornness of poverty and the complexity of its causes. He sensed the shoals ahead. He said bluntly to the then almost naïve Shriver: "You've got to understand right away that you've been given nickels and dimes for this program. You'll have less than a billion dollars to work with." Shriver replied that he was nevertheless quite excited about his first opportunity to spend a billion dollars! Many besides Harrington were skeptical. Said one columnist, the war is fine as a start, but it is not something that Sargent Shriver is going to overcome with a pilot project.[21]

Willard Wirtz, Wilbur Cohen, departmental representatives, union members, civil-rights activists, and social scientists now worked together despite serious divisions in their points of view and desires. One division was between those who favored seeking jobs and training and those who preferred activities involving community action. Harrington, Frank Mankiewicz, and Paul Jacobs managed to get Shriver to add to the recommendations some radical assertions that there would have to be basic changes in how Americans allocate their resources: that is, the American "system" needed massive "social investments" and "structural changes." Had this appeared in the day's headlines, translated into common speech, it could have been devastating. To the surprise of all, Johnson is said to have sent back word that if it took such innovations to complete the work done by the New Deal, then we'd just have to make them! An unrealistic scheme to attain universal American literacy within eighteen months was scrapped. A winner was something to be called community action (see below).

Members of the task force but not many others during those years were aware of the extent of the giant welfare programs already in existence. That March, for example, HEW alone had 120 programs that dealt in some way with aspects of the problem at hand. These had been requiring money in ever-increasing amounts, and knowledgeable persons saw a need for additional staff positions for such activities. There were programs in the Department of Labor, plus hundreds of state programs, as well as vast numbers of venerable voluntary agencies and church efforts. A comprehensive inventory and description of welfare agencies, laws, and programs for one large state during the 1950s had required 520 pages. Some churches—the Mormons, for example—took care of their own almost in toto; and Catholic, Jewish, and Protestant congregations devoted funds, effort, and buildings to people requiring assistance.[22]

Many names are associated with the famous antipoverty warfare. Aides to Shriver were Adam Yarmolinsky, Daniel Patrick Moynihan, and James Sundquist—a team of Eastern liberal-intellectual political figures then well within the Kennedy family establishment. It was not to be a Texas-controlled activity. The act would come to bear the stamp of Wilbur Cohen from HEW, of staff from Robert Kennedy's Juvenile Delinquency Committee, and of personnel from the Bureau of the Budget. Old-line bureaucratic types were largely excluded from the planning process. Experience gained in New Haven, Connecticut, proved beneficial, especially in community-action matters. The poor did not participate in basic planning; but there was input from the religious, trade-union, civil rights, and academic communities. The gestation period to mid March 1964 was one that the participants would not readily forget.

The OEO soon became decidedly controversial. It is surprising that a program begun at well under the $1 billion level and one that never exceeded $2 billion should have been the center of so much attention; for, as will appear, it faded by comparison with such money-payments programs then in existence as social security, the categorical-aid program Aid to Dependent Children, and veterans benefits. Critics or skeptics quickly focused on programs like the Job Corps, Volunteers in Service to America (VISTA)—something of a domestic Peace Corps— and community action. The most bitter opponents of the latter saw it as no more than a trial run for the government to teach the techniques of revolution to the poor.

One fact that had to be faced was that there was simply no definition of "poverty." The Committee for Economic Development adopted one in 1964, using a Social Security Administration standard of $3,000 for a four-person nonfarm family. By the standard that an individual needed $1,500 annually, it was decided in 1962 that 35 million people had been living in poverty. The standard was changed in 1965, and a census series was rooted in that. With a very slowly rising standard—from $3,089 in 1962 to $3,743 in 1969—the number of poor was said to have decreased from 38.6 million (21 percent) to 24.1 million (12 percent). In such reports, little is said about what role the draft and the war-occasioned prosperity played in the favorable results, but something in this vein should have been forthcoming. After all, from

1965 to 1973 the OEO cost about $15.1 billion—admittedly at a time when the total expenditures on Vietnam came to $120 billion.[23]

The War on Poverty has been criticized as being "3,000 people without a plan," lacking in clear objectives, and a skirmish rather than a war. Taxes were not enacted to fund it adequately; it tended to exclude the near-poor; and it addressed, so some knowledgeable people said, pieces of problems. It was dissected four days before the August 20, 1964, signing of the OEO bill in the first of many articles in the *New York Daily News*. One charge was that Mobilization for Youth, which had already been in existence, employed Communist sympathizers and had inspired riots in Harlem. Such charges would expand into an uneasy feeling nationally, even though such problems were limited in scope. The Job Corps would be attacked because it had temporarily housed youths in posh hotels. Some of its camps were not ready on time, and the locations for them were often resisted by those who lived nearby. The fact that the new agencies were not under the control of existing city political machines was resented in powerful quarters.

There was more. The hiring of radicals, especially from black enclaves akin to ghettos, soon gave some agencies a flavor that was unacceptable to middle-class whites. Radicals Huey Newton and Bobby Seale drew up a ten-point program for the Black Panthers in the office of the North Oakland, California, Poverty Center. Sociologist Tom Wolfe noted that some people in impoverished black communities quickly discovered that one thing the OEO could do well was to provide administrative jobs at good pay; so, activists gravitated directly to its units. Money, some said, was being "thrown at problems." The truth was quite different. It was laws that were being thrown at problems. Their funding was utterly inadequate to achieve the goals.

Passage of the OEO bill was arranged through devious strategy—as befit the master craftsman in the White House. The sponsor in the House was a Georgia Democrat, Phillip Landrum, since it was known that votes from northern liberals and some young Republicans were in the bag. Republicans on the ad hoc subcommittee were largely by-passed. Some seventy-nine witnesses testified, all but nine favorably. Questioning was perfunctory. Five mayors (including Richard Daley from Chicago) were for it. Robert Kennedy led the spokesmen for controversial Title II. Congress did not yet understand the dynamite buried in the sections on community action.[24] Congress added two new sections—funds for adult literacy education and for migrant farm workers; but it killed incentive loans for businessmen. Proposed out-right grants to impoverished farmers were replaced by loans. A trouble-some amendment, which would have given governors the right to veto aspects of Titles I and II within thirty days of a proposal, did not pass. The final vote on OEO was 61 to 34 in the Senate and 226 to 185 in the House. It is said that the price for support from the southern group in the House (which finally came to 60 affirmative votes, opposed by 40 negative votes) was a pledge that Adam Yarmolinsky—a master of relevant details and arrangements that were vital to the future success of the program—would not be appointed as Shriver's deputy. Passage was fast and easy, reminiscent of the steam-roller successes of Roosevelt's Hundred Days. But funding for the program was held to $800 million, about three-eighths of which already belonged to various departmental programs that were absorbed into the poverty bill.[25]

So, it has been said, there was "an outpouring of plans, proposals, demonstration projects, pilot projects, bills, laws, rules, schemes, devices, and propositions." On the surface, it appeared that the long arm of the federal government had transferred funds from the tax-paying segment of the general public to those who were in need. But, enroute, many groups found there was something in it for them, and some people in the middle and upper classes profited unnecessarily. In the case of legislation on housing, urban renewal helped downtown merchants, except for small businesses that were "renewed" out of their business location. City officials often seemed to be acting mainly on behalf of their constituencies. Ethnic leaders appeared to be justifying their existence and managed to stay in power even when they were contributing little or nothing to getting the program. Radicals and reformers rejoiced at approaching long-sought goals but did not stay to do the work. For members of unions, there was urban employment for those in the construction trades. At the end of the road there were some benefits for the poor, but in the case of slum clearance these were not the same poor as those originally in the slum. Neither before nor after the Johnson administration, it should be said, did slums give way readily to even the most ingenious governmental programs.[26]

Nevertheless, some partisans of OEO have remained lyrical, stressing slogans, ideas, and titles of programs while minimizing the evidence of the modest results. Sar Levitan says that the War on Poverty produced the most dramatic and sweeping social legislation since the New Deal. Yet much of it, he then judged, in *The Great Society's Poor Law* (Johns Hopkins Press, 1969), came, not from elite experts in the executive branch, but from earlier manpower policies, economic programs, and ferment during the Eisenhower and Kennedy Years. Whatever the fanfare by Johnson partisans, the war rested to an extent on past planning and action. Levitan minimized the role of presidential salesmanship, for he contended that civil-rights groups had been campaigning for these policies for some time.[27] Such opinions take too much from the Johnson presidency.

The president later mused in his memoirs: "There was no magic formula. We had to try a wide variety of approaches. Some worked better than others. Some failed completely. I heard bitter complaints from the mayors of several cities. Some funds were used to finance questionable activities. Some were badly mismanaged. That was all part of the risk."[28] Michael Harrington said that he could weep at the lost opportunity for innovation on the scale of the New Deal. He felt sure that Johnson had been prepared to do it, but "the Vietnam War overwhelmed him." The program was "underfunded and oversold"; therefore, people came to believe that social programs did not work.[29] One perspective, then, is that the War on Poverty was considerably smaller than many wished and that its programs had been too often untried previously. Another perspective is that the programs had many roots and that they would have stood some chance of making a real impact on a basic American problem if only they had been heavily funded then and later. By July 24, 1966, Shriver was on the defensive enough to indicate on CBS that if poverty were really to be licked, it would take an income-maintenance program—perhaps a negative income tax, as Goldwater's economic adviser Milton Friedman had been advocating. Here is an area for continuing debate.

When one considers in retrospect the famous War on Poverty, from 1964 to 1969 and later, other questions arise. Was it the right kind of approach—the right kind of "war"? Was it the right time for such a crusade, coinciding as it did with a massive grass-roots movement ("war"?) for civil rights by a tenth of the population, together with an increasingly unpopular actual war in Southeast Asia? Such questions do not yield easy or conclusive answers. Were the basic ideas and concepts appropriate to the task? There are valid questions of scale, for the rhetoric lavished on the war contrasts poorly with the level of expenditures. Contemporaries had much to say about high overhead compared with actual payments and services.

Why should there have been so many individual programs? Why was jurisdiction scattered about: in Labor, HEW, OEO, and elsewhere? It is tempting to give a simple answer, but there were many reasons. Programs had already existed before Johnson's coming, and these were deeply embedded in federal, state, and local governments. The first programs of 1963/64 were in the conduit already, and they enjoyed the sponsorship of various agencies and groups that lobbied for them. While one purpose of OEO was to start fresh and to give unity in administration, it was never intended to move the massive public assistance, social security, or veterans programs to its fold. Finally, the Great Society enterprise was not outlined in advance and then enacted. Rather, it evolved in response to continuing task-force inputs all throughout the 1965–1969 period. Thus, many bills and laws and many ultimate destinations for programs in the government were inevitable.

Several concerns will not go away. Did the emotional overpromising of results from the War on Poverty and the bold statements on the extent of deprivation help to create a mood of revolt? And did they finally lead to rioting, looting, and burning (i.e., revenge) in Los Angeles, Detroit, and the nation's capital itself? Was the determination to include "the poor" in community-action programs an acceptable one? Was it largely activists and radicals who stepped forward? On balance, should Lyndon Johnson be given a plus for initiative—whatever else may be said? His emphasis on the supremacy of the federal government, and on class and race division in America, must be noted. The inflationary results of new domestic expenditures, when coupled with costs of the war in Southeast Asia, were highly unfortunate, and the administration knew this. A noble presidential effort it all was, accompanied by moving language and some positive results; but the War on Poverty was hardly of a scale and type capable of eliminating poverty then or later.

4

★ ★ ★ ★ ★

ENLARGING ON AN INHERITANCE IN SOUTHEAST ASIA

Lyndon Johnson was to be a wartime president. "Sometimes a nation must do what it would not choose to do," he would say in midstream, for "sometimes men must die in order that freedom may live." Every one of the highest-ranking American presidents would have agreed. His war would not be for such a glorious cause as American independence, territorial integrity, "Cuba libre," to make the world safe for democracy, or to guarantee the four freedoms; but the Vietnam War would be big enough and bloody enough to be one of America's major wars—and its longest. Back on June 28, 1950, in a letter to President Truman, Senator Johnson had admired Truman's decision on Korea. Meaning was being given to freedom by the president's courageous response to aggression, he said; moreover, "having chosen this course, there is no turning back." Yet, in time, "peace will be restored and justice will assume new meaning for the oppressed and frightened peoples of the world."[1] Here, beyond any doubt, it would turn out, was a man who, remembering aspects of the past, partially misread them.

The figure of Lyndon Johnson is permanently associated with the war that was waged during his term of office and was left as a legacy to his successor. As he entered the Oval Office, Americans in and out of uniform were working closely with embattled Vietnamese troops; as he departed, a major war was in place. Command of American ground troops shifted during those years from Gen. Paul D. Harkins to Gen. William C. Westmoreland (June 20, 1964, to July 2, 1968) and then to

63

Gen. Creighton W. Abrams. The escalating commitment of air and ground forces was in response to defined crises and the development of new logistic bases that came under attack. An initial goal had been to protect the South Vietnamese from the terroristic tactics of a ruthless enemy; and this required ingenuity, changes in counterinsurgency tactics, and a variety of new initiatives. In general, the goal was to protect the integrity of South Vietnam as an entity. Another hope was to force the Democratic Republic of Vietnam in the north to concede that the southern Republic of Vietnam would be permanently free of the former's control. These were the early goals; but toward the close of the Johnson presidency an observer from afar might have thought that the whole enterprise had but one goal—namely, the purpose of achieving peace—for this came to be the objective that America's leader stressed repeatedly.

The origins of this war in earlier administrations and the manner of its termination in the 1970s lie outside these pages. The approach, in more than two chapters here, will be topical but with some sense of chronology. Those who are interested in the war independent of focus on the presidency may choose among the first generation of books, written primarily to sway contemporaries; a second generation, written after the Pentagon Papers appeared; memoirs of military figures; and a new generation of books, which strives for perspective.[2]

A battle has been joined between those who zero in on Kennedy's sending of advisers to Vietnam until the total came to over sixteen thousand, thus opening up a conflict, and those who focus on Johnson's escalation with troops and bombing. One fact is indisputable: President Johnson vastly enlarged his inheritance in Southeast Asia. Johnson, as Kennedy's vice-president, seems to have had no objection to Kennedy's "adviser" policies. He did, however, have strong reservations on the handling of President Ngo Dinh Diem that led to the latter's removal by South Vietnamese generals and his death at the hands of their soldiers. After visiting Vietnam for his president in May 1961, Johnson had reported that "the battle against Communism must be joined in Southeast Asia with strength and determination to achieve success there"; otherwise the Pacific must be surrendered as a "Red Sea." The struggle was not lost, he thought; there should be an alliance of free nations going beyond the Southeast Asia Treaty Organization (SEATO), new economic and military effort, and help so that countries could defend themselves. The "best people" should control, plan, and direct America's military aid program. Vietnam could be saved, he then wrote Kennedy, although there would be "very heavy and continuing costs involved." So, "At some point we may be faced with the further decision of whether we commit major United States forces to the area or cut our losses and withdraw should our other efforts fail." We could help—or "throw in the towel in the area and pull back our defenses to San Francisco and a 'Fortress America' concept." This secret advice, which is so revealing of this leader's mind, was declassified and published in a biography during the 1964 campaign.[3]

The impact of Lyndon Johnson's personal contact with Vietnam should not be overlooked. There was psychological meaning in a semiofficial letter that Lady Bird sent, at the State Department's request, to Madame Nhu in response to two letters: "They brought back to us memories of the warm reception we were given by the Vietnamese people which we shall always remember."[4] Lyndon Johnson and his countrymen as they faced the South Vietnam problem were armed with still other memories. There was the memory of victorious wars for democracy entered by the United States in 1917 and 1941. Johnson had served briefly—without training—as a lieutenant commander in the navy in 1941/42. There was the Korean "police action" during Truman's time. There was the awareness of historic treaty obligations and of fiascos such as Munich when these were not honored. There was, especially, the memory of how playing fast and loose with the threat of Chinese intervention in Korea had led to disaster. Many Americans remembered that the Republicans had charged the Democrats with having "lost" China to communism by both diplomatic and military mistakes. Johnson knew that President Kennedy had not quieted Southeast Asia very much when Kennedy had settled for a form of alleged neutralization in Laos.

Somehow, Johnson did not weigh heavily enough certain other knowledge that he surely had on Korea: 33,629 Americans killed, 103,284 wounded, and the unpopularity at home of that "police action" under the United Nations flag. He could have guessed that there would be a special emotional pressure in the Vietnam matter due to the million or so Catholic citizens living uneasily among a Buddhist majority. Gen. Omar Bradley had commented that Korea had been "the wrong war, at the wrong time, against the wrong enemy." Johnson could easily have questioned the analogy that because an independent South Korea had finally resulted from the conflict, using 400,000 American troops, a similar result could somehow be purchased in Southeast Asia.

Before overly stressing the influence of Kennedy's "bear any burden" attitude of early 1961, it would be well to recall the Republican party's sentiment of 1960: "We know that freedom can be preserved only by a people who are prepared to make any sacrifice for it." Yet Milton Eisenhower has recalled: "When President Eisenhower was in the White House there was absolutely no commitment, verbal, written, public, or covert that promised our use of military power on the side of South Vietnam. The only commitment was a SEATO commitment." Historically, it was not true that putting troops into Vietnam was but carrying out an Eisenhower commitment, he asserts. The vision of war had been expressed early and clearly by Rusk and McNamara on November 11, 1961, when they wrote Kennedy: "We should be prepared to introduce United States combat forces if that should become necessary for success. Dependent upon circumstances, it may also be necessary for United States forces to strike at the source of the aggression in North Vietnam."[5]

Johnson would recall later, "My first major decision on Vietnam had been to reaffirm President Kennedy's policies." The death of Diem had occurred on the eve of Johnson's taking office; therefore it seems clear that Johnson felt a burden for making the United States Government appear to be upright and honorable, for who knew when the media might uncover the Kennedy team's misconduct (or its indifference to Diem's welfare) during that tense period? Escalation would come fairly easily to the new president, who was absolutely convinced, said Hubert Humphrey later, that "aggresson unchecked was aggression unleashed."[6]

Many excuses have been made for the president's escalation of Vietnam into a major war. Perhaps the generals decieved him; or he had little choice; or he was pushed, or sank, into it; or he was never objectively informed about the situation; or, little by little, he found himself doing things he didn't really want to do; or it was his Texas heritage; or there was an impenetrable wall of advisers around him; or the polls supported him. Whatever the reason, he did barge ahead, rejecting difficult alternatives that were offered. He leaped before he looked. But one way out had been urged on him quite early.

The idea of "neutralization" as a way to leave Vietnam was much on the minds of sophisticated people during the early 1960s. In August 1963 Gen. Charles de Gaulle, president of France, made the point that the two Vietnams ought to be unified and neutralized (i.e., be neither pro-American nor pro-Communist) and that foreign forces should be withdrawn. The idea would be pushed on Johnson in private by Senate majority leader Mike Mansfield and later, in public, by columnist Walter Lippmann. In his memoirs, Johnson says curtly that this formula "would have meant the swift communization of all Vietnam, and probably of Laos and Cambodia as well." He criticized the concept of neutralization in a 1964 New Year's Day communication to General Dinh and again to Lodge in March. Fairly well known is the subsequent

Johnson liaison with Lippmann on neutralization, begun after Lippmann interviewed de Gaulle on May 21, 1964. Here, the columnist claimed, was an escape hatch: give limited support to Saigon while pressing Hanoi and Peking for neutralization, since the latter, while it was facing a collision course with the USSR, would surely like to have its own southern border stabilized. Lippmann spent some time with Fulbright, Bundy, McNamara, and Ball (in the State Department) and with the president, who wanted a guarantee that the Communists would not take over Vietnam during such an interlude. No guarantee was possible, Lippmann was told. Later, he attended a White House meeting with Johnson, Bundy, McNamara, and Vance; but his guarantee still was missing. Lippmann noticed that the advisers were pressing hard toward a military "solution"; therefore, nothing came of this idea.[7]

Johnson had long since been warned that even a conference on Cambodian neutrality needed to be turned down "definitively." The State Department had told him that North Vietnam was not interested, that the Soviets probably would welcome it, and that the Chinese seemed suspicious. Yet at the moment, at least, neutralization was not an enemy's idea. In a memo, Southeast Asia specialist Roger Hilsman at State assured Rusk that even talk of neutralization was "clearly very dangerous" and might be a self-fulfilling prophecy. Put a marine battalion in Saigon if necessary (allegedly to protect dependents, but actually to prevent more coups). Someone had written in the margin, "No one in Saigon agrees." Hilsman said "I believe we can win" if there would be vigorous and coordinated implementation, extension of the secured area, teamwork like that in Malaya, political stability, and rejection of orthodox military war methods.[8] There were many ifs.

Senator Mike Mansfield, who had long been familiar with Asia as a resident there, could not be ignored. (He was to be mentioned by Johnson in *The Vantage Point* three times as often as Fulbright, twice as often as Dirksen.) A critic of Kennedy's Vietnam policy, Mansfield met with Johnson in early December 1963, after which the Montana Democrat sent copies of memorandums that he had previously given to Kennedy. His argument, presented largely behind the scenes, reads persuasively *in retrospect* as an alternative to the Vietnam policies that were actually pursued during this presidency.

Mansfield had declared to Kennedy that the policy that says a war can be won through limited means in Vietnam alone "may be in error." If an effort, politically and socially, would be made by the Saigon government, if there were an astute diplomatic offensive involving France, and if an understanding policy were developed toward a Cambodia free of Chinese domination, something might result. Mansfield then thought Diem "a man whose integrity and honesty are unquestioned and without whom there would be no free Vietnam." Burma and Cambodia were then secure in their non-Communist independence without aid. Enduring American interests in the region were limited. Yet here was an annual financial and military burden of combat troops, propaganda, and "a possible conflict of indefinite depth and duration, dependent largely on our forces for its prosecution." So, Kennedy was on a collision course, he thought, warning that costs could reach as high as those in Korea. Vietnam was more important to the Vietnamese than to us. Our commercial and economic interests would not remotely justify even the costs already incurred. A devastated Vietnam would have but the illusion of freedom. He asked, what about peripheral situations elsewhere?[9]

On January 6, 1964, the president solicited additional comment from Mansfield. The senator said that we should not bite off more than we are prepared in the end to chew. Talk less about *our* responsibility and more about *theirs*. Think about peaceful solutions through efforts by other nations. Now, at Johnson's request, the growing Mansfield file was sent to Rusk and McNamara, with the order that each man had forty-eight hours to write "a personal memorandum of refutation [sic] which he [Johnson] can review and then use with Senator Mansfield if he wishes." The result was, however, a single two-page joint reply: "U.S. Policy in Vietnam." As to Mansfield, Kennedy's foreign-relations architects agreed, their basic objectives coincided, but not the means for attaining them. Diplomacy could not eliminate terrorism. *The North must be convinced it cannot win* (italics added). "We believe the fight against the Viet Cong can be won without major and direct United States involvement provided the new South Vietnamese government takes the proper political, economic and social actions to win the support of the rural people and uses its armed forces effectively." (Here was certainly a major caveat.) Neutralization must wait until Vietnam grows strong and aggression is frustrated, they judged. The overwhelming majority of the American people, they confidently assured their new president of six weeks, agreed with their views.[10] (If so, was it not because they were ignorant of the bad news their president now knew, which will appear shortly?)

Developments in Saigon and France soon led Mansfield to return to the attack. Sending copies of all of his previous documents on February 1, he told Johnson that coups could not help. "Legitimacy" had been destroyed with the assassination of Diem. (Here was an inescapable point, one notes, made much earlier in the 1942 book *The Principles of Power* by historian Guglielmo Ferrerro, when focusing on Italy. Seven different lean and hungry generals would lead the Saigon government in the year 1964!) The people in Vietnam don't want to crusade against the Viet Cong, wrote the senator. "We will find ourselves engaged in an indecisive, bloody and costly military involvement" that will escalate just to preserve the status quo. "Most emphatically" the senator opposed an American war that had no national interest to justify it. French efforts in Laos and Cambodia should be supported with an open mind.

A steady stream of memorandums giving the views of the Democratic majority leader in the Senate would go to Johnson clear through 1965 and 1966 in an effort to have his attention, ear, and acquiescence. Mansfield was not exactly ignored; yet neither was his advice heeded. He was treated by the White House team as a mixture of threat and nuisance on Vietnam policy. While Mansfield lost—as Johnson said publicly on March 20, 1964, that the idea of neutralization should be knocked down "wherever it rears its ugly head"—the harried president was by 1966 forced to think more kindly of neutralizaion. Then, as the government continued to propose that peace be restored to Vietnam, James Reston, after a briefing, was able to write of Johnson: "He is in favor of the neutralization of all of Southeast Asia, and he is prepared to let the peoples of South and North Vietnam decide their own political future, even if this means a coalition with the Communists or even a Communist Government." Douglass Cater, in the White House, immediately wrote of Reston, "I thought he hit the nail right on the head Sunday." It had been a column well worth writing, Cater wrote Reston, for people should be paying attention to what the president says.[11] The president's conversion was, at the least, several years too late.

Instead of pursuing diplomacy during the winter of 1963/64, therefore, the new president at once initiated activities designed to prevail against the odds. He shipped old CIA hands back to Vietnam in an effort to improve the collecting of intelligence. He presided over a split between civilian and military advisers on how much priority to give to punishing North Vietnam—thus getting at the "real enemy." There were meetings, shuttling of envoys back and forth to Saigon, endless discussions, briefings—in other words, interminable activity focusing on how to "get at" the North, rather than how to bring progress in the South, says William E. Colby, head of the CIA at the time. Meanwhile, the strategic-hamlet program ceased to work. The CIA's recommendations were in great part "neither welcomed nor adopted." Rejecting a diplomatic solution, the Johnson team still was not seeking a military victory, said Johnson later. Vietnam was allegedly "reassessed" every day.[12] *But not fundamentally.*

There has been much speculation on what Kennedy would have done had he lived; but it need not concern us here, for one side deals with facts and the other with hopeful conjecture. It seems virtually certain that Kennedy was not on a withdrawal course. Thus, Rusk remarked in regard to a possible Kennedy withdrawal, "Kennedy never said anything like that to me, and we discussed Vietnam—oh, I'd say hundreds of times. He never said it, never suggested it, never hinted at it, and I simply do not believe it." Kennedy told the Huntley-Brinkley program of NBC, "I think we should stay." George Ball judged, "I think you can safely say that escalation was proceeding fairly rapidly before Johnson took office." And Clark Clifford noted that Johnson had inherited a full house of top advisers from Kennedy, who thought their collective course was satisfactory and who "all felt that we were headed correctly in Vietnam." There was no thought of withdrawal, and no paper urged it as Johnson became president, says the State Department's William P. Bundy. One Kennedy intimate wrote, "Formally, Kennedy never made a final negative decision on troops." To a Texas audience, Kennedy said on November 22, 1963, "Without the United States, South Vietnam would collapse overnight." On the twenty-third he had planned to say, with regard to military aid for Vietnam and eight other countries, "Reducing our efforts to train, equip, and assist their armies can only encourage Communist penetration and require in time the increased overseas deployment of American combat forces." He believed wholeheartedly in the domino theory and he had no intention at all (after having been savaged by Khrushchev in Vienna) of letting the Communists have Southeast Asia. His representatives at the Vietnam Policy Conference in Honolulu on November 20, 1963, decided on a twelve-month program of covert operations against North Vietnam.[13]

Kennedy had deliberately built up America's conventional forces to handle limited war if need be; in public he took a consistently hard line on Vietnam. He was de facto head of the Vietnam Task Force. It was in the spirit of Kennedy that Hilsman wrote to Rusk in March 1964, "No matter what we do, our problems in Southeast Asia are not going to vanish overnight, and we must be prepared to maintain a strong military posture in the area quite indefinitely." There may once have been ambiguities in Kennedy's private view (expressed while chatting idly with Kenneth O'Donnell), but it is impossible for the reader of this record to agree that much in the way of withdrawal by Kennedy lay ahead. Considerable research on the then strikingly little publicized suggestion of McNamara and Taylor to remove one thousand personnel by the end of 1963 *if training was going well* revealed no indication it was much more than an irrelevant gesture, for Kennedy said at the time that "no formal announcement" was to be made. Johnson early established his policy on Kennedy's of October 2, and one looks in vain for protests from any of the Kennedy team in December as the scheme died a quiet death. Later assertions that here can be seen a "true" portent of what Kennedy would "probably" have done about Vietnam if he had lived are very unpersuasive.[14] To say Kennedy was waiting until after the 1964 election to withdraw the nation from Vietnam, as some of his partisans have claimed, is seriously to impugn his character, making him seem the cheapest of opportunistic politicians. Small wonder that Johnson so bitterly resented the idea emerging during his years—an idea with a long life—that if only the Massachusetts leader had lived during the long months after the killing of Diem, the escalation to major war in Vietnam would never have happened.

The administration of President Johnson inherited an entire team of officials which was responsible for developments in Southeast Asia. Secretary of State Dean Rusk, Secretary of Defense Robert McNamara, advisers McGeorge Bundy and Walt Rostow, and others had long cherished the idea that an American counterinsurgency effort could somehow thwart Communist guerrilla activity in that theater. While some would leave (Bundy and Hilsman are examples), most would stay the course to 1969. Decision making on the conduct of the war would rest with holdovers as well as with the new president—himself a holdover—and his new aides in the White House. Rostow was one who made the transition from the State Department to be close to the president's side. Also charged with responsibilities were the National Security Council and the Joint Chiefs of Staff and diplomats, military advisory groups, and military commanders in Saigon, Thailand, and on the high seas.

Always, it is convenient to refer to the chief executive as the decision maker, but even he, living frequent workdays of up to eighteen hours, had to rely on others for matters that were well above the routine level. His mail and polls revealed the unfocused public mind. *If Vietnam did not ultimately go well, in a democratic republic like the United States one must look at the Congress and the people themselves, for three national elections were held during the Johnson years.* In spite of talk of imperial presidencies, much machinery giving checks and balances in connection with decisions on Vietnam existed from 1963 to 1969. The media made sure that whatever went wrong got the full glare of publicity, at least to the extent of their knowledge. Under the circumstances, the president cannot be allowed to stand alone, either in triumph or in disaster. But from the very outset he did not level with the American people. For example, when on February 14, 1964, he set up a "small committee" to manage

American policy and operations in Vietnam, he said in secret National Security Council Memorandum 280: "It is my hope and expectation that the establishment of this committee will permit an energetic, unified, and skillful prosecution of the only war we face at present." Such a remark, if it had been made publicly at the time, would have been sensational, even though there was some precedent in President Franklin Roosevelt's unmentioned aid to Britain against Germany on the high seas in 1940/41.

So, the figure of President Johnson is still central when considering the unfolding of the Vietnam War: especially pertinent is his public defense of his war. This went through four periods: commitment, escalation, overcommitment, and reversal. At the outset he wished to be regarded as trustworthy and competent, exercising acquired authority. With growing opposition, he turned aggressive and defensive. Finally, he seemed outwardly indifferent to criticism of his chosen path. At first, he responded to questions but did not initiate discussion. After August 1964 he actively instituted discourse and sought consensus and trust in his judgment. By 1965 he became the active leader in charge. In 1966 he sought to oblige listeners to continue in their allegiance to him, whether they agreed with him or not. Personal aggression and anger became increasingly common. As 1967 progressed, his effort to seek public approbation ceased, so that in an AFL-CIO address he said in effect that he would no longer engage in dialogue with his opponents. Stoically, he carried on. The year 1968 found him assuming the guise of peacemaker, one who is sacrificing himself for the great cause of national unity and world peace. There was self-justification and self-congratulation.[15]

The idea of a national commitment due to membership in SEATO was taken seriously by Johnson and Rusk, whether it impressed others or not. According to the treaty: "Each party recognizes that aggression by means of armed attack in the treaty area against any of the parties or against any state or territory which the parties by unanimous agreement may hereafter designate, would endanger its own peace and safety, and agrees that it will in that event act to meet the common danger in accordance with its constitutional processes." On this point, the Senate Foreign Relations Committee had then said: "The committee is not impervious to the risks which this treaty entails. It fully appreciates that acceptance of these additional obligations commits the United States to a course of action over a vast expanse of the Pacific. Yet these risks are consistent with our own highest interests. There are greater hazards in not advising a potential enemy of what he can expect of us." So Rusk could say in 1966 that such a treaty was no mere "legal technicality."

To the administration, credible commitments (i.e., treaties) added up to credible threats (i.e., deterrence) and thus to containment. At the time there were forty-two treaties—or mutual security pacts—which called, in specific language, for defending countries when defense of them might be required. A scholar astutely suggested that persons calling for withdrawal from Vietnam "without regard to victory or honor" should remember these obligations.[16] Such considerations were always in the forefront of the president's mind.

At the same time, they were duly remembered by former presidents in the mid 1960s. As early as December 27, 1963, President Johnson told the press that he had enjoyed extended conversations with Hoover, Truman, and Eisenhower, during which constructive suggestions had been made. He was very grateful, he said. As time passed and Hoover died, Johnson was usually able to say or intimate that with an army in Vietnam he was merely following in the footsteps of his predecessors. But Milton Eisenhower corrected him; and after that, intimations in public that President Eisenhower approved of Johnson's military escalation stopped.[17]

One wishes to see the Vietnam obligation and opportunity as Johnson did at the beginning of his term. He was informed secretly by many routes of the factual situation. It would be absolutely essential, he early told Henry Cabot Lodge, that the CIA, the military, and the diplomats work closely and well together.[18] Rusk soon informed Lodge of Johnson's "deep concern that our effort in Vietnam be stepped up to highest pitch and that each day we ask ourselves what more we can do to further the struggle." So even though Washington was told initially (and believed) that the Vietnamese were in "a state of organizational turmoil" and that the Viet Cong had "a powerful capability for at least a brief period of intensified operations," there was little hesitation. The new president was not just carrying on; he would augment and improve—and eventually carry the day!

What the president got from the outset was very bad news. But bad news only spurred him on. The State Department's intelligence unit had just questioned estimates from Defense; gains since July had been erased. It had also been discovered that the Diem regime had been falsifying reports on the military situation and the strategic-hamlet program. Says Rusk's biographer, "The military situation in Vietnam was in fact far worse than anyone had imagined." The Viet Cong's skill in countering aircraft was improving; the infiltration of material seemed to be increasing; Saigon was losing many more weapons; "incidents were up; capture of Viet Cong weapons was down; recoilless rifles and material of Chinese and Russian manufacture were showing up." All of this,

Secretary Rusk told LBJ, meant the possibility of "protracted intensification" of the Viet Cong effort and possibly "increased outside aid," so that prospects for the future might be seriously deranged. Buddhists might persecute Catholics; local politicians and generals were jockeying for position; there were more Viet Cong attacks now than before the Diem coup.[19] No wonder Johnson would recall that as of November 23, "South Vietnam gave me real cause for concern."

What seems clear to the reader of quantities of secret documents (now in the Johnson Library) that reached the new president in December 1963 is that he knew full well then that the Southeast Asia adventure was not going well and that for a long period it was not likely to go well. This is important, for it indicates that the president was not really drawn into a quagmire over a long period of months and several years; rather, he knew from the very beginning that even a great American effort centered in Saigon would have a very slow payoff—and might not have any! One aide, Mike Forrestal, fresh in from a visit to Vietnam, informed Johnson on December 11 that members of the Viet Cong were strongly positioned in the provinces south of Saigon, much more so "than we had previously thought." While some 219 hamlets had been claimed by Diem, only 45 of these had been identified! This was important because money was allocated in accordance with provinces that Diem controlled. Recent reports were alarming; since the anti-Diem coup, there had been only inertia. How could the Saigon government win the peasants' confidence and support? Operations against North Vietnam had brought little success, Forrestal said. The trails in Laos were not the only conduit for supplies; the delta, Cambodia, and the sea were other common sources. McNamara should be told that a capability to strike at North Vietnamese targets should be developed.[20]

On December 17 a CIA document that was termed "as good a wrapup on the Vietnam situation" as could be found was transmitted to a president who quietly read such things in bed. There was "disturbing paralysis" in provincial administration. Weak pacification policies and a confused chain of command accompanied deterioration in the hamlet program. Long-term setbacks were imminent. The local press was being intimidated, even suspended. Ruling generals were arresting their competitors.[21]

The president was being warned. So too had been those, like McGeorge Bundy, through whom such material was routed. Suppose the new president had then been willing to take seriously the implications of so dismal a scene and therefore write off American operations at once, rather than forge on with the kind of determined resolve that said full steam ahead? Instead, George Ball cabled Lodge that a special effort should be made to reassure South Vietnamese leader Dinh on the neutrality question, for: "Nothing is further from USG mind than 'neutral solution for Vietnam.' We intend to win."[22] Such a devil-may-care attitude was certainly in the tradition of America's earlier wars and of the national penchant for enjoying the underdog role in competitive sports. It also saved face for the Kennedy holdovers in State, Defense, and White House offices. Errors would not have to be admitted; they would someday rise from the wreckage of the Diem fiasco, and all would be well.

The point is that the new president clearly did not think his way through his Vietnam inheritance in November and December of 1963. His knee-jerk decision was made in hours—not even in days. From the outset, the vice-president of the Kennedy years, facing the 1964 election, was determined on the necessity to carry on. He was even willing to enlarge on his inheritance. The secret National Security Action Memorandum 273, implemented on November 26, 1963, made that all too clear: "It remains the central object of the United States in South Vietnam to assist the people and government of that country to win their contest against the externally directed and supported communist conspiracy," it began. Contrary comment by readers was not welcomed: "The president expects that all senior officers of the government will move energetically to insure the full unity of support for established US policy in South Vietnam. Both in Washington and in the field, it is essential that the government be unified."[23] The tone was more like dictatorship than leadership.

Even though bad news accumulated during those first days and weeks of December, the nation's course had already been determined: the policy was to stand fast and to escalate American help as required to achieve goals in Southeast Asia. It made little difference, therefore, when McNamara soon visited Saigon and reported back that "the situation is very disturbing." It was, he said, well suited to producing in several months either neutralization, at best, or a Communist state at worst. "We should watch the situation very carefully, running scared, hoping for the best, but preparing for more forceful moves if the situation does not show early signs of improvement." The CIA reported glumly, "There is no organized government in South Vietnam at this time." Statistics on the powerful Viet Cong were grossly in error, and the "future of the war remains in doubt." Ditto political stability. Said the CIA's John McCone, "There are more reasons to doubt the future of the effort . . . than there are reasons to be optimistic about the future of our cause in South Vietnam."[24] What would the country have thought, said, and done if these gloomy reports had been released? They were not. In no way on the CBS program "Face the Nation" on December 29 did Roger Hilsman convey such bad tidings. Said Johnson, "We expanded our advisory effort."

The year 1964 brought continuing ferment over Vietnam. In early January an interdepartmental committee, headed by a major general, recommended that there be twelve months of covert operations against North Vietnam; the president gave his approval on January 16. In February the president assured Senator Stuart Symington that the latter had been right when he had said that losing Vietnam would mean losing Southeast Asia: "I am determined not to accept that loss." The man who had just inherited Oval Office leadership grandly assured General Duong Van Minh, "I speak for the whole American people in saying we are resolved to provide the necessary tools to assist in carrying out these tasks in every village and hamlet of the Vietnamese nation." On February 20 Johnson directed that "contingency planning for pressures against North Vietnam should be speeded up."[25] Behind the scenes, a March 1 memorandum from William Bundy in the State Department advocated the blockading of Haiphong, as well as air attacks on rail lines to China, road nets to Laos, cadre camps, and industrial complexes. Soon, the National Security Council (NSC) urged all kinds of preparation for possible future action on seventy-two hours' notice.[26] Yet Johnson's press conference on March 7 would be told only that administration interest in Vietnam was as high as ever.

March 1964 brought a dozen recommendations from Gen. Maxwell Taylor and McNamara after an investigation in Saigon. They had found much of the population apathetic or indifferent, with army desertions and draft-dodging common! They did not yet think "major additions" in United States personnel were warranted, nevertheless. The increased threat they saw was, astonishingly, to Burma, Malaysia, the Philippines, India, Australia, New Zealand, Taiwan, Korea, and Japan. Hot pursuit into Laos should be permitted, and that into Cambodia studied. Totally unwarranted, it now appears, was their estimate that American training forces could be substantially reduced before the end of 1965. They urged that direct action be taken against North Vietnam (described in a still-classified appendix). Mining of ports was only mentioned. While the United States clearly should increase overt pressure, such actions would be of an "extremely delicate nature"; how could a case for them be built? We should prepare, for "we may want to mount new and significant pressures against North Vietnam—for which thirty days notice would be required."[27] No one in the Joint Chiefs of Staff (JCS) opposed any of this; instead, they favored immediate action against the North. Meanwhile, the president confidently assured Vietnamese students "that the US will supply whatever help Vietnam needs to retain its freedom."[28]

In summary, the new president of the United States during his first months in office kept making unqualified public and private promises of support to South Vietnam, essentially a state in chaos. The American public simply had no idea that in the winter of 1964 their future had already been committed—if the nation's honor and integrity still had any meaning. There was no great national debate on any of this, even though the close reader of Johnson's public prose can now see that he occasionally showed his hand fully, as in a speech at UCLA on February 21. Faced with the option of publicly writing off an embarrassing setback or privately forging ahead with the financial and military effort, Lyndon Johnson took the politician's way out. He considered linkage with Kennedy absolutely essential to the success of his accidental presidency; Kennedy's men must therefore be upheld in their primary policies. For the incumbent Democrats it was an election year, and the uncertain trumpet had already sounded all too publicly at the Bay of Pigs.

Late April 1964 brought an assessment by *Time* that "the nasty guerrilla conflict in Vietnam is beginning to look more and more like a full scale conventional war." Within SEATO, the French wanted a political solution, but the other seven powers vowed that the defeat of the Communist campaign was essential not only to the security of South Vietnam but to that of Southeast Asia. Said Johnson at the time, "When the going gets tough the tough get going." He did inform a still inattentive nation on April 20, "We are in this battle as long as South Vietnam wants our support and needs our assistance to protect its freedom." Peace would come "once war seems hopeless." Notice had finally been given, but few noticed.

By June 2 the president was ready to list "four basic themes" governing U.S. policy for the region. "America keeps her word," he said, adding that the future of the whole area was the real issue. "Our purpose is peace." Here was not just a jungle war but "a struggle for freedom on every front of human activity." Linkage was made with Eisenhower's desire for "an independent Vietnam endowed with a strong government," thus stretching the famous letter of October 25, 1954 to President Diem to its ultimate limits. Said the outline before this leader at the time, "the American people must be convinced that containment of communism in the region is worthwhile."[29] We intend no rashness or major war, said Johnson June 23, but "they can count on our help for as long as they need it and want it." When Robert Kennedy volunteered to be the new ambassador to Vietnam, Johnson took the position that security there for Jack's brother was insufficient, although he would do the job "damn well." So Maxwell Taylor, coauthor with Rostow of the blueprint that had sent thousands of advisers into Southeast Asia, took over. By July 1964 some two hundred Americans had been killed in Vietnam, twenty-five hundred had been added to forces in being.

Several authors of books have written about the episode that would shortly arouse the slumbering public mind: the abortive attacks on United States destroyers in Tonkin Gulf off North Vietnam in the summer of 1964. The books and declassified documents are a reminder that this chance for dramatic reprisal against North Vietnam was somewhat thinly based. Among other things, the South Vietnamese had just attacked enemy coastal installations. Johnson sought support from a Congressional leadership meeting the evening of August 4. It is commonly believed that there was little opposition then. In fact, Senator Mansfield read a memorandum opposing retaliation. And Senator Aiken asked the CIA director about "the provocation, if any," for the second North Vietnamese attack. Senator Russell wondered if we could prevail with forces on land. Senator Leverett Saltenstall wondered if we had any allies. Concluded Aiken bitterly as to the draft resolution, "By the time you send it up, there won't be anything for us to do but support you." Johnson did get the votes, as an uninformed Congress quickly gave the president broad support in a memorable resolution. The national crusade for South Vietnam was now dramatically public. Although here was "a commitment undertaken with little domestic criticism or questioning," says one informed historian, "the precedent for U.S. military action against North Vietnam had been established."[30] Another historian notes that serious questions were subsequently raised about "the nature and even existence of the alleged attacks." Evidence would be "suspect," for administration officials were "obviously in a mood to retaliate," selecting whatever evidence "confirmed what they wanted to believe." The president supported his subordinates "without question" as he ordered air strikes in retaliatory overkill. When he sought his congressional resolution, however, he did not exactly seek at the time a blank check for later expansion of the war, because he did hope that limited means would somehow suffice to prevail. But the resolution protected him politically in an election year and so served multiple purposes.[31] Later the resolution would loom larger.

Tonkin Gulf was not Johnson's finest hour. "In presenting its case . . . the administration deliberately misled Congress and the American people," we are told, as silence was preserved on the covert raids being carried on at the time by South Vietnamese gunboats and on the electronic espionage being done by the *Maddox*—code-named DESOTO.

Embarrassing questions were raised by Senators Wayne Morse of Oregon and Ernest Gruening of Alaska, the latter suspecting a "predated declaration of war." But the House passed the resolution by voice vote, and the Senate, which was one-third full for the debate, passed it 88 to 2 after assurances by Senator Fulbright.

It is hard to agree that the Congress was deceived, whatever would be said later. At the time, the public raised Johnson's rating from 42 to 72 percent so that a nail was driven very early into candidate Goldwater's presidential effort. American retaliation by aircraft from the *Constellation* and the *Ticonderoga* against torpedo boats and oil-storage facilities nearby was considered by the Joint Chiefs "a pretty good effort." Ten percent of Hanoi's oil-production facilities was destroyed. The president apparently believed in the reality of the second North Vietnamese "unprovoked" attack, despite the flimsy evidence. "For all I know, our Navy was shooting at whales out there," he once observed in private. In any case, he used the action as a reason for escalating American military effort and especially to arouse American opinion in an election year behind the long-term Kennedy-Johnson posture in Southeast Asia. One historian concedes that "there is no evidence to show that the events of the second Gulf of Tonkin incident [of August 4] were the result of a deliberate provocation which would provide the US an opportunity for reprisals."[32] Still, only someone who wanted to escalate in order to prevail would have behaved as the president did.

Deterioration in presidential relations with the Congress on foreign affairs began with Tonkin Gulf, although that was not soon apparent, for a March 1966 effort at repeal of the resoluton failed by a vote of 92 to 5 in the Senate. One reason was that Senator Fulbright had laid his prestige on the line. When Senator Gaylord Nelson wanted to forbid the use of combat troops, Fulbright replied that the president had no intention of fighting a land war in Asia. Eventually, Johnson came to exclude Congress from his Vietnam planning procedures. A Congress so treated naturally turned to open resentment. From the base of Greuning and Morse, the hostile roll call came, after some months, to include Fulbright, Church, McCarthy, Hartke, and others. At the time, August 1964, there was rallying around the flag, as might be expected.

Naturally, there are misgivings when one reads how White House insiders as early as June had been preparing the way for just such a resolution. Said William Bundy, as he prepared drafts of a supportive resolution, "We can win if we stay with it."[33] The official final resolution supported "all necessary measures to repel any armed attack against the forces of the United States and to prevent further aggression." So the U.S. was prepared, "as the president determines, to take all necessary steps, including the use of armed force," to help SEATO members defend their freedom. The resolution would expire when the president found peace and security in the area "reasonably assured" or when the Congress terminated it by concurrent resolution.

The military naturally took satisfaction from the events of early August. When coupled with the political rewards accruing to a president who was evolving into a commander in chief, it can certainly be said that the mood in Washington in mid summer 1964, especially among Democrats, was euphoric. And the military envisioned opportunities. Adm. U.S. Grant Sharp told the Joint Chiefs of Staff, "Recent U.S. military actions in Laos and North Vietnam demonstrated our intent to move toward our objectives." Hanoi and Peking must learn "the cost of pursuing their current objectives and impeding ours." Momentum must be maintained, for "we have declared ourselves forcefully both by overt acts and by the clear readiness to do more."[34] His commander in chief had long since pointed out realistically that the nation could not oppose the spread of communism and promote the growth of freedom just by giving speeches.

An earlier Republican-party complaint, made on July 2, that the country had not been told what was going on in Vietnam had been easily by-passed. Although aides had advised Johnson to go on TV with a report to the nation, he chose not to do so; apparent attacks on our ships and the bombing of Hanoi's facilities soon eliminated the need. The president's explanation, given on August 4 on TV, would come when the nation's aircraft had already been in the air for one hour. The Chinese, it seemed, needed to know what was happening; and Hanoi would need to grasp the nature and purposes of the attack, yet still not be able to forestall it or make their own public explanation first. World reaction was initially favorable but was quickly diluted on second thought. The Japanese newspaper *Asahi* saw the United States as being "at the very brink" and warned against adventurism. The foreign press admitted that, based on what they knew, there had been provocation. The Communist press saw only aggression.[35]

The American attacks of early August would not be followed up with new ones, although both the Air Force and the Marine Corps hoped for additional enemy escalation. Covert operations against North Vietnam continued (but what was done remains classified at this writing). When the Viet Cong attacked an American air base at Bien Hoa on November 1, election eve, Goldwater's peace-posturing opponent could not very well retaliate; but contingency plans were being laid for bombing of the North at some future time. Reasons thought to be compelling were the aid to Saigon's morale, deterrence of the aggressor, display of will, and so on. The Air Force, then seeing little action, was restive. There was disagreement about what to bomb. Some advisers, especially George Ball in the State Department, questioned the bombing in toto, saying that it might trigger a vast flow of North Vietnamese manpower into the southern conflict, or, unthinkably, draw the USSR and China together. As the president's men got down to cases, it was the justifiable fear of collapse in the south that weighed most heavily. Opportunities to begin bombing were by-passed in December 1964 and in January 1965, but the time soon came in the ground war when General Taylor said, "To take no positive action now is to accept defeat in the fairly near future." Escalation, carefully delimited and more or less coordinated with efforts to institute negotiations, was now at hand.

The regular bombing of North Vietnam began on the morning of February 7, 1965, on direct orders from the president, in spite of the fact that Premier Kosygin of the USSR was then in Hanoi. The first strike by forty-nine carrier-based fighter planes was allegedly in response to an attack on United States barracks and helicopters at Pleiku, but the reprisal strikes had long since been planned. Not since the raids of August 1964 had anything so dramatic been undertaken. The commander in chief somehow saw the action as a limited response rather than as a permanent widening of the war, it is said; he very briefly suspended the action secretly in May while peace feelers were being sent out. In December 1965 and January 1966 there would be a thirty-seven-day pause. The policy of off-again, on-again bombing has been attacked. Historians have been critical of the presidential explanation for the renewed bombing during the winter of 1965/66. For example, one says: "The Administration was considerably less than candid in explaining to the American public the reasons for and significance of its decision. The air war certainly was not an appropriately measured response to the small attacks that had occurred against Americans and their facilities."[36] Since it showed few results, the next step would be to escalate still further. What had been modest in size became "a regular, determined program," though it was still personally restricted by the civilian president.

As for the army, in the early spring of 1965, Gen. William Westmoreland, who had taken command of the ground war in this theater, requested marine "landing teams" to protect the bombing base at Danang against Viet Cong raids. At the time, Danang was the most important American military base in the north. General Taylor was dubious, saying it would be "very difficult to hold the line." This first portentous commitment of ground troops would be made without the man in the street quite seeing it as the dangerous change in the war that it really was. Americans were now part of a ground war, beginning with the first thirty-five hundred marines who arrived on March 8, 1965. The Joint Chiefs of Staff sought a commitment of significant numbers of ground forces; the modest figure of forty thousand would be a compromise. Nevertheless, says the author of a general history of the war, "Consciously emulating the example set by Franklin Roosevelt in leading the United States into World War II, Johnson took the nation into war in Vietnam by indirection and dissimulation."[37]

But the titular leader of America, who was only too aware that he possessed the powerful twin titles of president and commander in chief, had no intention of seeking a declaration of war or even admitting publicly at the time that he was waging one. When on April 6, 1965, he approved an increase of eighteen to twenty thousand men in United States "military support forces," it was said to be for the purpose of filling out existing units and supplying needed logistic personnel. In the secret National Security Council meeting at the time he also approved the deployment of two more Marine battalions and a Marine air squadron plus headquarters and support personnel. A "change of mission" for the Marines was approved "to permit their more effective use." Yet President Johnson commanded that "premature publicity be avoided by all possible precautions." Thus, "The actions themselves should be taken as rapidly as practicable, but in ways that would minimize any appearance of sudden changes in policy." Only the secretaries of state and defense would handle official statements, he said, for the changes "should be understood as being gradual and wholly consistent with existing policy."[38] Here, to be blunt, was intentional deception on a most important matter of state. It could be said with certainty in spring 1965 that the nation was waging a Vietnam War. In June it was admitted that American troops were engaging in offensive operations, and use of thirty B-52 bombers on the eighteenth was warlike enough. But thanks to what amounted to presidential conspiracy against the public mind, there would then be few calls from leaders in high places for a constitutional declaration that a state of war existed. With one might have come censorship, allocation of raw materials, and wartime taxes or issuance of bonds. People were still hoping for the best. Such an ambiguous situation, however, could not long endure without countervailing reaction of some kind.

Not surprisingly, Mansfield sent a flurry of letters and memorandums to the president in June 1965, following a leadership meeting at the White House. In three detailed pages, Mansfield tried to induce Johnson to resist "irreversible extension of the war in Asia." Bombing Hanoi-Haiphong was doing just that, said the senator. It would not be effective; it would thwart discussions, push allies away from us, keep China involved, freeze-in Russia as an arms supplier, enlarge the ground war, and ensure carrying the war ultimately into North Vietnam and maybe farther. Do what Eisenhower did in Korea, urged the majority leader of the president's party: press your advisers to show what good bombing had done so far, compared with initial promises. No American interests warrant an all-out effort. Get to the conference table! Never, of course, did Mansfield think of a Communist South Vietnam as the solution.

The president soon replied by phone, thus stimulating three more pages of protest. To prevail fully south of the seventeenth parallel would take nearly a million American soldiers, Mansfield now guessed. To keep just the status quo, a half million might suffice. If negotiations were what we sought, maybe a hundred thousand troops might do; that is, if a powerful diplomatic peace offensive should be mounted. A discussion among these three options must be held, and Johnson could expect no initiative to come from the Congress. Look out! If you ask support for more ground troops, there will be "a wave of criticism."

Now, on the fourteenth, Senate majority leader Mansfield recommended the reconvening of the Geneva Conference, a call for a cease-fire, amnesties to be guaranteed by international occupation forces, and a declaration of willingness to withdraw when others should do so. The senator judged that world reaction would be "immensely favorable." As June 22 brought another leadership breakfast, there was another communication from Mansfield, who had received no written response from his first two efforts. Something had to give. Exactly a week later a none-too-apologetic McGeorge Bundy—to whom had been delegated the task of preparing a formal reply—answered all three missives as best he could. The delay, he claimed, was no measure of the interest the president had in the letters, for "the president greatly values your counsel."

Speaking for President Johnson, Bundy said that the administration was unwilling to make a clear choice among Mansfield's three alternatives. The administration's judgment was less pessimistic than Mansfield's. "Signs and signals" had already been thrown out on the diplomatic front, Bundy said. The current way of calling for a cease-fire was to "urge an end of 'aggression and subversion.' " There seemed to be areas of agreement, he thought. Anyone reading the list would doubt that Mansfield would have concurred. The administration kept studying these problems, said Bundy. "Doctrinaire rigidity" regarding a cease-fire proposal, he claimed, did not exist.[39] So the president's team had quietly, even casually, shelved a reasoned proposal that could have extricated the United States from Vietnam, yet possibly at the cost of a coalition government there that might or might not have become Communist—though perhaps not as Stalinist as what came later. It might even have been like Yugoslavia. Who can say with assurance? Anyway, the man in the White House forged on.

There would be great criticism during the ensuing war as to the alleged limited objectives of the nation. Many believed that war was customarily waged to be won—with the enemy conquered. Yet no less a figure than Gen. Earle G. Wheeler, chairman of the Joint Chiefs of Staff, could tell an elite audience in spring 1965 that although there were various goals in the struggle, the objective was very limited—"very similar to the Korean War." Thus: "As the president has said so often, all we want is to get the nations in that part of the world to leave their neighbors alone, free to find their own destiny without outside pressure. We want nothing more—no land, no special rights. We are willing to help all of the nations in the area to get back on their feet, including North Vietnam. This objective is a far cry from the classic objective of warfare—the overthrow and total defeat of the enemy."[40] Here was altruistic idealism, to be sure, which was astonishing when coming from a general in the armed forces and was lacking in credibility to world and national opinon and to vast numbers in the military itself. It was no wonder that opposition to the Johnson administration came from traditional patriots at the same time that it came from the New Left, pacifists, and many whose orientation was toward first protecting NATO allies and Israel, if need be.

Johnson's team seems to have had three basic assumptions when framing its military policy. First was the idea that escalating military pressure scientifically would ultimately induce Hanoi to stop supporting the Viet Cong—which it most certainly did not. Second, there was confidence that diplomatic signals and military actions could be coordinated in such a way as to send particular "messages" to the enemy. Many almost irrelevant events and confusions kept this academic idea from working out in practice. Third, there was the thought that the use of force could be carefully controlled—that is, turned on or off or modified in rhythm with changes in policies and responses. Like the others, this assumption proved to be ill founded, says a close student of the subject. It was just too difficult to orchestrate a distant Asian government and its military organization with such fine tuning. Moreover, the belief that the nation-seeking enemy would recognize the merits of rational cost-benefit considerations proved fallacious. The enemy proved to be complex in his own organizational patterns; his motives, goals, strengths, weaknesses, and options were anything but simple; his goal of an independent and Marxist unified state was unshakable.[41] Orchestrated escalation was a major failure of the Johnson administration overseas; at home, it led to overheated protests.

There is a myth that the United States was "defeated" by a third-world state using guerrilla weapons. But the arrival at Haiphong of Soviet and Warsaw pact ships with munitions was routine throughout the period of the war. And there was a rail line north. Only years later did China reveal that during the war years it had sent three hundred thousand soldiers to Vietnam, a thousand of whom were killed. The Hanoi government promptly denied this claim. Perhaps fifty thousand Chinese may have been there at any one time. These soldiers supposedly worked as antiaircraft artillerymen, road builders, railway workers, and logistics teams helping to keep supply lines open. Their work was exclusively in the north. Manpower was not China's only contribution. More than 2 million guns, 270 million rounds of ammunition, 37,000 artillery pieces, 18.8 million artillery shells, 179 aircraft, and 145 naval vessels constituted a much-needed contribution. Twenty thousand Chinese soldiers were engaged in building an all-weather road from Yunan Province into Laos.[42] Such extensive aid, added to untotaled but substantial Soviet assistance, gives the lie to any contention that the United States ineptly fought in vain against a small, backward, and primitive military force. In retrospect, North Vietnam's logistical basket seems to have been virtually bottomless; and its disregard of horrendous losses meant that a war of attrition would experience rough sledding. The extent of potential Soviet and Chinese aid simply was not taken into account by an overconfident administration.

Washington, nevertheless, saw its purposes as being served. McNamara's optimistic statements were assembled by a liberal columnist in the *New Republic* into a paragraph as 1966 approached. This essay made for devastating reading: "Our most notable modern prophet is Defense Secretary McNamara. His field: Vietnam. 'The corner has been definitely turned toward victory.' (May 1963) 'The major part of the US military task can be completed by the end of 1965.' (October 1963) 'We have every reason to believe that plans will be successful in 1964.' (December 1963) 'The US hopes to withdraw most of its troops from South Vietnam before the end of 1965.' (February 1964) We read, with mixed feelings, his latest effort last week: 'We have stopped losing the war.' "[43] Here was fuel for a later credibility gap.

Johnson, concealing obstacles, did have ample support in polls and incoming mail for his belligerent course in 1965, and he knew it. Former Republican candidate Thomas E. Dewey told him that "the vast majority know you are everlastingly right." Noting the rise in protest,

Dewey added that every president had to resist the clamor of the "confused and traitorous in doing the right but sometimes unpopular thing. You are doing it bravely and well and history will record it." Dewey added that his own speeches in support were being well received. Conservative Ezra Taft Benson said that Johnson should bear in mind that there is no substitute for victory and added, "Surely a nation which has spent almost one-half of its total budget for defense can clean up the mess in Vietnam." A correspondent said, on May 10, 1965: "Everywhere I go the same thought is expressed, 'Bravo for the president. He has guts as well as wisdom.'" A private poll of one thousand voters in New Haven, Connecticut, showed the public mood: "Do as we are, keep military pressure on but seek negotiation" (yes, 65 percent; no, 20 percent); "We should step up our military even more and win the war" (yes, 44 percent; no, 35 percent); "Forget the whole thing and clear out" (yes, 15 percent; no, 68 percent). They did not want the bombing stopped, nor did they want Hanoi or Red China to be bombed. The pollsters said that, overall, three out of four of those polled Americans supported U.S. policy with reservations. Moreover, pollster Harris assured his aides in June that there was a clear mandate for the president's course of action (65 to 35 percent). Some 47 percent said that he should send more troops in; 11 percent said to take them out. So, Harris found there was a notable rallying behind the president. Today's observer bears in mind, however, that such vigorous and well-reasoned memorandums of secret protest as that of George Ball from the State Department on July 1 were unknown to the public.[44] The Farleys, Deweys, and Bensons praised the president in ignorance of the cases being mobilized by the Mansfields and Balls. The polls but measured a public opinion framed in ignorance, as my reading in 1975 of many boxes of incoming mail on Vietnam at the Johnson Library showed clearly.

A crucial moment for public opinion came on July 28, 1965, when the president told an afternoon TV audience and a packed press conference that troops in Vietnam would increase from 75,000 to 125,000 and that the draft would be doubled, for "we are guardians at the gate." The effort was decidedly low key; it was no "day of infamy" oration. One writer now said gloomily that here was "a land war in Asia against which all experts have warned."[45] The public began to take increasing notice.

The time was at hand for a great debate on fundamentals. Instead, there would be simplistic protest, mixed with further automatic support from those who held traditional views. One of the latter, James Farley, said comfortingly, "It is good to see that you continue to enjoy the wholehearted support of the American people in your position on Vietnam and on the other problems which face you from day to day." He thought that Johnson's legislative record was the greatest in the history of the republic.[46]

A form of protest called teach-ins had already begun at the University of Michigan on March 24, 1965, and was immediately emulated. Some thirty-five hundred students and professors were crowded into four lecture halls as the sessions continued until dawn. The administration sensed many dangers: to the truth, to the president's prestige, to the Democratic party, and to the war effort, especially since many of the campus affairs were weighted against the government position by antisystem and anti-Vietnam organizations. For a time, contingents from the State Department, the Agency for International Development (AID), or the army were sent to defend the administration's orthodoxy. McGeorge Bundy performed yeoman service. Organized disorder—such as hooting, jeering, and constant interruptions—made such campus visits intolerable for the men from Washington. Paperback books with edited speeches, extracts from documents, books, and articles—all cleverly loaded—resembled scholarship but gave the president's case no quarter; students who were uninformed on methodological proprieties quoted paragraphs as from Scripture. Spokesmen for the Johnson administration were astounded at the remote and uninformed sources of "proof" that protestors relied on, including the quotation of uncompromising conclusions voiced by some journalists and by pacifists whose time anywhere in Asia, if any, was sometimes measured in days. But the superior attitude of some who came on behalf of the White House was duly resented, too. One professor said, "The consensus President Johnson always talks about must mean the consensus of those who agree with him."[47]

The Johnson presidency was not involved in every social change that took place in the 1960s and 1970s. In 1965 at Berkeley there was born a "free university" movement, one in which academicians would not choose or veto the curriculum, tuition would be free, and courses would be, to say the least, untraditional, involving drugs, New Left preaching, and orientation toward Asian mysticism. "Alternative newspapers," which were anti-Vietnam and were entranced with total sexual liberty, came into being. About forty of these still exist in the 1980s. Their causes were opposition to the draft, apparent excesses of the CIA, techniques of fighting in Vietnam, alternative life styles, and the newly discovered generation gap. Such ferment was only partly attributable to the occupants of the White House; esprit de corps from opposition to the draft, protest songs, generation-gap solidarity, and other factors held much of this together.

As Vietnam evolved, many people hoped that the government really knew more than it seemed to. While the White House always has access to staggering amounts of information on just about any subject of interest to it, the president nevertheless may act in partial ignorance of both the facts and the policy options. Cabinet officials have their own research staffs; and some, like those in the Department of Defense, can, if they wish, make extensive use of think tanks—research organizations in the private sector which do research in response to government contracts. It is a fair, but largely unanswerable, question whether President Johnson's mind was always well served by the research machinery in existence at the time.

A case in point is the assumption that the premier research organization on national defense, the RAND Corporation, served both the Kennedy and the Johnson administrations through its intermediary, the Air Force, with relevant information and impartial findings on the Vietnam War. For the most part the assumption is in error, for the nonprofit Santa Monica- and Washington-based think tank was not funded to study such regional matters and tactical considerations; its central diet consisted of strategic, intercontinental, and long-range studies and fundamental research. Some relevant research titles (such as a study that was critical of the bombing) did reach the White House; but while impressive and pertinent to the needs of leadership, these are a negligible part of the research effort that—with encouragement—could have been brought to bear on Vietnam by RAND's more than five hundred doctorate-holding specialists, many of whom were dubious quite early about the prospects in Southeast Asia.

The blame for this loss of guidance rests largely on the Air Force, which (controlling only half of the American aircraft in Vietnam in the mid 1960s) saw the Southeast Asian war as having only peripheral interest for it. Interviews of prisoners and resulting predictions (perhaps overly optimistic) were a RAND contribution that reached desks in the White House. Hard-headed suggestions on the organization of troop units and on changes in Air Force equipment fell on deaf ears in the military; and the existing anti-"whiz kid" feeling, which was so frequently expressed by leaders in uniform, constituted something of a guarantee that many out-of-tune evaluations would not be routed to Johnson. It was widely charged that Alain Enthoven, of McNamara's staff, enjoyed influence that was somewhat beyond his years and his staff's capabilities. But David Novick, another RAND alumnus, would revolutionize his assigned area of cost-benefit analysis, and Charles

Zwick would rise to become director of the Budget Bureau. James Schlessinger made the move from RAND in 1967, starting an influential government career as director of strategic studies.[48]

It is true that during the 1960s some RAND staff and alumni, as well as other people, were studying the subject of "coercion" in international politics as a substitute for all-out war of an older type designed to bring an enemy to final surrender. Stressing "gradualism in escalation," "signals," and "orchestrations," a literature of books and articles came into being in the 1960s created by RAND consultants M.I.T. political scientist William Kaufman, Harvard economist Thomas Schelling, and alumni like strategist Bernard Brodie at UCLA, Hudson Institute founder Herman Kahn, and others. While one vigorous book has described nuances of their thinking, there is little evidence that they had either direct contact with President Johnson or compelling influence on top officials. In 1966, Schelling, inventor of the idea of gradual "compellence," was offered a post with the executive branch by McGeorge Bundy, but he declined. Yet there certainly was a coincidence between the way the administration fought and negotiated and the untried but logical enough ideas of such intellectual authors.[49]

While the shooting war escalated during the spring and summer of 1965, the president pursued other approaches to "solving" Asian problems. He enlisted the aid of Eugene R. Black, an investment banker from New York City, to help get from the Congress the Asian Development Bank, which would presumably provide the investment funds that would help countries in planning and research. The initial appropriation would be $200 million. A Mekong River redevelopment commission was sought. Thirty-two countries joined the bank as it set up headquarters in Manila, and some loans were made. Johnson, who had pushed the building of dams in Texas, naturally singled out such a project in Java for favorable comment in his memoirs. But such activities had little to do with ending the troublesome war that was beginning to haunt decision makers.

Those who were close to the president at the time were generally in favor of what had transpired from the time of Tonkin Gulf through the initiation of bombing and the sending of American troops. But Hubert Humphrey would later recall that he, at least, had opposed the February 1965 bombing, had not been a part of the decision making, and had found that his views were not particularly welcome. At the time, he had sent a long memorandum to the president, arguing his case, contending that "we will be taking big historic gambles" and that "the moral dilemmas are inescapable." Cleverly, he associated this escalation with Goldwater's position in 1964, with an allegedly Republican military solution, and with the loss of approval in Europe. Humphrey's case: Why risk Chinese intervention? Why support an unstable country? Don't overreact. Weren't more Democrats than Republicans in the opposition? Avoid becoming the prisoner of events. The political risks were great. He would support the administration, but "these are my views."[50]

Now the president from the Democratic party had lost the intellectual allegiance of both his vice-president and his Senate majority leader; soon the Democratic chairman of the Senate Foreign Relations Committee would go off the reservation. A journalist with extensive experience in the Orient, Robert S. Elegant, wrote that the United States faced a major commitment of not less than ten years in Vietnam; there would be a "protracted stalemate." At the Ranch that month, Johnson would say, typically, "Until independence is guaranteed there is no human power capable of forcing us from Vietnam." But sometimes even he had misgivings. Once when a plane was shot down, he blurted out to a National Security Council meeting, "Where are we going?" In response, Gen. Curtis LeMay wanted much tougher action. Exiting, the president said in an aside, "I get anxious and look for the fire exits when a general wants to get tough. LeMay scares the hell out of me."

Reactions to what was happening varied across the spectrum. Inside the family, George Ball at the State Department thought the cause hopeless; William Bundy at the nearby Southeast Asia desk favored escalation to perhaps 85,000 to show good faith, then exit gracefully. Gen. Maxwell Taylor opposed American involvement in a ground war. But Dean Rusk had put his reservations aside in his concern over Communist aggression: send troops, but don't use them—except to deter, he hoped. Elsewhere, Joseph Alsop wondered if Johnson were "man enough" to stand up to the Communists in Vietnam. Truman spoke warmly: "The president is dead right—I'm 100 percent back of him." The president was acting in the spirit of Churchill's principles of the 1930s, directed at the Nazis, Truman thought.[51] *U.S. News and World Report* for June 17, 1965, would summarize: "War involvement in Vietnam is to grow in size and complexity. Bombing, unless greatly expanded, cannot be decisive. Ground operations, if they are to be depended upon, will take substantial U.S. forces. Vietnam war, right now, looks as if it will be a long haul." Soon, on July 28, Johnson announced that fifty thousand more troops were going. But when the vice-president got ready to say, in a Detroit speech in July, that the nation must be prepared for a "long, costly, and ugly" war, the word from the president was that this would not do; unfortunately the text was already out, so Humphrey only muted it in delivery.

Soon it became common to say that "the war" (which was no longer referred to merely as a counterinsurgency action) was being "Americanized." The expression would live on.[52] Given the historical thrust and deep significance of the word *America* in modern world history (i.e., movement toward freedom, democracy, opportunity; helping the emancipation of peoples in Europe and Asia), here developed a most unfortunate linguistic practice. When applied by Westerners to what happened in Vietnam from 1965 to 1975, it is decidedly inappropriate if not downright wrong. For the war was fought in Vietnam, not in Iowa or Maryland; the number of Vietnamese military casualties and the number of civilians killed and maimed vastly exceeded those from the United States.[53] Generals Westmoreland and Abrams never achieved the unified command over forces in uniform that they sought. The final consequences of the war to the United States, bad as they were, proved not even remotely as devastating as those to the people and landscape of North and South Vietnam alike. Only in the origins of weaponry and in the innovation in strategy and tactics, perhaps—and in the peace negotiations—was there true Americanization. The proper terms for what happened after spring 1965 are "escalation" and, perhaps, "intensification."

Either Lyndon Johnson was not facing up to the inevitable consequences of what he was doing, a year and a half into his presidency, or he hoped that others would not be stimulated to do so. Whether he knew it or not, a great national debate, like no other since the War between the States, was about to erupt, for many really wondered if this war in so remote a theater was really necessary. After spring 1965 an office he had won overwhelmingly in the election of 1964 would never be for him the same rewarding office. Yet, both legislative and partisan politics would continue to offer relief and a feeling of accomplishment to this restlessly determined president.

5

WINNING BIG: 1964

As the new president had looked toward the session of the Congress facing him in 1964, he saw the first order of business to be the passage of major elements in President Kennedy's stalled program. Anything else would be unthinkable. Johnson's speech to the Congress on November 27 signaled this approach clearly, not the least on civil rights. There was the felt need to fight for a tax cut in the vicinity of $11 billion to stimulate the economy. Since all knew that Johnson was a brilliant legislative tactician, he felt special pressure to be completely successful in his congressional relations—not merely to carry on in the late president's name. Carrying on did not mean that his efforts would be lacking in personal commitment, for there had been much coincidence of viewpoint between Kennedy and Johnson. The differences of early 1960 had faded.

So, the year was to be one for major decision making and presidential action. An attack on poverty, a law on civil rights, attention to relations with the Soviets, and a need to implement policy on Vietnam were crucial matters indeed. To blend his personal staff with that of the Kennedy holdovers involved considerable strain, as did the move into the White House—the latest home away from Texas for the president, Lady Bird, Lynda, Luci, and brother Sam Houston Johnson. Other emotion-draining matters centered about food service, patterns in entertaining and interacting with persons of great consequence to the nation, the social activities of both daughters, and relations with the media, which were anxious to get the story behind the story. But

Johnson had once sought the very office he now held. He had long since sensed its possible frustrations when, as Senate majority leader, he had interacted with President Eisenhower. Of course the new office would have its built-in challenges and annoyances! Lyndon Johnson had every reason to know in advance, however, the many opportunities available to one who would accept the obligations of leadership.

By the end of the first months of 1964 the president could point to achievement. On January 3 he had appointed civil servant Esther Peterson to be the special assistant for consumer affairs and had created the President's Committee on Consumer Interest. Years later (in 1980) these actions would win Johnson a posthumous award from the National Consumers League for "enhancing consumer representation in government decision-making." On January 8 the War on Poverty was declared a future program, and on the twenty-seventh came a request to the Congress for a stronger public-housing and urban-renewal program to provide—somehow—"a decent home in a decent neighborhood for every American family." Meeting with a group of older citizens on January 15, he strongly supported a plan of hospital insurance for the elderly. "Dignity and self-respect," he said, should not have to be traded to get hospital and nursing-home care. The means test (to see if income was low enough) should go. Nevertheless, the budget he submitted had been the smallest in proportion to national output since 1951. He got his tax cut. Minimum-wage legislation was extended, and $600 million was provided in aid to wheat and cotton farmers—an amount only $200 million less than what the War on Poverty would get. The constitutional amendment to abolish the poll tax was sent to the states for ratification. Proposals to minimize the arms race were sent to the Geneva Disarmament Conference. It was indeed a busy time.

One task had been to set in motion forces that might achieve the enactment of a civil-rights law, which had long been pending in the Congress. To this need and opportunity the Texan unexpectedly brought an inclination that had shifted appreciably through time. Very early, he met with distinguished Negroes Roy Wilkins, of the National Association for the Advancement of Colored People, and leaders Martin Luther King, Jr., James Farmer, A. Philip Randolph, and others to establish lines of communication, give assurances, and solicit ideas.[1] On November 26 Johnson was told by the Council for United Civil Rights Leadership (composed of the NAACP, the National Urban League, etc.) that there was particular urgency about civil-rights legislation.[2] By coincidence, he was meeting that very day with Democratic Senator Richard Russell of Georgia, who would turn out to be the leader of those who viewed as anathema any federal intervention to change old

Southern ways. The *Washington Post* for November 24 carried the opinion of veteran columnist Roscoe Drummond: "I have read every major speech Mr. Johnson has delivered in the past year. It is evident that no man in public life has done more to demonstrate to the American Negroes that the conscience of the American people and the conscience of the government are on their side in the fight for equality of opportunity and status—and to stir and strengthen that conscience." Gone was the Texan of 1957, for whom the Civil Rights Act of that year had been weakened as a price of his support. Pointing this out, university president Milton Eisenhower, the former president's brother, once judged: "There is no question that when Johnson became president, he became the most militant civil rights leader in the history of the country. He was now obviously doing what he felt the people of the United States wanted done or that he felt the people ought to want to have done." After all, "what one stands for at any time in his life depends a good deal on what his responsibility is."[3] This was a good assessment by one who knew this leader personally.

A brief chronology of civil-rights events during the Johnson years will provide guidance. There was the struggle, for many months, which was finally successful, to pass the Civil Rights Act of 1964. Then came racial disorder during the summer and the sad events in Selma, Alabama, the following March. Johnson's famous speech of March 15, 1965, began the campaign for voting rights. The Voting Rights Act of 1965 would be signed on August 6, but then the Watts riots took place in Los Angeles during that turbulent August of 1965. The president felt he had to say on August 15, "We must not only be relentless in condemning violence, but also in taking the necessary steps to prevent violence." More legislation was thought to be in order. Nevertheless, an effort to get a 1966 act with a fair-housing provision was thwarted by a filibuster. As a result of a Detroit riot in July 1966, the Commission on Civil Disorders was appointed, and the earlier Civil Rights Commission was given five more years of life. The assassination of Martin Luther King, Jr., on April 4, 1968, along with ensuing riots in the capital and in 125 other cities, brought rapid passage of the Civil Rights Act of 1968 only six days later.

Cause and effect seem perhaps too evident in this chronology, for each act had independent roots and was framed and virtually ready for passage before violence occurred. But the dates of passage were certainly related to the assassinations of Kennedy and King; the violence and property damage in Harlem, Watts, Detroit, and Washington, D.C.; and mass demonstrations or property damage and loss of life in scores of other cities. Surely it must be said, reluctantly, that passage of the civil-rights acts of the 1960s was accelerated by acts of violence. Physical confrontations could have their price, however: increased fear and distrust, property damage, disabilities and deaths, and uneasy relationships between the races. In an ideal world, other means of expediting equity and justice would have been possible. In any case, the civil-rights acts owed much to the aggressive president, to those working closely with him, and to the leaders and organizations in the black communities and in white communities who took risks and struggled so hard to obtain for racial minorities what others in America already had.

It has become the custom to treat "The 1960s" as a unit, an entity, a period—one that can be held up to view and comprehended in each of its many facets.[4] This periodization puts a nearly intolerable burden on the student of the Johnson presidency in such areas as civil rights, protests by the black community and by students, increase in crime and in the use of drugs, and other social issues. After all, when Johnson came to power, CORE already existed and the NAACP was decades old. Many other related events had taken place—the August 28, 1963 March on Washington; Little Rock, Greensboro, the Freedom Riders, and Birmingham; formation of the Student Nonviolent Coordinating Committee and Students for a Democratic Society; the early commitment to activism of Tom Hayden, Mario Savio, Allard Lowenstein, and many others. Martin Luther King, Jr., had become a national figure before Johnson's presidency. Campus unrest, though at first directed at alleged university mismanagement, was already a reality. Radical essayist Paul Goodman had a following. Both King and the student movement would, during Johnson's years in the Oval Office, convert to new causes that were directly traceable to his policies in office, however. With regard to periodization, the ten years from 1963/64 to 1973/74 make for a better decade than "The 1960s" for a serious social study.

A charge against the chief executive is that he fought tooth and nail for the Civil Rights Act of 1964 only because he wanted to prove that he was a better president than Kennedy would have been. Psychologically, the argument is plausible, but it flies in the face of well-marked changes in Johnson's conduct. In Detroit, on January 6, 1963, he had said: "To strike the chains of a slave is noble. To leave him the captive of his color is hypocrisy." A few weeks later he told the Cleveland Urban League that the problems left unresolved by the Emancipation Proclamation must be settled. In May 1963 he told the National Press Club that half a loaf would not do. His most noted declaration was at Gettysburg on Memorial Day: "Until justice is blind to color, until education is unaware of race, until opportunity is unconcerned with the color of men's skins, emancipation will be a proclamation but not a fact. To the extent that the proclamation of emancipation is not fulfilled in fact, to that extent we shall have fallen short of assuring freedom to the free." He argued his cause forcefully inside the administration. Birmingham, to him, meant an end to compromise. If his new language and sentiments were not those of the earlier senator and representative, we have his own retrospective judgment, from 1972: "I do not want to say that I've always seen this matter, in terms of the special plight of the black man, as clearly as I came to see it in the course of my life and experience and responsibility."[5]

A common perspective on Kennedy and Johnson is that the former "really cared" about Negro problems, while the latter, imbued with a southern white man's perspective, only rushed in after Dallas to gain liberal support for his 1964 election. Yet the *southwestern* Johnson, as vice-president, early sensed the true need and possibilities. In mid 1963 he was giving advice about civil rights for the black man to Kennedy men behind the scenes. A mysterious typed transcription of a secret Edison Dictaphone recording of an impassioned telephone plea that he made on June 3 to Theodore Sorensen seems to prove his dedication, as well as his critical posture toward the hesitations and vacillations of the Kennedy team. Kennedy, he said, should deliver in the South a presidential speech of commitment to Negro rights, while looking people "straight in the face." There must be "a moral commitment." Neither confrontation nor a hasty bill was the way to go: "It might cost us the South, but those sorts of states [sic] may be lost anyway." In six months they hadn't passed anything. Said Sorensen rather lamely, "Well, I think we could have done better"; he would tell the president what Johnson thought.[6] Kennedy's next civil-rights speech did show somewhat more fire, for whatever reason.

By some people, Johnson's record on civil rights has been the most praised of his activities; by others, he has been given credit only for good intentions; to a few die-hards, the whole record is one of lasting damage to majority rights; and radicals think he should—somehow or other—have done more. To some extent the facts speak for themselves: there are the 1964 act, which prohibited discrimination in public places and aided in ensuring fair employment and desegregated schools; the 1965 voting-rights act, which outlawed literacy tests and poll taxes; and the 1968 act that prohibited discrimination in the sale or rental of housing. Aide Joseph Califano, who later became Jimmy Carter's Secretary of Health, Education, and Welfare, correctly says that in 1964 Lyndon Johnson "devoted a staggering amount of his time, energy, and political capital to breaking the Senate filibuster and passing the act."[7]

The 1964 State of the Union message had scarcely begun before the president said, "Let this session of Congress be known as the session which did more for civil rights than the last hundred sessions combined." But in this speech he said practically nothing else on that subject, as coverage of many themes brought seventy-nine interruptions for applause. The time for details and exhortation would come in a few months. Meanwhile, his deadly seriousness on the matter was apparent to a few. On New Year's Eve 1963, he was instrumental in integrating the faculty club at the University of Texas in Austin by the outwardly simple gesture of bringing with him a black woman, one of his secretaries. That did it. "We were all startled," wrote Barbara Jordan later about reaction in the black community as the 1964 act took shape, "that this was really what he wanted to do, that this man in the White House was really going to push this."[8]

The first draft of the civil-rights speech of March 31, 1965, was prepared by staff attorneys in the Attorney General's Office in response to events in Selma, Alabama; but its early thrust was out of keeping with the mood in the White House. A new version by Horace Busby would be the basis for work by the president and Richard Goodwin right up to the time of its delivery in person before both houses of Congress and a nationwide TV audience. Its final sentences were dramatic. Saying that Selma was symbolic of the effort of Negroes to secure for themselves the full blessings of American life, the president said with great deliberateness: "Their cause must be our cause too. Because it is not just Negroes, but really it is all of us who must overcome the crippling legacy of bigotry and injustice." He concluded with: "And we shall overcome!" using the language of the marchers nationwide. Jotted a liberal columnist in the press gallery, "Seems from the heart . . . his best speech." Johnson's words were brave and influential, but violence aimed at the Selma march would shortly gain equal attention.

The long struggle to pass the Civil Rights Act of 1964 has been traced in detail.[9] Much drafting work on the bill itself had been done during the Kennedy years, and the conversion of House Republican minority leader Charles Halleck, a few days before the assassination, was important. Another person who deserved credit was Senator Everett Dirksen, a powerful Republican from Illinois, who engineered the passage of eleven amendments to the legislation. Hubert Humphrey recalled how determined Johnson was from the outset to see that Dirksen had every chance to "look good" in connection with passage of the bill. Humphrey was ordered to see, drink with, talk to, and listen to Dirksen. "I courted Dirksen almost as persistently as I did Muriel [Mrs. Humphrey]," he said, claiming that no day had passed without his mentioning some part of the bill to the Illinois orator. Humphrey appealed "to his sense of fairness and spirit of nation." When the bill passed, he told Dirksen, "It would be his bill and the biggest Republican boost since the Emancipation Proclamation." Dirksen did come to feel that it was his bill, Humphrey thought. Insiders, such as political strategist Larry O'Brien, knew how important Dirksen's role was, and told him that his approach was reasoned, cooperative, and courteous, helping to make a remarkable record. When Dirksen died on September 7, 1969, the memorial speeches in Congress said that he had not engaged in opposition for opposition's sake, had employed the art of "objective compromise," and had helped to bring major legislation into being, while he was beloved by the people of the country.[10] If Senator Johnson aided Eisenhower, so did Senator Dirksen aid Johnson.

The president's version of events appeared early in a letter drafted for his signature by Bill Moyers. From the beginning, Johnson said, he had anticipated that the bill would pass. "A number of factors prompted my optimism, notably a feeling on my part that the general consensus of the American people had caught up with the legislative demands of their fellow citizens who had been dedicated to justice and equality." The times were historically ripe. "No doubt President Kennedy's death provided a dramatic and important catalyst for consideration of the legislation, but I believe he would have been able to pass the legislation had he lived." Here was a generous concession. But stress must nevertheless be laid on Johnson's personal concern. No detail was too small. Debate was finally limited by invoking cloture, after which the favorable vote in the Senate was lopsided. As passed, the act contained a fair-employment-practices provision and one that restored the teeth that had been deleted in 1957 as a price for passing that bill. Johnson had gotten his bill (and Dirksen's) without compromise on essentials. "Under Kennedy," say contemporaries Evans and Novak, "it is quite probable that one or both of these sections would have been sacrificed in the Senate in exchange for the public accommodations section and to eliminate or at least shorten a Senate filibuster. But Johnson refused any compromise whatsoever."[11]

Signing of the act was staged with a flourish, complete with live TV, in the rotunda of the Capitol; but unfortunately, riots in Harlem erupted within two weeks, so that better race relations would not be a visible result of passage of the bill. Johnson quickly gathered black leaders together and pleaded with them to get their followers to curtail, if not observe a moratorium on, "all mass marches, picketing and demonstrations" until after the November election. It would be self-defeating if they did not. One person who attended the meeting says that while most of those present agreed to a *pro forma* truce, the leaders of the Student Nonviolent Coordinating Committee (SNCC) and the Congress of Racial Equality (CORE) refused. Implementation of the act became Johnson's personal concern. He was generous when in the fall Martin Luther King, Jr., won the Nobel Peace Prize. "This is a tribute to the leadership you have given to the movement for individual dignity and equality of opportunity"; the award honored the nation as well, Johnson wrote aboard Air Force One. Each man had indeed tried to do his part: King with the marchers and eloquence of speech; Johnson by adding to the laws of the land. (Only later would the FBI files on King begin to bulge with tapes and transcripts as the concern of J. Edgar Hoover over certain of King's associates and King's growing antagonism toward the Vietnam War mounted.)

Effective blows were struck during those years at local and state racial barriers, both public and private, in many areas of American life. Before the decade had closed, the guarantees of the thirteenth, fourteenth, and fifteenth amendments would be on the road to firm implementation throughout the land in such areas as voting, education, and public accommodations. Housing and employment, however, did not respond rapidly then or later, for discrimination had long historic roots, and many other important economic and social factors were involved in the lack of progress.

A proper perspective would be that the acts of 1964, 1965, and 1968 built on a foundation laid in the acts of 1957 and 1960. The 1964 statute was more comprehensive and well beyond what the Kennedy team had sought. Voter registration and literacy requirements must be applied fairly; most public accommodations must be open to all. Now the attorney general could intervene in civil-rights suits and could sue in order to guarantee desegregation of public facilities, including schools; and other aid to this end could be given by the federal government. The commission's life was prolonged, and it was given more authority. Federal funds could be withheld when discrimination had been proved. It tried to guarantee an end to job discrimination because of race, color, religion, sex, or national origin, using the new Equal Opportunity Commission. The Census Bureau would henceforth aid the commission by collecting statistics on voting. The Community Relations Service would help in solving civil-rights problems.

A Johnson concern during the first months in office was passage of his tax bill and reduction in government spending. In these twin tasks the president was in his element, reveling in the opportunity to count noses, manipulate the minds and emotions of legislators, and struggle in tandem with overworked staff to achieve goals that were not too far away and that would be immediately noticed by men of power in New York City and financial circles worldwide. He proved to be more than up to the task.

A second concern was allowed to slide for some months. This was to coin and then round out a slogan that could become a Johnson election-year trademark—as in his lifetime "Square Deal" was Theodore Roosevelt's; "New Freedom" was Wilson's; "New Deal" had served Franklin Roosevelt; "Fair Deal" had worked for Truman; and "New Frontier" had so brilliantly been identified with Kennedy. The timing and manner of Lyndon Johnson's selecting and announcing his choice of "Great Society" has much interest, for here was what T. V. Smith had called an operative symbol, one that "begets anticipation"; Smith had also warned that anticipation can lead to frustration.[12] His was an opinion from an earlier decade that Lyndon Johnson might well have weighed more carefully.

The term selected was a happy choice. Eric Goldman says he suggested "good society," from the book of that name by Walter Lippmann. Speechwriter Richard Goodwin liked "great society" better, a term that had appeared in a book by the Socialist Graham Wallas in 1914, although Goodwin seems not to have known it. Henry Luce had used it in 1939; so had a textbook in 1958.[13] But Jack Valenti drew his chief's attention to its potential: "Why not enlarge the theme, coupling the phrase with a new outline of what the president felt would be his philosophy, his précis of his move to the future, his aims and objectives for this country here at home."[14] Public use of the term seventeen times early in 1964 failed to interest the media. Terms such as "better deal," "glorious kind of society," and "greater society" did no better. The opportunity was seized to use the chosen expression at the University of Michigan's commencement ceremonies on May 22, 1964, in such a way that it could no longer be ignored by the image makers.

The Great Society speech opened with the vision of a utopia with "abundance and liberty" for all. There would be an end to poverty and racial injustice; knowledge would be readily available; and even leisure would involve, not boredom and restlessness, but a chance to build and reflect. Moreover, the "desire for beauty" and "hunger for community" would be served by "the city of man." There was much more in this academic vein. The places to build were the cities, the countryside, and the classrooms. There was sturdy affirmation on conservation: "The water we drink, the food we eat, the very air that we breathe, are threatened by pollution. Our parks are overcrowded, our seashores overburdened. Green fields and dense forests are disappearing." Beautiful America was endangered.

The area of education was targeted by saying that the society would not be great "until every young mind is set free to scan the farthest reaches of thought and imagination." Classrooms were overcrowded, curriculums were outmoded, and teachers were underpaid and many of them were not qualified. Henceforth, "poverty must not be a bar to learning, and learning must offer an escape from poverty." Moreover, "we have the power to shape the civilization that we want." Enrich the life of mankind! The oration evoked twenty-nine outbursts of applause from members of the graduating class and their families. Afterward, the speaker was described as being euphoric and exuberant.

Stress has been placed on the creation of this key Johnson expression, not because there is anything unusual about ghost-assisted presidential speeches—at least since President Hoover composed with a pencil, unassisted. Rather, it is a reminder that all major speeches in this and other administrations bear the stamp of officials and staff members and emerge after give-and-take with the president; thus, one should take care, when analyzing such addresses, to avoid discovery of alleged key facets of presidential personality, character, or point of view. This utopian speech was not at all in line with Lyndon Johnson's motto, "Strive for the impossible; settle for the possible." But it was illustrative of his opinion, expressed in an interview, that "the satisfaction one gets out of life is really what you live for." He said that some people get pleasure from making money or from being heroes, but "doing something for humanity" gives "the biggest kick and thrill." If he had to start life over, it would be as a teacher, preacher, or politician. Whether the Johnson of the Great Society speech, which was framed by Goodwin and Valenti, is the "real Johnson" is conjectural; but what the president then said in public does reveal his willingness to dream big in public.

Others will have to delineate, in outline and with subheadings, a social philosophy for this leader, after carrying out minute research into his authentic words and actual deeds. Here is a problem of no little magnitude, for (a) the words quoted must be verified as really *his*, and (b) the actions cited must be those deriving from *his* initiative, or at least from his genuine enthusiasm, free of imminent political gain. Richard Goodwin's edited words and the brainstorming of task forces cannot be added together to equal the inner reaches of Johnson's mind, emotions, and soul. There is an ancient saying, "Speech is a mirror of the soul: as a man speaks, so is he" (Publilius Syrus); but surely the words used must be those of the leader himself. The work of separating out the Johnson-inspired acts of this busy administration has not yet been done. In any case, Johnson was pragmatic, earthy, and generous in the large, had unshakable confidence in action taken by the national government, and was determined to realize maximum personal credit for whatever good was achieved. The historian who is concerned over LBJ's social philosophy will simply have to dig deeply or be patient.

Johnson spoke expansively to his Great Society theme in New York City on May 28, 1964, saying "no child will go unfed and no youngster will go unschooled." Every child will have "a good teacher and every teacher . . . good pay, and both have good classrooms." Every human being would have dignity; every worker a job. Education would be blind to color; employment would be unaware of race. The Great Society would be "where decency prevails and courage abounds." Speaking at the Civic Center Arena in Pittsburgh on October 27, he said, "The Great Society is when America's promise and her practice come together. . . . It is as real as tomorrow, and it is yours for the working at it. . . . The Great Society under a Democratic president cares." Now came elaboration: "It's the time—and it's going to be soon—when nobody in this country is poor. . . . It's the time—and there's no point in waiting—when every boy and girl in this country . . . has the right to all the education that he can absorb." There would be "full social security" for "every older man and women," plus meaning, purpose, and pleasure. And "a job for everyone who is willing to work, and he is going to be paid a decent wage." Moreover, "false distinction" among people would no longer make any difference. Henceforth, "every slum" would be "gone from every city in America." The country would be beautiful. Man, under God, would have full dominion over his own destiny. There would be peace on earth and good will among men. (The speechwriters were working overtime, and election day was certainly approaching.) Said the president as candidate, "The place is here and the time is now."

The latter-day reader can only deplore such unrealistic exaggeration and raising of false hopes. Seldom from responsible public figures, even during an election, does one hear balderdash such as this. Did the president of the United States think that such promises could be made without arousing hopes that could only be dashed? Only a leader who was hopelessly indifferent to his spoken words (or a demagogue) would promise that his program would lead to dignity, decency, and courage. Such talk would taper off, fortunately. In 1965 the term Great Society would be used in public twenty-nine times; in 1966, thirty-one times. But in 1967 there were only five mentions, and in 1968/69, but three. So, Lyndon Johnson buried his own term in his own day. The Great Society, says sociologist S. M. Miller, was based on a belief in "cost-free liberalism," which held that improvements could be financed out of economic growth, not out of the taxpayers' pockets. "That mistaken judgment, coupled with the failure of some programs to achieve results commensurate with their rhetoric, prompted public disillusionment,'' he says. And some programs created unfortunate side effects.

The year 1964 would prove to be an astonishing election year, one that would bring elation to the new president and his supporters and dejection to his Republican opponents. Great effort had been exerted during the eight months after the tragic event in Dallas to portray Democrat Lyndon Johnson of Texas in a favorable light. Journalists and writers for magazines received energetic cooperation from the president's men in the White House. An early book that was somewhat more than the usual campaign biography was the effusion of William S. White, the Pulitzer-Prize-winning Johnson intimate. Here was a ringing endorsement for one who was said to have ''the gift of empathy,'' the ''power of personal persuasion,'' and ''an instinctive, sensitive awareness of the inner feelings'' of those with whom he interacted. The political gift of ''The Professional'' was compared to that of a great violinist, born to the violin. Johnson was compassionate; he functioned best in ''disaster.'' ''Lyndon Johnson's intellectual processes have always been, under great stress, almost reflexive, of an instantaneous, tactile sensitivity unique in my experience as an observer of public men,'' judged White. Johnson distrusted ''doctrinaire solutions to political problems'' and eschewed ''absolute, all-or-nothing stands.'' He rejected irrationality in anything and bore being misinterpreted with ''patient fortitude.'' There was not an ounce of demagogy in him.[15] In much of this, White missed the mark. A pleasant book by Johnson's friend Booth Mooney hewed to conventional lines, giving a totally favorable portrait without pretensions to being either objective or lasting literature.

The election gave political writers a field day as they pitted an alleged southerner-turned-liberal against a ''doctrinaire'' conservative. Moderate Republicans agonized as they deserted the head of their ticket, who said he offered ''A Choice, Not an Echo.'' There were dirty-tricks activities by reactionaries opposed to Johnson; meanwhile, some liberals and snobs reveled in the chance to defame the plain-spoken high-school graduate and department-store man from Arizona. The basic Johnson strategy was to stress ''consensus,'' speak of great goals to be served by his coming Great Society, and make certain that his opponent appeared in the image of an extremist reactionary rather than just as a conservative with a conscience. The South would be courted— by Lady Bird especially, it turned out—while Johnson strove to appear presidential, saying at first, ''I guess the best thing for me to do . . . is to stay around here and let people know I'm real busy tending the store, that I'm taking good care of their business."[16] Trips away from the capital would be tied in with the election: a fourteen-hour tour to observe poverty areas in Appalachia, a flight over the flooded Ohio River area, and visits to places where public works were being dedicated. Prosperity was an ally, as the Dow-Jones industrial stock average rose. Highly visible meetings with labor and business leaders demonstrated continued consensus, and Henry Ford II's support made heads turn. The chief advisers would be James Rowe and lawyers Abe Fortas and Clark Clifford. When appealing to moderate Republicans, Johnson's kind words were for Ike, Governor William Scranton of Pennsylvania, Milton Eisenhower, and Henry Cabot Lodge, who had been Nixon's running mate in 1960. "I'm not sure whether there is a real Republican candidate this time," Johnson remarked, as he duly courted and flattered former followers of Nelson Rockefeller and George Romney.

Inside the White House there was constant speculation during the election campaign about how the voters were viewing the nation's involvement in Vietnam. From memorandums that were passing back and forth in White House corridors, one can see what the major questions were presumed to be. Johnson was told that the public seemed to be asking, Why are we in Vietnam? After so long a time, Why haven't we been able to train Vietnamese to do their own fighting? Why can't we win? Or, Why not turn it over to the locals? What would happen, anyway, if we did pull out? Why must we stand and fight? Why not turn it over to the United Nations, à la Korea? An aide suggested that the president could handle such questions in a simple fifteen-minute broadcast, complete with maps; the goal: to depoliticize the issue. Wrote this assistant, "Unless we can extract the issue from politics, we are hard put to follow it through. If we can persuade some Republican leaders of stature and influence to join this line, we can tab the others as extremists and malcontents—and thereby stabilize our plan of action for some time to come."[17]

One of the oddest of Johnson's moves took place within family privacy early on the morning of June 12, 1964, when, astonishingly, he quietly dictated and showed to his wife a secret draft statement saying he would not be running for election after all. Now Lyndon Johnson could not be charged with "politics" with regard to the Vietnam issue! He moaned that people were saying he was power hungry; that the Congress had no sense of urgency; that the office needed somebody capable of recruiting higher-caliber people like Rusk and McNamara. There had been so much criticism. So it went in this moment of self-doubt. But Lady Bird wooed the temporarily unnerved heart-attack victim of 1955 back to the first principles of politics, one of which is not to quit unnecessarily under fire.[18] The TV folk and eager columnists never had the chance to turn this private action into a major human-interest story—or scandal. Suppose the story had surfaced during the campaign?

As always, many interesting events took place behind the scenes. Averell Harriman objected to Dean Rusk's calling his Department of State *nonpartisan*. The word used by Senator Arthur Vandenberg had been *unpartisan*, Harriman wrote the president. Factual attacks by Senator Barry Goldwater should be answered by the secretary or his deputies; if they would not do the job, Harriman said *he* would. At one point, former minister Bill Moyers suggested to Johnson that an opportunity existed "to arouse many religious groups to oppose Goldwater," using someone at the Democratic National Committee. Wrote Johnson, cautiously, "I agree with this, but let's get somebody else to do it." Walter Heller advised that while Eisenhower had had three recessions, Kennedy and Johnson had had none; something could be done with this. Truman sent word he was "pulling all the strings he knew of to assure your victory in the upcoming campaign and that he was most confident that your opponent did not have a chance."[19]

In what was visible to the president and the public in spring 1964, there seemed little indeed to bring concern to Democrats. Never, said some in the media, had a president shown such raw energy in performing the duties of his office. *Time* was overwhelmed. In a single week of late April, it noted, the president had made nearly two dozen speeches, traveled 2,983 miles, held three press conferences, been on national TV three times, appeared in person before nearly a quarter of a million people, and made his right hand bleed and puff up from handshaking. It was all "breathtaking, nerveshaking, totally implausible"; a handsome Johnson face would grace the cover of the May 1 issue. Republicans had been preempted.

The loyal opposition at the time shared in idealist *goals* but differed sharply on the *means* to be used in achieving them. A real warning was to be found in Republican emphasis on limited government and limited expenditures. Congressional members who rooted their political thinking on such principles would be hard—perhaps impossible—to win over. Whether Republican dedication to peace through strength could be drawn upon to gain support for a crusading war that was not targeted for victory was uncertain.

The probable candidacy of Barry Goldwater in opposition to Lyndon Johnson became apparent as the hopes of the former's moderate Republican opponents faded. Goldwater was ready to crusade. After the State of the Union message, he had said of the president, "It is my impression that he out Roosevelted Roosevelt, out Kennedyed Kennedy, and even made Truman look like a piker. There is no single field in which he is not going to move in and take over your lives." At the same time, Senator Russell had described Johnson's civil-rights plans as "shortsighted and disastrous legislation," so the conservative candidate of the Republican party could hope that much of the South might be his. He would have preferred Kennedy as an opponent. Once Kennedy had talked of such a contest, advising: "Don't announce too soon, Barry. The minute you do you'll be the target. If you give them [the moderate Republicans] eighteen months to shoot you down, they will probably be able to do it." The two even talked about campaigning together before the same audiences! Unfortunately for Goldwater, Johnson could not be charged squarely with the failures of those years, especially the Bay of Pigs. Worse, Goldwater recalled, while a good campaign would be one that involved opposing without hating, "All my contacts with Lyndon Johnson had instructed me to believe he would be incapable of opposing without hate."[20]

Much would go wrong. The slick efficiency of the Rockefeller team rapidly made Goldwater's off-the-cuff candor a major liability. His earlier comments on social security (in a book) and his remarks about using America's strength to win victory in Vietnam stereotyped him as "a trigger-happy, pugnacious, somewhat uninformed candidate," he recalled. He came to consider the campaign a "season of untempered abuse, vindictive falsehood, desertion of civility." The famous use-the-atom-bomb-against-Hanoi remark was actually no more than a suggestion that at some point we might interdict the supply trails in Vietnam by "defoliation of the forest by low yield atomic devices." Thus he did not suggest using giant hydrogen or atomic bombs, but the AP and the UPI promptly said that he had—a story that was retracted only by the latter. Another cross that his campaign had to bear was the divisive tone of his party's convention in San Francisco's Cow Palace. He endured criticism throughout 1964, much of which was well based, from moderate Republican leaders. Scranton offered the epithet, "shoot from the hip," and Lodge, "trigger happy." Columnists like Walter Lippmann and Joseph Alsop took after the candidate.

John S. Knight, publisher of a newspaper chain, who did not support him, wrote in an editorial on June 21: "I can no longer stand silently by and watch the shabby treatment Goldwater is getting from the news media." TV commentators were discussing him "with evident disdain and contempt." Columnists, cartoonists, and editorial writers were no better. Said Knight, quite accurately: "The Goldwater movement represents a mass protest by conservatively-minded people against foreign aid, excessive welfare, high taxes, foreign policy, and the concentration of power in the federal government." Nevertheless, it was the public posture of some moderate Republicans during the primaries that was responsible for the size of the fiasco of the Goldwater effort in the fall.

The disastrously fragmented Republican party collapsed at the polls in 1964, due to the passions of John Birch Society members, desertions by moderates, rumors about the candidate, and internal accusations. Goldwater's odd yet spirited words—"Extremism in the defense of liberty is no vice and . . . moderation in the pursuit of justice is no virtue"—were widely quoted with astonishment. Even Eisenhower asked him what they meant. These words had originated in a speech by Cicero. The standard-bearer had voted with President Eisenhower only 12 percent of the time—a fact that Johnson revealed gleefully in his speech at Johns Hopkins University.[21] Observers of such phenomena were sometimes open-mouthed, both in public and in private, whatever their views on partisan politics.

The choice of a running mate for Johnson should not have aroused much interest then—or later. Determined not to let the post go to Robert Kennedy, Johnson simply announced, "I have reached the conclusion that it would be inadvisable for me to recommend to the convention (as my running mate) any member of the Cabinet or any of those who meet regularly with the Cabinet." First, in a tense meeting, he so advised the late president's brother (his own attorney general)—after which Robert Kennedy of Massachusetts somehow ran, with Johnson's help, for a New York seat in the United States Senate. Humphrey would recall that within hours after John F. Kennedy's death, he had been called by friends and political leaders about his availability for the 1964 vice-presidential nomination. The majority whip of the Senate was told in May that if nothing arose to put an obstacle in the way, he would be the choice. Desperately wanting the job, he responded fully to two searching private cross-examinations by Johnson's aide Jim Rowe. At Rowe's request, Humphrey called the president and said: "You can rely on me. I will be loyal." But time passed. Johnson gave him a full lecture on presidential/vice-presidential relationships, born of the strains of his own experience from 1961 to 1963 (and a reason, to appear in chapter 12). Johnson said, "I think we make a great team." Humphrey would be fully capable of carrying on if anything happened to him, Johnson added.

So Humphrey accepted the task without illusions—a point that has often been overlooked. Barry Goldwater once asked Humphrey why he had submitted to such patronizing treatment. "You and I have been around long enough, Barry," Humphrey said without rancor, "to know an uncooperative vice president could cut the man in the White House to ribbons. . . . We just went over the rules. I told him I knew the limitations and would observe them. We were in deep trouble in Vietnam. There were riots in the cities. He was doing his best to cool the civil rights question. As I read him that day, deep down inside he was scared. He wasn't worried about beating you. His problem was how to run the country." Goldwater agreed. It is not true that Johnson kept the Minnesotan at arms length at the time. He called him twice on August 18 and again on August 20, 23, 24, and 26. The Humphreys were guests at the Ranch on the twenty-ninth. There were four calls on September 2. When Johnson announced his decision at the convention, it was termed by a columnist "the annointment of Hubert Humphrey"; corny, but good theater, and carried out "in the grand manner." Humphrey says he loved every minute of the ensuing campaign, for he was the president's full partner, speaking and campaigning day and night. "It was a happy time" with victory obvious.[22] Humphrey's time of trial would come four years later.

The Atlantic City convention was astutely called "a dreary wasteland of Lyndon-knows-best." The president's acceptance speech was worked on by Horace Busby, Willard Wirtz, Bill Moyers, McGeorge Bundy, and Richard Goodwin—all to no good effect, for they produced a patchwork that the candidate read uneasily without verve. One overstatement (though it was true in a sense) was unfortunate. Said the commander in chief, the strength of the nation "is greater than the combined might of all the nations, in all the world, in all the history of this planet. And I report our superiority is growing." This laid an unfortunate foundation for the Vietnam stalemate soon to come and should have attracted more attention then and later.

Goldwater requested and was granted a secret meeting with the president on July 24. He said that while divided by party and philosophy, they were united in love of country. Replied Johnson, "You know damned well, Barry, that the nation is first in my thinking." The Republican candidate continued: "The war in Vietnam is a national burden. The people are already divided. The legitimacy of our presence is being questioned. The conduct of the war is being criticized. My views on this matter are clear and, I think, well known. I asked to see you because I do not believe it is in the best interest of the United States to make the Vietnam War or its conduct a political issue in this campaign. I have come to promise I will not do so." Johnson seemed greatly relieved, Goldwater recalled, speaking with passion about such problems of the war as distance and the conflicting reports coming from intelligence sources and the press. Recalled the Arizonan as to civil rights: "I said if it became a political issue it could polarize the country. I told him I would not attack his position. I hoped he would refrain from challenging mine."

So the war and civil rights were never to become major issues in the 1964 campaign, thanks to secret connivance between the opposing candidates! "I don't recall a single statement from the president or the White House which could be regarded as in violation of that private agreement," recalled Goldwater, adding, "Perhaps I was quixotic," for Johnson "was vulnerable on Vietnam." As if this conspiracy were not enough, Goldwater claims that, through his military contacts, he had "a very clear picture of what had taken place" in connection with the murder of Diem during the Kennedy-Johnson period. He guessed that if the voters had known what Johnson knew about the role of the United States government, they might have turned against Johnson, for President Diem had been a South Vietnamese hero who had fought the French and was anti-Communist.[23]

Sensitive people cannot read such sensational revelations without being concerned about how the American political system is to work if there are to be secret, even conspiratorial, agreements between top political opponents, including concealment, by the overly loyal opposition, of official wrongdoing. Sportsmanship, patriotism, or keeping the public calm are not adequate motives. The nation was at peace! Barry Goldwater and the president must be faulted for what they did, considering that open discussion could have made a real contribution in the long run to the national interest. The public was entitled to a debate on the timing and nature of civil-rights legislative efforts. The people would have profited by a full airing in 1964 of Vietnam issues that arose only belatedly in the campaigns of 1966, 1968, 1970, 1972, and even later. Americans should not have had to wait for the revelations of the Pentagon Papers on withdrawal of support for Diem, Tonkin Gulf, and conditions in Saigon. It is not clear exactly how much reserve Brigadier General Barry Goldwater actually knew about such matters in the fall of 1964; but it could easily have been a great deal. Public knowledge might have expanded rapidly if he had gone public.

A reading of the files "Republicans for Johnson" in the Johnson Library brings realization of the fears that were engendered in moderate Republicans by their candidate. Partisans such as Arthur Larson and Arthur Fleming wrote about their new convictions. But most who knew Goldwater personally were not swayed by innuendo. Jack Valenti recalls that Johnson considered him, not a deadly enemy, but a fellow rancher who cared about the land and its resources. Both liked the honest, determined, forthright, open man who spoke his mind. Liberals in the media varied in degree of attack. Goldwater "preaches a moral revivalism with a mystic quality," said a columnist, portraying Goldwater as dashing, sun-dusted, boyish, and attractive, one who says "the most extraordinary things in a low-keyed, matter-of-fact way."[24] Charges by zealot psychiatrists that he was mentally unstable were later refuted in legal action, but too late.

The Democratic campaign really got under way behind the scenes on August 5, as nine Johnson aides met to clear strategy and to assemble tactics. Lines of authority were worked out. Positive themes in the Democratic campaign included the Great Society, praise for consensus approaches, and some portentous statements on education, which were generally overlooked as mere campaign rhetoric. Thus Johnson said at Denver, "I intend to put education at the top of America's agenda . . . : that regardless of family financial status education should be open to every boy or girl born in America up to the highest level which he or she is able to master."

Much of this utopian excess disclosed the raw political mind of a master at work, aided by some strikingly irresponsible speech writers. A researcher concluded that when Johnson was in the South, he spoke as a southerner; when in the West, he spoke as a westerner.[25] One way or another, he built on the image that he had created four years earlier, so that columnist David Broder would finally judge that in 1964 Johnson had built a vast and enthusiastic personal following of his own and was no longer just Kennedy's successor; rather, he had become "a towering political figure, with a constituency that is his, and his alone." Lyndon Johnson, whose first two Senate campaigns had been inauspicious and who had barely been selected and elected vice-president, focused throughout on an overwhelming victory. His determination was hardly ameliorated by the striking and overly lyrical account of "The Kennedy Record," which was written by a Kennedy-ite for the handbook of the Democratic National Convention.

Speaking in Chicago, Johnson linked himself firmly with the long past of the party: "So we tonight, assembled here, pledge ourselves to democracy's greatest tradition, the New Freedom of Wilson, the New Deal of Roosevelt, the Fair Deal of Harry S. Truman, the New America and the New Frontier of John Fitzgerald Kennedy, and after Tuesday, November third, the Great Society of Lyndon Johnson and Hubert Humphrey." It may be a bit unfair, but it is certainly relevant to mention that Wilson, Roosevelt, and Truman all led the nation in major wars; certainly the speaker did not mention their leadership of a nation at war.

Continuing his identification with his party's past, in Austin the candidate announced that he had long known that "government is not an enemy of the people. It is the people." Here again he identified with his idol, FDR, whose remark "The state is just people" was basic to the increase of government during the New Deal. A Johnson discovery in his speech was "that poverty and ignorance are the only basic weaknesses of a free society and that both of them are only bad habits and can be stopped."

A much-noticed event in the autumn was the death of Herbert Hoover, the nation's most decorated leader. Wrote Brooks Atkinson, drama critic for the *New York Times,* on October 27: "There has never been a better American than Herbert Hoover. . . . Neither of the candidates for president today has anything like Hoover's high-mindedness." He recalled that Hoover, in his ninetieth-birthday message, had said that "we alone of all nations fought for free men in two world wars and asked no indemnities, no acquisition of territory, no domination of other peoples." Here, too, was part of the American tradition that Johnson was obligated to uphold in foreign affairs.

During the campaign the president made more than two hundred speeches in forty-five days of exhausting campaigning, going out to the crowds and wearing down the press corps. It was not at all the campaign he had once intended to wage. In Pittsburgh he observed that Kennedy had left him an inventory of fifty-one major bills sent to the Congress; looking through that list, Johnson had discovered that every single one had now passed the Senate and all but four or five had passed the House. Thus was his own competence highlighted. Whenever Goldwater attacked Kennedy, the aides who had formerly worked with the latter duly rejoiced and planned to give the attacks maximum circulation. They were certain of their hero's reputation.[26] Throughout, the Johnson team was deadly serious. Said one columnist on September 5, "The White House these days is not a very emotion-stirring place, nor is it blessed with much humor." The office of Paul Southwick prepared for release on October 10 a 124-page document, "Nineteen Sixty-Four: A Year of Progress," whose title page carried a Johnson quote from January 8: "We must be strong enough to win any war, and we must be wise enough to prevent one"—words that read better then than they would later.

The inept Republican campaign failed to get appropriate publicity for Johnson's blockbusting statement in Manchester, New Hampshire, which was possibly his most important utterance of the whole campaign: "I have not thought we were ready for American boys to do the fighting for Asian boys. What I have been trying to do, with the situation that I found, was to get the boys in Vietnam to do their own fighting with our advice and our equipment." Johnson followed up this appraisal on October 21 in Akron, Ohio, with, "We are not going to send American boys away from home to do what Asian boys ought to be doing for themselves." Possibly he remembered that his hero Franklin Roosevelt had easily lived down his promise, "Your boys are not going to be sent into any foreign wars."

Democrats were justifiably incensed over the appearance and distribution of the free-swinging paperback *None Dare Call It Treason.* Both hate literature and bad history, it went through fifteen printings with a total of three million copies; Averell Harriman correctly called its recital of betrayal in the Department of State and of treasonous conduct, which even included Eisenhower, "cleverly prepared half-truths."[27] Although technically it had a price, many copies were mailed free of charge or given away by groups like the John Birch Society. It seems not to have had any official tie with the Republican party. An analysis of it by the political-science faculty of San Fernando Valley State University, in a pamphlet titled "None Dare Call it Reason," unfortunately reached few members of the public. Among the uncritical, the *Treason* book may have done widespread and lasting damage to the credibility of United States government officials.

Comments turned toward political hardball. The Republican candidate had permitted "In your heart you know he's right" to become a slogan; a snotty reply was "In your guts you know he's nuts." From no less a person than Walter Lippmann had come the pompous decree: "We all know of demagogues and agitators who arouse the poor against the rich. But in Barry Goldwater we have a demagogue who dreams of arousing the rich against the poor." Liberal journalist Richard Strout even wrote on September 5, "Are there enough zealots and bigots in America to elect a team like Goldwater and Miller?" The Arizona senator was "the next thing to a crackpot." A student of press coverage of Goldwater's speeches concluded that nearly half of the time the theses of his speeches were not reported, while full accounts of charge and countercharge submerged his constructive proposals. Interpretive commentary in news accounts was often negative; thus his failure to develop points was often noted, but no commentary indicated that a point had been well developed.[28] The media bias against Goldwater was well marked, and intelligent contemporaries were well aware of it. But only a few called for even-handedness.

Thoughtful Democrats were disquieted by a series of commercials that their party aired in order to discredit Goldwater as a responsible person, making him seem to be unfit for leadership of the nation's

113

military might in a nuclear age. A later study produced devastating conclusions: "Not one of them would have been approved for broadcast had they been required to be judged by television standards for product commercials. All six would have been guilty—at the least—of being deceptive, misleading, and unfair. None of them could have been modified successfully to fit the network code without losing the one thing they all had in common: an unfair and largely unwarranted attack on the Republican candidate."[29]

The decent man from Arizona had been permanently slandered. That publicity would be abandoned, but not before the damage had been done. The commercials are said to have helped bury Vietnam as an issue in the campaign by their theatrical tactics. Says Valenti: "Even the president thought Moyers and I . . . had gone too far with the famous TV message of the little girl with the daisy. . . . He ordered it off the air."[30] Not since the subsidized defaming of President Hoover in 1932, perhaps, had a candidate for the nation's highest office been so maligned. The "truth squad" activities of Democratic aide Mike Feldman, which involved pursuit of the candidate after a few days with quick rebuttals, were resented but were much closer to legitimate politics.

A dramatic moment was the president's decision in New Orleans to discard his bland prepared remarks on civil rights and to "wing it" with force and verve. He launched into a story of how Senator J. W. Bailey had once told Sam Rayburn that the people of Mississippi really ought to hear what they had not in thirty years: a *Democratic* speech. According to a tape of the address, he now said: "All they ever hear at election time is 'nigra, nigra, nigra.' " The audience was stunned. Yet the man from southwestern Texas forged on: "Whatever your views are, we have a Constitution and we have a Bill of Rights, and we have the law of the land, and two-thirds of the Democrats in the Senate voted for it and three-fourths of the Republicans. I signed it, and I am going to enforce it, and I am going to observe it, and I think that any man that is worthy of the high office of President is going to do the same thing." It was an act of political courage—whatever the impending Democratic sweep. The president knew from his many contacts with Negroes—who were increasingly calling themselves "blacks"—that moods were changing. White liberals were still crusading for integretation, but many Negro leaders were now seeking black identity and the new label. Martin Luther King, Sr., in his autobiography, explains the ferment very well indeed: "We were running out of time. The excuses had been used up. People wanted answers that made sense for a country surging through the most technologically advanced period in history, when disease was being conquered, when the machinery in our lives gave us travel and enormous comfort in all our working and social lives. We could speak to people thousands of miles away on the telephone but not a seat away on a city bus."[31]

Johnson's final speech on TV before the election was considered by many to be one of his finest and the prelude to an enormous victory that Valenti said was all they had hoped for and more than they had expected. Roy Wilkins reported in with: "The people have not spoken; they have shouted. Congratulations!" The incumbent took forty-four states for 61.1 percent, compared to FDR's 60.7 percent in 1936 and Harding's 60.3 percent in 1920. Johnson's percentage of the total two-party vote was less than theirs; still, it was most satisfying.[32] In addition to his 486 electoral votes, he could exult in the gain of over 500 Democratic seats in state legislatures, as well as the taking of 12 state governorships from Republicans, a Senate that would be 68 to 32, and a House of 295 to 140. As for coattails, 61 Democratic seats in the House had been won by less than 55 percent, 37 of them by less than 52.5 percent.

Stratification in the election may have been unprecedented. An analysis done by the University of Michigan Survey Research Center seemed to show *no* black support for Goldwater. People making under $3,000 a year were 74 percent for Johnson; those above the $10,000 figure were, even so, 56 percent for him. Only 17 percent of the union members voted for Goldwater, and only 20 percent of those with only a grade-school education and 16 percent of the unskilled did so.[33] The figures showed that, except for hard-line Republicans, a majority of every kind of voter—classified by sex, age, color, income, education, religion, and all other categories—favored Lyndon B. Johnson. The election was a catastrophe for a party that, with its eyes wide open, had committed temporary suicide with an able but outspokenly conservative candidate, a zealot who was ahead of his time but clearly prepared the way for one who someday would come.

Leading Democrats rejoiced in the astounding results of November 3. "It was a glorious victory," crowed Clark Clifford, for "there is no substitute for intelligence, experience, incredible industry—*and being right.*" Since many in the Congress would not have made it without him, Johnson should know that "this is the time to be president"; there were limitless opportunities; "this can be the most thrilling and the most rewarding decade in our history." President Truman had conveyed his congratulations months earlier, saying that Johnson possessed the "well earned right to lead us for another four years with the skill and success that you have already manifested in the brief period that you have occupied that office." To the candidate the telegram then had "meant more than all the rest" and had "made my spirits soar."[34] A month after the campaign the president's popularity in the polls stood at 69 percent. (Others at the same point: Truman, 50; Eisenhower, 68; Kennedy, 56; Ford, 47; Carter, 51.) The day before the election, the happy apparent victor, who envisioned some kind of Great Society, observed triumphantly, "I have spent my whole life getting ready for this moment."

6

SECOND MANDATE: ENDORSED WITH VOTES

Lyndon Johnson was absolutely convinced that the lopsided result of the 1964 election had given him an unlimited mandate to follow his inclinations at home and abroad. There can be little doubt on the matter. Exactly what that mandate was—for example, in connection with Vietnam—remains unclear. Was his deeply dedicated, no pull-back policy understood? The mandate at home seemed to have something to do with a Great Society, the War on Poverty, civil rights for minorities, and, maybe, expanding educational opportunity. Late in 1964 even the president did not really know the details of what he would seek to do, for there would be continuing interaction between White House staff, agency officials, and task-force experts and intellectuals. Who could say what might now be suggested and, in the light of his mandates, enthusiastically adopted?

The Great Society theme was picked up by at least two major publications, beginning with the *New Republic* of November 7, whose fiftieth-anniversary issue was entitled "America Tomorrow: Creating a Great Society." Read years after publication, it seems terribly dated. The second special publication was a twenty-page magazine insert of the *Washington Post* for January 20, 1965, entitled "The Great Society." Here, the Johnson dreams were treated with the kind of respect that is normally reserved for the Sermon on the Mount (the analogy is appropriate). But then, in his State of the Union message for 1965, the president had just said that "we know that history is ours to make," as he rejoiced in "the excitement of great expectations." Notable was a new caution. "We are only at the beginning of the road to the Great Society," he warned, noting that every American "for many generations" would need to have faith in the destination and fortitude to make the journey. (The campaign was clearly over!) One fuzzy paragraph would win special notice: "The Great Society asks not how much, but how good; not only how to create wealth but how to use it; not only how fast we are going, but where we are headed."

One source of the administration's legislative ideas were the task forces. Assigned to such subjects as income maintenance, urban problems, intergovernmental fiscal cooperation, transportation, cost reduction, foreign economic policy, national resources, education, and preservation of natural beauty, they reported after varying amounts of interaction and study. While they go unmentioned in *The Vantage Point*, they were referred to by President Johnson in public forty-four times, even though he had insisted on establishing them on "a completely off-the-record, confidential basis." Members were told that "their membership and their report would not be publicly released and that they were being asked to prepare a confidential report solely for the use of the president." This insistence on secrecy, the president later admitted, was "one of the most controversial characteristics of the task force operation," but he considered it to be central. When one reflects that their personnel supposedly included "experts from every region, academics, administrators, practitioners, business leaders and labor leaders," a staff director from top levels in the executive branch, and a liaison person from the White House, it is astonishing that secrecy could be kept so completely. It is a tribute to Johnson's famous powers of persuasion (and perhaps to the media's disinterest in such a serious activity). The president said that he wanted to leave participants free to ignore their public images and to make them more critical. What were the president and cabinet doing wrong? What ought to be done—"no matter how radical their ideas might seem to be." He did not want formal documents that would be examined by the Congress and circulated in academia. The task forces did not have to do "a thorough, detailed job."

For the most part the reports appeared on the president's desk only after the 1964 election, when they became, according to Johnson, "the basis for most of the 1965 legislative program, such as the Elementary and Secondary Education Act of 1965, the Higher Education Act, and the Clean Air Act." This appraisal is somewhat overdrawn. The system was expanded in 1965 to include interagency task forces made up of cabinet officers and agency officials. Here, said the chief executive, was a "rather unique device" that enabled the president to take a comprehensive look at various governmental activities. By 1966 and 1967 the process had been expanded to the point that some fifty to sixty groups were being formed annually, allegedly covering "every major area of domestic concern and providing a basis for a comprehensive program for both legislative and administrative action by the federal government." The collection of ideas became institutionalized as a staff member was added to work exclusively on the legislative program for the next year. Some one hundred and fifty academic leaders were reached by letter or in person in 1965 alone, and bright young people had some input. Ideas were reviewed by Johnson's staff, the director of the budget, and the chairman of the CEA. Then they went to the president, who had long been a consumer of paper work.

The reports of the task forces were self-generating: some task-force reports resulted in the forming of new task forces. The coming State of the Union address each year was a prime target; so were major messages. The observer must admire the cooperation that was obtained and the energy that was expended; the concealing of the process from the electorate brings less admiration. Here was secret government, and not on behalf of national security. Most of those who participated, it seems likely, were unknown to the democratic process of election and to membership in the civil service. The media were frozen out completely.

There is something to the Johnson argument that he and his team were too swamped with work to reflect very much on the formulation of new policy or to do research on or to evaluate future programs; so he was reaching out to the country for its "best thinking." It is claimed that when leaders found out that the task forces were actually going to be important in policy formulation, there was almost no reluctance to serve on them.[1] Few "radicals" are said to have been among the two hundred and fifty who were invited to participate in task forces. Selection was supposed to be on the basis of "commonsense soundness" and "perspective" and "freshness." Professors were, admittedly, overrepresented; associations were underrepresented. From one association naturally came the complaint, "The task forces represent the worst form of intellectual and educational elitism."[2] Secrecy meant, said one hostile HEW executive, that the reports "don't really pollinate anything." Only late in the game did increased participation on the part of the agencies ameliorate this. The 1968 legislation on education and housing was to be helped considerably.

Previous presidents had relied on departments, agencies, staff in the White House, and personnel in the Bureau of the Budget to frame bills. Thus, whatever innovation there was had to come from the appointed or civil-service bureaucracy. Because of channels, the daring

119

innovation that reached the president was minimal, and compromise was all too common. Johnson knew of Kennedy's experiment with preinauguration task forces. But LBJ was determined not to let so-called intellectuals dominate his effort, and he sensed that the future inevitable leaks that he was seeking outside advice from experts could only be helpful to his reputation.

The later task-force reports picked up steam, as a person like Laurance Rockefeller headed the natural-beauty task force and position papers were furnished by the Bureau of the Budget. It has been said that without the task-force effort, the administration and Congress would not have pushed so hard for programs relating to supplementary educational centers, regional education laboratories, rent supplements, and model cities. The reports provided a mine of ideas and judgments on possibilities. Johnson is said to have read the early ones, plus Budget Bureau analyses.[3] Once Johnson told members of his cabinet that the task forces on budgetary savings should help them to save. After he had talked to those in eleven task forces, he said, "We think we have the best people available in these respective fields in the country." The education task force had probed with "a bold spirit of innovation and imagination," and economies on military personnel might ensue. Such references lent prestige to contemplated actions.

We must remember that there were other inputs to the legislative mill. Each spring, Joseph Califano and his helpers visited a number of university centers, seeking ideas for programs; and inside government, some "idea men" were allowed to by-pass channels. A resulting loose-leaf book displayed ideas by category for the president to view. What survived then got further distribution; but what impact the reviewing process had is obscure.

Public commissions also carried out some studies during the Johnson years, with variable impact. The Kaiser committee on urban housing, the Heineman commission on income maintenance, the commission on crime, and the Kerner commission on civil disorders came and went—leaving, in some cases, an unpleasant taste because of their adverse judgments on current practices. Follow-through was erratic in any case.[4] No wonder Johnson greatly preferred the task-force approach, for here were outward partnership between public and private figures (i.e., consensus), safe secrecy, and "interest group liberalism" of a kind that was quite controllable.

Contemplating all this, it is not surprising that the "host of ideas" shortened the route to putting laws on the books. It is also no wonder that so many impractical and/or untested laws emerged, laws that much later would require modification, amendment, abandonment, or repeal.

The right of senior staff to dominate the selection of task-force personnel provided an effect of self-fulfilling prophecy, because people who were in favor of what the staff wanted naturally turned up on the task forces. The president automatically approved most of those who were nominated, although he would grumble at the predominance of East Coast and West Coast names. Didn't anybody with brains live in the middle of the country? Johnson would grouch: "You think the world consists of Boston, New York, Washington, San Francisco, and Los Angeles." One result of the elaborate process of task forces and commissions was the involvement of so many persons in the governmental process, if only temporarily. The long-range effect of this on the professors and their students, then and later, cannot be measured easily. Perhaps the minds of Washington's locked-in bureaucracy were somewhat expanded by contact with strangers who were far removed from the political routine of the nation's capital.

Looking back, Lyndon Johnson later recalled that he had "made a personal decision during the 1964 Presidential campaign to make education a fundamental issue and to put it high on the nation's agenda." His biggest political concern was the church-state issue, as it related to possible federal funding for parochial schools. An intellectual crutch turned out to be the findings of a task force headed by John Gardner, president of the Carnegie Corporation. "Every society gets the schools it deserves," the group declared. "We favor federal aid to education"—especially to disadvantaged areas.

As President Johnson was facing the State of the Union message for 1965, there was ample input by cabinet members, staff, and friends such as Abe Fortas. Every Christmas season this chore encroached on a relaxing holiday, as those close to the center of power saw the chance to insert a paragraph or a sentence that might somehow change history. Entire drafts were junked. Willard Wirtz was especially persistent this year in demanding that the idea of opportunity for employment appear in the message. He insisted on the phrase "I propose we commit ourselves to a policy of full employment opportunity for every American." The final draft gave him his wish: "We seek full employment opportunity for every American citizen." Every speech writer sensed the importance of what went in—and what lost out. Said aide Harry McPherson: "In pressing hard for change he took great risks, both for himself and for the country. He had to convey, not only a poignant sense of the misery to be relieved, but confidence that money and organization and skill could relieve it. Otherwise men would do nothing." So the writing of messages was a political art form, "as orthodox as a classical string quartet." "First," he says, came "the passionate description of a problem—sometimes widely recognized, like crime, urban decay, the paucity of medical care for the poor; sometimes esoteric, like the need to reorganize a government agency. . . . The purpose of this part was to hit the mule across the forehead, to get its attention. The future was bleak—unless the people chose some expensive commitment to change."[5]

The 1965 address certainly was of this type. "We built this nation to serve its people," was its premise. The proposal in education was to begin a program to ensure that every child would attain the fullest development of his mind and skills. Negroes, the poor, and the elderly would have new opportunities. The president sought $1.5 billion to improve preschool, elementary, secondary, and college education. Another goal was better health through research, regional medical centers, the education of doctors and dentists, and community centers to aid the mentally retarded. A department of housing and urban development was sought. America must be made more beautiful. He wanted a national foundation for the arts. Meanwhile, waste was to be eliminated. In foreign affairs the president noted that communism was wearing a more aggressive face in Asia, certainly in Vietnam, where its aggression would not be ignored. "What is at stake is the cause of freedom and in that cause America will never be found wanting." Few listeners guessed how important the hundred or so words relating to peace in southeast Asia would turn out to be during the rest of the Johnson years. The Democratic National Committee was delighted to be able to put out a summary of glowing editorial reaction. The *New York Post* thought the president's goals must be taken seriously because of his skills as legislative leader. The president showed sober confidence, thought the Hearst press. The *Kansas City Star* was almost alone in catching the emphasis on searching for "peace": If he wished to be successful in doing things at home, it said, he would have to avoid failing in that search.[6]

Johnson was determined to make his Inaugural Address reveal how central was his Great Society concept. John Steinbeck wrote a draft at Johnson's request, but most of it was killed by self-confident speech writer Goodwin, after which, at the chief executive's insistence, two sentences were put back in: "The Great Society is not the ordered, changeless, and sterile battalion of the ants. It is the excitement of becoming—always becoming, trying, probing—falling, resting and trying again—but always gaining a little" (Valenti had finally substituted *excitement* for Steinbeck's *miracle*). The center of the speech was a sterile disquisition on "the American covenant," a subject that was more meaningful to his liberal-arts specialists than to his heartland audience.

When read after the lapse of years, and bearing in mind the raw force the Johnson's own basic language could have when the chips were down, the speech is disappointing. It does not sound at all like him. But it drew ten waves of approval and a tide of applause at the end. Gerald Ford was greatly impressed. Senator Dirksen thought it eloquent, and Charles Halleck considered it magnificent. Senator Mansfield found that it spelled out the American Dream.

Determined to put the entire power and prestige of the presidency behind the major education bill, Johnson and his staff consulted all the power centers in the Congress. One obstacle was the chairman of the House Rules Committee, Democrat Howard W. Smith of Virginia, whose slogan was "No rules for schools." Jack Valenti served as liaison with Catholic entities; Lee White dealt with Jewish organizations; and Douglass Cater worked with education lobbies. The bill spent three months in the Congress. Gradually, despite troubles as outwardly irrelevant as the expense accounts of committee chairman Adam Clayton Powell, it moved forward. Sometimes there were hourly reports on progress. With Senator Wayne Morse as floor manager, the bill was saved from eleven amendments that would have taken it to a conference committee and an uncertain future.

The true significance of the education bill, in Johnson's judgment, was that "it established a foundation on which the country could work toward educational achievement, with equal quality and opportunity for the future." He had weakened the "fears of federal encroachment," which he judged a real plus. Those who are awarding credit for the various activities of the administration in education should not pass over a footnote in the president's memoirs: "My determined efforts on behalf of education bills were stimulated and inspired by Mrs. Agnes E. Meyer, an old friend who, I believe, did more to influence me on federal education measures than any other person."[7] Wilbur Cohen says Lyndon's borrowing of seventy-five dollars to help pay for his first college semester "influenced him in all that he did about financial aid for higher education. He wanted to make it easier for people to borrow or get scholarships to go to college. That was a very important experience for him."[8]

Among public remarks that sound genuinely from the heart are some from the president's address to the National Conference on Educational Legislation, March 1, 1965. The enemies of mankind are "ignorance, illiteracy, ill health, and disease," he observed to fellow educators. "I do know that I am proud of this democracy and I do genuinely believe that education is its guardian and is its steward, and that a trained mind is the best possible insurance premium we can buy to preserve our freedoms and our liberties and to keep us from being slaves.'' Vice-President Humphrey judged him to be ''a nut on education. He felt that education was the greatest thing that he could give to the people; he just believed in it, just like some people believe in miracle cures.''[9]

The funding of American education during the years of Lyndon Johnson's youth had been relatively simple. At the elementary and secondary levels, public schools were financed by tax funds raised by school districts through property-tax levies. Private schools were funded by religious denominations, gifts and endowments, and tuition payments. In time, school districts came to be aided by subventions from state, county, or city authorities who used various sources of funds (income taxes, sales taxes, property taxes, etc.). Parochial schools received little or no funding from public revenues. Except in the cases of so-called impacted schools (which were located where numbers of government employees worked in their tax-exempt installations) and except for the federal school-lunch program, the public schools received little help from Washington. They were not sure that they wanted any. Local autonomy in educational policy making had deep roots.

Higher education had been largely a state responsibility (aided, in the case of land-grant universities, by federal funds); private colleges and universities were funded in the same way as private schools. Localities financed two-year colleges, or districts did so. Sputnik I had induced a flow of funds for scientific research; and national health institutes were funding medical research in tandem with heart, cancer, and other private health organizations. Critics noted that some states provided almost free college education for those who could house and feed themselves; elsewhere, tuition and fees retarded higher education for the poor and nonveterans. Disparities between black and white enrollments were enormous; in high schools the dropout rates were high. Vast differences in taxing capacity among school districts made for inequities in the quality of physical plants. *Brown* v. *Board of Education*, in 1954, was intended to be a blow against segregation in schools by race. Earlier, the NYA and several GI bills had helped many to get educations that would otherwise have been denied to them. In the early 1960s some leaders wondered if the federal government could not do something to help finance individuals, school and college plants, and the upgrading of teachers; but many others feared control from the top. Programs like the National Defense Education Act and that of the National Aeronautical and Space Administration had shown that financing of graduate programs, certain costs, and student grants could be helpful in the physical sciences. Medical schools had received federal support; Hill-

Burton had financed the construction of hospitals. The road had been paved.

Leadership for change came from many individuals. Anthony Celebrezze, the holdover secretary of health, education, and welfare, was succeeded in 1965 by John Gardner. When holdover Francis Keppel left in 1965, Harold Howe took over as commissioner of education. Democratic Congresswoman Edith Green from Portland, Oregon, closely studied and tried to modify administration proposals, and black Congressman Adam Clayton Powell from New York helped to push bills through. International education was the assignment of Charles Frankel. After May 1964 Douglass Cater performed strategic and brokerage roles in order to further both education and health programs. The education area was complicated. One thinks immediately of HEW; but at the time that Gardner was in charge there, his department controlled less than half of all federal expenditures for education. Twenty other agencies occupied the field, contracting in such areas as research on space, atomic energy, and defense. Gardner created the Office of Planning and Evaluation, under William Graham, a former RAND economist, to strengthen the functions of management.

President Johnson, who was determined to make a difference in American education, probably was unaware that historian Henry Adams had once told the young Franklin Roosevelt that "nothing that you minor officials or occupants [of the White House] can do will affect the history of the world for long." Johnson would certainly make his mark anyway, but he did not win total approbation from educators, since he had little of the smooth and suave personality that they tended to admire. But his heart was obviously in the right place, as evidenced by a letter to Truman: "I hope and believe the bill will help us do many things in education that the country ought to have been doing for a long time."[10] In 1965 Johnson was asked what he considered to be the major problems in public education and how he would solve them. His heartfelt reply was: "If every person born could acquire all the education that their intelligence quotient would permit them to take—God only knows what our gross national product would be—and the strength we would add to our nation, militarily, diplomatically, economically is too large even to imagine." The important things were "an economy adequate to keep children in school, well-trained teachers, and sufficient books and buildings." Crime, slums, and certainly poverty programs would be eliminated through education! Still, "We just don't want to bite off more than we can digest at one time."

He was also impatient over apparent detours. He wrote to Frankel, "You're not going to make a program for those Ph.D.'s are you? I want to do something for that little boy at the end of the line who can't read or write.'' The idea of having a cabinet department of education died for lack of a constituency at the time. The White House Conference on Education, July 20–21, 1965, went well, displaying Johnson's interest in the subject and leaving the president gratified.

The public was vaguely aware of precedents: the Morrill Act in 1862 had been responsible for the creation of large numbers of land-grant universities; Smith-Hughes in 1917, Lanham in 1940, the GI bills of 1944 and the Korean War, the National Science Foundation of 1950, and NDEA in 1958, as well as funding for impacted areas, showed the potential in federal action. The Higher Education Facilities Act of 1963 helped to finance the construction of buildings. To these were added the blockbuster bills of the Johnson years: the Elementary and Secondary Education Act, which was aimed at disadvantaged children in slums and deprived rural areas; and the Higher Education Act, which arranged for federal scholarships for needy students, helped college libraries, and started the Teachers Corps. The OEO was aiding preschool children as well as adult education. As the result of such bills, spending by the federal government on education increased considerably—but *not in Johnson's day* by as much as is generally assumed. (There was, however, a coasting effect.) Education spending from 1963/64 to 1967/68 increased from $36.2 billion to $54.6 billion, a considerable increase to be sure. The federal share of the national total grew from 4.0 to 7.2 percent, while the local share decreased, even though its total in dollars increased. Funding for higher education increased from $11.3 to $18.8 billion, with the federal part increasing from 9.7 to 11.7 percent. The direction of growth was well established by the 1970s.[11]

The legislative program for education may be summarized briefly. The initial Higher Education Facilities Act of December 1963 provided loans and grants for the construction of libraries and classrooms. In August 1964 came the provisions for educational aid (work-study, Upward Bound) of the Economic Opportunity Act. The Elementary and Secondary Education Act came in May 1965. November saw the Higher Education Act, with its student loans and grants for needy students, its aid to developing colleges, and its money for instructional equipment and libraries—including the training of librarians. The Teacher Corps and funds to get colleges involved in community service were covered by this omnibus legislation. Amendments in October 1968 provided funds for educational technology, law schools, and cooperative and graduate education; student-aid programs were refined. An October 1966 law created the Sea Grant Program—a boon to marine research; and in that same month an international-education act provided aid to centers for international studies and for improving undergraduate instruction in the field. Much noticed by the thousands who were affected was the Education Professions Development Act of June 1967, which provided funds to train teachers and administrators in the entire educational system, grade school through college. Former President Johnson would say a year before his death, "I take great pride that I was referred to, when people tried to be generous, as the education president." Said a learned publication, "Many observers believe he earned that title."[12]

One of the promises he had made when campaigning in 1964 had been enactment of medical care for the elderly, a program long sought but never enacted into law. An omnibus bill along these lines had been introduced in 1951, had been sponsored by Congressman Aime Forand in 1957, but had been defeated in 1961, 1962, and 1964. There was nothing new about federal expenditures for health: they had risen during Eisenhower's years from $221 to $840 million and, in Kennedy's, to $1.6 billion. Kennedy had sought to use the Social Security mechanism to help solve medical problems of the aged. He admitted that some $25 billion was already going from public and private funds for health services, but he thought that both the quality and the distribution were inappropriate to the needs. Here was the foundation stone for Johnson's recommendations. The AFL-CIO, in November 1963, adopted a resolution calling the provision of health care a moral matter and asked for action. Dr. Michael E. DeBakey was one of many physicians who worked during the Kennedy and Johnson years for such ideas as regional medical centers, increased appropriations for heart and cancer research, and hospital construction, although the private groups concerned with heart disease, cancer, polio, and other illnesses were very effective. Volunteer activist Mary Lasker, says DeBakey, did more than anyone else to push public medical programs and to insert a strong plank in the Democratic platform of 1960.[13]

Armed with the overwhelming victory of his party in congressional races, Lyndon Johnson saw that a battle that dated back to the Truman administration could be won. Medicare for people who were on Social Security, he said on January 4, 1965, must come first. Wilbur Mills, chairman of the House Ways and Means Committee, gave prompt consideration to what were called S-1 (Senate) and HR-1 (House)—the first bills introduced. He unified several health proposals into one, and the American Medical Association decided not to boycott the program; therefore, Medicare, under the guidance of Wilbur Cohen and others, working in Johnson's name, became law. The goal, said Johnson expansively in a 1966 speech, was to achieve in ten years "modern

127

medical care for every person, of any age, of every race, of every religion, of every region, whatever his means." The federal government's expenditures on health did, of course, bring more medical and hospital care to the poor. In ten years, infant mortality among blacks was nearly cut in half, and life expectancy for blacks rose by three years, while still lagging behind that for whites. Enactment of Medicare inevitably brought demands for a parallel program for those on traditional welfare programs; this would be the new Medicaid program.

Beyond any doubt there would be a dramatic increase in the quantity of medical care, because of these programs, and in quality, because of the fruits of research and technology. Yet in 1975/76 a study could show that 61 percent of the public was still of the opinion that there was a "crisis in health care." Back in 1963, however, only 49 percent of blacks "saw a doctor"; the figure for 1976 was 74 percent. For whites the figure of 68 percent rose to 76.[14] Dissatisfaction with costs would escalate. Many of the needy ill continued to be treated free by physicians and to be housed in hospitals at a cost absorbed by paying patients, as doctors said was the case when they were fighting the Forand plan in Truman's day. The new medical programs lifted this burden to an extent from doctors and paying patients alike in the case of the poor and the aged.

In 1967, the Carnegie Commission on Educational Television brought out a report entitled "Public Television: A Program for Action." A quick outgrowth of this was the Public Broadcasting Act. Public radio and television stations now emerged; they emphasized higher cultural standards in programing and were free of commercials, except when soliciting funds from the public. Twelve years later, after the formation and after the operation for a decade of public TV and radio stations, the Carnegie group issued a second report, "A Public Trust." Its conclusion was that the original conception, as implemented, was not working.[15] The 1979 judgment was: "We find public broadcasting's financial, organizational and creative structure fundamentally flawed. There is little likelihood that public television and radio might consistently achieve programing excellence under the present circumstances." It would appear that the rapid creation of the system by the Johnson administration ran well ahead of public demand and understanding. But it seemed to be a good start. The second Carnegie report concluded that there had been some good, even great, programing; but the Corporation for Public Broadcasting would have to go, it thought, because it was vulnerable to political influence. This result was in line with Johnson's own apprehensions: "Considering that the thrust of the Great Society in general was toward the poor and minorities, it is worth saying that the emphasis in public broadcasting turned out to be toward an elite audience,'' he complained in his memoirs. Meanwhile, others were objecting that news and commentary in public radio were too liberal, and sometimes radical. By the 1980s the top eight funding corporations of public TV would be oil corporations, however, and restrictions on commercials were being eased. Certainly, public radio and TV were innovative, while still less than revolutionary.

A tense area continued to be civil rights. The year brought the Civil Rights Act of 1965, sometimes called the Voting Rights Act, which targeted the problem of guaranteeing southern Negroes the right to register and vote. Its statistical basis was the figure for voter turnout in the 1964 election, but it would be amended to include the next two presidential elections. Where minority turnout proved to be less than 50 percent (which suggested that intimidation had been used), federal officials could do the registering and supervise the polls. Changes in state election laws would have to be approved by the federal government. A bilingual provision was targeted at areas in which at least 5 percent of the population spoke a language other than English. By 1975, it has been stated, the law was responsible for more than a million new voters. Fulsomely praised then and later by black leaders, the act was vigorously attacked by constitutionalists. Years later an editorial in a financial weekly would declaim: ''The 1965 Voting Rights Act was a brutal measure that should never have been necessary in a free society.'' The presumption of guilt and direct federal intervention were termed highly offensive, even crude, although the act was admitted to have been triumphantly successful.[16] Advocates of increased black registration and voting in the South, needless to say, showed little concern with such matters then or later.

There is the temptation to see the quantity of legislation in the years 1965 and 1966 as totally traceable to Johnson's mandate at the polls, forgetting that the president and his team had to work together effectively to achieve their ends. This took time, especially since Kennedy's had not been a winning system. Joseph Califano says that upon his arrival in the White House in July 1964, the situation was very unsystematic, chaotic, and anarchic. In August he and Charles Schultze got Johnson to try to put into effect a planning-programming-budgeting system for domestic matters, since the data base was ''terrible, just terrible.'' But talking to some cabinet members about cost-benefit ratios was like talking to a wall.[17] Still, rather surprisingly, Califano himself brought a limited knowledge base with him to the center of power: ''I knew nothing about domestic programs, nothing about social programs, and indeed, I hadn't even ever thought much about them.'' So he gave himself a crash course of reading and meetings. Liaison with specialists at universities soon helped. For example, he, Cater, and McPherson interacted with some Harvard faculty members in June 1966, after which Califano wrote to one of them: "We are particularly interested in these questions: Where should the Great Society go from here? What needs have we left unmet? What new problems do we create as we solve old problems?" He would be meeting with other groups, and he wanted "to block out those areas of concern to the people of this country."[18] It was alleged that the president was receiving ideas from these faculty members, and he was appreciative.

Government was a well-oiled machine in those years. The congressional staff of the White House consisted of five full-time and four part-time people; others could be available as needed. They met weekly, sometimes with Johnson and other times with Humphrey; the president was kept informed. A daily summary of congressional contacts was one output. The group probably got the same kind of advice that he gave Valenti: "The most important people you will talk to are senators and congressmen. You treat them as if they were president. Answer their calls immediately. Give them respect. They deserve it . . . ; they are your most important clients. Be responsive to them."[19] Said the politician-president in 1965, "I keep hitting hard because I know this honeymoon won't last." And, "Every day I lose a little more political capital. That's why we have to keep at it, never letting up. One day soon, I don't know when, the critics and the snipers will move in and we will be at a stalemate. We have to get all we can, now, before the roof comes down." One member of the liaison group has said that he never worked so hard as he did during the period from February to June 1965, urged on personally by a president who was in a hurry.

Several figures on the Hill were much on Johnson's mind. One was the House majority leader, Carl Albert, Democratic congressman from Oklahoma (from 1947 to 1977). Of impoverished origins, he was a Rhodes scholar and lawyer who managed to keep a low profile as he endeavored to get administration bills passed. He could make suggestions to colleagues, such as that public-works money might not be forthcoming if support for such items as OEO were not given. Republicans, he once claimed, as a partisan, had been "blind for 35 years" in opposing progressive legislation and in their disregard for human beings. He was in solid with Johnson, especially since he was supportive of both foreign and domestic matters. Senator Dirksen has been mentioned earlier. He and President Johnson met at least three hundred times, he would recall, with the meetings on civil rights seeming "almost endless." Said he, "The president and I are actually intimate friends."[20] In him, Johnson found special qualities in addition to his resonant voice and old-fashioned oratory. The two professionals avoided personal enmity regardless of what might be said in political battle. Much the same could be said of Johnson's interaction with Oregon's independent Senator Wayne Morse, who had broken away from the Republicans in the early 1950s, a former law professor with whom the man from the Ranch happened to share an interest in cattle breeding. Morse developed a deep-seated hostility toward Vietnam policy after he failed to get the log books from the *Maddox* after Tonkin Gulf. His defeat by the youthful Robert Packwood in 1968 brought a colorful career to an end.

The ideas for a 1966 program came, with very few exceptions, from individuals outside the government, according to Joseph Califano. Much of the package was put together during the last six months of 1965, despite interruptions from domestic crises such as Watts and fights over the prices of basic metals. Califano saw and dined with Johnson frequently; he also met with outsiders and Budget Bureau officials. He had read all of the existing task-force reports. He prepared small charts for Johnson's benefit. Down at the Ranch, the nation's leader was taken through what had been developed. "He sort of said, 'Yes, No, Okay, go ahead, I want to think a little more about that.'" Thus did Johnson make his decisions. All of this had an impact on the State of the Union and special messages of the coming year, much as had happened when plans were being made for 1964.

The next stage was work on various bills. The appropriate agency head or cabinet officer would be briefed on the program that was headed for the Congress. Some congressmen were given special instruction on the legislation, so that they would be able to say something nice and have an input if they so desired. Tough legal questions were handled by the Office of Legal Counsel in the Attorney General's Office. The formula for the model-cities bill was literally written by Califano and Schultze the night before the message went to Congress. The enthusiast for task forces will want to bear all of this action in mind when weighing their true influence. The next step was to make a head count of the Democrats on appropriate committees; here Johnson moved toward the forefront. Someone would have to brief the press. And there would be technical briefings for departmental people.[21]

Not even remotely was this president isolated in the White House. After he had retired, Lyndon Johnson claimed: "I think it is fair to say that I was getting a wider variety of information, of ideas, of opinions on a broader range of subjects than any man in or out of government during the more than five years I was in the White House." Data and ideas came from newspapers, magazines, TV, daily contact with congressmen; letters from friends and enemies, the informed and the uninformed; task-force reports; and meetings with leaders and specialists.[22] It is nonsense to say that he heard only what a few advisers told him or that he was limited to only what they wanted him to hear. Even cursory examination of the telephone logs in the White House Diary will show the vast amount of time spent in direct communication with well-informed individuals nationwide, people in positions of real power who had their own avenues to inside information. He read high-circulation newspapers and listened selectively to the people's pundits on TV.

Cabinet meetings were another source of input to the Johnson mind and program. A profile of one such meeting—where a record is available—shows Johnson's interaction with the cabinet. On October 18, 1967, Larry O'Brien and others spoke on the outlook for passage of legislation. The ambassador to Indonesia told about conditions there. Ramsey Clark reported on that week's peace demonstrations in the capital. The subjects for immediate legislative concern were air pollution, election reform ("nothing new"), flammable fabrics, truth in lending, highway beautification ("not a prayer"), and flood insurance. The Senate was about to act on mental retardation, a "partnership for health" bill, and Title V (civil rights). Everything would need "a strong push." A military-pay bill was due to be acted upon. Some of the items on the agenda are still classified.[23]

There were the influential Tuesday luncheons with distinguished outsiders, of which much was made at the time. The president's view was that these had a "regular agenda that was thought out in advance and well prepared, and the pros and cons of every item on the agenda would be called for and given, and the facts were elicited, the conclusions were drawn, and the recommendations made, and the president then considered them and disposed of them." While he did not end up knowing all that there was to know on each question, he felt, expansively, that he came "as near knowing as any person in the country." Here, however, there may have been some "groupthink." Looking back, Eisenhower in 1960 had had one bipartisan meeting with legislative leaders and had met five times with Johnson' and ten times with Rayburn. In 1963 Kennedy met with Dirksen eleven times and with Halleck eight times. By April 1, 1964, President Johnson had already met with Dirksen and Halleck ten times. O'Brien kept a weekly file of items to be taken up at routine legislative breakfasts.[24]

The Republicans, meanwhile, had decided, at Eisenhower's urging, after the debacle of 1964, to form a policy group that would include Goldwater and a handful of other leaders. The president quickly saw to it that this group met frequently with him in the White House during the first six months of 1965. On one such occasion, Goldwater told Johnson privately that he felt McNamara was pursuing a policy of parity with the Soviets and should be replaced. Johnson offered no defense but said that he just couldn't do that. From John Kenneth Galbraith came the praise, "He was far better than Kennedy (and I think than Roosevelt) in winning the requisite response from the Congress."[25]

The time would come when the term "imperial presidency" would be dredged up in part to describe Lyndon Johnson's (and Nixon's) posture. But this round of executive domination, one historian tries to remind us, began with Kennedy and only reached a climax under Johnson; here was a period "when the White House systematically ignored the Congress in making major foreign policy decisions in regard to Cuba, the Dominican Republic, and Vietnam." Congressional leaders were "informed of, but not consulted about," major steps. Johnson inherited an office in which there was a Bay of Pigs effort, about which Congress was not consulted, and a Cuban Missile Crisis on which Kennedy "did not even bother to consult with representatives of Congress" in arriving at the quarantine decision. Kennedy's ad hoc group on the crisis had included no one from that body. Only two hours before Kennedy announced his plans to the public did he meet with some of them. Here, it is said, was a dangerous precedent. While one can disagree with some of this, as Walt Rostow did,[26] the interaction of Johnson with the Congress, as portrayed here, seems to contradict assertions that he often acted without consultation. He often met with Mansfield, Albert, Dirksen, and other leaders. But there was ample high-handed conduct. Determined to halt a threatened nationwide rail strike in April 1964, the president intervened personally, kept the contending parties hard at work, conspired behind the scenes with their members, intimated that certain rewarding or punitive legislative results just might follow a settlement, and twisted arms. At length he won.

What Lyndon Johnson did so successfully was first to develop a program of legislation, then to forge the necessary coalitions to carry the bills, and finally to perfect the timing that would be crucial to pacing consistent achievement. He used his enormous knowledge of the congressional mind to work out practical rewards and punishments—if those are the right words; and his were the decisions that built the congressional liaison staff into such a potent force—taking nothing away from the astute Larry O'Brien. Some of the groundwork for stroking egos had admittedly been laid during the Kennedy years. Where Johnson excelled was in knowing who in Congress were "the whales and the minnows''—the ones who could move bills or stop them, and the ones who would follow along.

A staff member claims that this era was the most creative period of progressive legislation in the history of the nation. Carl Albert said it was a great legislative performance: "far greater than Roosevelt's," even though Roosevelt was helped by the times. Columnist Tom Wicker thought, in August 1965, that the list of Johnson's achievements already read better than those of most two-term presidents. The research division of the Democratic National Committee issued a 140-page document, "The Johnson Administrative Record: First Session of the 89th Congress," which compares platforms and promises, treats "the obstruction of opponents," indicates by categories (such as youth and minorities) who were served and how much, and concludes with a statement on goals and achievement of them.[27]

A price had to be paid by the president for his succession of victories. Tiredness entered his very bones. "Very few people," he said, "have any idea of the long and tedious and grinding work that goes into every presidential day."[28] It was not too hard, for example, to tell Califano, in the summer of 1965 at the Ranch, that he wanted transportation and fair-housing programs, plus a case study that would demonstrate how to rebuild a ghetto, which resulted in model-cities legislation. But to turn such a desire into legislative reality meant keeping track of seniority among the congressmen, watching bills that were expiring for lack of action, and attending to a multitude of annoying and even very petty matters. It was part of Johnson's style to involve himself—surely unnecessarily—in the thousands of secondary judgments relating to the federal budget. Its director at the time says that Johnson came very close to reaching totality in this respect when making his first assault on the budget.[29]

Victories were what made life worthwhile. It was a staggering performance when a calculation showed that during the first ten months of 1966 some 90 of his 115 legislative recommendations had been signed into law. Yet full appreciation never seemed to come, or to be loud enough, or to be from the right people, to stroke Johnson's enormous ego. Part of the problem was put well by Wilbur Cohen: "I think he tried to do too much and worked too hard at it with too many small things mixed in with the large. The average person was unable to comprehend it all; it was too big; too much for him to swallow all at once."[30]

The following subjects were dealt with in memorable laws passed during 1965, many of which had an important impact in the 1960s but some of which came into full flower only during the next decade: Medicare; aid to education; higher education; the four-year farm program; the Department of Housing and Urban Development; housing; increases in social security; voting rights; fair laws concerning immigration; older Americans; programs dealing with heart disease, cancer, and strokes; law-enforcement assistance; the National Crime Commission; drug controls; mental-health facilities; the health professions; medical libraries; vocational rehabilitation; the antipoverty program; the Arts and Humanities Foundation; aid to Appalachia; highway beauty; clean air; water-pollution control; high-speed transit; manpower training; presidential disability; child health; regional development; aid to small businesses; weather-predicting services; increases in military pay; community health services; the Water Resources Council; water desalinization; control of juvenile delinquency; arms control; strengthening of the UN Charter; an international coffee agreement; retirement for public servants; the Delaware Water Gap Recreation Area; the Whiskeytown National Recreation Area; the Assateague National Seashore; and life insurance for GIs.

The system of accounting for funds within the government was drastically altered during those years by PPBS—the Planning-Programming-Budgeting System. Introduced into the Department of Defense by former RAND Corporation experts in 1961, it was only during the summer of 1965 that the system, which had been envisioned as early as 1949 by the Hoover Commission, was mandated in federal departments and agencies. After a time the president would be able to tell the Congress that the system was bringing "the most advanced techniques of modern business management" to government. Fundamental questions were routinely asked. Departments must henceforth develop objectives and goals, evaluate programs by weighing benefits against costs (i.e., by cost-benefit ratios), examine alternative means of achieving objectives, and shape budget requests in the light of analysis and long-range planning. Now the White House sought funds to provide trained personnel, more data, better cost accounting, and new methods of evaluation. A year later the president could tell the Congress that— especially in connection with vocational rehabilitation, veterans pensions, and job creation by the Department of Commerce—PPBS had proven worthwhile.[31]

The RAND alumni who brought PPBS to government—especially David Novick, Charles J. Hitch, and Alain C. Enthoven, who was backed fully by McNamara—were not members of Johnson's White House family; nevertheless, their influence was profound. Soon the subtly different terms "cost-benefit analysis," "cost-effectiveness analysis," and "systems analysis" were being heard throughout Washington and were quickly spread to state capitols and then throughout American local government.[32] The environmental-impact statements of the next decade would owe much to this technique.

The winter and spring of 1964/65 was an important period in American history; for it was then that a commitment was born in the emotions of a first lady and a president to an area of activity they termed the New Conservation, but that would soon be nicknamed environmentalism. Between them, with encouragement from leaders in the private sector and figures in government, they set America on a course that would have the most far-reaching results. Several presidents had long since made their mark in conservation, reclamation, or concern for the national estate. The Johnson family would move this activity to new ground. Lyndon generally labeled the beautification program "Lady Bird's business," but her able press secretary, Liz Carpenter, says that he "was there every step of the way, rallying, telephoning, cajoling for the needed votes, scolding, flattering—pouring on the Johnson treatment." Apparently, here was virtually a form of recreation compared with worry over the war. "He would brag about her role, then tease her about it." Johnson would say wryly that if he were lucky he'd get a little nap in the afternoon; more likely he would be hearing his wife and Laurance Rockefeller "planting daffodils in the next room." Once he told the cabinet: "I love that woman, and she wants that . . . program . . . so let's get it done."[33]

In those days, Americans were still showing a certain ambivalence toward "the land" or "the great out-of-doors" or the "national heritage" or "the landscape." Sometimes they behaved as would conquerors, raping the land and disposing of its assets with abandon and slight regard for tomorrow. Yet they could follow pioneers like Frederick Law Olmsted (Central Park) and John Muir (Yosemite National Park), preserving, planting, and restoring. Various presidents had rescued scenic areas for national parks or, like Herbert Hoover with the Skyline Drive area of the Shenandoah Valley, had paved the way for successors to do so. Franklin Roosevelt of rural Hyde Park had been distressed about soil erosion; John F. Kennedy had been alerted by pioneer environmentalist Rachel Carson to the dangers of DDT and other chemical pollutants. In garden-club circles there had long been interest in the control of billboards. Nevertheless, by the time of the Johnson administration, the United States had developed into a land with many threats to its resources, landscape, and the health of its people.

In President Johnson, the country had acquired a water-respecting and horizon-loving southwesterner who incorporated much of the American duality between preservation, restoration, and enthusiastic growth-oriented developmental activities. With his support, much of his native Texas land had been flooded through construction of dams on the local Colorado River, and he had never been one to be critical of the Corps of Engineers as they flooded much of Oklahoma and Arkansas or engineered other vast projects, some of which were at least questionable. Yet he was decidedly sentimental about "the land" and was easily swayed, during his White House years, toward leaving American air, water, and vistas better than before.

In Lady Bird Johnson, the president had an educated colleague who was well suited to being the organizer, propagandist, spokeswoman, and recruiter of talent for her cause of beautification. It was nearly too late. The national capital, which was planned at the behest of the founding fathers and which received praise each spring for its rows of cherry trees given by Japan, was by the 1960s a neglected piece of real estate, abused by both the public and the private sectors. While the wife of each president is mentioned routinely in accounts of the nation's chief executives, Claudia Taylor Johnson—"Lady Bird" to all—ranks with and even above members of the cabinet and aides with regard to some aspects of this program. India Edwards, of the Democratic National Committee, thought that Lady Bird was "one of the great women of all time," a remarkable asset to her husband.[34]

It was after the 1964 election, apparently, that the president's wife and partner decided to concentrate her energies on one area of concern where she might make her influence felt. Secretary of the Interior Stewart Udall encouraged her to stress conservation and beautification. From a dialogue with him at the Ranch, it seems, was born the determination to beautify the capital as a beginning. The resulting Committee for a More Beautiful Capital met on February 11, 1965, at the White House. Soon $2 million would be pledged from private sources. There would be plantings of traffic circles and grassy triangles; the problems of the Potomac Basin would be studied. Among those especially involved were Mrs. Albert (Mary) Lasker, the Rockefeller Foundation, and even the Japanese nation. Azaleas, cherry trees, close to a million bulbs, and other landscaping materials were planted. Certain areas of severe blight were rehabilitated. Two malls were created in the downtown business area. Annual beautification awards gave a sense of accomplishment. Gatherings, such as the National Youth Conference on Natural Beauty, attended by five hundred, spread Lady Bird's enthusiasm. The Redwood National Park in California was a direct result of her effort. Inside the White House a communication in early 1965 urged that a strong statement by the president would constitute a "conservation milestone"; there should be a massive effort to save the countryside: set aside more parks, seashores, and open spaces; and preserve the unspoiled sections of the rivers.[35] There proved to be a receptive audience for such views in the Interior Department, the Congress, and soon in the country.

In a major message of February 8, 1965, the president emphasized the protection and improvement of the landscape. "What we have in woods and forest, valley and stream, in the gorges and the mountains and the hills, we must not destroy," he said as he transmitted details of the progress that had been made since the establishment of the National Wilderness Preservation System on September 3, 1964. He claimed that "only in our country have such positive measures been taken to preserve the wilderness adequately for its scenic and spiritual wealth." Here was "the New Conservation." The same day he transmitted a long special message on "Conservation and Restoration of Natural Beauty." Subjects treated were the cities, the countryside, highways, rivers (especially the Potomac), trails, pollution as the enemy of clean water and air, solid-waste disposal, pesticides, and the need for research on such things. In conclusion, he referred to the carelessness that Americans had often shown toward their "natural bounty" and called the beauty of the land "a natural resource linked to the human spirit."

The two messages of February 8 did not change very much very quickly, but they were clear signals that America was on the verge of a whole new area of activity and controversy. Reference was made to the Clean Air Act of 1963, with this warning—one that Johnson scarcely imagined would prove so prescient: "One of the principal unchecked sources of air pollution is the automobile. I intend to institute discussions with industry officials and other interested groups leading to an effective elimination or substantial reduction of pollution from liquid fueled motor vehicles." In such sentiments was a beginning toward cleaner air—and much later of at least a temporary economic catastrophe for the American automobile industry!

It would be a mistake to assume that the president broke new ground with every aspect that he chose to focus upon in his addresses. The attention of the nation had earlier been directed at pesticides. Johnson asked that the burden of proof of safety be placed on "the proponent of the chemical." Water pollution should be controlled at its source, and government would zero in on the most polluted rivers. "We will work with Canada to develop a pollution control program for the Great Lakes and other border waters," he said, presaging a campaign that would someday have its impact on Lake Erie in particular.

Substantive legislation was passed. The call for a national system of trails recognized that a hundred thousand miles of trails already existed but that "each community has opportunities for action." The request for a national wild rivers system would help to bring results. The effort to control billboards along federal highways came hard on the heels of earlier ineffective efforts, but the targeting of junkyards and auto graveyards was a worthwhile new thought. Johnson hoped to make the existing Open Space Land Program more effective in urban areas, with the goal being small parks, squares, pedestrian malls, and playgrounds. The call even got down to the level of benches, outdoor lighting, and other ways of having the federal government show cities and towns how to serve their own people through "thought and action." Overall, the man from the open spaces was joyfully attacking the "ugliness that can demean the people who live among it." Beauty (that is, nature) would add to the quality of life.[36] Such talk was completely in character for a leader whose experience of city living was largely limited to blighted and neglected Washington.

The State of the Union Address in 1965 had been the first ever to use the word *beauty* in its text; an entire column dealt with "The Beauty of America." Said Johnson: "For over three centuries the beauty of America has sustained our spirit and has enlarged our vision. We must act now to protect this heritage." He envisioned a fruitful federal partnership with states and cities to make the next decade a conservation milestone. A massive effort would be to establish, "as a green legacy for tomorrow," more parks, seashores, and open spaces. Highways should be landscaped, and so should city streets. Little did contemporaries realize how far-reaching would be the arm of the next paragraph: "We will seek legal power to prevent pollution of our air and water before it happens. We will step up our effort to control harmful wastes, giving first priority to the cleanup of our most contaminated rivers. We will increase research to learn much more about the control of pollution." While more ideas would emerge from a conference he was soon to call, the president said that the Potomac should become a model. Among individuals who cared deeply were Laurance Rockefeller, Stewart Udall, and Mary Lasker—termed by Lady Bird "that most sophisticated, most intelligent of women." Said she of the Manhattan resident, "Mary has that rare quality of making suggestions in a way that, somehow or other, winds up by getting them done." When there was a Women Do-er's luncheon in the White House, on February 5, to kick off the beautification program, she was a featured speaker.

The Committee on Beautification held its first meeting on February 11, 1965, in the Blue Room of the White House, with Lady Bird as hostess. Secretary Udall, called "the real captain of the project," was there, along with representatives from the National Capital Planning Commission, the Public Housing body, and the Pennsylvania Avenue

Plan, along with assorted architects and planners and many delegates from the private sector, such as the National Organization of Home Builders and the American Petroleum Institute. Recorded Lady Bird: "What are there more of than filling stations? And if each of them, or many of them, should adopt even the idea of neatness, what a boon it would be, and it would be even greater if they had a minimum of landscaping and some excellence in design!" No meeting would be complete, she said, without her dear friend Katie Louchheim; then there were representatives from the Fine Arts Commission of Washington, the Committee of 100 for the Federal City, Mrs. Kit Haynes of the National Capitol Garden Club League, and "that Number One conservationist," Laurance Rockefeller.[37]

The featured talk by Lady Bird began with a moving quotation from a former British diplomat, who in 1913 had estimated Washington's potential: "Your admirable river is quite as beautiful . . . as that which adjoins any of the capital cities of Europe. . . . No European city has so noble a cataract in its vicinity as the Great Falls. . . . You have such a chance offered to you here for building up a superb capital, that it would be almost an act of ingratitude to Providence and to history and to the men who planted the city, if you did not use the advantages that you here enjoy." To her committee Lady Bird said, "I think I have here in front of me today, you who set the true value on these things."

The first lady told delegates to a White House Conference on Natural Beauty (May 24–25, 1965) that people must be educated to the idea that the beauty of the land depends on their own initiative and will. The cities and the countryside must be rescued from blight just as we had moved to save the forests and the soil. Citizen and governmental action and education would be the tools. Research, better coordination, and more money would all be needed. "Over the next forty years we are going to rebuild this country. We will build as many houses as we have since this country was first settled. We will build enough offices and factories to create at least one and a half million new jobs each year. We will complete and expand our network of interstate highways and rebuild our system of secondary roads." Her unqualified promises, so like those then being produced by her husband's speech writers, were extravagant. Still, "dream no little dreams," a great Chicago architect once said, for they have no power to move men's minds. Lady Bird suggested that "perception of beauty and action to preserve and create it are a fundamental test of a great society."[38] The conference involved more than speeches. The president was handed reports by State Senator Fred Farr, of California, on highways; by Edmund Baron, of the Philadelphia Planning Commission, on cities; by William H. Whyte, of the American Conservation Association, on the countryside; and by Mrs. Arthur Whittemore, of the League of Women Voters, on ways and means of accomplishing goals.

In accepting these reports, President Johnson ad-libbed nostalgic memories of an earlier pristine Texas hill country. Today's youngsters might not have the privilege of growing up in a wide and open country, but they could feel "a little of what the first settlers must have felt, as they stood unbelieving before the endless majesty of our great land." More formally, he observed that natural beauty had acquired two major enemies—technology and urbanization. Protection and restoration were needed. As he saw it, "the natural heritage of beauty" was one cornerstone of the Great Society. So there would be new legislation. Activity would be pushed out to the state and local levels. Said salesman Johnson, he was counting on his audience to get in touch with their legislators so that the job would get done.

Lady Bird proved to be extremely effective. Her proud husband declared that "the work done by a concerned and compassionate woman" had touched "a fundamental chord in the American people with her quiet crusade to beautify our country. She enriched the lives of all Americans."[39] He saw himself, moreover, in the mold of a New Conservationist, by which he meant one who was taking action against pollution. For example, the president reflected on the "considerable resistance" encountered prior to his signing of the Water Quality Act of 1965. There would have been less furor, perhaps, had the people at HEW not accidentally armed the president with the erroneous charge that "sulphuric acid" was being poured into waterways. Soon it had to be confessed that what he should have said was "sulphites" (the HEW staff had just thought "sulphuric acid" sounded better!).

The president would have other occasions to refer to environmental themes in 1965. On September 21 he spoke at the establishment of the Assateague Island National Seashore, a dream thirty years in the making. Fire Island National Seashore had been acquired a year earlier. "I intend," he said, "to find those oases of natural beauty which should never have been lost in the first place, and to reclaim them for all the people of this country." On October 2, on signing the Water Quality Act of 1965, the president observed, "No one has a right to use America's rivers and America's waterways that belong to all the people as a sewer." The banks of the rivers were one thing; the flowing waters were something else.

When signing the new Solid Waste Disposal Act and amendments to the Clean Air Act on October 20, Johnson said, "When future historians write of this era, I believe they will note that ours was the generation that finally faced up to the accumulated problems of our American life." His administration did indeed start the ball rolling; but over a decade later a wrap-up on clean air in the *New York Times,* written by three journalists, showed how difficult the problem of cleaner air had become. From Albany: "Almost 10 years after Congress passed the Federal Clean Air Act, the air in and around metropolitan New York City and the rest of the state is somewhat cleaner, but not up to Federal standards. Controversy over the law's implementation has been almost continuous."[40]

The final environmental action the president took in 1965 was the signing of the Highway Beautification Act on October 22. Soon $66 million would be allocated to begin eliminating billboards and for scenic easement. But victory would not come during Johnson's presidency. Of this act, he admitted, "It is a first step, and there will be other steps." To those in the East Room, he said that unless he missed his guess, "history will remember on its honor roll those of you whom the camera brings into focus today, who stood up and were counted when that roll was called that said we are going to preserve at least a part of what God gave us."

The spark plug for the antibillboard campaign was a group of Lady Bird's friends and persons whom she had recruited. A newsworthy effort by the first lady was a May 1965 landscape-landmark tour into Virginia by chartered bus of a group that included the cabinet wives, the Laurance Rockefellers, and officials from the Bureau of Public Roads and the Park Service. Of primary importance was the role of forty reporters, including personnel from the three networks, for the trip was well calculated to build a local effort into a national crusade. Another day devoted to beautification was January 12, 1966, during which her party looked at school playgrounds and community parks. There were "dreams of a future full of alleys of cherry trees beside the water" near Washington's Haines Point.

It is entirely too easy to forget the role that persons outside the government play in making its wheels move. At one point, Mrs. Lasker played a considerable role in getting the Post Office Department to issue large photographic stamps on beautification and conservation themes. Said the first lady, her "list of projects, her suggestions of how government can help do good things, is endless." Her good rapport with the Johnson family was essential. Her apartment was always available to the two Johnson daughters on New York shopping trips; she donated a valuable rug and other rare items to enhance White House furnishings. As the campaign to beautify the capital began, she gave 800,000 daffodil bulbs and 2,400 dogwoods for planting. So this

leader—whose name could be equally associated with the arts committee or with medical legislation, such as the grants for regional medical
centers, and who held no elective or appointive post—is one to be
remembered. Dr. Michael DeBakey was certain that she had a persua-
sive influence on Lyndon; certainly when Mrs. Lasker wanted the
famous surgeon to do things in the medical area, he would drop
whatever he was doing in order to accommodate her.[41] She would be
awarded the Medal of Freedom as one of Johnson's last presidential
acts.[42]

As is often the case, the beautification crusade had its opponents,
some of whom could mobilize clever and relevant arguments for going
slow. The signboard lobby fought Lady Bird to the wire. The billboard
law was passed by only a single vote; that it passed at all was due to
Johnson's belief that the personal honor of his family was involved. One
person who worked in the Congress said that he had never had a
rougher time dealing with clearance from senators than on that beautification program. In 1966 Congressman Gerald Ford indicated a desire
to cut the beautification program by $100 million or to eliminate it
entirely, but Laurance Rockefeller swung into action at once on behalf of
the Citizens' Advisory Committee. At Johnson's suggestion, Rockefeller
wrote Ford that outdoor recreation and scenic beauty were major goals
of society which were worthy of bipartisan support. At stake was the
total quality of the environment and of the life we achieve. Rockefeller
also called on Ford when concerned about what impact on beauty
certain highway construction would have. On reporting back to the
president, Rockefeller was told by LBJ that "making contacts of this sort
is vital."[43]

Two quite different organizations worked on recreation and beauty.
Vice-President Humphrey was chairman of the President's Council on
Recreation and Natural Beauty, whose members came from the cabinet
and governmental agencies. Rockefeller chaired the Citizens' Advisory
Board on Recreation and Natural Beauty, whose members came from
various sections of the country. Both bodies issued printed materials,
press releases, and lists of speakers. In an executive order of May 4,
1966, the president quoted Thoreau to good effect—"It is a noble
country where we dwell, fit for a stalwart race to summer in"—and
added that a nation that calls itself great must have "poetry as well as
prosperity." For those who predicted that the coming regulations would
cut into profits, the concept was questionable.

Like its predecessors, the administration pursued a water-develop-
ment program. Emphasis was on construction of facilities, with maintenance a close second. The Army Corps of Engineers, the Bureau of

Reclamation, the Soil Conservation Service, the Tennessee Valley Authority, and the Public Health Service were active in the Interagency Committee on Water Resources and the ad hoc Water Resources Council. Research and planning were stressed in these bodies and in many minor agencies.[44] Given the relative affluence and ease of mobility during the 1960s, it may be that Americans could afford a higher level of dissatisfaction. This intriguing theme may be relevant to Johnson's emphasis on urban and highway beautification, amendments to the Clean Air Act, measures to control solid waste and pesticides, and clean water.

In 1965 and 1966 the president came down hard on pollution. There would be a "clean rivers demonstration program," complete with commissions established under the 1965 Water Resources Planning Act. Ambitious plans to increase expenditures for a program of construction grants flourished, but the cost of the Vietnam War meant that during the final two years the administration cut back considerably. In the Congress a growing environmental bloc kept tabs on all this but was helpless in the face of the expensive escalating war. Still, one result was a congressional white paper on the environment. One White House aide guessed correctly that there existed widespread support across party lines for expenditures in this new area.[45] Neither the emerging environmentalists in the White House nor those in the Congress believed that laissez faire in development would any longer serve the public interest. In northern California, the redwood-forest-products industry disagreed. The president observed, in a speech on March 4, 1968, "A beautiful America can be a proud America." So the new legislation had in mind partly the health—both mental and physical—of the public and partly the beauty of America and its land. From these considerations came such major bills as the Water Quality Act, the Clean Water Restoration Act, and action directed at automobile emissions and billboards. Somehow, with all the other heady issues of presidential election year 1968, quasi-environmentalism did not get very much attention from the candidates. Intensity of views lay ahead.

One must be careful not to overstate either the breadth or the depth of the tentative environmental crusade of the 1960s. Much in the way of legislation and expenditure lay ahead during the Nixon and Carter years, and massive change for the better was slow in coming, except of course, in the District of Columbia. When the American Academy of Political and Social Science in July 1979 issued its volume *Environment and the Quality of Life,* it covered themes, activities, and ideas that in many instances were not part of the pioneering of the Johnson years. The whole struggle over economic growth—its basic desirability versus the problems that it creates—came later. The Club of Rome's *Limits to Growth* (1972) and Herman Kahn's utterly different *The Next 200 Years* (1976) struggled with ideas with hardly any audience during Johnson's years. Contamination of the outer atmosphere; environmental law; land-use planning; Environmental Protection Agency regulations—all belong to a later era. Nor had radicals yet decided that environmental problems were due to capitalism per se; corporations were not yet buried in regulations; and statements regarding environmental impact lay ahead, along with crusades to save the whales, harp seals, and various endangered species.

But the spark for such struggles was ignited during the years in the White House of the Johnson family, only irregularly and incompletely noticed by commentators or the average person. The president would say to Lady Bird's White House Conference: "Today I worked and thought about problems in Vietnam and the Dominican Republic. I had to consider decisions which might affect the security of this country, the lives of Americans, and the destiny of other nations. Yet this may be the most important thing that I have done and am doing today, and I am confident this is the most important group that I will see. For this is part of what all the rest is for." Those around Johnson naturally sensed his personalized relationship to the push for conservation and tried to accommodate to it. One effective response was that of Orville Freeman, secretary of the Department of Agriculture (which included the Forest Service), who saw to it that the 1967 yearbook of his department was on the appropriate theme. Called *Outdoors USA*, its four hundred pages of text and pictures dealt with the big forests, water, beautification, and the countryside; it made for inspirational reading and viewing by people on congressmen's mailing lists.

Land preservationists, hoping to set aside maximum portions of America from development, fought a last-gasp fight in 1968/69 through Secretary Udall, but they scored only a partial success. On July 26, 1968, the head of the Interior Department asked the president to use the Antiquities Act of 1906 as authority for setting aside enormous areas of the public domain. Other presidents, notably Herbert Hoover, had done this, he stressed; but aide DeVier Pierson directed Johnson's attention to the provision that parcels should be "confined to the smallest area compatible with the proper care and management of the objects to be protected." In the fall, Udall detailed his proposal to earmark 7,617,200 acres, which would have increased the national park system by 25 percent. Postponing any action to the very last minute while he was dressing for the inaugural ceremonies, the president finally authorized only 300,000 acres. His hesitation seems to have stemmed from a threat by the House Interior Committee's chairman, Wayne Aspinwall, to seek repeal of the Antiquities Act itself, from his own edict that the cabinet should take no lame-duck action that would be binding on their successors, from concern over any criticism as he left office, and from his love of consensus. In any case, he shrank from using the power that was his, and he behaved with untoward hesitancy and propriety. Critic and wilderness extremist Justice William O. Douglas would condemn this "consensus conservation," saying bitterly that Johnson "gave the heritage of America away to the fat cats and the official vandals who have despoiled us." Udall left office furious with his chief, but Johnson was sure he had done the right thing.[46] The decision had been of a kind with the more general decision to by-pass the possibility of reorganizing the administration of federal land resources. Nothing so fundamental as a merger of the Forest Service and the Bureau of Land Management would be forthcoming.

Meanwhile, the commemorative conservation stamps appeared, complete with slogans on beautifying cities and planting in parks and along highways and streets. The infant environmentalism was about to take off in the next decade, when action would be taken under the clean-air and water acts and provisions for waste disposal, control of strip mining, withdrawal of lands from grazing and deforestation, restrictions on land use, and regulation of agricultural chemicals. Laws passed during the Nixon administration and later would provide new teeth. The 1960s were not the decade of environmentalism, for the heading "Environment" in the *Readers' Guide to Periodical Literature* did not even exist in 1960, had but seven entries in 1967, bloomed to a page and a half in 1969, and reached two and a half pages by 1979. The future battleground was prepared between 1962 and 1969 beyond doubt. The groundwork in environmental ("New Conservation") legislation was laid during the Johnson years, but the time of outdoor harvest and of controversy in the marketplace and the media lay ahead.

7

IN THIS CORNER: THE MEDIA

Presidents of the United States quickly find that to lead the nation and retain a modicum of support there must be much wooing of the media—the press, TV pundits, columnists, even some book authors. White House occupants have sought affection and respect from those whose job it is to tell the world what the president is doing, has said, apparently plans to do, and perhaps hopes will happen in the future. John Steinbeck explained the problem in 1966 exceptionally well. The people demand, he wrote the White House, that the president "be greater than anyone else but not better than anyone else." The leader must be above reproach; yet the people reserve the right to question his motives. Perfection inspires dislike, said the novelist, judging that Lyndon Johnson had been successful so far in nearly everything he had undertaken. But "a presidential slip of the tongue, a slight error in judgment—social, political, or ethical—can raise a storm of protest." So, "we wear him out, use him up, eat him up," and "exercise the right to destroy him."[1] It was in this spirit that the visiting Charles Dickens observed about Americans in the 1840s: "Any man who attains a high place among you, from the President downwards, may date his downfall from that moment." One working newsman, who became the top information official for the Department of Defense, summarized the role of newsmen: "The press tends to go to extremes, and the responsible press exhibits extremism in pursuit of truth—which is a virtue. The press wants to know everything. It wants to know now."[2]

The former representative and senator knew the awesome power of the media, not just to report news, but to make it; here was a power he also possessed. Historian Eric Goldman narrates matter-of-factly how, during the presidential-election year 1964, when he was working in the White House, he personally gave information about possible misconduct on the part of William Miller, the Republican vice-presidential candidate, to aide Walter Jenkins, who passed it on to columnist Drew Pearson. After this was published, "other news media picked up the story and played it hard. Of course Miller cried smear, but he was labeled in a way that he did not shake off throughout the campaign." The memory would bother the liberal professor later, even though he was still sure Miller "had about him a slick sleaziness" which even yet made the White House assistant for cultural affairs "wince." While the deed gave him pleasure, he admitted, the tactic might have been wrong. Years later, President Nixon would call such tactics "playing hardball," while the press labeled them "dirty tricks." The newsmen did have the power to alter public perceptions of the famous. After leaving office, Johnson told a CBS producer what had changed in politics during his years in it: "You guys. All you guys in the media. All of politics has changed because of you. . . . You've given us a new kind of people. Teddy. Tunney. They're your creations, your puppets . . . your product."[3]

Johnson tried too hard to win over press and TV people during his first months in office. He associated with them and tried at first to treat them as friends, even buddies. He tried his usually effective flattery, not quite realizing that what worked on a one-to-one basis sounded peculiar when spoken to a group. He should not have said, for example, on January 25, 1964: "I never enjoy anything more than polite, courteous, fair, judicious reporters; and I think all of you qualify." The laughter was hollow. By July 14, 1965, he was ready to lay it on the line toward what he nicknamed "the Georgetown Press." After an ironic "The press helps me. The press is one of the best servants I have," his brother says he blurted out: "Somebody ought to do an article on your damn profession, your First Amendment."

The role of TV in building, shoring up, or diminishing the presidency in the eyes of the public became a real capability in the decade before Johnson. It was a fact with which presidents had to live. Aides could not fathom why he watched the screens at every possible moment, with three different channels on three sets, even when conducting unrelated business. First to last, television was for this president the flame that drew the moth. He needed it; the networks needed him. But neither showed much trust. The screen built him up in 1963/64 only to treat him as an adversary when Vietnam warmed up.

The presidential press conference has been a problem for many occupants of the White House. Johnson was duly told of aide James Rowe's opinion that the press conference is the president's instrumentality; therefore, he should shape it so as to help him carry out his responsibilities. Don't abdicate your powers. Be like Roosevelt, although he would not allow anybody to quote him after a conference without his permission. But the new president knew full well that times had changed. In the Washington press corps were foreign newsmen. Early in the game, Johnson was briefed on media people in preparation for a White House dinner staged for them on December 12, 1963. Among those present were representatives from Reuters and from papers in Switzerland, Canada, Japan, India, West Germany, and the USSR.[4] Press conferences involving such outsiders could not be treated too high-handedly.

The press secretary was bound to be a key figure in good public relations. In Eisenhower's day (1959) there were nine employees in the press office; these became ten in Kennedy's day (1963); and in Johnson's day (1966), over sixteen. But in the last analysis the task of creating and maintaining an image has to be the responsibility of the president himself; for although the press secretary may be somewhat instrumental in projecting or altering images, the policies and decisions—and the image—come from the president. It is inevitable, says Bill Moyers, that a president's words and deeds will not always be consistent with each other, for he must sometimes reach conclusions from inconclusive evidence. Moyers became an informed doubter who, on leaving office, advised his successor to work hard and keep a sense of humor. Before he had developed his own, however, Moyers tried setting up a system for making a record of every outside call made to a member of the staff; but this aggressive activity was soon dropped.[5]

Any discussion of the role of the press during the Johnson administration involves consideration of a so-called credibility gap, which was often in the forefront of discussion in the press room by columnists and by commentators. While the problem is often treated as having hinged upon the administration's alleged dishonesty over Vietnam—and especially body-count figures—the matter is far more complex than that. Lyndon's realistic and blunt brother Sam Houston concedes: Lyndon "often hinted the opposite from what he meant; omitted important elements of some report; made outright denials of things that were obviously true; avoided direct answers to simple straightforward questions; needlessly kept the press guessing about certain things he planned to do; waited until the last minute to tell where he was going; and often treated reporters as if they were 'the enemy.'" Even the former head of public relations for the Defense Department readily admitted that the administration simply failed "to explain to the citizens of the United States that our bombing mentality was destroying homes and killing civilians." There was too much intimation of "surgical precision." So it was easy for Harrison Salisbury of the *New York Times* to be shown some damage in Hanoi and proceed to humiliate the administration with generalizations. Again, when marines were committed to Danang in March 1965, the fact was readily admitted by the State Department's press officer, Robert McCloskey. The president was furious, and said flatly, but falsely, that there had been "no change."[6]

It was the White House correspondent for a newspaper that was normally partisan to the Democratic party who codified the mass of complaints that Johnson had created a "credibility gap" in the presidency. Wrote James Deakin in a short paperback: "Somehow, Lyndon Johnson as president has seldom been able to state a major position or make an important announcement in a straightforward and unequivocal way. Somehow, his pronouncements turn out later to have been full of weasel words or hidden meanings or downright deception." Having run in 1964 as an apparent dove, Johnson soon emerged looking like a hawk, which is said to have been the "chief reason" for the credibility gap. Many a gripe was directed by the Washington press corps and others toward the president from Texas. There was Johnson's vanity: he considered his left profile to be more photogenic. He avoided wearing his glasses and got some contact lenses; but finally he went back to glasses. His penchant for constantly giving gifts (a photograph of himself taken with each reporter was a favorite), though appreciated, was still resented. Frequent visits to rural Texas were wearying experiences for the press; and Lyndon's glorification of his hill country, with its symbolic restored birthplace, his boyhood home, and his grandfather's log cabin, exposed him to charges that he was memorializing himself while still alive. His name on a state park, on a lake, on the plaque of an electric cooperative, and on the projected Johnson Library was an irritant. His inexhaustible energy, demonstrated in speeding down narrow roads and lurching across fields, was easily placed in a bad light, even though some of the roads were not public highways.

Many reporters thought of Johnson as the great American Yahoo, a "big-talker whose specialty is the off-color joke"; some referred to him in that guise behind his back. Prose about him could not help but be affected. "Yes, he certainly had faults; we delighted to recount them," recalls a senior newsman. It has to be said, in partial extenuation, that the media were dealing with a caricature of the traditional Texas caricature! How easy it was in the angry 1960s to be a penetrating H. L.

Mencken or Sinclair Lewis; how difficult to be a gentle Will Rogers. Johnson did seem to have an endless supply of tasteless anecdotes about political rivals, which were filled with innuendoes directed at usually private aspects of their lives. His total awareness and obsessive curiosity evoked wonder. The newsmen, no slouches at using profanity, were totally outclassed by the cattle-raising Texan. "Johnson's jokes and similes are heavily animalistic and scatological," said Deakin; "they emphasize bathroom functions." Here, he thought, was "the bravado that overcomes insecurity." The Johnson biographical literature abounds in unsavory examples of gross crudeness in his stories and comments, but it would be only compounding the tastelessness to dignify them by printing them here. Walt Whitman said: "Be sure to write about me honest. Whatever you do, do not pretify me: include all the hells and damns." Nevertheless, the extremes of LBJ's language are virtually unprintable in a book such as this. Yet cabinet member Wilbur Cohen thought him "earthy" rather than "crude"; so it may be a matter of taste. One who lived a full life and knew six presidents finally insisted that "style is man" and personal traits are essential components of style,[7] but as can be seen in these pages, I do not fully agree. Official actions and consequences are what make a presidency meaningful at the time, and later. Oliver Wendell Holmes once issued a reminder that suggests a certain humility to journalists and historians alike: "The world's great men have not commonly been great scholars, nor its great scholars great men." Too often the media wasted their time, and the public's, from 1963 to 1969.

Other Johnsonian characteristics—dwelt on by some media people in private, and sometimes in public—were his alleged disinclination to read and quote from *books*. On this, it should be said that during his adult life he had sweated through endless thousands of pages of heavy government reports and substantive correspondence on major topics of every possible kind. The president was portrayed as a bully who humiliated his subordinates—a sometime thing. To the tender Deakin, an example was Johnson's telling an aide, "If you ever keep Hubert waiting again, I'll kick your ass down that hall." On the other hand, Johnson has been faulted for not treating Humphrey politely.

The development of mutual dislike and distrust took time; each year it got worse. Some say that the downfall of key aide Jenkins was the breaking point for Lyndon. Mutual opposition to Goldwater did bring the media and the president close together during the last months of 1964, when Larry O'Brien judged, "It is obvious the press generally is engaged in a total drive to stop Goldwater."[8] The bottom was reached for Johnson when he read the *Baltimore Sun* for January 16, 1967, which featured the "credibility gap" problem right on page one. He kept it around for several weeks while Fred Panzer conducted a research study on problems that previous presidents had had with the media back to 1933. Panzer should have gone back to 1929. The game was the same; only the wrinkles were new, he learned. Unfortunately, the charges against Johnson had become a smear technique, partisan, filled with half-truths, and hard to answer without adding to the problem, Panzer thought. In Kennedy's day the term "news management" had been used, said Panzer, who offered devastating examples from cautious and reputable columnists. It seems that Johnson had inherited an unhappy press from Kennedy, which he would have to woo for many months.[9] When the *Baltimore Sun* said in 1967 that "the war with newsmen and commentators is fought with public jibe and private recrimination," what Johnson was then saying about them in private would have made even their eyes pop. He hated to be put on the psychiatrist's couch, he once said, by "amateurs" (a later biography would do just that).

The Johnson team was concerned with which columnists were being read in a whole area like New York City. When that area lost the *Herald-Tribune*—leaving only the *Times*, the *Daily News*, and the *Post*—this was seen as a "decrease in communications," which would mean future dominance by the *Times* and *Post*, and this could have "a real political effect." Joseph Alsop would be lost to that giant audience, leaving "no strong columnist support" on Vietnam except for Drew Pearson, although James Wexler continued to be an intimate friend. "Obviously, the television news shows become more and more important," moaned Robert Kintner to the president. By 1967 the days were far behind when *Time Magazine* could say, in an article, "Mr. President, You're Fun." TRB, in the *New Republic,* reported that the president was seeing groups of newsmen informally much more often; but he was just holding forth, justifying himself, which "apparently gives him relief." The president evidently did not know how to gain the trust of the newsmen, the country, or the world: "He finds regular, candid communication with public opinion and its representatives distasteful. His alternative methods are only partly successful."[10]

Vietnam was a problem that could not be surmounted by better interpersonal relations. Here the gap was basic: how Johnson viewed the war and how the media increasingly viewed it. By the late 1960s "there were more journalists who opposed the war than favored it," says David Halberstam. One intellectual who spent some months in the White House recorded: "The country hasn't been suffering from a 'credibility gap' but from an 'incredibility gap.' People can't believe that the president and the secretary of state really believe what they say. But they do.'' He especially noticed the gap between what members of the staff said in private and what they said in public.[11]

The president from Texas was what he was, and nothing much could be done about it. He seemed to gravitate toward secrecy in small and large things alike. Denials could be followed by the predicted action; transcripts of speeches and talks were not always trustworthy. Thus, ''again and again the reporters, and through them the American public, were misled.'' From the president's point of view, however, the media were the ones at fault. Later a mammoth two-year study concluded that ''the networks actively slanted their opinion coverage against U.S. policy on the Vietnam war''; this was seen as a clear violation of the FCC fairness doctrine. This was true enough, although the study in question was ignored or condemned by those who had been accused. How could the media ignore the Pentagon's switching in 1966 from revealing ''sorties'' over Vietnam to listing ''missions''—an act that automatically reduced the size of daily statistics, since a mission normally involved only four planes? Still, there was justice in Johnson's conviction that his Texas, and therefore Confederate, heritage and his more or less southern accent were insuperable barriers to his being accepted by the primarily northern and eastern newsmen. President Carter would suffer similarly.[12]

Was the Washington press loaded against a person like Lyndon Johnson? For years it has not been a demographic reflection of the nation, for one such newsman wrote: ''We are younger, whiter, more male and far better educated than the people for whom we write and broadcast.'' Half have had graduate training, and the Northeast has been overrepresented. A full 96 percent agreed that there has been a liberal bias among Washington media representatives. Such a bias could, in peacetime, be an asset to a Democratic president. But an aide early advised Johnson that the local press the chief faced was a ''wolf pack'' at attacking public officials; but, like sheep, they followed the bellwethers: their leaders were Walter Lippmann and James Reston, who gradually replaced Arthur Krock on the editorial page of the *New York Times*. So far—1964—the president had them in his pocket. Don't lose them! Keep worrying that ''the one thing the northern liberals place above principle is winning.'' Nevertheless, reporters did not have to stand for personal rudeness and inconsiderateness. Not really atypical was the president's sudden decision in 1968 to go to Puerto Rico by way of Beaumont, Texas, and Marietta, Georgia, so that the White House reporters—for whom the trip was really compulsory—had nothing tropical to wear as they scrambled to be on their way. ''What kind of crap is this?'' snapped one. Their wives and families were not amused at such unannounced trips.[13]

On the other hand, the sophisticated minds that were occupying the White House knew that some reporters wanted to have power as well as to report about it. Press secretary Reedy asserted, "Many newspaper stories and a much higher number of columns are written solely for their impact upon the president." Members of the press could sniff out manipulation. They knew that the White House briefed the press so as to be in full control of the first four paragraphs of any story about a new bill or some Johnson activity. "That's what tells most of America," said one staffer.

The president's problems with the media over Vietnam were central. The aging Lippmann, for example, was widely considered to be the dean of the American columnists, along with the elderly constitutionalist Krock. Lippmann was an Ivy League northeasterner who quickly switched his allegiance from Kennedy to Johnson. As Lippmann called on the country to support the new leader, he instantly reaped Johnson's affection and was even given the opportunity to comment on the drafts of some speeches. Birthday gifts, personal telephone calls, private luncheons, and inclusion at state dinners marked this period. When Lippmann's discontent with Vietnam became public, he was farmed out to McGeorge Bundy for an indoctrination that did not go well, especially since Lippmann espoused the neutralization ideas of French President de Gaulle. Soon Bundy did not "like the tone" of a column, replying that Asians were glad that our policy was to stand firm "even if they do not praise it in public." Bundy even tried to refute the columnist in letters to others. Now, said Johnson, "Every time I pull my chair nearer that guy, he pulls his chair farther away." Said Lippmann, "I'm just going to have to take out after Johnson's foreign policy and show that it doesn't work." To him, the president was exercising "unlimited power." All courting stopped. A typed "book" of Lippmann errors over the years circulated inside the White House. The journalist conspired, successfully, to get a new anti-Vietnam editor for the *Washington Post*.[14]

Since the situation was getting serious, an aide advised the president, "I think we should stop attacking Lippmann, the press, and the broadcasters." But Johnson checked the "Yes" box when asked if the story should be leaked that Lippmann had been dead wrong on Hitler and aggression on May 19, 1933. Cutting jokes were fed the president, as the columnist griped that the incumbent was "the most disagreeable individual ever to have occupied the White House." In 1968, Lippmann supported Nixon over Humphrey, thus astonishing many. The war was nothing but "savagery"; Americans were ashamed of it. "Nixon is the only one." Johnson would later use Lippmann as a case in point when generalizing about "tireless assaults on me and my administration" and lack of support from the press corps or media.[15]

The Johnsons owned media outlets and had enjoyed a long personal and business relationship with Frank Stanton of the CBS network, going back to World War II. Lyndon understood when aides suggested in late 1967 that a live TV interview by three commercial correspondents might have the same success as a similar effort had had in 1964. But he could not quite grasp what his conduct and policies had done since then to affect the kinds of questions that were apt to be asked. The taping, on December 18, 1967, would be tense. Said TV newsman Dan Rather before beginning, "I wouldn't like the job of staring you down, Mr. President." A nasty crack by Johnson would be edited out before broadcast. Many questions were repeated several times before being answered "live" for national viewing. Between takes, everybody looked ill at ease and fidgeted.[16]

Johnson used the media for his ends; and this was naturally resented, even though his ends were, in his view, also the nation's. Twenty-eight times from November 1963 through November 1966 alone he would preempt network TV programs in order to make announcements of one kind or another. While he dreaded in advance all of his televised news conferences, which might have had perhaps four hundred and fifty people present, he ended each session, says Reedy, with a distinct improvement in his public image. Once when he experimented with a lapel mike to give himself freedom of movement, he did far better, but somehow the practice did not survive.

Press secretaries, in the age of TV, came to have high visibility. Johnson was well served by George Reedy, Bill Moyers, and George Christian. Reedy was religious, honest, experienced, comfortable to be around, and informed. Yet he seethed inwardly against his dictatorial boss of thirteen years and played a role of questionable propriety. He saw his task as providing a source of accountable information for newsmen, whatever the roadblocks. He did not have to prepare daily one-page press summaries of newspapers because "the president would have read the papers before I have." Newsmen could go directly to administration officials—but Reedy expected to be informed. He delivered their requests and queries to the chief and anwered media questions fully, but he bore in mind that his leader kept his own counsel; there were dangers for Reedy in this. He later emerged critical of the presidential office, even referring to an "American monarchy," where rashness was not uncommon and long-range thought was rare.

Johnson, he said, was rarely candid and thought of reporters as transmission belts.[17] Moyers would revel in the job of press secretary, taking some risks while doing so; Christian was less adventuresome.

Press conferences, judged *Newsweek* in February 1965, are a kind of prearranged show where some reporters get to stand up and be on TV. They also presented occasions for much staff preparation and not a little strain on the chief. Before Johnson's first conference he was urged by Pierre Salinger to tell the reporters his plans for them and to settle the format; McGeorge Bundy disagreed, suggesting that Johnson only issue a statement of appreciation for what the press had done during the first two weeks since the assassination. Johnson did neither. There would be close checking to make sure that the frequency of his conferences would at least match that of Kennedy's. The score, after 914 days, was Kennedy 50, Johnson 53, but the latter had held some 40 "little conferences," fortunately. By the critical 1,076-day point, it would be Kennedy 66, Johnson 76, so all was well. By mid 1967, a survey showed that Eisenhower had averaged 24 a year; Kennedy, 18; and Johnson, 24. Johnson finally held a total of 135 official news conferences, with 1966 being the high year, with 41, and 1965 and 1968 the low ones, with 17 and 19; 1964 saw 32. At impromptu conferences, some twenty to forty newsmen would be present.[18] Of the first 39 conferences, 8 were live on TV.

Newsmen complained of having little advance notice, meeting rooms whose small size limited the attendance, and the exclusion of specialists who might ask penetrating questions. The complaints reflect some of the wary cynicism into which the press drifted during those trying years. Yet the newsmen had every right to view every logistical move made by the White House public-relations people as self-serving. Said a White House memorandum on techniques during one major struggle: "To make the Cronkite show or Brinkley, this would have to be released no later than 3:30 unless the news is so hot that they will pick it up from the ticker." After 4:00 it would have been impossible to make the *Washington Star*. A White House release before 5:00 P.M. would get into the first edition of the morning *New York Times* and most of the morning papers, as well as some of the late news TV shows.[19] So a correct view is of professionals against professionals, with the goal being the molding of the public perception.

The president had many things on his mind other than the convenience of the working representatives of the media, a fact that they sometimes found hard to remember. For long periods, Johnson would refuse to meet with the press. Moreover, he would not hesitate to rake a reporter over the coals. Still, slow walks around the White House grounds with reporters often produced printable news. Both president and reporters, even under the best of circumstances, were not completely comfortable. But is this not entirely natural? One source of gratification by the press was the absence of off-the-record speaking at the press conferences. Johnson experimented with a variety of formats, trying—largely in vain—to emulate the success of Roosevelt and Kennedy. The more informal the situation, the better he did. Try as he might, the White House reporters remained critical and emphasized his frequent lapses from truth, his secrecy, his tendency to propagandize, and his alleged lack of candor. Mere technique could not ameliorate these complaints, especially since he hoped to use the conferences to get publicity, defend his actions, explain his purposes, and guard his image.[20]

There was usually a long opening statement, sometimes with details and statistics. Repetition was used to good effect. Policies were proclaimed, and critics were frontally attacked. There could be drama. News could be made. The president's conduct was marked by attacks on some reporters, pointed questions, interruptions, and sarcasm; yet there was some humor as well. Johnson would argue, use an arsenal of tactics to avoid answering, and refer questioners to other officials; quite often he would manage not to reply at all. So, his conferences were not such as to generate good will. If one agrees with Clinton Rossiter's judgment that the presidential press conference is "the most influential channel of public communication to and from the president," these adverse judgments give pause.[21]

A tactic that was most annoying was the scheduling of Saturday press conferences. Newsmen thought that these were designed to reduce attendance. A journalist said in 1964 that Ike's conferences reduced tensions; but Johnson's "controlled affair" was chiefly aimed at spot news regulars, who had a self-interest in retaining tolerable relations with the White House. From the conferences came rumors, revelations among gossip columnists, and personality sniping. By 1967, a newsman complained, "Mr. Johnson holds sudden, informal gatherings attended by the thirty or so reporters regularly attached to the outer lobby of the White House."[22]

President Johnson's shifting standing in the polls may be easily checked in compilations. Attentive observers tried their hand at the time. In March 1964 Senator Abe Ribicoff told Abe Fortas that the president's popularity with the people was very high. By April a traveling journalist-lecturer found hardly any hostility. The public, except in New York City, found Johnson "sympathetic" and "understanding." And so it went. The whole subject of presidential popularity is filled with rocks and shoals. With all presidents there have been great swings of popularity, depending on matters both great and small. All presidents from Eisenhower to Reagan have seen their standing with the public, as measured by the polls, rise and then decline. Snapped President Johnson to his news conference on July 31, 1967, "We don't base our actions on the Gallup Poll."

The whole subject of popularity, polling, and acceptance by the people was intertwined with presidential relations with the reporters, columnists, anchormen, and the institutions that employed them. The situation gave rise to bone-numbing cynicism among top aides and was sometimes responsible for almost diagnosable depression in the president himself. As Johnson left office, he told Spiro Agnew: "We have in this country two big television networks, NBC and CBS. We have two news magazines, *Newsweek* and *Time*. We have two wire services, AP and UPI. We have two pollsters, Gallup and Harris. We have two big newspapers, the *Washington Post* and the *New York Times*. They're all so damned big they think they own the country. But, young man, don't get any ideas about fighting." Such words are an indication that here was the first president to realize that big media had come to replace big finance as his chief rival in running the nation. Said a British journalist, "The American press fulfills almost a constitutional function"; to which a journalism professor in the 1980s added that "they have acquired the authority and sometimes even the power of a shadow government."[23]

Such descriptions of the media are graphic and contain some element of truth, but all had not been black in Johnson's relations with the press. There had been friendships: for example, the Johnsons hosted a dinner at the Elms on December 3, 1963, for publisher Katherine Graham and columnist Joseph Alsop. And there had been recognition of Johnson's problems by Henry Graff in a special article in the *New York Times*. "I thought the article was both fair and well done," Moyers wrote Graff. "The president, too, was pleased with it. All in all it was a very good show." Stewart Alsop would later be sympathetic to Johnson's problems with the media. "It certainly is true that the press has been unfair—sometimes bitterly unfair—to President Johnson," he wrote, adding that one must feel something like pity for this "strange, proud, cruel, sentimental, insecure, naïve, and bitterly driven man." Johnson himself told the cabinet during his final year, "I think we have been terribly neglectful in telling our story." With such an admission the president by no means intended to grant the excesses in Deakin's credibility-gap book, which said with deep bitterness: "The president has diminished himself. He has detracted from his accomplishments in other fields. . . . Moreover, he has impaired the faith of the American people in their government, and this could have profound implications for the democratic system."[24]

But what of media conduct during the 1960s? One writer has said that the evidence shows overwhelmingly that in the 1960s and early 1970s we had a full-fledged "imperial media" in America. Another view, presented after unloading a series of hostile comments on Johnson's treatment of the press, was also critical of the aggressiveness of newsmen: "The sad conclusion is that Johnson and the press failed each other and in so doing, they both failed the country." Says one White house occupant: "Johnson hated the Press. It didn't matter how effective he was, the Press still pictured him, not as a statesman and leader, but as a boor."[25] A most important note was sounded when George Christian told reporters to their faces, "I know you don't like your 'cornpone president.'" After all, the people had overwhelmingly elected the chief executive; but only in a remote sense had they chosen the newscasters and commentators; therefore, in the frequent clashes between the two camps, it was as much certain parts of the media as it was the president who exhibited "arrogance of power."

In judging the degree of fairness of the media, some attention should be paid to the depth of the president's ultimate passion against his enemy. After his withdrawal speech in 1968 Johnson took the opportunity, aboard a plane bound for Chicago, to let ten hapless correspondents have it between the eyes. "Well, you fellows won't have me to pick on anymore," he said. "You can find someone else to flog and insult. And I want to tell you here and now that this damned credibility gap you've been harping about is something you've all created yourselves." The reaction was grim. As early as 1966 he wrote to the ailing Eisenhower: "Perhaps I should also thank you for distracting the eager doctors of the press from my person. I find many of them are frustrated surgeons at heart—but you would know about that." Once, he even wanted to make a speech attacking his adversaries but feared it would be interpreted as an attack on freedom of the press.[26]

Johnson said later that he sometimes had talks with the press where all of their questions were on one subject. "I couldn't get them away from it where they would ask a question on anything else." Then they would report that he was "preoccupied" with that subject, although he really cared more about half a dozen other subjects. Warming to this theme, the irritated man declared: "I do believe that the press can do considerable harm and has. It can create false impressions, it can provoke and encourage dissension on issues. I think they did that on the Vietnam question." Soon it became "intellectually fashionable" to oppose the nation's stand in Vietnam. "I think that the East is still the molder of opinion and the leader of thought and one of the most influential, if not the most influential, section of the country." It has powerful academic communities, financial power, Wall Street, and newspapers and magazines with the fullest accounts; it is also the headquarters of the three networks, he added.[27]

Lyndon Johnson came to be loaded on the subject of media derelictions. His own obsessive viewing of TV and reading of columns made him an expert on this, and his awareness of the personal lives of the news gatherers was greater than his responsibilities warranted. His dear friend Jack Valenti would say: "Mr. President, . . . who the devil reads all that stuff you read? Sure, some people in Washington, but very few of the citizens out there know what is being printed. You take too much of this to heart. Forget it." Johnson would only grunt at such helpful advice. Well-meaning staff fed him memorandums that kept him stirred up. Who but Johnson would ever know that a *Newsweek* article with twenty-seven statements had five (that is, 19 percent) that were inaccurate? After North Korea captured the *Pueblo* in 1968, was it really necessary to know exactly what ten TV newscasters had then said? (Staff told him.) Asked once if he would grant an interview to Cabell Phillips, who was only writing on Truman, Johnson checked the "no" box and scrawled, "He has always sold out against me." Consistent, into his retirement years, in his appraisal of media performance, Johnson put the press off limits at the Ranch, saying: "I've served my time with that bunch, and I give up on them. There's no objectivity left anymore. . . . So to hell with it." The "cornpone president" had been scratched, from 1963 to 1969; even as a private citizen he was still bleeding. Press secretary Reedy endured the rack for a decade; in a 1982 memoir he finally got even, and then felt better. His final conclusion on LBJ as an individual: "There was no sense in which he could be described as a pleasant man. His manners were atrocious—not just slovenly but frequently *calculated* to give offense."[28] Yet some visitors found the man at his desk in the Oval Office warm and winning as he focused total attention on them. Two weddings in the White House years (Lynda and Luci) showed all the Johnson family to good advantage. But most of the press found the president too often to be unpresidential, at least in the sense of John F. Kennedy as a role model.

This account of combat is not exclusively descriptive of the Johnson presidency, for other presidents and other media representatives have behaved somewhat similarly and shared these emotions. During later administrations the reporters and commentators would seek to identify credibility gaps and media manipulation as they searched for "The Truth." The intensity of mutual distrust during Johnson's administration, however, may be unexampled—except for the depths during Nixon's final years. Cartoonist Jules Feiffer even said later, "I didn't have it in me to hate Nixon the way I hated LBJ." One must agree with the understatement of Hubert Humphrey on the overall media situation in the Johnson presidency: "He and the press were hardly in love."[29]

The reporters and commentators were what they were—no better, no worse. In their self-image they were "keenly professional" and "strongly disposed to seal off personal reactions and render highest respect" (Deakin's own portrayal). The reporters did not admit their own imperfections, which occasioned frontal attacks by Eisenhower ("sensation-seeking columnists and commentators"), by Goldwater (many examples to choose from), and now by Johnson. Their self-image making was, to say the least, flattering and self-serving. But they did suffer and endure slurs and slights.

President Johnson, like other executives, hoped to be the first to release spot news, and he hated leaks. But he seemed to have a thing about any astutely correct guess made by a commentator and was not averse to making changes in impending events just to prove a newsman wrong. This could happen with regard to appointments, trips, and even important policy making. It was an unpleasant aspect of the Johnson incumbency and the source of lasting enmities; for as one journalist correctly judged: "The White House correspondents, who would almost rather be called warlike than inaccurate, got badly burned." It made them both wary and hostile.

In all of this, there was the public welfare to be considered. The reality of the functioning presidency was well within the public interest; so, portraying the total character and personality of the incumbent president was a duty. The press was absolutely entitled to try to reveal the nature of the passing scene and the life of the most powerful man in it. Indeed, they were, as the price of enjoying First Amendment freedoms, obligated to do so. With a tad more humility during the Johnson years, the media could have performed its functions just as well. If Vietnam furnished largely bad news, that was the nature of the message; the media's role naturally developed into that of messenger. While the president's best side was often missing in his dealings with the media, one must at least weigh the calm biography later written by wire-service reporter Frank Cormier. Then there is the conclusion of *New York Times* journalist Max Frankel that nobody would ever suggest that Johnson was unfair in his dealings with the press. Drew Pearson saw nothing worse in the interrelationship than is normal between president and press. Such judgments are hard to reconcile with Reedy's memoir, with its hostility toward the newspeople and the president alike. Interviews with reporters by oral historians in the 1970s elicited a startling diversity of opinions about Johnson's true conduct during his term, but most of those interviewed were big-name columnists or TV personalities.[30] The working White House press were the ones who suffered personally and seem to have shown the most distress. The reader of the record as presented here, with its recriminations from both sides, and the effect of such strong emotions on what Americans read and viewed, cannot be overly charitable toward either Johnson or much of the media he faced in that day. It was a bad interaction for both, with the public too often the loser.

8

★ ★ ★ ★ ★

AMERICA:
CUSTODIAN OF THE WORLD

As president of the United States, Lyndon Johnson had the same constitutional responsibilities toward foreign policy and foreign relations as other presidents, but much of this area of his concern has received scant attention from those focusing on Johnson's performance. Any retrospective view of foreign affairs during the Johnson years must take account of the president as he looked back on his record from the perspective of several years. His memoir *The Vantage Point* gives weight to matters that students of Johnson barely mention. India's food crisis from 1965 to 1967 has an entire chapter to itself, culminating with an account of passage of the Food for Peace Act of late 1966, which the president thought to be ''the beginning of one of the most important tasks of our time.'' For a year, he recalls, an average of two grain ships a day arrived in India, so that one-fifth of all American grain went to that crisis-torn nation. In the twenty-three chapters of this book, Vietnam gets five. So foreign affairs, including war and peace, get eleven out of twenty-three chapters from a man whose chief hope was to be remembered for his work in education, poverty, and civil rights.

As President Johnson surveyed the world with the help of associates in December 1963, he saw a varied picture. In a briefing memorandum prepared for his view on December 12, it was duly recorded that in Europe, de Gaulle was a problem but not a major one. The basic objectives of the Kennedy administration regarding trade should have Johnson's support. The lines of communication opened toward the Soviet Union during the Kennedy years could be sustained—the wheat deal would continue. The spread of communism in the Western Hemisphere and in Southeast Asia would be resisted. Indonesia's possible adventurism in Malaysia should be watched.[1]

Faced with the problems of financing a limited war in Southeast Asia and with legislative experimentation at home, the Johnson administration would not pioneer in the field of foreign aid. The Food for Peace Act with aid for India was helped by new miracle grains (wheat and rice) that were the result of work by pioneering scientists. Walt Rostow says that Johnson not only gave the matter of world agricultural policy an extraordinary amount of time, energy, and resourcefulness, but he also got bogged down in such tiny details as the dates of grain shipments, guiding every negotiation, checking on rainfall on the subcontinent, and studying the state of Indian grain stocks. It almost sounds like a hobby; if so, granting that he is said never to have lost the sense that the fate of hundreds of millions of men, women, and children was involved,[2] his time could have been spent in far worse ways.

The president also exercised personal control over the Agency for International Development, which made loans or grants of five to ten million dollars to foreign governments, and all Food for Peace (PL480) sales or grants, especially after 1965. Kennedy had not done this. Somehow Johnson considered these loans or gifts part of his obligation for political leadership. Indefatigable in seeking to change things, he wanted to force India toward birth control and to redirect its efforts from industry to agriculture. He proved to be ''a wise developmental administrator in what many of us at the time railed at as heartless,'' recalls an associate.[3]

The administration inherited AID, which had been created in 1961, when the idea had been to further major development rather than to provide short-term assistance. Development was supposed to eliminate monetary aid in time. Because of criticism, its staff was reduced and cuts were made in economic—but not in military—assistance. The foreign aid request for 1964 was lower than any of Eisenhower's, and the $3.38 billion requested for 1965 was the smallest up to that time. Because cooperation with the United States was declared to be essential to getting help, some fourteen countries were taken off the rolls, but other countries were added. Critics of the AID program said that it contributed to the gold drain, but some 80 percent of the funds was really spent at home. Economic aid exceeded military aid until the astronomical figures for Vietnam mounted up. There was some effort to change directions: for example, there was increased awareness of the relationship between the inexorable growth in world population and the availability of food to feed the new millions. An area of interest was health and education overseas. There was some shifting to multilateral methods of conveying aid, such as use of the Asian Development Bank, the Inter-American Bank, and the International Development Association of the World Bank. Nevertheless, while other nations expanded their contributions, the American share in official development assistance fell from 61 percent in 1964 to 51 percent (of a higher total) in 1968.

There was some emphasis on developmental aid for Latin America, as lending increased by two-thirds; but the same old problems remained at the end as in the beginning. Major states—Argentina, Brazil, Bolivia, and Peru—moved under military rule, and inflation plagued the area. No administration, it would turn out, could easily bring progress, prosperity, contentment, and self-government to intractable Latin America with dollars, with friendly speeches, or by extending the nuclear umbrella.

Figures on aid during the years 1964 to 1968 reveal little in new commitments. Military aid (excluding Vietnam) went steadily downward. Loans and grants for development dropped. But total economic assistance was little changed—at $3.9 billion in 1964, $3.5 billion in 1968.[4]

Account must be taken of the hostile charges that President Johnson had no background for, or much understanding of, foreign affairs. An experienced State Department official and diplomat, looking back at the 1960s, did not agree with this assessment. He said that Johnson both knew and cared much about foreign affairs.[5] There is no doubt whatsoever that President Johnson went far out of his way to study the international scene, to meet foreign leaders, and to listen to viewpoints. He gave this area an outsized share of his time. But one aide later claimed that Johnson had no real grasp of foreign cultures: what made the Vietnamese Vietnamese, for example. "He was a people man, and he thought people everywhere were the same." (Of course, he could have learned this "truth" from almost any grammar school in the country.) One biographer thought that this lacuna was Johnson's greatest weakness as president. The constant assessment that Johnson's "education" was something obtained during his youth in some history or international-relations courses or through study of textbooks and reading of some collateral books is unrealistic. He spent thousands of hours in committee meetings during his adult years, and he read weighty reports on innumerable subjects. There was contact at home and abroad with foreign leaders—an activity denied to most critics. His was the education of the work place. Major roadblocks in his mind were preconceptions rooted in party loyalty and overfamiliarity with and regard for earlier Democratic decision makers, such as Wilson, Roosevelt, Truman, and Kennedy.

The president was thereby oriented, unfortunately, toward such twentieth-century national characteristics as risking major wars, standing up for principles no matter what, expecting good to come ultimately from waging apparently just wars, and expecting history to reward the wartime president. To him, the crusade in Vietnam strikingly resembled Truman's in Korea, Roosevelt's for the Four Freedoms, and Wilson's to fight a "grim and terrible war for democracy." If he had not been so admiring of his own party's former presidents, if he had not himself "learned" by living through three major wars, he might have been able to pursue different policies. He did not see history whole: that Wilson's war did not end horror in Europe; that Roosevelt's opened the door to Communist expansion worldwide, exposing America to Soviet strength; and that while Truman's showed that limited war could be waged even in a nuclear age and then ended with establishment of a stable state, all depended on United States forces staying indefinitely on the Korean peninsula. Even victorious wars could have fallout—a fact that Johnson should have weighed more seriously.

During his first six months the new president held nine bipartisan meetings on foreign affairs with members of the Congress. Such subjects as the relative strength of the U.S. and Soviet armed forces, Panama, foreign aid, Southeast Asia, and Vietnam were agenda items for groups in which not only his own party but congressional Republicans were represented. By June 1964 Johnson would have received twenty chiefs of state and heads of government; this compared with Kennedy's twenty-nine in all of 1961, twenty-seven in 1962, and twenty-two in 1963. Eisenhower had received ninety-one during his two terms; and Truman, sixty in nearly two full terms. On November 26, 1963, the brand new chief executive early met with a variety of heads of state. He also spoke with Deputy Prime Minister Anastas Mikoyan, using the occasion to ask that a letter be delivered to Nikita Khrushchev. Johnson tried to make it clear that the nation had no intention of invading Cuba despite the Soviet presence and Castro's support of hemispheric subversion. The president's briefing card for the meeting advised that he avoid specifics and be on his guard, especially since his visitor would be looking for departures from Kennedy policies. An interesting reaction from the Warsaw Pact came a few weeks later from a Communist news service in Budapest: "At the end of the first month of the 'Johnson regime' we can reaffirm that the new president was not sparing with tranquilizing statements and declarations of desires for peace. What we regret is the absence of concrete facts, new initiatives, and efforts to develop practical Soviet-American relations."⁶ Wooing Communist leadership with words might prove to be a waste of time.

The onset of the Kennedy-Johnson administration had coincided with a vast wave of political independence among European colonies in Africa. At the same time, in Asia, a tide of nationalism was blending with absorption of various forms of Marxism to produce a ferment that would show itself in many forms. While United States leaders continued to hope that there would emerge a flowering of democratic practice and a new birth of freedom everywhere, the facts were soon plainly displayed: authoritarianism, adventurism, repression, and outside efforts to implant communism or achieve economic gain were loose in what would come to be called the Third World.

The Kennedy legacy in Soviet-American relations was one of Cold War being waged openly by both powers. But an odd initiative toward establishing better relations after 1963 came from the late president's widow. Writing in the White House on December 1, whether with help or not is not known, Jacqueline Kennedy addressed a handwritten letter to Nikita Khrushchev! Thanking him for sending a representative to her husband's funeral, she said that relations with the Soviet leader had been "central" in Jack's mind. "You and he were adversaries, but you were allied in a determination that the world should not be blown up. You respected each other and could deal with each other. I know that President Johnson will make every effort to establish the same relationship with you. . . . I know President Johnson will continue the policy in which my husband so deeply believed—a policy of control and restraint—and he will need your help."⁷ Apparently no reply was received.

From abroad, early reactions to the loss of Kennedy had been: from London, nervousness—for the British had supported Kennedy's approach to British-American and East-West matters; and from the Soviets, hope for a continuation of improved communications. The French were said to have regretted losing the Kennedy of Young America. The Germans recalled how their hearts and imaginations had been captured by Kennedy in Berlin. Italians thought of Johnson's visit in September 1962. India was concerned about future aid, and the Japanese deplored the recent cancellation of bilateral trade talks. What would Johnson do? Argentina allegedly thought that it would be impossible to re-create the emotional commitment once felt toward Kennedy. In Washington a columnist expressed hope that people overseas would try to keep a sense of proportion, for acceleration in Kennedy mythology would be a substantial disservice.⁸

The Soviet Union would preserve a self-imposed moratorium on criticism of Johnson and his announced policies for some weeks. Continuation of Kennedy's policies would be welcome, guessed the United States Information Service. "The Soviets report the president's activities promptly and with reasonable accuracy, emphasizing statements which indicate a continuing American recognition of the need for peace." However, some policies were criticized: the presence in Vietnam, policies regarding Cuba and NATO, and the arms race. McNamara was the scapegoat. The assassination of Kennedy had been a plot by ultrarightists who were trying to change "progressive" directions in U.S. policy. China saw Johnson as carrying forward Kennedy's "two-faced tactics." Latin American countries admired the orderly succession under our constitutional system. In general, the press abroad began in late November with uncertainty in viewpoint but became increasingly gratified as Johnson took hold.[9]

President Johnson considered that his policies on Europe were unified around strengthening the Atlantic community. United States ties with Great Britain would remain close. Both problems and opportunities lay in securing Europe against the Soviet Union, in seeking equity in trade relationships, and in hoping to improve America's adverse balance of payments. There would be numerous meetings with heads of state and negotiations over the integrity of NATO as the French cut back on military participation. There was the ever-present temptation to engage in personal diplomacy. The president could not hope to match Eisenhower's prestige with Europeans, however, and a repeat of Kennedy's "Ich bin ein Berliner" triumph could not be expected. A trip to Europe was always a possibility, but Johnson was counseled not to go. The tall Texan did seem to strike something of a spark among Europeans, nevertheless. A 1965 report from the Paris embassy said that people in Europe were speaking about him with awe as well as affection. "There is great admiration for your monumental achievements, but at the same time it's almost as if you were a Paul Bunyan or some super human mythical figure beyond their comprehension. They've simply never confronted anyone like you." He really should come and be seen.[10]

In the summer of 1966, advisers told Johnson he should make a detailed statement on European policy. Rusk transferred a New York City speaking engagement of his to him, so that the National Conference of Editorial Writers on October 7 became the opportunity. In a serious frame of mind, the president saw three necessities in a Europe that had been at peace since 1945 but was still living under the threat of violence: NATO should be modernized, Western Europe further integrated, and progress in East-West relations accelerated. In those days it was still possible to refer optimistically to "the unification of Germany" as something to work toward.

With an eye on the Soviets and their Warsaw Pact, the president uttered his key phrase: "Our task is to achieve a reconciliation with the East—a shift from the narrow concept of coexistence to the broader vision of peaceful engagement." Endorsed was the Soviet-supported Oder-Neisse border between Poland and East Germany—a border that was then totally rejected by West Germany. This somewhat unorthodox move was accepted by Bonn in 1970, to the former president's gratification. An effort was made in this speech to further the cause of nonproliferation of nuclear weapons—a concern that would continue.

The Soviets did take note of the Johnson announcement of minor changes in trade policies toward them and the easing of credit restrictions. But Leonid Brezhnev would quickly assert that the United States was evincing a strange and persistent delusion when it announced such changes while continuing to wage the war in Vietnam. In so doing, he was proclaiming something that would later be called "linkage" and become part of the international vocabulary—to arise from our side when the Soviets brutally invaded Czechoslovakia, in 1968, and Afghanistan more than a decade later.

An area of strain was continuing American support of Radio Free Europe and Radio Liberty, whose long hours of anti-Communist foreign-language broadcasts originating from studios on the Continent appeared to be wholly financed by private donations. Revelation that they were being heavily funded by the CIA was embarrassing. As for the USSR, its Radio Moscow and its Radio Peace and Progress continued their shrill attacks on the West, twenty-four hours a day, matched to a degree by the quieter Voice of America and the prestigious BBC. The war for men's minds continued unabated during the 1960s, whatever the soothing but sometimes deceiving words used by diplomats.

Not, perhaps, since Herbert Hoover had received Ramsay MacDonald at Rapidan Camp in Virginia was a statesman received so informally as was Chancellor Ludwig Erhard of Germany in December 1963 at the Johnson Ranch in Texas. Wrote a local reporter: "The shining green foliage of the live oaks of the hill country, the shallow flow of the Pedernales and the fresh emerald patches of the small grain fields added the only color to the barren soil of a rainless fall and winter. This was the setting of this meeting." When Johnson delivered a short prayer, an astonished Texas reporter said it was the first time he had heard Johnson do that. "It impressed me. The presidency is sobering Lyndon Johnson as it has all those who preceded him." Since it was the Christmas and

New Year holiday period, it was not strange that Erhard's visit gave the Johnsons the chance to entertain old friends and associates, Texans all and persons of consequence in ranching and local life. The German culture in the region added much to the visit, impressing journalists who accompanied Erhard to America. Johnson was deeply gratified by the aura of friendship and cooperation that grew out of the visit. The most successful discussions, he thought, were those when the two talked frankly alone. Relations with Germany would surely be close in this administration, observers soon agreed.[11] Lady Bird felt correctly that "we had put a little more cement into the building of good relations."

Interaction with France during these years was considerably less satisfactory than with West Germany. This was an inheritance from Eisenhower's quarrel with de Gaulle over NATO's French headquarters; part was personalities; and there was sharp difference of opinion over the future of Southeast Asia. The personal enmity stemmed partially from a report that reached Johnson before his meeting with de Gaulle in the White House on November 25, 1963. The French leader apparently had told an Allied ambassador that the United States could not be counted on if the USSR invaded Europe. But when talking with Johnson, he said Frenchmen *knew* they could count on the United States. "I stared hard at the French President, suppressing a smile," records Johnson, noting how France had criticized how this nation lived up to its SEATO commitment. He resolved to avoid petty bickering while ignoring de Gaulle's future attacks on American policies. He proved to be careful indeed, at least in public. But it made neutralization an even less viable alternative in Vietnam.[12]

President Johnson naturally moved slowly in the policy areas of foreign affairs. His principles and plans appeared in a major address to an Associated Press luncheon in New York City on April 30, 1964. America's world policy began, he said, with protecting the country and preserving the liberty and happiness of its citizens. The nation sought no new territory, but the freedom of others was a continuing concern. To allies, we would be the most dependable and enduring of friends; to enemies, the most steadfast and determined of foes. Surrender anywhere would mean defeat everywhere. Here—with Southeast Asia as backdrop—was what the teacher in Johnson considered "inescapable teaching."

Military strength was to be the bedrock of our foreign policy. Resistance to Communist expansion without "purposeless provocation" and "needless adventure" was called a tested principle. Strengthening allies, and encouraging the independence and progress of developing countries, while still pursuing lasting peace, had been principles of American policy since 1945 and would continue to be basic. There were certain "areas of concern." First: to build military strength of unmatched might. Second: to resist efforts by Communists to extend their dominion and expand their power. Remember the Berlin airlift, the Korean War, the defense of Formosa, the Cuban crisis, and the struggle in Vietnam. Third: there had been work to revive the strength of allies, to oppose Communist encroachment, and to protect the American future. Fourth: to aid the independence and progress of developing nations and to help them resist outside domination. Fifth: to pursue peace through agreements that would decrease danger without decreasing security.

The principles were remarkably similar to those proclaimed by the State Department during the Kennedy administration, both in language and in thrust. Partisan politics, thought Johnson, would have to yield to national need. (The remark could be amplified: Republicans and other opponents should leave foreign policy to his team.) Areas of major concern to America were the relationship with the USSR; the development of the Atlantic partnership, the Alliance for Progress commitment in Latin America, together with the OAS effort to isolate Cuba, and the mixing somehow of anticommunism with economic progress. A "battle for freedom in the Far East" (for South Korea) had "proved the futility of direct aggression." The United States could wage a war against poverty in the new nations of Asia and Africa. In conclusion, the United States could never again retreat from world responsibility and would have to get used to working for liberty abroad as well as at home. The struggle would be unending, as dangers replaced dangers, challenges replaced challenges, and new hopes replaced old hopes. There would be no turning away. The inherited Kennedy team of speech writers had duly helped to preserve continuity; unfortunately, the ringing declaration to "bear any burden," et cetera, had already been used.

The speech to the Associated Press, with its linkage between the Kennedy and the Johnson administrations, was considered compass setting by the media. It was also seen, even this early, as something of a reply to Senator William Fulbright, chairman of the Foreign Relations Committee, who had been intimating that United States policies toward communism were rooted in myths. A new announcement in the speech was that production of weapons-grade nuclear materials was being reduced by the United States and the USSR; nevertheless, a new Hanford reactor would be able to replace the cutbacks if need be.

The solidly anti-Communist posture of the Kennedy-Johnson administrations, as well as their predecessors and successors, has been much noted; and by many liberal, radical, pacifist, and New Left circles it has been bitterly condemned. Yet the conduct of Moscow and Peking during those years was certainly of a kind to evoke suspicions and fears. President Johnson would be informed, for example, that in 1964 the Chinese had exported some 15 million books and huge quantities of seventeen periodicals, at a cost of about $25 million; the Third World was the chief target for what was almost entirely propaganda. For its part, Moscow spent $70 million for export of 45 million books and pamphlets in thirty-nine languages and another 28 million publications in twenty-four languages of the less-developed countries. Some 2.5 million pieces of Communist mail entered the United States monthly, a million of it from the USSR.[13] That the Communist forces on the planet were taking seriously their conflict with non-Communist governments and peoples seems, in the light of such astronomical figures, altogether clear. Small wonder the president stuck to his guns and considered that those who refused to admit the existence of a Communist threat were either naïve or culpable.

In Latin America, the administration inherited the mixed legacy of earlier years and two inescapable facts. Despite rich cultural heritages, the region was largely populated by undereducated and often impoverished masses who were ruled by undemocratic, even dictatorial governments. Eisenhower's Act of Bogota had seen the beginning of an assistance program called Operation Pan America. The next step had been Kennedy's Alliance for Progress. Disorder and poverty, it was hoped, would be targeted by a good neighbor United States. Yet Johnson also had to live with people's memories of the Bay of Pigs and other CIA projects in the hemisphere. Moreover, United States relations with the Organization of American States seemed to Latin America to be self-serving, domineering at the worst, and at best an afterthought on the part of the Yankee government. The president would struggle to make progress on these fronts during his years—only to move counterproductively later in response to some crises.

The task of focusing on a single administration in connection with hemispheric diplomacy is a thankless job, for exciting events tend to drive out the less exciting. Quiet diplomacy makes few headlines. Milton Eisenhower, when interviewed about Johnson's years in office, did not hesitate to assert, "I think there were more changes in policy toward Latin America by the United States during the Eisenhower administration than in any before that or since." Thus: "the basic legislation for the entire Alliance for Progress was not passed in the Kennedy administration, but in 1960 under Eisenhower. All President Kennedy did, very candidly, was to get a new euphonious name." This was reminiscent of Franklin Roosevelt's earlier adaptation of the Good Neighbor performance from Hoover. Johnson knew he was building on the past. When speaking of the Charter of Punta del Este of 1961, which created the Alliance for Progress, he linked it with the earlier Act of Bogota in 1960, for, said Milton Eisenhower, the language is "about word for word."[14]

With his year as a teacher of Spanish-speaking youngsters in Catulla, Texas, still fresh and warm in his mind, President Johnson took personal pleasure in finding any opportunity to forge warmer relationships with Latin American countries; he especially tried to strengthen the Alliance for Progress. While most Americans at the time had little interest in its well-being, scholars have been committed to the health of that Kennedy-launched body. Its start had been stumbling, as the per capita GNP failed to grow in the region. As Johnson came into office, the new body seemed to be on the verge of failure. This is worth remembering when one reads that during Johnson's years the alliance failed in its basic tasks.[15] Efforts to strengthen it often ran into opposition from major states in the region, however, and from European powers as well.

The president was destined to face problems in Panama, Brazil, Cuba, Peru, and Chile. His responsibilities in the region were carried in considerable part by Thomas C. Mann, Johnson's choice for assistant secretary for inter-American affairs. The two Texans agreed on a business-oriented and anti-Communist approach, avoiding disorder even at the cost of takeovers by the military within the country. No less than thirteen governments south of the United States would be taken over by the military during those years. Such events uniformly distressed many, while they concerned others very little, for increased order always had to be weighed against the risks in unaccustomed and sometimes disorderly democracy.[16] The Johnson administration would produce a Mann Doctrine in March 1964, whereby private United States investments would be protected; economic growth, furthered; and social reforms, not overly stressed. There would also be nonintervention, except that Communist factions would be kept from engineering takeovers à la Castro. Stability was valued, especially since many of the revolutionaries of the 1960s favored Marxist overthrow far more than creation of self-governing and reformist states. The Johnson policies could therefore be criticized as being baldly anti-Communist. The administration's posture throughout a coup in Brazil will emerge as archival documents are used more fully in the future.[17]

The president's most important noncrisis personal participation in Latin American affairs was attendance at the 1967 meeting of presidents at Punta del Este, Uruguay, where the Alliance for Progress had been created six years before. From April 12 to 14 the president engaged in "days of work as intensive as any I had experienced, except during a major crisis." Both bilateral and overall problems were discussed. Although a pledge to create a common market in the 1970s was made by the group, it did not emerge. America was a "junior partner" in the negotiations and plans; so, criticism was muted. The president was pleased, for he wanted governments to shift from tacit partnership with the United States to partnerships with each other. Rostow says, realistically, that the population problems of the region remained, rural modernization lagged, and there was continuing instability.[18] The president's conduct and performance were good, in any case, and he probably deserved the thrust of praise from friend Abe Fortas. "This is one of the historic achievements of your administration."[19] The president's pleasure should be emphasized, for venerable Democrat James Farley had written him very early, on his Coca Cola Company stationery, as he prepared an initial visit southward. "I will tell them . . . of your residence in Texas, on the Mexican border; that you have traveled extensively, and of your sympathy for the Latin countries, which is well and favorably known at least by the heads of those governments," he wrote.[20] For Johnson, it was a good feeling to think that one was building in areas of one's unique suitability.

The Dominican Republic, sharing with Haiti the island of Hispaniola in the West Indies, which had been Spanish for three centuries and was troubled with insolvent and antidemocratic government, was the locale of a crisis in 1965 which brought President Johnson into a no-win situation. He would later be charged with sending marines and keeping them there contrary to good neighborliness and an alleged obligation to let the OAS police the region. The event and Johnson's role in it created a sensation at the time, although he trod in the steps of Kennedy. His defender Rostow later termed the administration's response "the reluctant acceptance of a high posture."

The background can be quickly sketched. Its long-time dictator, Rafael Leonidas Trujillo y Molina, was assassinated in 1961; his successor lasted only briefly, after which the apparently Democratic Socialist Juan Bosch was elected president but was soon deposed. Now came a military junta; but on April 24/25, 1965 some of the army seized control of Santo Domingo in the name of Bosch, while a new junta took control elsewhere. Leftist forces in the city issued arms indiscriminately to the populace, so that in the face of actual disorder and the promise of much more, decisive action seemed to be indicated. A colonel now headed a new junta, which asked the United States to help "restore peace to the country." Our ambassador was not convinced at first, but he soon cabled that the situation was "deteriorating rapidly" and that "American lives are in danger." He and fellow officials agreed that "the time has come to land the marines." Evacuation of Americans was one problem, and security of all embassies and foreigners was another; general order was the sought-after goal.

President Johnson was certainly oriented toward the well-being of the Dominican Republic, for as vice-president he had been sent to that troubled island on a mission. As was usual with him, this circumstance meant that subsequent events became far more vivid and personal—a consequence of human nature. Having received cables begging for strong action, including one from the head of a political party and one from the chairman of the Dominican senate,[21] Johnson was not to be dissuaded by indecisive debate among OAS ambassadors in their council. By now, diplomats on the scene were fearful for their lives and took a more realistic view of the need for intervention than did leaders from the same countries who were safe in distant capitals, Johnson records. He also was persuaded to act by a conference call with Ambassador W. Tapley Bennett, Jr., who surmised that a Communist government might well emerge from a rebel victory; Bosch would then become a powerless figurehead. Food, medicines, and supplies were short; the lives of innocent people were at stake. "We were not using force to impose a political solution," says Johnson, noting his efforts to gain uniform action from major OAS members. This was finally achieved but well after the marines had landed and had the situation pretty well in hand.

Reactions in the domestic press to the energetic American action at first were favorable. Walter Lippmann backed the president, saying that United States action could be defended on the old-fashioned and classical diplomatic ground that the Dominican Republic lay squarely within the sphere of influence of the United States. It was only normal for a great power to insist that within its sphere of influence no other great power should exercise hostile military and political force; such spheres were fundamental, he thought. The *New York Daily News*, a newspaper that fully accepted the Vietnam adventure at the time, linked both matters, gushing: "It may be that Lyndon Johnson is a man of destiny, assigned by fate to clean up all or most of his inherited messes and thereby start world communism toward its downfall. Stranger things have happened, and we'll see what we'll see." The Castro takeover of Cuba was often mentioned as having taught a lesson. Americans in residence and visitors did have to be protected. It was assumed that there was need for the marines, who would surely leave routinely. Former President Eisenhower approved; Fulbright thought it right and proper; Senators Mike Mansfield, Frank Church, and Wayne Morse also favored the action. Taking a Cuban threat seriously, Latin American leaders and editors both applauded. So, it looked initially as though the president was on firm ground.[22] Judging from his press conference on April 27 and statements that he made on April 30 and May 1, the American action had not been based on a Communist threat.

Johnson soon justified his action, however, by telling the nation how he had thwarted communism. Local forces had been "really seized" by leaders trained in Cuba. They then "overthrew that government and became aligned with evil persons who had been trained in overthrowing governments and in seizing governments and establishing Communist control," he asserted. The slant in these speeches was hardly accidental. Bill Moyers wrote at the time to Richard Goodwin, "The president says to start outlining the kind of speech he will give if he has to on increased and/or continued U.S. intervention in D.R. He wants to tie it, of course, to the preservation of liberal and progressive goals in a hemisphere constantly under the threat of Communist perversion [sic] where every legitimate social revolution is a struggling infant subject to the ravages of disease, etc."[23] Soon the American liberal media turned hostile on such intervening to prevent another Castro-type Cuba, since correspondents on the scene could find few signs of Communists in positions of leadership. A concerned Justice Arthur Goldberg called Jack Valenti to suggest the appointment of someone who had unimpeachable liberal credentials as Johnson's personal representative to the Dominican Republic; this would quiet the liberal critics, he predicted.

Johnson may have been on firm legal ground in his counterintervention.[24] But American embassy and military personnel showed uncertainty about this when questioned. The White House staff nervously contemplated the bad situation that had developed with regard to their chief's credibility. Jack Valenti and Douglass Cater advised: "Some overriding questions that might be explained: Did we move too quickly, not consulting the OAS? Was it really true that the D.R. was within hours of a Communist takeover before we moved in? What should now be the goals for that country? Will we do it again elsewhere in the hemisphere?" They attached a CIA memorandum, "The Communist Role in the Dominican Revolt," saying that the president "could display it to the group without actually letting them see what is in it. This publicizes the fact that we have specific evidence of Communist takeover." Now greatly worried, Valenti wrote his boss, "We spent the entire day X-raying the report on Communist takeover in the Dominican Republic. It needs more work. That work is now going on. It will be ready about Monday. We thought it best to make ABSOLUTELY certain before anything was released.''[25]

The White House was, by mid May, well aware that its problems with the media over the Dominican Republic were: Why had the United States acted on April 28 without consulting the OAS? and, Were the Communists really in charge by April 30? Valenti told his chief, after study by a task force, that while there were ample Communists and ''we know they were taking over,'' we ''can't prove it without doubt.'' American agents must not be exposed. ''One key point in establishing Communist intrusion: we must not make our case for Commies so strong that it becomes *the* reason for our sending troops—instead of our stated and truthful reason which was to save American lives.'' Meanwhile, OAS support developed belatedly. Keen lawyer Fortas pointed out to Valenti that the United States had a plan for getting rid of Communists in the Dominican Republic; but after a three-man committee of the OAS might take over, would we be able to share control with them? He thought not; he wanted to see his old friend about this.[26]

What President Johnson did on April 28 was to send four hundred marines, with an eye to preventing any acceleration of the disorder; then the next day he landed the force that would reach a surprising twenty-two thousand, intending to prevent the apparently Communist-dominated forces from taking over the country and intending to move toward free elections. Says Rostow, he faced ''not a doctrine but a situation.''[27] By June 1966 the Dominican people would, in a free election, turn away from Bosch—who had been the object of so much favorable publicity in the American media and one whose fortunes had been eclipsed.

The event left scars and bad memories among Latin American specialists and among Democratic Socialists in the hemisphere. But the president had acted much as Kennedy had acted in the Berlin Wall and Cuban missile crises and as Truman had in Korea. He wanted no setback *anywhere* in the global Cold War. The cause of progressive government, but not Marxist government, in the Dominican Republic was advanced. Observer Paul Nitze later judged that both our action and the size of our commitment were appropriate, and Gen. Andrew J. Goodpaster believed that ''given the premises on which he was operating, it was very effectively and quickly conducted.'' But Milton Eisenhower told Johnson privately that he had overreacted. The president had strolled with him around the White House lawn, explaining the matter in detail, after which they had root beer in a tiny room next to the Oval Office. When asked what he thought, Eisenhower replied that the initial sending of marines had been in harmony with international law. But sending more forces to intervene in the civil war in order to avoid a Castro-type activity had been wrong; a few days of waiting and the use of the OAS would have been better. He talked twenty minutes while the president first sat down and then rose and paced silently around the room. Now the president invited Eisenhower to have lunch with some staff members and himself, on which occasion the president repeated almost word for word what Eisenhower had said, although at the time the visitor had wondered if Johnson was listening! He repeated the recommendations that had been made. In time—for whatever reason—he ended up doing exactly what his visitor had suggested.[28]

There was definitely a need for making a rapid decision. The consequences of doing nothing, of waiting for joint agreement followed by joint effort, could well have proven bloody. (Yet the action, overall, cost nine marines killed and thirty wounded.) At Punta del Este in 1962 it had been agreed that communism was "incompatible with the principles of the inter-American system." When endangered by communism, the member states could "take those steps that they may consider appropriate for their individual and collective self-defense." Unfortunately, it was impossible to line up any Communist fifth column for inspection by American media and critics; so Johnson had to stay on the defensive. McGeorge Bundy wrote to the veteran Socialist Norman Thomas: "I think that our position, all along, has been plain—full support for OAS efforts in behalf of a political solution which will be satisfactory and responsive to the majority of the Dominican people." Some have accepted at least the assessment that there was a future Communist threat; thus, Castro-ite forces indeed might have emerged someday with control of the state. Few have forgiven the administration for allegedly weakening the OAS and the entire concept of achieving democratic change without revolution.[29] At home, Senator William Fulbright, chairman of the Senate Foreign Relations Committee, never recovered from the shock of Johnson's intervention—a loss for the president that had ominous overtones.

As the Johnson administration considered its relationship with mainland China, it had to keep in mind the anti-Communist sentiment of the American people. The nation possessed treaty relationships with China's neighbors to the East—South Korea, Japan, the Republic of China, and the Philippines—and saw these as part of a containment policy of the kind represented elsewhere by NATO. The United States remembered the World War II alliance with Chiang Kai-shek, as well as the Red Chinese intervention that had proved so costly in the Korean "police action." A rift between China and the USSR in the late 1950s meant that there seemed to be no pressing urgency in seeking closer relations with Mao's government, and chaotic internal conditions in mainland China (i.e., the Cultural Revolution) favored the lack of action in diplomacy.

The Johnson policy of not aggressively seeking rapprochement with China met with little general resistance, for scholarly opponents were handicapped by the public memory of China's intervention against the United States during the Korean War and the plain fact that the Chinese were supplying weapons to the North Vietnamese. An effective though muted voice was the American Friends Service Committee, which declared in 1965: "The United States and the People's Republic of China have become almost completely separated by a wall of mutual hostility. There is no cultural exchange, no trade, no intervisitation, and no diplomatic contact except for occasional official encounters in off-the-record talks at Warsaw since 1954." The atmosphere was "war, not peace." The Quakers made it clear that they favored a world security community to replace violence. In actuality, United States contacts with China at Warsaw added up to more high-level diplomat contact than with all the Western nations who maintained relations in Peking.[30] Sessions might deal with charges of aggression in Laos, Vietnam, or the Taiwan Strait; a missing yacht; or Chinese exposition of a grand plan for world disarmament.

At first, Peking seemed remote. But the explosion in the atmosphere of the first Chinese atomic device in 1964 focused attention on a possible future threat. In speech after speech during the fall, candidate Johnson used the event to good effect, reassuring the public that the new development meant little to American security. Our nuclear superiority was overwhelming. We were prepared! There is no discussion of China policy in *The Vantage Point*, but Johnson personnel were aware that wars of national liberation were being aided by the Chinese in Malaysia, Laos, Indonesia, and perhaps Africa; foreign minister Chen Yi boasted in 1965, "Thailand is next." In Asia there seemed to be developing a "Djakarta-Hanoi-Peking-Pyongyang axis," to which Cambodia and Laos would be added in time.

There was a continuing struggle over the future of Red China and of Nationalist China in the United Nations during those years. Lines were sharply drawn, with many articles and vigorous letters to the editor displaying uncompromising attitudes on both sides. Neglect—hostile rather than benign—seemed as good a political posture to Johnson as it had to his predecessor. In his first address on foreign policy, he said, as to China, that so long as they pursued aggression and preached violence "there can be and will be no easing of relationships." America had an "unalterable commitment" to the defense of "Free China." Mainland

179

aid to North Vietnam in the 1960s made it seem unwise "to get into any debate publicly on the subject of policy toward China," says Paul Nitze. This went so far that when Nitze wrote an article in 1967 about problems then existing between China and America and had it accepted by *Foreign Affairs*, the State Department prohibited publication of it, quoting a rule that "no one was to discuss policy toward Communist China."[31] Rusk had endured a similar humiliating restriction during the Kennedy years.

Meanwhile, the administration had to grasp at straws when assessing Chinese intentions. One clue appeared in the *New Republic*, on February 27, 1965, which revealed that Mao Tse-tung had told Edgar Snow (author of *Red Star over China*, a sympathetic account of Mao's rise to power) about the possibilities Mao saw in Vietnam. "First, a conference might be held and United States withdrawal would follow. Second, the conference might be deferred until after the withdrawal. Third, a conference might be held but United States troops might stay around Saigon, as in the case of South Korea. Finally, the South Vietnamese front [the Viet Cong] might drive out the Americans without any conference or international agreement." While there was hope for improved Sino-American relations, it would take time, said Mao; maybe there would be no improvement during this generation. Snow paraphrased him as concluding: "He was soon going to see God. According to the laws of dialectics all contradictions must finally be resolved, including the individual." There was little in the suggested options to cheer up those who were seeking closer ties soon. Still, Secretary Rusk told the House Committee on Foreign Affairs on April 20, 1966, that the nation sought eventually to establish friendly relations with China—at the very moment when the United States was for the first time bombing the environs of Hanoi.

The administration was perplexed. Should a major speech on the subject of China be delivered to clear the air? In early November 1967, staff member Al Jenkins prepared a full-dress speech on China for possible presidential delivery. It began, "Tonight I want to talk about Communist China and its relation to others, including the United States." No such speech would be delivered. Here is what seemed possible at the time: first came a catalog of Chinese setbacks, including the failure to prevail in Indonesia and the expulsion of diplomats from many African states. However, "It is obviously impossible to identify any direct causal links between the allied stand in Vietnam and Peking's reverses." America was not waging a holy war against all things labeled "Communist," and "we pose no threat to the Chinese government or territory"—unless provoked. The more humanistic, eclectic, practical traits of the Chinese might soon prevail; when that happened, both the hand and the heart of the world would be extended. We were not implacably hostile; we looked forward to a time of "reasonableness" and would engage in "mutual endeavor" if the Chinese ceased to use force.[32] Here is a vignette of what might have been tried, but what might have been ignored, by Mao. James C. Thompson, Jr., said later he had researched thoroughly in the State Department the question of Vietnam's relationship to the fact that Indonesia had driven out communism, but he had found none. Yet qualified experts thought that a connection was possible; therefore, Vietnam provided some payoff for those who believed this way.[33]

Could Lyndon Johnson have visited the People's Republic of China in the late 1960s and worked out an agreement along the lines of the Shanghai Accord of February 27, 1972, after something like Nixon's "extensive, earnest and frank discussions" on normalization of relations? It certainly would seem not, considering that the public then thought of China, correctly enough, as a supplier of munitions that had killed American boys and as our enemy during the Korean War. There would be new possibilities only when Chinese-Soviet enmity intensified and when a fresh face entered the White House.

The United States government paid little attention to Africa and its affairs during these years. From having twice been to Senegal, Johnson thought he had as vice-president gotten some perspective into "what life in an African village was like and what its problems were." He knew the continent's statesmen hated being considered pawns in a game played between Communist and non-Communist nations. There would be correspondence between the president and the heads of African countries, and he invited them to Washington to share ideas and work out plans for cooperation. Johnson says he knew that there was need for "a coherent American policy to deal with the African continent, at least that portion south of the Sahara." Dealing on "a buckshot basis" was to be eschewed; there should be continuity in operations, ideals, and programs. Assistant Secretary of State G. Mennen Williams, a former Democratic governor of Michigan, early spelled out African policy for Johnson as he saw it: The United States would oppose South Africa's apartheid policy by continuing the arms embargo; but economic sanctions were considered to be impractical. The Angolan people should have self-determination at such time as Portugal set up more democratic institutions there. African unity would be supported—that is, "Africa for the Africans"; and "What we want for Africa is what the Africans want for themselves."[34] Specialists who were aware of African regionalism—north and south of the Sahara, east and west, and the South

African nation as a special area—would have recoiled from such slo-
ganeering.

A big public push in connection with the once-dark continent came
on May 26, 1966, the third anniversary of the Organization of African
Unity, when the ambassadors of thirty-six African countries and three
hundred guests came to the White House. "I made the first address by
an American President devoted wholly to Africa," Johnson records
proudly. He decried living by a double standard: professing abroad
what we do not do at home. While the United States had ties to Europe
(NATO), Latin America (OAS), Southeast Asia (SEATO), Australia and
New Zealand (ANZUS), coupled with bilateral arrangements with
Japan, South Korea, and Nationalist China, we knew the new Africa
"wanted to handle its problems alone as much as possible." He offered
help in training Africans to develop modern communications and
transportation systems. Aid to education was extended. Soon the
president would have a major report, prepared by Edward M. Korry,
ambassador to Ethiopia, which the chief executive claimed much later
was "the most comprehensive study of Africa and our role there ever
compiled for a President." But at the time, October 5, 1966, in NSC 356,
he ordered it kept secret. Its thrust: in Africa we had become enmeshed
in an unmanageable range of projects without having competence in
any. To implement the report a committee of experts in the State
Department and AID was formed, together with White House representatives; and a steering committee from the United States, the United
Kingdom, Italy, Belgium, and Canada did consider the plans. But,
"Economic and social development is a slow business, especially among
nations in a very early stage of modernization," said the president.

Johnson's noteworthy address at Howard University on race relations had an impact in Africa, since a defamatory book called *The
Invisible Government* was being used in Africa against the United States.
"Among the questions most frequently asked," wrote one journalist,
"are those about American civil rights, the CIA and the young people,
American national politics, Vietnam [and] foreign aid."[35] Preoccupation
with Vietnam and the strategic struggle with the USSR kept African
affairs on the back burner, even though routine misery on that continent
measurably transcended that in Southeast Asia. Growth of interest in
the once Underdeveloped, then Developing, and now Third World
nations lay years ahead, even though an encyclical letter by Pope Paul
VI in March 1967 on their many needs attracted attention in America.

There was powerful but quiet intervention to prevent Greece and
Turkey from going to war over Cyprus in August 1964 and in November
1967. One observer has said that negotiator Cyrus Vance performed

"one of the most remarkable jobs that I think has ever been done . . . ; without [him] there would have been a war between Greece and Turkey." This is memorable, for "few people in the world can say that they stopped a war." On another occasion, White House intervention at John Kenneth Galbraith's initiation saved the Greek scholar Andreas Papandreou from probable execution and helped to obtain his release from confinement. Such unqualified successes would not be numerous, however. An insider has said, "The Johnson years were obviously preoccupied with Vietnam, and the political niceties of Italy [for example] were only a secondary matter." Still, negotiations related to Vietnam could spill over to involve states in the Asian theater, for better or worse. There were, during the last days, 39,300 U.S. servicemen on 146 bases in Japan. Politician Johnson, strangely, told Prime Minister Eisaku Sato in November 1967, that the question of the complete reversion of Okinawa could not be settled until after the 1968 election. After one Asian negotiating trip, the president was told by old hand Averell Harriman that "the Manila Conference and your trip to Asia were well received everywhere—by the governments, and in the press."[36]

During the post-World War II period the ancient stresses between Muslims and Jews accelerated with the creation of a new Israeli state, which incorporated shrines that were holy to both peoples. In June 1967 there erupted the sudden Six Day War between Israel and Egypt, in which the former attacked first because of concern over the closing of its avenue to the sea. The event was bound to evoke emotions in the United States, where Christians and Jews alike venerated the Holy Land. A president from a Democratic party that was financed noticeably by many Americans who had a deep personal interest in the security and welfare of Israel would predictably give the Middle East his full attention. Very early, in the fall of 1963, he told an Israeli diplomat: "You have lost a very great friend, but you have found a better one." On another occasion he observed, "I have always had a deep feeling of sympathy for Israel and its people, gallantly building and defending a modern nation against great odds and against the tragic background of Jewish experience." He seems to have given Arab concerns far less attention.

War in the Sinai, if it came, might spread to involve the great powers, some thought. Since the United States was the leading arms supplier to Israel, any president would have had difficulty in being nonpartisan, of course. Israel's president had said almost to himself when he left the White House in early 1964, "I go back to Israel confident and cheered by the knowledge that the man in the White House is a friend of our cause."[37] When Egypt closed the crucial Gulf of

Aqaba, an Israeli sea highway, the war then begun by Israel, which was said to be preemptive, became an immediate White House concern, not the least because Syrian involvement seemed likely.

Walt Rostow asserts that "Johnson tried hard, but failed, to keep Israel from initiating hostilities on June 5 [1967]."[38] The fact of failure should be stressed. Faced with the difficulty of getting Nasser's Egypt to reopen the international waterway, Johnson leaned on Foreign Minister Abba Eban, especially in a meeting of May 26, telling him very carefully, "Israel will not be alone unless it decides to go alone." This was repeated "very positively," in the hope of preventing an Israeli attack. "All of our intelligence people are unanimous," he unwisely added, however, "that if the UAR (United Arab Republic) attacks, you will whip hell out of them." Could this have been translated by the listener into: "If you proceed, you will easily prevail"? Israel wondered if the United States, the British, or maybe the United Nations would be able to achieve Israel's goals for it. There was this odd remark by Johnson: "I am fully aware of what three past presidents have said, but that is not worth five cents if the people and the Congress do not support the President." By this, Johnson meant, he says, that his own bitter experience showed that Congress might again "turn tail and run if the going got rough."

On the weekend of June 3, on the eve of the attack, Johnson had the opportunity to tell the heavily Jewish audience at a dinner given by the New York State Democratic party how unthinkable war was regarded by the United States. But he only referred to "concern" and said he was in "contact," adding, "To go beyond this tonight would not serve the cause of peace or would not be helpful." This was hardly a public demand for Israeli patience or a public notice that, one way or another, the straits would eventually be opened. So, Johnson deferred to Israel—with an eye on domestic politics—and he failed to preserve the peace. When it was all over and Israel had acquired vast new territories, Abe Fortas was one who said enthusiastically to Johnson: "You've handled the Israel-Arab problem magnificently."[39] Much depended on one's point of view.

Johnson, Rusk, Rostow, and others seem to have thought they had a commitment from Israel to hold up action for two weeks. "During those trying days I used all the energy and experience I could muster to prevent war. But I was not too hopeful," claims the president. Many Vietnam doves would have had to convert themselves into Israeli hawks to get a resolution of support for executive action through the Congress, he says. He thought his position of weakness was one that the dynamic Israelis could easily sense. And they were uncertain if a four-nation task force would ever challenge the closing of the Gulf of Aqaba; they considered the UN ineffective, for the French were refusing to take a stand. Rusk candidly told our ambassadors in a cable that "Israel will fight and we could not restrain her." Why, then, did the attack begin? "Only the Israelis themselves can describe and assess the reasons for their decision," says Johnson, who was, not surprisingly, unwilling to call it "aggression."[40]

Could a different American president, one less politically handicapped, have better conveyed the unacceptability of such a devastating and destabilizing strike? Possibly it is an illusion that a great power can control the ultimate policy decisions of any beleaguered but powerful small one. A State Department briefing officer said on June 5, "Our position is neutral in thought, word, and deed." Then Dean Rusk had to add that the word "neutrality" absolutely did not involve "indifference"! The press was not satisfied. "Mr. Rusk, under our concept of neutrality, would it be a violation of one of the countries involved to raise funds by financing or floating bonds in this country in your judgment?" Rusk was noncommital. "*Are* we neutral in thought, word, and deed?" The reply: "I don't, I think, need to get into particular phraseology that goes beyond what the president has said and what I have said. Thank you."[41]

A shocking event of the war, which got little attention then or later, until 1982, was the brutal Israeli attack on the United States communications ship *Liberty* in the Mediterranean on June 8. Final American casualties came to 34 dead and 171 wounded. At the time, the ship could have determined the order of attack in a possible war between Israel and Syria, and perhaps have ended the Israeli news blackout on the extent of conquests. The press quickly lost interest in the attack. Only one question was ever asked in a presidential press conference, with the commander in chief replying evasively, "I think you know about as much about it as we do." Johnson's memoir gives only the very low initial casualty figures and calls the event an "accident," an "incident," and an "error." But the State Department on June 11 told Israel, behind the scenes, that the attack was "quite literally incomprehensible" and showed "military irresponsibility reflecting reckless disregard for human life." Initially, the American dead were buried at Arlington with a plaque "Died in the Eastern Mediterranean," but this was changed under pressure in 1982 to "Killed—USS *Liberty*."

There is need for a carefully crafted professional book on this episode. A few facts were revealed in 1970, when Phil Goulding, former head of public affairs at the Pentagon, discussed it in his memoir.[42] The United States court of inquiry convened by the navy stayed out of sensitive international questions, he admitted. The reason for tough orders given to ship's personnel to preserve permanent silence on the episode was *Liberty's* function as a technical research and electronic intelligence gathering (i.e., "elint") ship; this resulted in an effective cover-up. An article for a navy audience appeared in 1978, and the next year there was a little-noted book, *Assault on the Liberty,* complete with interviews and pertinent documents, prepared by the ship's angry cryptographic officer. Some documents were used at the Johnson Library, but much more exists.[43]

The facts make for ugly reading. In execution of direct orders from the Joint Chiefs of Staff the ship was in international waters, some fourteen miles off the coast (fifteen miles north of the Sinai Peninsula) and some fifty miles from Egypt. A change in orders specifying a move to a hundred miles from shore failed to arrive. *Liberty* was a former Liberty (merchant) ship now covered with sophisticated antennae, and over complement with a crew of more than three hundred. Its simple armament consisted of four machine guns. The number GTR5 appeared in very large letters (the figure 5 was ten feet high) near the bow; LIBERTY was on the stern. Speed was five knots, and the wind made the national ensign fly smartly in the breeze. Israeli planes had circled and inspected the ship thirteen times over a 16-hour period. The two-stage daylight attack consisted of a 20- to 25-minute strafing by Mirage and Mystere jets with rockets and napalm, followed by a torpedo-boat attack with torpedoes and deck guns. (During the attack a 7-by-13-foot flag was added but was perhaps obscured by smoke.) Helicopters and two extra jets hovered and circled overhead.

Communications were inhibited by the total destruction of normal gear, but it is said that when emergency gear was used, the Israelis heavily jammed the channels. Those aboard the *Liberty* had no idea what government was striving to obliterate it, nor did the Sixth Fleet when it first received sketchy details. Even the White House was ignorant for a time both on this and the attack by the aircraft, but the Israeli government hastened to admit responsibility, apologized, and offered to pay damages. The failure in official communications by the United States must be stressed, first to last. It was of a kind with the failure at Pearl Harbor; a similar case was the sinking of the U.S. cruiser *Indianapolis* in 1945 without word being spread appropriately. Messages received and memoranda created at the White House were error-filled and must have made for uneasiness from the beginning.

There is no doubt at all that Israel, engaged in waging war, used its air force and navy to try to totally destroy a ship near the war zone, one that was clearly marked and beyond the twelve-mile limit. It has become my opinion that no prima facie case has ever been made for the idea of an intentional attack on an identified ship on the orders of the Israeli civilian government. Given highly visible prior reconnaissance, it simply cannot be assumed that top military officials knowingly ordered an attack on this American ship, whatever the importance of possible gains in operational secrecy during the war. An investigation by Israel in a few days produced a number of plausible and rather fantastic reasons why the mistake could have happened without command error per se. Commenting on these to his superiors in a cable, the naval attaché of the United States in Tel Aviv at the time could scarcely contain his disgust and anger. He said that when he had been asked to comment informally, he had simply kept his mouth shut and made no reply, pretending he had not heard the question.

While indignant at all insinuations of deliberate wrongdoing, Israel quickly paid $3,325,500 to next of kin of the thirty-four dead. A year later, under pressure, it also paid $3,566,457 in claims to the wounded, although private lawyers took a noticeable share of this. For years there was no payment for the ship itself, but in the 1980s, with renewed publicity, Israel paid a niggardly $6 million for destroying a sophisticated ship valued at some $33 million. This long-delayed result can be partially explained by the public silence of President Johnson throughout and the handling of government protestations in June 1967 only behind the scenes at the State Department level. The contrast with the dramatic tactics that this presidency used in connection with Tonkin Gulf is marked. Perhaps the difference is attributable to certain realities in the financing of American political parties and the power of nationwide solicitude for a hard-pressed religious homeland. After all, as the Pentagon bitterly told the world on June 10, 1967, "the identification markings of U.S. naval vessels have proved satisfactory for international recognition for nearly two hundred years." All marking on the *Liberty* and the flag had been clearly visible, it insisted. Oddly, the Pentagon told all hands who had survived this awful event "that they were to pipe down." The public-affairs chief says that the attack "was no accident—mistaken identity perhaps, but no accident." Johnson used the hot line to tell an impressed Chairman Kosygin that we were sending aircraft to investigate the attack, even though we didn't. A prominent Israeli figure, Chaim Herzog, wrote in 1982 that the United States just "saw fit" to position an intelligence-gathering ship off the coast of a friendly nation in time of war without giving any warning whatsoever and without advising of the position of the ship. In final comment on this episode, we may want at least to consider the observation of a historian who is well versed in the episode: "Nations do not have 'friends.' They have only interests. . . . In any given set of circumstances nations are guided to action by what they perceive to best serve their own interests." Dean Rusk said in 1981 that the attack on the *Liberty* "was and remains a genuine outrage."[44] The conduct of the Johnson administration in reaction was not much better. Only a full congressional hearing, it appears, will ever reveal the full facts and clear the air on an episode that has been swept under the rug too long.

A tense moment in the Middle Eastern conflict occurred on June 10, when for a time in the Situation Room the staff thought that the movements and intentions of the Soviets were in doubt. On the hot line, Kosygin spoke of "a very crucial moment" having arrived, and warned of a "grave catastrophe." Israel must halt operations within a few hours, or the Soviet Union would take "necessary actions, including military." The word "military" was checked over and over for a possible error in translating by the Johnson team, who would remember that moment as a time of utmost gravity. CIA Director Richard Helms later recalled that personnel used "the lowest voices I had ever heard in a meeting of that kind." The United States fleet was ordered to change course, with confidence that the Russians would notice, and Kosygin was informed that Israel was indeed close to a cease-fire. This Soviet-American crisis was soon over, with Johnson later crediting the hot line for much of the result.

To a National Foreign Policy Conference for Educators on June 19, 1967, the president was now ready to state what he called "Five Great Principles of Peace in the Middle East," which were: recognition of the right to national life; justice for refugees; maritime passage; limits to the arms race; and independence and territorial integrity for all. The parties concerned must learn to reason together. Rostow says that Johnson, to the end of his term, made it clear to Israeli officials that he regretted their decision to go to war on June 5, but that he did this "without rancor or moralizing." The partisan Middle Eastern policy of those years seems not to have been America's finest hour, especially since the president resisted efforts to draw the United States too deeply into the negotiating process.[45] This was a decision that the next Democrat to occupy the White House would reverse with a flourish.

The full dimensions of presumed American commitment against communism in the 1960s were impressive. The nation had treaty obligations, as Rusk testified in 1966; these were to 42 countries out of the 117 on the planet at the time. But the United States, he said, would "in the appropriate way" (meaning in the United Nations or elsewhere) "presumably give aid and support to those who are victims of the kind of aggression which would have worldwide implications." If we have a base in a country with or without a treaty it "clearly signifies an interest and concern on our part with the security of that country." Thus, "No would-be aggressor should suppose that the absence of a defense treaty, congressional declaration, or U.S. military presence grants immunity to aggression." Here was a most impressive commitment to police the planet, at least most of it.

Among those listening to this assertion of broad responsibility was Senator George Aiken. "Are we bound to fight communism wherever it exists?" he asked. Said Rusk, "No, sir, no sir, we are not, we are not." We were not fighting communism to destroy it as a social or political organization; rather, we were assisting allies to meet Communist aggression in one way or another under one circumstance or another, said the secretary of state of a nation that was already overinvolved in distant Southeast Asia.[46]

One scholar observed in 1968 that for twenty years there had been a "grand consensus" in United States foreign policy. It had been agreed, said Seyom Brown, that the primary threat to the national security was Soviet expansion. The Soviets wanted to expand; growth in their power would bring eventual control over us. It was agreed that the only critical obstacles to such expansion would have to come from the United States; only military power would suffice. Finally, establishment of additional Communist regimes, plus expansion of those in existence, would add to the Soviets' global power and would increase their capability for expansion. The Communist powers were assumed to be allies—or at least they were considered to be a unit or unified.[47] Understanding this is basic to understanding foreign affairs during Johnson's presidency.

Some sophistication is required when judging the attitude of the United States toward the United Nations during these years. For extreme partisans of world-order planning and for those who were unwilling to admit that there were flaws both in the UN Charter and in performance, nothing short of surrender of American sovereignty would do. For example, how far should the nation go in joining with UN members in conventions on various subjects? Such agreements as those on genocide, slavery, forced labor, and women were not ratified by the United States. When, in 1966, one on racial discrimination came up for signature, it was our policy to sign but not to push for its ratification. It would have no legal effect, Walt Rostow told the president. One might wonder why a civil-rights administration should have stood back from recommending ratification, but the agreement contained controversial issues: an international committee could request information on civil rights; there was reference to discrimination in "any field of public life"; and what would happen to freedom of speech if dissemination of racist ideas were prohibited? The International Court of Justice might impact United States sovereignty.[48]

No amount of praise lavished on the United Nations in presidential speeches sufficed for critics at the time, not even the message on its twentieth anniversary, when Johnson said: "Mankind has found a forum in the United Nations. Man's hopes have leaped and his fears have shrunk because of the force and influence of the United Nations."[49] Criticism quite naturally revolved around the refusal to center Vietnam peace negotiations with Hanoi at Morningside Heights, New York City, site of the UN. Nevertheless, President Johnson did pay his dues to United Nations partisans. He gave three major speeches before that body, beginning on December 17, 1963, when he made clear the continuity of American purposes and policies following the assassination of Kennedy. Next came the twenty-fifth anniversary meeting in San Francisco, where he spoke on June 25, 1965. On June 12, 1968, he again addressed the world body. Appointment of so strong a figure as Justice Arthur Goldberg to represent the nation in the UN was a dramatic bid for support. Few said that Lyndon Johnson, a man with a background so remote from Morningside Heights, had done enough. There was, fortunately for him, a massive decline in United Nations prestige among typical Americans in those years; a continuing Gallup poll on "United Nations performance" saw a "good" rating of only 49 percent in 1967 drop to 44 in 1970, 35 in 1971, and 33 in 1975.[50] Even though Johnson saw himself in the image of internationalist (he still lashed out at "isolationism" after he was out of office), he knew full well the limits of UN performance and popularity, even if the naïve could not.

The UN Charter had indicated that efforts at revising it might be made after ten years. In September 1965 two amendments took effect, but a general overhaul of the charter was resisted within the organization, which was increasingly subject to the desires of the many small developing nations of the Third World. A new group in America, World Peace through World Law (renamed the World Law Fund) became active, and an impressive line-by-line rewrite of the charter appeared as a proposal in book form at the hands of two Harvard professors. Such scholarly effort had an impact on a handful, but there is no sign that President Johnson saw any merit in so esoteric an exercise as unilaterally redrafting America's most comprehensive treaty obligation—given the apparent political disinterest. There was also no mileage in creating a stir when there was no prospect of victory in the UN, for in that body during these years, there was a sharp decline in the ability of the United States to prevail in votes. The new enlargement of the Security Council (to 15) and the expanded Economic and Social Council (now 27), together with new geographical-distribution requirements in seating, showed how the nonpermanent Council members were scoring gains over the large nations that had been victorious in World War II.

President Johnson was determined to outdo his predecessors in the field of foreign affairs. He frequently had his staff make a count of what he had done and then lay it side by side with the performances of other presidents. One such comparison was between his meetings with heads of state and those of his predecessors. It was gratifying to learn that the total was 301 for his five years, compared with 97 for Kennedy, 185 for Eisenhower, 70 for Truman, and 97 for Franklin Roosevelt (the terms were of different length, however). And 101 of his meetings had been outside the United States in 21 countries (Kennedy—14; Eisenhower—35; Truman—5; Franklin Roosevelt—23; Hoover—10). So "performance" in foreign affairs had been duly quantified, though little was said about the proliferation of new countries![51]

Few of his countrymen had any idea of how much raw effort went into his role as diplomat. Repeatedly, there was burdensome preparation for meetings with heads of state, ambassadors, and media representatives. Staff members offered guidance, while old friends provided sage counsel, it was certainly hoped. There were innumerable memorandums on problems and opportunities abroad, as well as meetings with their drafters. Typical was Walt Rostow's advice on a forthcoming meeting with historian Henry F. Graff in early 1968. Make sure he knows that Vietnam concerns do not inhibit conducting a global foreign policy, the president was told. Concerns are regionalism and holding the line in Europe, with or without de Gaulle; some progress has been made with the USSR; note improvements in policies regarding trade, money, water, food, population, and so forth; be confident on world movement away from extremism. In short, show that while others were focusing just on Vietnam, the president was building "a structure of world arrangements of partnership."[52] Given Johnson's fabulous memory, it was certain that professional advice like this was never wasted.

The time ultimately came for the former president to tell a team that was creating drafts for his memoirs the intimate details of earlier decision making. Pressed on the Dominican Republic episode (apparently by Harry Middleton in July 1969), he finally said wearily: "I remember very little about that period. The reason is, it happened so fast. When you're in the presidency, and when you've got a major decision to make, you just put everything out of your mind and focus on that decision like a laser beam and when the decision is finally made you just put everything else out of your mind because there's another one right behind it and then you've got to focus in on that."[53]

Given his early hopes and expectations, Johnson would feel both satisfaction and dismay with the emerging world of the 1970s. In 1970/71 Freedom House found that the United States was "dangerously polarized" at home when debating foreign-policy issues, even to the point where it was "superpatriots" versus "antipatriots." An anti-Communist crusade was meeting head-on with the popular illusion of détente. World peace was in jeopardy.[54] Fortunately, the man at the Ranch could always speculate that things might have been different if only the Democrats had prevailed in the 1968 presidential election! His total impression of foreign affairs from 1963 to 1969, overall, must have resembled the assessment in a partisan book of 1968: "Confident of the ultimate support of the American people, he subordinates passion to prudence, and politics to policy, as he pursues a steady course with formidable energy and imagination."[55] In any case, one possible conclusion emerges clearly: Motivated by a combination of political sagacity and idealism, Lyndon Johnson took very seriously his responsibilities in foreign affairs, although naturally with mixed results both at home and abroad. This politician had done the best he could to be a world statesman—given his own abilities, his built-in limitations as a dedicated partisan, the kind of advice available to him, Soviet and Chinese hostility, the albatross of Vietnam in image and reality,[56] and the sheer magnitude of intractable world problems.

9

★ ★ ★ ★ ★

BUILDING POWER
ON EARTH AND IN SPACE

The Cold War and man's long quest for knowledge about his universe blended as the Johnson administration engaged in research and development of space vehicles and futuristic weapons systems from 1963 to 1969. Strategic deterrence of the Soviet Union was one goal; placing a man temporarily on the moon before the end of the decade was another.

In Lyndon Johnson, the nation had probably the best qualified among leading political figures for leadership in the new age. Formerly chairman of the Senate Subcommittee on Preparedness, he was familiar with issues of the 1950s on weapons and strategy. Entrusted with responsibilities for space efforts during the Kennedy years, he was one who helped to create the National Aeronautical and Space Administration. He knew about the Kennedy administration's push toward giving the nation a far better capability for fighting limited wars with conventional weapons. And to a degree, he was aware of efforts in the academic community and think tanks to develop the new knowledge in mathematics, physics, and other disciplines which would be necessary in order to attain our national goals. Johnson also knew well that charges and countercharges (in regard to missile gaps, real and imaginary) could help to win or lose elections.

The administration inherited influential reports and decisions from earlier years: National Security Council (NSC) 68, from the Truman era, on rearming America; the Gaither Report, which sought hardening for missile sites, secure communications in time of attack, more research, and better-balanced armed forces; and the report of the Rockefeller Brothers panel, which found many deficiencies and lack of power in the office of the secretary of defense.[1] Johnson himself had called in 1958 for increases in the development of ballistic missiles and manned bombers.[2] It had been embarrassing when extreme charges by Democrats of a "missile gap" in 1960 had been discarded as being untrue soon after a narrow victory in the election.[3] The United States was belatedly found to have "a substantial superiority over the Russians in numbers and effectiveness of missiles," says one expert.[4]

When planning strategy, presidents had long been able to consult leaders—both civilian and military—from the Defense Department and from the army, navy, and air force. This same advice-giving machinery was available to Johnson. But well before he assumed office as commander in chief and throughout the 1960s, there would burgeon a new battery of intellectuals who devoted full time to the new world of defense strategy. Fanning out from an elite, government-funded, non-profit research organization in Santa Monica, California—the RAND Corporation—these think-tank personnel, consultants, and alumni became almost indescribably specialized on weapons-systems capabilities, moves and countermoves, scenarios of what might be, and recommendations on how to make the United States and the world safer. Their secret reports went to numerous influential civilian and military figures in policy-making roles; and their succinct briefings (which were fully outlined, rehearsed, and complete with audio-visual aids) offered the chance for congressmen, top brass, and even presidential candidates to engage in face-to-face confrontation and to test their own ideas against facts that had sometimes undergone computer testing. Master briefers could make life miserable for advocates of strategies that had been good enough to win earlier wars. Gen. Curtis LeMay would chomp on a cigar and glower; but the briefing fraternity considered reservist Maj. Gen. Barry Goldwater to be both knowledgeable and alert.[5] Minds were swayed, and opinions were molded behind the scenes, long before the media had even discerned the nature of issues, much less the "options." Public opinion in a democracy had therefore come, during the 1960s, into the era of the monopolistic expert, equipped with government secrecy clearances, who could reach even into the White House without the public's knowing the facts, the issues, the recommendations, or—often—the final action. The new need for planning, restraint, and subtlety required more intellectuality than the uninformed people of the previous decade possessed.

For those who were willing to read, the situation had changed when, in 1960, physicist Herman Kahn of RAND managed almost conspiratorially to have the enormous book *On Thermonuclear War* published outside the security system by a university press. Sales and awed reviews of the book were extensive. Its specialized vocabulary—Doomsday Machines, recovery time, Will the Survivors Envy the Dead?—became household words only two decades later during the nuclear-freeze debates. Said Senator Hubert Humphrey on the book's jacket: "New thoughts, particularly those which appear to contradict current assumptions, are always painful for the mind to contemplate. [The book] is filled with such thoughts." Hollywood's reaction was the 1964 movie *Dr. Strangelove*, which featured Peter Sellers as a weird but funny scientist from one "Bland Corporation." As the satirical volume *Report from Iron Mountain* put it, Kahn was responsible for the vogue that soon developed of writing about counterforce strategy, minimum deterrence, and credible first-strike capability without "getting bogged down in questions of morality." The author indeed had dared to "think about the unthinkable" with rationality.[6] Soon, columnists and academics who hoped to command any hearing either had to master the giant book by the modern Clausewitz or perhaps attack its author personally and hope for the best. Not surprisingly, the Peace Research Society was soon founded, for most study of a possible central (nuclear) war and what RAND strategist Albert Wohlstetter, updating Winston Churchill, called "the delicate balance of terror" was in reality a peace-loving and, it was hoped, peace-preserving, activity!

The Johnson administration, like those before it, was aware of the technique of policy analysis that was called operations research during World War II. That was an effort to quantify the value of alternative solutions to military problems. By the time Johnson took office, a much more sophisticated technique—systems analysis—had been developed and was being taught at RAND, so that both intellectual capability and use of computerization became *de rigueur* among Pentagon experts. The cost-benefit and cost-effectiveness approaches came to be applied to budgets, expenditures for weapons, and strategic planning. Models and scenarios were designed with an eye to improvement in making predictions; war gaming, decision theory, and simulations also came into being.[7] By serving the Air Force, RAND also served, to a degree, the executive branch.

The president stood at the pinnacle of this pyramid of complexity, though he was protected from its detailed workings to some extent by his brilliant secretary of defense. But as one who had long been familiar with testimony on weapons systems, Johnson was willing to let the Planning-Programming-Budgeting System be superimposed over the usual fiscal process. This major revolution in management was resented by high-ranking military personnel, since bright and sometimes brash youngsters, who ate and slept in the new intellectual climate, could use numbers to prevail over hard-won military intuition. Production of new ships, planes, and exotic weapons, as well as growth in manpower, could rest on computer runs and war games that were played in simulated environments. While computer and space-era civilians infiltrated the Pentagon during the McNamara years, many such new-type civilians had become virtually as partisan to the military as the military was itself, a fact little allowed for by critics. Those buried in the think tanks cherished a more scholarly attitude.

As vice-president, Johnson had strongly supported the building of a supersonic bomber. The British, he said, had led the world for centuries because they had dominated the seas; we had assumed leadership because we had taken over the air. Johnson sent a two-page letter to Kennedy, urging action. Soon Johnson said to Theodore Sorensen: "They'll ridicule him for it. They'll laugh at him, just as they do the space thing. But my friend, if he didn't do it he'd be in worse shape."[8]

The struggle between advocates of bombers and advocates of missiles raged all through the 1960s. There were other disputes. It was during the Kennedy years that the administration began to concentrate on building both deterrence forces and so-called war-fighting or war-waging forces. As for the ever-present outcry for unilateral disarmament, just how did one guarantee defense against the USSR and its Warsaw Pact allies while at the same time negotiating arms control? The "mix" of weapons systems was of interest; so was the "optimum" balance between nuclear and nonnuclear (soon to be termed *conventional*) forces. A specialist would term this latter problem "perhaps the most important issue" of the time.[9] There was talk of achieving flexibility in deterring and resisting aggression. Long lead time in research and development (R & D) was considered essential by the more sophisticated.

Such problems and issues permeated the Johnson presidency for those who had been introduced to the new issues and the now exotic vocabulary of national power. To Robert McNamara, two points seemed axiomatic. First, "the United States is well able to spend whatever it needs to spend on national security." Second, "strict standards of effectiveness and efficiency" needed to be applied. So, strategic retaliatory forces were to be improved, if possible; nonnuclear forces were to be increasingly emphasized; and "a general upgrading of effectiveness and efficiency in the defense establishment" was to be instituted.[10]

When President Johnson began to face the basic problem of security in regard to the Soviet Union, the fact that his was the finger on the button and that the buck would stop with him on matters involving central war or peace forced him to make certain resolutions. He early decided to avoid unnecessary name-calling of the kind associated with the long Cold War, because he thought that emotions should not be stirred up unless something could be accomplished. Such expressions as "captive nations" and "ruthless totalitarians" were among those ordered to be especially avoided in White House releases. He told the United Nations on December 17, 1963, "The United States of America wants to see the Cold War end, we want to see it end once and for all." A letter from Khrushchev in January 1964, which contained attacks on "colonizers" and "imperialism" but failed to address issues, was not considered helpful. Johnson therefore decided on a gesture: the United States would shut down four plutonium piles and some nonessential military installations. He tried to get Soviet agreement to cut back production of U 235, which is used in H-bombs; failing in that, he unilaterally announced an American cutback. He did these things despite advice from McGeorge Bundy, on the eve of a visit from science adviser Glenn Seaborg, that the Kennedy staff's guideline on the problem of the cutoff of nuclear production had been "to defer any visible decision during 1964."[11] Here had been advocacy of politics as usual.

Johnson would later claim to have caused a thaw in the Cold War during his presidency. Opinions will certainly differ as to this, for there were appearances, and there were realities. During his term, agreements were indeed made; conflict in terms of weapons was avoided; and rhetoric from the State Department was muted. Yet any observer of the next decade and later would be hard put to discern any durable thaw. The USSR underwrote the enemy in Vietnam; did little to facilitate negotiations to bring that war to a close; continued to achieve major-weapons capabilities; boldly dared to crush Czechoslovakia while Johnson was in office; and entered the 1970s measurably stronger than ever vis-à-vis the United States, which had been a nation of unexampled power after World War II and had once held a nuclear monopoly. The former president was justified in reflecting later, "No man should think that peace comes easily." Nor could *any* American stop or arrest the Soviet side of the arms race.

It was on January 15, 1964, that Johnson declared: "We are determined that this nation is going to be strong enough to secure the peace and to protect this country, but we are not going to throw our weight around. We hope we are going to be wise enough to prevent the necessity of ever using that strength." In Seattle, on September 16, he said that the nation's nuclear weapons were "under careful control" and would continue to be so. The Johnson administration had a policy designed to guarantee this. The weapons would be released by presidential action alone; "complex codes and electronic devices" would prevent unauthorized action; two or more men must act independently before any firing; and electromechanical locks had been in place since 1961. Many missiles were underground or beneath the seas, and there was "constant communication" between the strategic forces and their commander in chief. Work was being done to prevent nuclear spread, together with a striving for arms control. America's action to modernize and expand conventional forces was considered a step toward peace, said the commander in chief.[12]

Thus, the increased size of ground forces and of the tactical air force and new airlift capabilities were both linked with peace, not just with their use in Southeast Asia. Conflicts were being avoided, he said. Remember that for nineteen dangerous years, national survival had been furthered, along with survival of our freedom and our race. Although this was an election-year speech, here was a very sensible effort to calm a public that was just getting introduced, somewhat, to the new world of atomic strategy.

For the alert citizen and the military veteran, there could be consideration of new weapons entering the national arsenal. There were the new fighter aircraft F-4 and F-111. Polaris was another impressive system to be fully developed during the Johnson years; here was an absolutely first-class system. Over-the-horizon radar and laser-beam technology dazzled those who were privy to secrets. Air-to-ground and air-to-air missiles; the Sentinel ABM system, then under R & D; new developments in underwater sound devices; and MIRV (multiple warhead) technology made up a new world of military items for those who had tuned out after V-E or V-J day. Quietly, physicist Sam Cohen of RAND was lonesomely devoting the 1960s to research on a nuclear device he called "a neutron bomb," about which he secretly briefed an elite in the federal establishment.

The nation, with its nuclear capability during these years, was without doubt the free world's umbrella. In October 1964 the president said that if nonnuclear states should need our strong support against some threat of nuclear blackmail, they would have it. The secretary of state explained that if a country were threatened with the use of nuclear weapons, it "would have the entire international community, including the United States, register its support in whatever appropriate way would be necessary in the circumstances." Johnson was carrying on a long American tradition when he postulated, while in office, the righteous superiority of American motives with regard to international power politics.[13] Everyone assumed that a United States first strike was unthinkable. The Soviets, presumably, were not so sure.

On January 18, 1965, President Johnson presented to the Congress the first comprehensive presidential message devoted to defense since Kennedy. During the four years of the Kennedy-Johnson presidencies, he said, strategic nuclear power on alert had increased threefold; tactical nuclear power had expanded; the special forces had multiplied by eight; combat-ready army divisions had increased by 45 percent; and the marines had grown by 15,000 men; airlift capacity had doubled; and the tactical fire power of the air force had increased by 100 percent. He was proud of McNamara's budgeting process, which by then was very controversial; and he defended administration planning, decision making, and the close tie between the military policies of the Department of Defense and the foreign policy under the secretary of state.

American military strength, said the president, had come to consist of over 850 land-based ICBMs, 300 nuclear-armed missiles in Polaris submarines, and 900 strategic bombers—half of which were ready to be airborne within 15 minutes. Older missiles and bombers would be phased out, because brand-new weapons systems for effectiveness in the air, on land, and on and under the sea were being developed. He paid only lip service to defense shelters and to an antiballistic-missile system. The Post Attack Command and Control System was being developed. About $2 billion would be spent on R & D. Military pay was up, he said, and he planned to realign the army reserves and the National Guard. Overall, the defense budget had grown, but reductions in costs were impending. The president reminded Congress that "the defense of freedom remains our duty—twenty-four hours a day and every day of the year," for "to be prepared for war is one of the most effectual means of preserving peace."[14] These themes would have long lives.

Such Johnson-McNamara efforts to convince Americans that their strategic defense was in good hands did not prevent unremitting attacks. Little noted by reviewers, yet by far the most widely distributed such book in the heartland—in hundreds of thousands of copies at $1.00 or even free—was *Strike from Space,* a paperback book that appeared in November 1965. Phyllis Schlafly and retired Rear Adm. Chester Ward, who had earlier collaborated on two antiadministration books that had vast quiet circulations, claimed that American defenses were so weak as to invite a Soviet "strike from space." They focused on the cancellation of the development of certain weapons, they supported manned bombers, and they alleged that new weapons were not being stressed. The hard-hitting but physically unimpressive book was filled with carefully arranged facts and many charges. It must have helped to increase the hinterland's distrust of McNamara's civilian-dominated Pentagon. Years later, Mrs. Schlafly still thought the Great Society had been financed with funds detoured from strategic defense. On December 22, 1964, at the Ranch, several adversaries—but no specialists—argued over the building of "somewhere" between nine hundred and two thousand Minuteman missiles. The commander in chief finally opted, on the spot, for one thousand.[15] Here, it would certainly appear, was questionable decision making, far from Washington and in the absence of experts.

United States relations with the Soviet Union necessitated the creation of high military doctrine, rather theoretical in nature, designed to avoid thermonuclear war. The 1950s had inherited the Truman doctrine of *containment* of the Russians, which had been born of the vast superiority in atomic weapons in American hands. The Democratic party had at first been divided over containment, and Henry Wallace had been forced to resign from the cabinet largely over this issue. The Eisenhower administration at first embraced another doctrine, *liberation*, by which was meant policies designed to "roll back" the Soviets from their successful occupation of Central European countries and domination of those populations. But liberation proved abortive. *Massive retaliation*—which was advocated by John Foster Dulles, the new secretary of state—using the threat of total war as a way of furthering credible containment, became a doctrine. We would "strike back where it hurts, by means of our own choosing." Vice-President Nixon explained that the "retaliation" could be by methods other than atomic—as Dulles amended his views. Some advised *disengagement*, but that sounded too much like retreat.

At the close of 1967 the administration took stock of how the nation was handling its overall defense effort in the light of Vietnam's demands. NATO, during these years, moved from a massive-retaliation concept to *"assured destruction."* Next came a *flexible response* strategy. Consultation with the European powers on the use of nuclear weapons improved a great deal. The free world was aware that Minuteman ICBMs now numbered one thousand, and the forty-first Polaris ballistic-missile submarine had been commissioned. The Strategic Air Command (SAC) took delivery of the SR-71 strategic-reconnaissance aircraft. The Sentinel System to provide protection against a Chinese ICBM and any accidentally launched missile moved toward possible production. Seventeen satellites transmitted high-priority traffic, including photographs, for the military. Focusing their eyes on the ground and air war against North Vietnam on evening TV, people at home and abroad showed little sensitivity to such matters, being virtually unaware that "first strike" and "second strike" were to become a permanent part of the world's vocabulary. And who could tell if the president was really guarding the nation's strategic interests?

Other areas of concern were addressed. Research programs continued to be awarded to several score of colleges and universities. To government officials this seemed progress, but to articulate liberal and radical observers this amounted to reprehensible infiltration of the purity of the academic process in America. Meanwhile, entrance standards for draftees were lowered, even though the services clearly needed a plentiful supply of those who would be able to read increasingly complex instruction manuals. Spending for the military went up; yet substantial cost reductions were claimed. It was maintained that genuine competition among the competing defense contractors had become routine.[16]

All of this provided comfort to the commander in chief and gave him the chance to put America's military activities in a better light whenever he was challenged. Unfortunately for him, few political points were to be scored by even the most impressive progress in the complex strategic theater or in the administration of the Pentagon's multitudinous concerns. In his memoirs, Johnson mused on how the national obsession with Vietnam had diverted attention from such fateful matters: "A favorite argument of those who opposed our involvement in Vietnam was that the war prevented us from reaching any agreements with the Soviets or resolving areas of difference between Washington and Moscow. Many critics claimed that I was so preoccupied with Southeast Asia that I was neglecting Europe and passing up opportunities to ease Cold War tensions with Russia and Eastern Europe. The Soviet propaganda machine fed this notion, both openly and through informal contacts with individuals. The argument was not true, but few people took the trouble to compare the allegation with the facts."[17] One can sympathize with him, but his denial can be challenged.

Not surprisingly, the apparent military budget climbed substantially—from $51 billion in 1963 to $76 billion in 1968. The contrast between the funding of the strategic forces and the general-purpose forces is jarring. The area covering the missiles and other nuclear elements declined from $10.4 billion to $7.6 billion; meanwhile, the conventional part grew from $17.9 billion to $32.4 billion! Waging the war in Southeast Asia and the stressing of conventional capabilities were therefore costly in more ways than one, as funding to prevent or wage central war suffered. By the end of the Kennedy-Johnson period, the United States had 429 major installations and about 2,000 minor ones, located in almost every non-Communist country. Thus was brought to fulfillment the desire to strengthen conventional forces in order to spread America's power on the planet and to expand freedom by bearing any burden. Moreover, it had been revealed as early as 1964 that 334 American guerrilla teams were at work in forty-nine countries to train the local military in defense against subversion. The hostile expression "the world's policeman" was frequently heard, along with "arrogance of power." But strategic strength vis-à-vis the Soviet Union was a casualty.[18]

Those who were charged with working on strategic matters in the Johnson White House often used two sets of initials: NPT meant Nuclear Nonproliferation Talks; SALT was the long-hoped-for dialogue on Strategic Arms Limitation Talks. There came to be a mutuality of interest and, ultimately, agreement between the United States and the USSR by 1966 that nuclear weapons not be expanded beyond themselves and Great Britain, France, and mainland China. Countries that seemed to be possible candidates for the "club" were West Germany, Japan, India, and Israel. The sovereignty of free states was involved in what Rostow called "essentially, a constitutional arrangement" for the organization of the nuclear world. Proliferation could someday affect collective security and alliances alike.

Nonproliferation, if effective, meant that democratic and undemocratic nations, which were far removed, were coming under the American nuclear umbrella. Said Johnson on October 18, 1964, "The nations that do not seek national nuclear weapons can be sure that if they need our strong support against some threat of nuclear blackmail then they will have it." There would be tangible rewards for self-denial by the nation, as well as a vast increase in the assumption of responsibility—an aspect of raw power—by the United States. This responsibility would be spelled out to the United Nations on June 17, 1968: "The United States affirms its intention . . . to seek immediate Security Council action to provide assistance . . . to any non-nuclear weapon state party to the . . . [treaty] that is a victim of active aggression or . . . a threat of . . . [nuclear] aggression."[19] While the USSR and Great Britain said much the same thing, it was the American promise that was credible to the free world, given weapons realities at the time. A major impact was being made on the post-Johnsonian world, one that was little noticed at the time.

The bilateral SALT talks were rooted in the realization that the NPT commitment implied an obligation to try to reduce the planet's nuclear arsenal. McNamara saw the talks as a way in which the great powers could come to fathom the psychology of each other: the hopes, fears, and modes of thought of the opponent. The talks began in considerable ignorance despite preparations, for as late as March 6, 1967, the head of the Joint Chiefs of Staff told Congress candidly that we "don't know whether the Soviet overall objective is strategic nuclear parity, or superiority." In any case, a gigantic nuclear capability on the part of the Soviets would certainly facilitate their global aims at conflict levels less than general nuclear war, the secretary admitted. Uncertain whether any SALT talks would be possible, the administration finally decided on an antiballistic missile (ABM) straddle: a limited system would undergo R & D. In a San Francisco speech announcing this on September 18, 1967, Robert McNamara decided to use in public for the first time some of the new sophisticated vocabulary of thermonuclear threat and war, thus raising public consciousness at last.

Once, in a private interview, Johnson had commended the slogan "Peace Is Our Mission" to those at an air-force base, saying that the B-52s stationed there had a potential of being used for another twenty years. These weapons served humanity! Few doubted (and certainly not their leader) that the United States had the capacity to devastate the USSR if by some amazing reversal of American morality it should deliver a surprise first strike. But would the United States have any bombers left to use if a Russian strike came first? *Could* we strike *second*? Here was the cause of continuing debate over ABM capability. Although much had already been spent, if researched, produced, and deployed, the ABM could only protect us in later decades.

Research on intercontinental attack and defense weaponry did continue during the Johnson years, despite the often-stated opinion that surely our technology and weaponry were already far ahead—to the point of "overkill." Always, the assumption was that we would profit from ample warning! Americans were naturally jarred in February 1967 when the Soviets claimed that they had a workable ABM of their own. Now the president stepped up efforts to arrive at some kind of arrangement whereby neither ABM system would have to be deployed. After all, it was McNamara's firm belief that no defense or shelter system or miracle weapon could defend against either American or Soviet ICBMs; gradually this view prevailed. The brief shelter fad disappeared except in Moscow, where, among other precautions, the gigantic subway system was programed.[20] Civil defense would remain a Soviet, but not an American, concern.

At the close of the Johnson years, one who was extremely well qualified quietly assessed national strength as part of an oral-history interview. Russia's land-based megatonnage had rapidly accelerated, so that it soon would have more land-based missiles than the United

States. The Soviets' missiles, at least their SS-9s, were "more powerful than any of ours." But in submarine-launched ballistic missiles, our force was superior. The Russian SA-5 air-defense system seemed to be "a very effective system against high-altitude bombers." The Soviets put more dollars into R & D. As the administration drew to a close, the nation had 1,056 ICBMs, the Soviets 900. Still, in submarine-discharged weapons United States superiority was 650 to 75; in intercontinental bombers, over 600 to 150. In deliverable nuclear warheads, overall, it was 4,200 to 1,200. Indisputably, the Soviets were gaining; yet, multiple warheads were in the offing.[21]

One of the legacies of the Kennedy confrontations in Berlin and in the Cuban Missile Crisis was the Soviet mood of determination that such humiliations would never be inflicted again. In the 1960s the USSR had turned single-minded effort to the planning and production of weapons for use on the seas, on the land, and in the air, and even in the upper atmosphere, for all that anyone could then be certain. In 1965, their strategic arsenal had come to but 220 ICBMs. Soviet determination was a frightening legacy from the Kennedy and Johnson years for later presidents to have to live with.[22]

There was another legacy: the research and development of future weaponry. In response to great pressure, the nation did decide on an ABM system, but its implementation was delayed. The United States opted for MIRV (multiple warheads), flight testing them in 1968. The Minuteman ICBM and the submarine-launched Poseidon SLBM, while impressive, were relatively lighter weapons created in a period when the Soviets were going in for heavy payloads. Since the lead time for such weapons was then at least six years, this meant that America's defenses during the 1970s had to be largely determined in the 1960s—an awesome theme preached by the think tanks. "Inexorably, the over-whelming preponderance that we had enjoyed in the Forties and Fifties," says Henry Kissinger, "was being eroded first into equality, eventually into vulnerability, of our land-based forces." National safety now came to rest, it certainly was hoped, on allegedly superior American accuracy and dependability.[23]

Perception of Soviet limitations, stability, and strength played a part all through the 1960s in American planning for the future. The nation watched in fascination as Nikita Khrushchev was unexpectedly replaced by a new focus of power in the Kremlin. Writing later of this—almost in the spirit of an aging Roosevelt emphasizing personal relationships with "Uncle Joe" (Joseph Stalin) in 1944/45—Johnson said, "I knew I would have to start all over again and get to know the new man, or men, who decided Kremlin policy." Another whose light dimmed in the Soviet Union was Andrei D. Sakharov, a distinguished physicist and nuclear expert. His lengthy essay in the *New York Times* for July 22, 1968, offered a plan for rapprochement between the two contesting nations and showed the intensity of some very limited dissent in Moscow. The times, he said, were full of danger from possible thermonuclear war, overpopulation, and famine in the poorer half of the world; chemical pollution of the environment; police dictatorships; and encroachments on intellectual freedom. Sakharov's opinions evoked numerous columns and editorials and had an effect on persons of thoughtful bent.

With an eye on mutual trade, the president appointed the Special Committee on U.S. Trade Relations with Eastern European Countries and the Soviet Union in February 1965. In a matter of weeks the committee issued what the president grandly, yet perhaps correctly, called "probably the most definitive report" on such trade yet made. As trade was sought with the Warsaw Pact powers, free of special tariff barriers, the Department of Commerce quickly ran into old mistrust and potent objections. Are we to trade with Communists while fighting them? The congressional answer was not affirmative. So, "We lost," Johnson says, simply; the concept was a "victim of the war in Vietnam." Still, travel between the United States and the USSR increased somewhat, and some commodities went off the U.S. banned list. An area of growth during the 1960s was in the numbers of Soviet-bloc official personnel who were permanently stationed in the United States. Excluding their dependents, the 654 of July 1964 grew to 957 by July 1969. Soviet spying continued apace, although it was laughed off or sneered away by many who were not charged with responsibility.

There is opportunity for fruitful research on the role of the CIA during the Johnson years and on the president's use and control of it. Yet much is already known. Covert operations were handled by a committee of the National Security Council called the 303 Committee, a name deriving from NSC Memorandum 303, which set forth the committee's responsibilities. Early in the Nixon years it would be renamed the 40 Committee. Revelations by the magazine *Ramparts* with regard to CIA funding of the National Student Association and the funding of trade-union liaison with unions overseas distressed the White House. An aide advised Johnson: "Re the CIA publicity, which is of course going to increase with ramifications, would it be a good idea to get President Truman, even though I know he is ill, President Eisenhower, and Allen Dulles to defend the necessities, the proprieties of the CIA authority?" It was vital to give strong support to the agency. But there had been so much CIA activity, which was still continuing, that it was hard to know where to begin a defense. Kennedy and Johnson had authorized the CIA to spend nearly $4 million to avert a Communist takeover in Chile during its elections of 1962 and 1964, for example.

A moment for decision came in the fall of 1967 when there was to be a CIA awards ceremony—the agency was to be twenty years old. Peter Benchley prepared a draft speech from CIA materials, and this was edited and approved by Harry McPherson. The speech was never given; a message was sent instead. In the aborted speech, the CIA's self-image was depicted as that of a professional intelligence service second to none, an "efficient and resourceful organization with clearly defined goals," and a permanent institution of government. "It is not a comfortable thing to serve your country in secret and unpopular ways." It did its job "in the spirit of a democratic community" and was in a sense "the conscience of the government," forcing us to face unpleasant facts, keeping us worried and alert. Truman had called it "a necessity to the president"; Eisenhower, "indispensable"; and Kennedy, "essential." Intelligence, in short, meant national strength.[24] Such open support would certainly have been welcomed; why it was not forthcoming is not clear, but one suspects "politics." Johnson's presidency-justifying memoirs would mention the CIA only in passing, discussing neither its contributions nor its problems.

The information-gathering activities of the FBI, the CIA, and military intelligence agencies during the 1960s would be explored in a series of confirmation hearings in the mid 1970s at which Theodore Sorensen, Warren Christopher, and Joseph Califano were questioned. It was ascertained that some 54 agencies had kept 858 files which contained 1.5 billion records on individuals, many of which were rooted in a worthy purpose but some of which went much too far in invading civil rights. It turned out that the Johnson administration's response to the 1967 riots and its concern, apparently legitimate, over extreme antiwar activities had been the prime mover. A White House meeting of January 10, 1968, with the president absent, had dealt with the collecting of domestic intelligence, especially by the army, whose record had been soiled by misjudging the number of protesters to be anticipated in the October 1967 march on the Pentagon. An army unit stupidly photographed protesters at the Democratic National Convention of 1968.[25]

Testimony before congressional committees in 1977 revealed that the CIA had maintained liaison at home and overseas during the 1960s with journalists and publications. A 1965 book, *The Pentovsky Papers*, while purporting to be a diary kept by a Soviet double agent, was in fact compiled from CIA interview records by a KGB defector working for the CIA and by an employee of the *Chicago Daily News*. Here was deception. Sometimes, stories planted by the CIA overseas were picked up by journalists and then printed in the domestic American press. CIA agents posed as reporters, or they paid legitimate reporters; both true and false information was selectively fed to journalists during CIA briefings in McLean, Virginia, but veteran Asian reporter Keyes Beech later commented favorably on the accuracy of CIA briefings in Vietnam.[26]

Only intensive fair-minded research will show the relative culpability of the Johnson administration versus, say, those of Kennedy and Nixon-Ford. Actually, FBI abuses extended from Roosevelt to the early months of the Carter administration. Whatever the goal of keeping communism in check at home and abroad, CIA ownership and/or subsidy of more than fifty newspapers, news services, radio stations, periodicals, and other communications entities and the writing, production, or financing of some two hundred and fifty books by "the agency" shocked Congress later. Much of this nation-protecting activity took place during Johnson's presidency, with, or doubtfully without, his knowledge; and it must figure in any serious assessment—always keeping in mind the nation's need to survive in the face of dangerous enemies overseas.

The White House may or may not have spied on the Republican party. It is career CIA official Howard Hunt's memory that a CIA division officer told him in 1964 to have some people obtain information from the Goldwater campaign headquarters: "This was a White House matter, I was told, President Johnson being keenly interested in the plans and utterances of Barry Goldwater." He says Republican press material, position papers, and advance speaking schedules were "picked up frequently" on some pretext or another and taken to Chester Cooper, a CIA officer attached to the White House. As a professional, Hunt did as he was told, although he was a vigorous Goldwater partisan. He found this "disturbing."[27] Is this the truth? Such stories emerge, but the records on which to base judgment are locked up or gone or never existed.

When Johnson came into office, there had already been tapping of Martin Luther King's telephones, with memorandums going to Kennedy; use of tax agents to spy; and creation of a "watch list" of twelve hundred citizens. Johnson continued such activities, being a person who was abnormally curious about the intimate personal lives of others, and especially so as the 1960s became tense and dangerous. Anna Chennault, a friend of the Republic of China, was spied upon during his administration. When an FBI agent hesitated to check the phone records of the Republican vice-presidential candidate, Spiro Agnew, Johnson himself "came on the phone and proceeded to remind [the agent] that he was commander in chief and he should get what he wanted."

Johnson aides used presidential powers to push agents to check on matters they thought promising. One aide even asked the FBI to monitor Senate hearings and debates to check on "Communist party line" remarks. The CIA ran a quiet secret war in Laos during the 1960s. It also checked on domestic dissenters, hoping to find foreign connections; this was an activity that the public thought was reserved to the FBI. The CIA's Operation CHAOS compiled 13,000 files on 7,200 American citizens. The editors of *Ramparts* were spied on by agents after its sensational exposé, and Rostow got a report on radical editor Robert Scheer. A reporter for the Knight newspapers, writing on all this, concluded that when Nixon took office, the government was already riddled with the kind of abuse and misuse of federal agencies that later led to Watergate.[28] Still, the Freedom of Information Act in 1966 was a step in a somewhat better direction, whatever certain flaws in its provisions. The question of whether expansion of the National Security Agency at Fort George G. Meade in Maryland was excessive in size, scope, and power in these years must be left to the research of others.

President Johnson was a person who inhaled every detail of the national budget, kept track of the votes and predilections of even the most obscure congressman, and had time to find out many obscure things. It stretches credulity to think that he did not bother to find out about such activities. Concentrating on the civil rights of minorities in a "civil rights" administration, did he never consider that noncriminals had the right to privacy? Johnson certainly knew about the secret taping of telephone conversations in the Oval Office, for it was done by a secretary on his signal. He even had two different systems. Six boxes of these tapes (all that remain?) were very belatedly admitted to still exist, despite long delay in finally depositing them in the Johnson Library, but in 1973 the Johnson estate closed them for fifty years! Some cabinet meetings in 1968 were certainly taped. A White House employee who was in a perfect position to know says that he once had physical possession of "hundreds" of Johnson White House tapes produced from bugs and/or microphones. "Thousands" of conversations were taped then, by many persons other than the president, says the then chief of communications.[29] So, Johnson continued a Kennedy practice, and Nixon continued a Johnson one—a simple truth, indeed. National safety and, sometimes, personal power were placed above the Constitution and the law in those years. Here was a legacy to be pondered in the 1970s and later.

Twice during the Johnson years the nation's air force lost hydrogen weapons in the full glare of international publicity. When a B-52 and a KC-135 tanker collided in 1966 southeast of Cartagena, Spain—fortunately without any unusual explosion—nothing was revealed about hydrogen weapons for three days. As time passed, says our military public-relations director at the time, "the wrath of much of the press corps turned into incredulity and the incredulity into disgust."[30] Three of the four hydrogen weapons aboard were quickly recovered, but it took months before the last could be retrieved from a depth of 2,850 feet six miles off the Spanish coast. Deferring to Spain, the United States government made its official disclosure only after a 45-day delay. The search at Palomares could easily have been a story of navy heroism, for the bomb was retrieved after a dangerous multimillion-dollar search. A hundred newsmen finally viewed an American H-bomb in a most unusual spot—lashed to the deck of a submarine. Only during World War II had so long a period of government concealment of a major news event been maintained.

The second distressing episode was the crash of a B-52 bomber in Greenland on January 22, 1968. This event involved fewer problems, because the Danish government rose above its hostility toward hydrogen weapons in order to permit more candid public relations. Again there was heroism, this time by men and dog-sled teams working at a temperature of $-25°$ F. The unlucky Pentagon public-relations team got little credit for its new candor, however, as a sensational spy-ship episode, analogous to that of the Liberty, took place off North Korea and quickly seized center stage.

On January 22, 1968, the Pueblo, an American intelligence ship cruising in international waters off Wonsan, North Korea, was boarded by a North Korean patrol ship and taken into port with its eighty-three personnel. Messages reaching Washington did not clarify the fate of the ship or its crew. Air-force planes were launched from Okinawa, but they were ordered back for what were then termed good reasons: approaching darkness and the ship's probable movement into Korean waters. As late as 1982 the Pueblo's commanding officer was still seeking, in vain, for "the truth" on why fighter planes from South Korea never came to help him.

It can be seen that this episode had in it the seeds of a public-relations disaster for the commander in chief. Word-for-word copies of messages could not be released, given the fundamentals of cryptography, but the Congress did get fifty-two pages of documents. Among them would be the revelation that there had been wounded aboard, that the Pueblo's guns had not been uncovered, and that many key lists and items of sensitive equipment had not been destroyed on time. Destruction was called "incomplete," so "several publications will be compromised" (large numbers of them were).

The *Pueblo* incident would linger in the public craw for a long, depressing eleven months before the abused crew would cross the Bridge of No Return in Korea, homeward bound. Throughout, the White House knew few hard facts—a situation that was difficult for either the media or the public to accept gracefully—and several embarrassing errors were made in press releases. On January 26 President Johnson called the event "a wanton and aggressive act" which clearly "cannot be accepted." But his TV audience heard him say that nothing effective could be done. Of course, the nation could have risked consequences such as those occurring after the sinkings of the *Maine* in 1898, the *Illinois* and three other ships in 1917, the *Arizona* and its companions in 1941, and the attacks in Tonkin Gulf, for example. Vengeance was prohibited to the activist but now totally frustrated president. He reported lamely that he understood that "the men are being treated well." This would eventually turn out to be false. He said that getting the ship and crew back would take time. On this he was all too right. "Precautionary steps" would be taken henceforth, he said without giving any explanation. (In fact, the use of intelligence ships was very quietly abandoned altogether.) A belligerent speech was prepared under the date of January 31 but ended up in his personal secretary's files. An eighteen-page effort aimed at linking both *Pueblo* and the Tet attack in Vietnam, it was presumably intended for dramatic delivery in person to the Congress. Next to an explanation of why the *Pueblo* was where it was appears the handwritten notation "weak." The whole effort was shelved.

Another try at toughness was the draft of a speech for February 5—this time for TV, 3,184 words in 28 pages, on "the recent grave events in Korea and Vietnam." On the *Pueblo*, it was charged that the commander "did not sense the gravity" of the situation. *All* personnel would have their terms of service extended up to one year if Congress agreed, and those in Vietnam would have their twelve-months' tours extended to eighteen. The number of strategic weapons on alert would be increased. The Fourth Marine Division and Air Wing would be called up. These steps were called "cautious determination" and not an impetuous or extravagant response. All this was said to be in the spirit of Kennedy's famous "pay any price" speech and the 1961 actions in Berlin and the 1962 actions in Cuba. Our grit and good sense were being tested; let's show them—and persevere. This speech, too, was shelved.[31]

The course that was actually taken, instead of the aborted speeches, was a humiliating February 5 press conference, where little was said or revealed. Was the president confident we would get back ship and crew? "No, I am not." It would take time. In a news conference of

February 19 he simply said, "We feel very deeply our problem connected with the *Pueblo*." A full $100 million would soon be recommended for South Korea. But the gratifyingly tough responses remained buried in the files. The government settled down for a long and ignominious wait, one that would be like water torture on the world's allegedly most powerful leader.

Johnson says that the *Pueblo* incident was "the first link in a chain of events—of crisis, tragedy, and disappointment that added up to one of the most agonizing years any President has even spent in the White House."[32] Oppressed and tormented, he was not amused when Republican candidate Nixon, noting the lack of protection for *Pueblo*, called it a "tactical blunder." In his defense the president said that cost alone would keep such ships from being adequately protected; actually, the protective ships would have been highly provocative to governments along whose shores the ships cruised. He defended the failure to send aid and said wanly that the help of the Soviet Union had been sought in attempts to obtain the release of the ship and its crew. "We believed that the capture of the *Pueblo* was premeditated" and part of a harassment program aimed at South Korea, he said later. Today's observer can only say that the commander in chief was commendably determined at the time to avoid another war in Asia, no matter what the loss of face for the nation. The risk-taking Johnson of the Tonkin Gulf response was no more. When at last, on December 22, 1968, he was finally able to announce the release of the ship's personnel, he paid tribute to the patient negotiations conducted by Maj. Gen. Gilbert H. Woodward, who had "preserved the integrity of the United States" during the long process.

It makes one pause to think that the *Pueblo*'s mission had been recommended by the field commanders, approved by the military commander in the Pacific theater, and then considered by a committee composed of top officials of the State Department, the Defense Department, and intelligence agencies. All certainly underestimated the risk. Twelve times in press conferences and addresses the president had to discuss it. Why had the government's performance seemed so inept to the general public? There was little time to react before the vessel had been towed into port. Every retaliatory action seemed unwise. Any attack might mean that the men might never get back. Specialist Paul Warnke judged that "something as irrational and outrageous as the seizure of the *Pueblo* presents a country like the United States with a problem for which there is no satisfactory answer." When his brother told Lyndon that the nation should turn aggressive, the president replied: "There's a lot you don't know about this. And you may never know. My first impulse may have been the same as yours, but I can't go around giving in to the first impulse that hits me. I'm the President of this country and my responsibilities are to the whole world on something like this. I've got to hold back on a lot of things that could lead to a third world war—or maybe the last one. So I'm not going to let myself start shooting without giving the matter a lot of good hard thinking."[33] Someday, perhaps, long-buried truths will finally emerge on why the intelligence-gathering ships of 1963 to 1968 were so important to the national interest. Sophisticated judgment on both the *Liberty* and the *Pueblo* episodes has been rendered by a person who was aboard the former and angrily watched the first tragedy reenacted because the Pentagon had failed to learn anything between the episodes. "*Pueblo*, like *Liberty*, was lightly armed, unescorted, unprotected and ill prepared to protect herself against an armed enemy; *Pueblo*, like *Liberty*, failed to receive fighter protection or any other armed support; *Pueblo*, like *Liberty*, could not be protected because the nearest aircraft were equipped only for a nuclear mission and because conventionally armed aircraft were too far away and lacked refueling tankers."[34] One, maybe both, of these public humiliations of the United States could and should have been either avoided or handled better. Presidential discretion in foreign affairs is fully displayed, in any case, by the choice of dangerous escalation toward war in the case of the minor *Turner Joy/Maddox* skirmishes but not in the costly *Liberty* catastrophe or in the total *Pueblo* humiliation.

On July 1, 1968, the United States and USSR at last signed the Treaty on the Nonproliferation of Nuclear Weapons. Under negotiation since 1964, this effort to approach the complexities of what specialists were calling the Nth Country Problem was a step in the direction set by Kennedy's Partial Test Ban Treaty of October 1963. That treaty had outlawed nuclear testing in the atmosphere and space as well as underwater; underground testing had not been forbidden—a serious and unnecessary mistake, according to expert Glenn Seaborg.[35] An agreement on civil aviation was finally achieved, so that the first direct flights between Moscow and New York took place in July 1968. While in his first UN address the new president had said that he hoped to prevent the spread of nuclear weapons, he would not succeed, because China and France joined the nuclear club. But a new cultural agreement with the Soviets was reached after some delay. The Consular Convention, negotiated in 1964, ran into a Senate roadblock and delays in Moscow; it took effect only in 1968. Strategic Arms Limitations Talks (SALT) began only during the next administration, a delay that distressed President Johnson.

After its success on the nonproliferation treaty, the administration turned to the question of the design, manufacture, and deployment of antiballistic missiles (ABM). Since the probable costs were considered to be "colossal," Johnson wrote Kosygin on January 21, 1967, and again on May 19, 1967, about the domestic pressures being placed on him to proceed. The result of these initiatives would be the two-day talks in Glassboro, New Jersey. Kosygin was "reserved but friendly," changing the subject every time the subject of ABMs came up. The Israelis must withdraw from conquered territory before other matters could be addressed, the Soviet premier reiterated. Here again was linkage. When Johnson urged a one-week meeting annually henceforth, the Soviet leader merely praised hot-line contacts to date. ABM and ICBM must be linked in talks, he asserted. Says Johnson "I left Glassboro . . . with mixed feelings—disappointment . . . but hope." He told reporters that the world was now a little less dangerous, although no agreement was readily in sight on the Middle East or Vietnam. It had seemed to help, in any case, "to sit down and look a man right in the eye."

Some progress seemed visible in mid 1968 as the Nuclear Non-proliferation Treaty was opened for signatures. The Soviets said they were ready to announce that talks on the reduction of nuclear weapons, both delivery and defense systems, were in order. The two countries did make a simultaneous announcement on July 1. Nothing was to come of this, for in August, Soviet tanks rolled into Czechoslovakia, shocking the world. So was abandoned the idea of a Johnson visit to Moscow during the first ten days of October. (Would such a dramatic visit have elected Humphrey?) Informed by Ambassador Anatoly Dobrynin about the invasion of Prague, Johnson killed the nuclear talks and quickly informed the Republican candidate. Johnson later claimed, correctly, that our government was "as well prepared as a government could be for the historic effort ahead."[36] The Senate did not ratify the non-proliferation treaty until March 1969.

For most Americans, the "space age" had been born in 1957 with the launching of Sputnik I by the Soviet Union. Soon a pioneering book-length report of the RAND Corporation was published by the government, and later by Random House, under the title *Space Handbook: Astronautics and Its Applications;* it received very extensive distribution. The product of thirty-six researchers, this account made public in 1959 was a resource for magazine writers in its candid rendering of Soviet pioneering and well-based predictions of things to come—including the naming of 1969 as the ideal year for a moon effort. "In astronautics," it said, "lies the possibility of improved performance in important public and communal service activities; weather forecasting, aids to navigation and communication, aerial mapping, geological surveys, forest-fire warning, iceberg patrol, and other such functions." So the Age of Space was born in the minds of obscure researchers long before the headlines took over.

Lyndon Johnson as senator and vice-president had been deeply involved in America's intense preoccupation with the conquest of space. In 1957 he had heard physicist Edward Teller expound to the space committee on the idea that people could someday go on a round trip to the moon. While RAND's *Space Handbook* footnoted many of its research personnel's studies of 1956-58, it remains unclear exactly who first issued a credible plan for a manned moon landing and return to earth. Certainly it was not a political figure! Says NASA's great administrator for the 1960s, James E. Webb, "It is not possible for me to say that one person suggested in a relevant environment the concept of the moon landing." Johnson's own commitment of long hours and leadership before becoming president needs to be recorded, especially, whatever his occasional desire to be elsewhere in a more vibrant committee or conference environment. He knew early the anxiety of his senatorial colleagues to "catch up" to the Soviets. When asked by President Kennedy what he would like to do in the new administration, he said he wished to continue his interest in space activities. "I think he was relieved to have me take it on," he later recalled when referring to his time as chairman of the Space Council.[37]

The man on the moon project of the 1960s had political origins beyond doubt. Three days after the Bay of Pigs fiasco, Kennedy asked Johnson whether it might be feasible governmental policy to try to put a rocket on the moon, possibly with a man in it, and make the return trip. "Is there any other space program which promises dramatic results in which we could win?" At the time, Johnson was what amounted to a hawk on space activities. After eight days of interviews and con-ferences—in which the views of Webb, McNamara, and Edward Welsh, soon to be executive secretary of NASA, predominated—he reported back: "The U.S. can, if it will, firm up its objectives and employ its resources with a reasonable chance of attaining world leadership in space during the decade." He had come close to *demanding* that NASA accept a dramatic major program. The opinion proved to be momen-tous, as president and vice-president recognized that the Soviets had as yet nothing remotely resembling a moon-project capability. The United States conceivably could be first. On May 25, 1961, Kennedy announced the unimaginable project of the decade to Congress. It was projected, behind the scenes, to cost twenty to forty billion dollars. The vice-president, unfortunately, had been sent to Asia and was given no media coverage as the one who had undergirded the Kennedy announcement.

As fate would have it, Lyndon Johnson was therefore present at the creation of the moon project; moreover, he would very nearly carry it through to the great event itself. Having urged it on his leader, who announced it, he knew, he recalled, "that if the program had gone wrong life would not have been pleasant for the Vice-President." Attacks on the space "boondoggle" grew until on July 31, 1963, the man from rural Texas would publicly defend the growing scientific and engineering program as a "solid investment." Later, of course, NASA's budget had to compete with many other interests of the Johnson administration; while interplanetary and pure research would not get optimum funding, the moon race did well. The Johnson-Webb team handled Congress brilliantly. Says Johnson: "People frequently refer to our program to reach the moon during the 1960s as a national commitment. It was not. There was no commitment on succeeding Congresses to supply funds on a continuing basis. The program had to be justified, and money appropriated year after year. This support was not always easy to obtain."[38] McNamara, denied military dominance from the outset, competed for scarce funds. The chairman of the Senate Aeronautical and Space Sciences Committee, Clinton Anderson of New Mexico, was a strong resource; so were Senators Robert Kerr of Oklahoma and Styles Bridges of New Hampshire. And outside the political arena the dedicated R & D effort at think tanks and burgeoning specialized corporations carried the project through intellectually. An important Johnson decision was to continue unchanged the Kennedy practice of keeping space policy under Webb rather than with the Science Advisory Council, which had many competing fish to fry.

The race to the moon gave great satisfaction to TV viewers and the White House—when all went well. Thus, 1965 saw astronauts whose names were then known across the land make two-man flights, spend 190 hours and later 330 hours in space, and hook up to a second space vehicle. Men walked in space. But a fire on the launching pad, which killed three astronauts on January 27, 1967, shocked the nation. (Johnson heard about it just as a toast was being offered to the new treaty on the use of outer space.) Still, there would be a successful three-man Apollo mission and, in his final full month as president, an orbital flight around the moon, complete with unforgettable pictures of that body and of what would soon be conceptualized as "Spaceship Earth." This image had a profound, almost spiritual, impact on philosophers and lay persons alike. TV spectaculars entranced the world. Unfortunately for Lyndon Johnson, it would not be until July 16, 1969, in the next administration that Apollo 11 successfully placed men on the moon and brought them back. President Nixon made sure that his predecessor was present at the launch site, a gesture that was doubly welcome since for years the possibility of a disaster had always made his presence at such events while chief executive inadvisable, and the public persisted in attributing the success of the moon race to his vibrant predecessor in office.

Two important treaties concerning space were signed with the USSR and other countries in these years as futuristic discussions began about a new field to be called Space Law, which was stimulated by a pioneering 1959 conference.[39] Among the areas of progress was provision for safe legal return for astronauts and for space equipment that might land in other countries. Weapons of mass destruction would be banned henceforth from outer space. Here was a "peace building" agreement, UN delegate Arthur Goldberg would tell Johnson privately.[40]

There have been a multitude of results from the dramatic space effort, too many and too far-reaching to be set forth here or attached to a single presidency. Johnson's astute retrospective view was that "space was a platform from which the social revolution of the 1960s was launched," by which he meant that "new ideas took shape" in many areas of activity and aspiration. He phoned the astronauts on one occasion, "You have taken all of us over the world into a new era." To the press he said, "We have come so far, so fast, so good."[41] At the time, twenty-two years had passed since the creation of the little known pioneering RAND engineering study of May 2, 1946, *Preliminary Design of an Experimental World-Circling Spaceship*, which had concluded that "modern technology has advanced to a point where it now appears feasible to undertake the design of a satellite vehicle." By the 1980s it would be possible for the head of NASA to declare pridefully that his agency's research, spin-offs, and applications had become "critical to our national security, a major positive factor in our balance of trade, and crucial to the growth of our national economy."[42]

Leadership of the public mind in space matters was handled adroitly by President Lyndon Johnson. Richard Nixon stated simple truth in his memoirs: "President Johnson was an enthusiastic supporter of NASA, and under his administration [and certainly James E. Webb's] the Apollo program made great strides." America's innovative leadership in space came to be much noticed by peoples of the world, diluting the initial triumph of Sputnik. Many messages came from overseas to the White House; one from the president of Brazil said that mankind would be able to benefit greatly from these new scientific conquests if their results should be applied with wisdom and a spirit of international solidarity.[43] This was a good sentiment, looking toward the future. Such encouragement was doubly welcome in view of the habit of radicals and some humanitarians to snipe at the space effort as an antisocial diversion of resources from needy humankind. Actually, it provided employment for thousands. Time would reveal the vast spillover onto people's lives from this administration's able stewardship of the space effort.

Federal agencies like the Veterans Administration, the Peace Corps, and HEW, for example, contracted during these years with the System Development Corporation (a spin-off from RAND in Santa Monica, California) to bring their information-retrieval systems into the modern world through the use of computer programs. Still other think tanks, such as MITRE, ANSER, the Stanford Research Institute, the Aerospace Corporation, and the Jet Propulsion Laboratory, utilized dramatic new methods to push the military and space efforts toward the cutting edge of new knowledge. Soon the private sector would move in the same direction, as some profit-making companies also placed scientists and engineers in freedom-giving atmospheres that were conducive to fundamental research. Here, overall, was a true revolution, which had been gestating gradually during several earlier presidencies but only now was beginning to pay off in exciting new developments and esoteric trained personnel. Thus the American way in business management and educational instruction in the 1970s and later had been given a vast computerized push into the future in the 1960s, born from government contracts with the nonprofit bodies. There would be an impact on peasants in deserts and rain forests alike, on sophisticates planning distant weekend trips, and on worldwide communications, as well as on military utilization of space. From governmental contracts, on the whole, would be developed "silicon valley" in California and smaller equivalents elsewhere in the new Age of the Computer.

In 1964 some people had supported the Johnson-Humphrey ticket precisely because they had hoped that its stewardship in the arena of thermonuclear responsibility and perhaps arms limitation might somehow decrease the awesome threats. Yet, Americans continued to be as threatened by the Soviets at the close of the administration as at its beginning, whether more or less credibly would be difficult to say with confidence. The nation, as this presidency unfolded, did enter the ages of space and of the computer. It also got five more years of freedom from nuclear attack and from the waging of thermonuclear war—an absolutely vital fact that was little noted by a public that as yet seldom thought profoundly about such unthinkable things.

10

★ ★ ★ ★ ★

THE GREAT SOCIETY
IN LAW AND IN PRACTICE

Certain generalizations on the Great Society seem to be warranted. The problems, it would appear, lay in (a) unrealized expectations, (b) faulty assumptions in the federal government's strategies for bringing about change, and (c) poor administration.[1] We have already witnessed the first of these and have placed the blame squarely on Johnson and those who drafted his speeches. His rhetoric was total oversell. There was no chance of bringing children to anything like equality or equality of opportunity with Title I of the Elementary and Secondary Education Act, for schooling is but one facet of a child's twenty-four-hour day. Yet the overall program had lesser successes, and so did the legislation that was aimed at crime, even though American society did not eliminate its criminals. There was unbridled optimism for a time among the specialists who inhabited the offices concerned with the War on Poverty and the education effort, even though some of the programs on which they relied were clearly destined to be short lived, some would be ineffectual, and many were supported by too few dollars. Model cities, for example, did not last long enough or have enough money to allow an educated appraisal.

An assumption that did not pay off was the idea that R & D techniques that were being used successfully in the space and weapons areas would bring fruitful innovation in the social arena. Local institutions could not profit readily from ideas they did not grasp and, fundamentally, did not want. Out in the country, many new programs quickly went down the drain when the federal dollars ran out. Worse, there was opportunistic diversion of new program funds to other local concerns; this might have been expected. The reality is that the opportunity for the federal government to reach down into local school districts in order to implement change was severely limited.

That the wars on crime, poverty, and educational deprivation in the United States can, in retrospect, be called "unusually weak, sometimes hopelessly muddled, and hardly ever efficient" (not by Republican politicians but by deadly serious think-tank researchers) will not surprise anyone who lived through the period. "Bureaucratic morass" was used to describe the guidelines and requirements that bogged down organizations and officials who could not keep the cumbersome machinery afloat. Those in Washington seldom grasped the reality of local conditions and the impossibility of achieving uniformity throughout the vast reaches of the nation, either then or afterwards. It might be added, as an educated guess, that some former professors-turned-administrators had weak if not nonexistent backgrounds in personnel management and program administration—a situation clearly believed fervently by a skeptical president.

Those who consider the Great Society in concept and result tend to focus on three areas—poverty, civil rights, and education; nevertheless, the total list of meaningful legislation throughout the Johnson years embraces many other fields of activity—for example, conservation and criminal justice. At the close of 1967 an effort was made by a team of White House staff members to identify areas of recent "major legislation" on the basis of its public appeal. They knew that they were making a subjective effort, but they did what they could. Aide Matt Nimitz led the effort.[2] The list for 1966 and 1967 is mind-boggling.

1966: food for India, child nutrition, the Department of Transportation, truth in packaging, model cities, rent supplements, the Teachers Corps, the Asian Development Bank, clean rivers, food for freedom, child safety, narcotics rehabilitation, traffic safety, highway safety, mine safety, international education, bail reform, tire safety, a new GI Bill, increase in the minimum wage, urban mass transit, reform of civil procedures, federal aid to highways, military Medicare, public-health reorganization, Cape Lookout Seashore, water research, Guadalupe National Park, Revolutionary War bicentennial, fish and wildlife preservation, water for peace, anti-inflation program, exchange of scientific knowledge, exchange of cultural materials, foreign investors tax, parcel-post reform, civil-service pay raise, stockpile sales, participation certificates, protection for savings, flexible interest rates, and freedom of information.

1967: educational professions, the Education Act, control of air pollution, partnership for health, increases in Social Security, age discrimination, wholesome meat, flammable fabrics, urban research, public broadcasting, the Outer Space Treaty, modern government for the District of Columbia, benefits for Vietnam veterans, the Federal Judicial Center, pay for civilian postal workers, the Deaf-Blind Center, college work-study, summer youth programs, food stamps, settlement of the rail strike, Selective Service, Urban Fellowships, the Consular Treaty, the Safety at Sea Treaty, the Narcotics Treaty, antiracketeering, the Product Safety Commission, aid to small businesses, and the Inter-American Bank.

Many such laws of the 1960s built on earlier foundations—on ideas, work, and legislation that went back for decades. But many were virtually new in concept, some so new as to have virtually no constituency. Some were passed with little lobbying or public attention. Some resulted only after battles in which the president himself was the force that made all the difference. Some of the titles that read impressively never attracted funding that was adequate to implement their language. Some are seriously overtitled. Some with modest enough titles later became enormous in funding and bureaucracy and, thanks to zealous administrators, became major factors in American life, far beyond anything the administration had dreamed of (the food-stamp program is a good example). In any case, the Johnsonian legislation remains an unprecedented show of effort, ingenuity, and movement.

The "movement" was, unfortunately, not just toward reform and good works and improvement and a better society. It was also, in a major way, a movement toward expanded federal regulation of individuals, businesses, and organizations. "The Great Society programs are all compulsory," observed New York Times columnist Arthur Krock irritably at one point. The groundwork was laid for future inflation of the dollar, because the costs of that day plus the costs of the next decade simply were not fully funded or anticipated then, and later they proved difficult to fund. Those who were old enough to have attacked the New Deal along similar lines hardly knew where to start in making an attack against so comprehensive an effort by a determined Democratic president who was equipped with compliant Democratic majorities in the Congress.

Lyndon Johnson had his favorites among the array of laws passed during his time in office. Asked three days before leaving office what he regarded as his "greatest accomplishment," he said at the National Press Club that it was the response of Congress to "my Voting Rights Act." It would make democracy real, correcting an injustice of decades and centuries. Reflecting further, he said that the "greatest single individual act that meant the most to me that I wrote and authored" was the Space Act in 1958. Later he praised (really, overpraised) the tax bill of 1968; next he ventured to call the housing bill of 1968 one of the ten landmark pieces of legislation in all of American history! Medicare would be mentioned only in passing. But had time permitted, he might have said something expansive, such as the words near the close of his memoirs: "I would not have abandoned a single major program that we instituted. I would not have postponed a single law that we recommended and passed."

The percentages of Johnsonian legislative successes are awesome: 1964—58, 1965—69, 1966—56, 1967—48, and 1968—56. These percentages are illuminated by such low-point previous years as 1957—37, 1960—31, and 1963—a low 27.[3] Johnson's program achieved massive support from Democrats. For example, in the House, his party supported him on 81 percent of all votes, compared with 83 for Kennedy, and 68.7 for Carter during his first three years. House Republicans supported Eisenhower by 68 percent, Nixon by 72.5, and Ford by 65.[4] Party regularity was alive during the Johnson presidency in spite of the controversial nature of much of what the president desired. No wonder he could tell his close friend Arthur Krim about "the wonderful members of this amazing 89th Congress" who had sent him "so many good bills to sign." Thus, " 'by their fruits ye shall know them.' "[5] Yet a technicality was responsible for much of this favorable action. Said Carl Albert later, the decision of the House leadership to pass a 21-day rule made all the difference; that is, if the Rules Committee did not report a bill within that time, the chairman of the committee involved could get the permission of his committee to ask the Speaker to recognize him to call up the bill without a rule. The change was vital to Johnson's program.[6]

This presidency made its mark in education. During 1965 the Elementary and Secondary Education Act was passed almost exactly in the form in which the administration wanted it. Title I gave funds to school districts on the basis of the number of children from low-income families (i.e., those who made under $2,000 a year or were on public assistance). A 1966 shift in the formula greatly aided the poorer states: for example, Mississippi's receipts nearly doubled in one year. Districts had the freedom to decide how to spend the appropriated funds, provided "educationally deprived children" were helped. Children in private schools received some benefits. An initial surge in construction tapered off as stress on better instruction and improved services increased. By 1968 some 6.7 million poor children were being covered, and other children benefited as a spillover.

Title II provided federal grants to the states for school-library resources, textbooks, and instruction materials. The purpose of Title III was to induce innovation and to help areas like art, music, languages, counseling, and educational media. Title VI, targeted at handicapped children, is said to have helped 225,000 of them during the Johnson years. Bilingual education was the mission of Title VII, but it was underfunded. Title VIII, as amended, was supposed to lower the dropout rate and to help rural schools; the money for it was completely inadequate. In such cases, the gap between public-relations claims and reality was wide. The language in the act was designed so as to prevent federal domination over curriculum, personnel, and books and also to prohibit the use of these funds in transporting students for the purpose of integrating schools (i.e., bussing). But a district was supposed to comply with the 1964 Civil Rights Act, eventually, or it would lose its funds. This presented a problem.

The Higher Education Act of 1965 provided federal scholarships for undergraduate students, which were based, not on promise or ability, but on "need." Loans from private lenders were to be federally insured, so that the interest rates charged would be lower and even some risky loans would be approved. This kind of program had long been sought by Johnson as a legislator, and Kennedy had tried for it in 1963 in vain. The act provided for many kinds of aid to colleges and universities, including help for libraries. The contribution of the Higher Education Act was chiefly in offering to those who could not afford to go to college the means to do so, thus building on the two GI Bills—of 1944 and Korea—which, however, contained no provisions for need. The famous Work-Study Program for college students and the even-more-noticed Head Start Program for preschoolers were enacted to be part of OEO.

Overall, aid to higher education amounted to meaningful figures. For fiscal 1968, grants reached $131 million; loans, $182 million; and work-study, $134 million. These impressive enough figures may be compared unfavorably with the existing GI Bill's $429 million the same year. Many of the act's titles obtained only minor appropriations during the Johnson years. In 1968 the National Defense Education Act (1958) was greatly broadened, and the National Science Foundation (1959) was assigned new activities.

The National Endowment on the Arts and the National Foundation for the Arts and Humanities were born in 1965, although Johnson had asked only for the former. While the money was not what many hoped for, this was a daring breakthrough in federal funding of the creative arts, carried out in spite of plausible warnings of possible invasions of creative freedom. Perhaps they owed their passage to guilt feelings over the overly generous funding of science as well as to a favorable study of the subject by the Rockefeller Brothers Fund, which seemed to say that any dangers to freedom in the arts could be handled.

Some figures showing changes in educational patterns during the Johnson years are meaningful. Enrollment in elementary and secondary schools increased from 39 million in 1962 to 46 million in 1970. There had been a shortage of teachers during the early 1960s; by the end of the decade it was gone. The federal share in expenditures for higher education grew from 14.9 percent in 1959/60 to 19.1 percent in 1967/68 but would sag again to 15.0 percent by 1976/77. The percentage of college graduates in the population rose from 17.3 percent in 1962 to 23.4 percent in 1976.[7]

An event in education was the 1965 White House Conference on Education, which was attended by 650 delegates and was chaired by John Gardner. Resolutions on policy were prohibited from the outset; nevertheless, panels quickly found a multitude of flaws in the existing educational scene. While an earlier conference in 1955 had been notably pessimistic, this one met in an atmosphere of coming change and gave participants a real lift.

Other programs of these years aided training facilities for the deaf, helped to build large numbers of student dormitories, enlarged the long-existing programs for impacted areas, and aided international aspects of education in America. The bill for this last program was signed in Bangkok, Thailand, as the touring president said expansively that here was the first step in spreading Great Society goals all over the world, thus confirming one of the predictions and fears of the defeated opposition in Congress.

Such growth in the federal role in education was bitterly contested, and many sensible objections were made; but its proponents tarred all doubters, constitutents, and opponents who wanted States' rights and local control, calling them callous to the needs of young people, especially when these opponents were seeking to make over the funding of many programs into block grants to the states, thus hoping to cut back on costs and control by "Washington." Many plans of the multitude of task forces never did pass, in spite of pressure from the White House. Some possibly fruitful ideas of the opposition also failed, including income-tax credits for the costs of college education.

By 1968, violence on college campuses made passage of new higher-education bills difficult and put the continued funding of old ones under fire. In that year there were five efforts to cut off funds to students who had been involved in criminal acts. Various approaches were tried, but both the constitutionality and the effectiveness of the measures were in doubt, and there was much indecision. Yet, most people agreed that it was intolerable that those who had destroyed property and endangered lives could be in college—and free of the draft—thanks to federal grants or loans.

Aspects of the Johnson effort to spread and improve schooling at every level have been studied, weighed, evaluated, praised, and condemned. Some figures are central. For example, there was a gap, by the 1969 fiscal year, between funds *authorized* for elementary and secondary education ($3.9 billion) and the amount actually *appropriated* (only $1.5 billion)![8] This is far too large a disparity to go unmentioned while we are concentrating solely on the number of bills passed and their admittedly exciting titles. Perhaps it was hoped that someday, with the war in Southeast Asia over, programs would be fully funded. The figures certainly tell, in capsulized form, the chasm between claim and reality in education during these years.

Too much should not be taken from the enthusiastic and hopeful president, who in a moving and entirely personal speech (i.e., free of ghost writing) at his old Welhausen Elementary School, Cotulla, Texas, on November 7, 1966, made abundantly clear how personal was his educational crusade. A substantial part of the speech was dictated over the telephone two hours before it was delivered, and some of the rest was just ad-libbed—a fact that is revealed through a close comparison of the taped speech and typed versions of it.[9]

There were a number of counterproductive side effects of the massive legislation on education. Shouldn't teachers teach rather than do research and administer so much? Was legislation being stretched by bureaucrats after being passed? Was there equity between universities and colleges, public and private, research and instruction? Initial evaluations of the effectiveness of the various programs brought a rash of studies, most of which were directly or indirectly financed by the taxpayers. Whether fully scientific or not, some hurt. A 1969 study of Head Start by Westinghouse Ohio found that the program was ineffective, thus nearly destroying it. There were positive findings in some later studies. But there would be many adverse assessments of programs, then and later. In 1968 a pair of critics judged that evaluations of the elementary- and secondary-education effort to that point had been "largely impressionistic and self-serving," although the evidence that was relied upon was "devastatingly pessimistic." Other efforts of this type could be "depressing in the extreme."

Some obvious results are not debatable: There were new buildings; newly trained or updated teachers; and students who had been kept in school or financed into college and then turned up as graduates instead of dropouts. Junior colleges became "post-secondary," divorced from high schools. Teachers colleges graduated to the status of state colleges, and some even became state universities, at least in name, during the next decade.[10] While GI Bills had (of necessity) chiefly aided men, the new programs aided men and women alike—a dramatic but seldom noticed change.

Lyndon Johnson celebrated early. Contemplating his Great Society legislation on November 13, 1965, he told fellow party members: "You have much to celebrate as Democrats. Foremost is the tremendous record of the first session of the Eighty-ninth Congress. It was an historic do-something Congress that will long live in the memories of all Americans. The vast Democratic majority must be credited with these accomplishments." In such a politicized attitude lay the seeds of trouble and, in the 1966 off-year congressional elections, it turned out, a degree of party repudiation, as the Republicans gained forty-seven seats in the House and three in the Senate. Joseph Califano felt that he and his colleagues got far ahead of even educational pressure groups after 1966. "If the president is dumping a dozen major education bills on the Congress every year, and he's moving into educational television and a public television proposal and something for bright kids and Head Start and . . . 'educational parks' . . . you've given them the agenda," he said. A scholarly observer felt that educators kept right on, as usual, asking such questions as how to improve education for the disadvantaged, how to upgrade the educational development of teachers and administrators, how to focus more effort on urban education, how to better finance higher education, and how to somehow link together vocational and manpower-development programs.[11] Was there no limit to the bottomless education pit? some wondered.

One result was certainly clear to any who looked closely: Education at every level fell, during those years, increasingly under the direct or indirect control of the federal government. What had been started would accelerate as the bureaucracy swung into administrative and regulatory action during the 1970s, putting flesh and blood on the words and phrases of the new legislation. Former professor and then Senator Daniel Patrick Moynihan said glumly that by 1980 "the federal government has acquired the power to shut down any university it chooses." And more generally, "The conquest of the private sector by the public sector . . . continues apace." Said *Harper's* as it printed these views, "In exchange for federal aid, universities and colleges have surrendered their independence to the government."[12]

But results could be measured: the number of people in their late twenties who had a high-school diploma rose from 60 to 75 percent of that group during the 1960s; the percentage of blacks doing so increased from below 40 to about 60. College attendance among the 18- to 24-year-year-old group jumped from 22 to 32 percent in a decade. No doubt the draft played a role in this, and so did war-induced prosperity. Anyway, between Eisenhower and Nixon, the median years of schooling among the adult population rose from 10.5 to 12.2 years. Yet, long-run improvement was to prove hit or miss. A government commission in 1983 would claim that 13 percent of seventeen year olds were functionally illiterate, with illiteracy at 40 percent among minority students.[13] The quality of education received earlier may have been better in some respects, for there certainly was a dilution of some standards and of grading patterns. Many newcomers in college classrooms were not competitive, and anything like excellence in all aspects proved hard to obtain or maintain.

There were indeed changes, both positive and negative, from the approximately sixty pieces of legislation that Johnson, his men, and the Congress created in the area of education. Johnson said, at Stonewall, Texas, when signing the Elementary and Secondary Education Act on Sunday, April 11, 1965, before an audience including his first teacher and former classmates, "As President of the United States, . . . I believe deeply that no law I have signed or will ever sign means more to the future of America." Later he asserted that "a dream" had been fulfilled. Legislation and all the dollars did leave their mark on educational *opportunity*, at the very least. According to one evaluation in 1978, since the mid 1960s the percentage of three- and four-year-old children in nursery schools jumped from 10 to 32, and students in college from 6 to 12 million. The number of black students in college quadrupled (from 274,000 to 1,100,000), to become 10.8 percent of the total. A Teachers College (Columbia) professor saw the resulting glass as being half full, rather than half empty. Mere growth in population could not have been remotely responsible for all of this. On the other hand, limited funding, then and later, undoubtedly limited the quantitative progress; and the sheer bulk of legislation nearly swamped those in the federal bureaucracy who were charged with implementing the fine print. A perceptive commentary a decade later generalized thus: "Having become dependent on the billions in federal money that supported educational activity over the last two decades, few school districts, universities or colleges can imagine life without it."[14]

While few would seriously claim that the man from the Pedernales River was personally enthusiastic about either the fine arts or the performing arts, a lover of galleries, or an eager inhabitant of concert halls, it would be inexcusable to minimize Johnson's contribution in such areas, as aided by other leaders and institutions. His was a lasting mark. Armed with federal dollars, art galleries and museums achieved explosive growth, and public attendance mushroomed; professionals would have called these phenomena impossible, assessed the critic for the *New York Times*. Said the critic for the *Washington Post*, in very brief perspective, "LBJ did more for the arts than all his 35 presidential predecessors combined." One who did yeoman service was Roger L. Stevens, who was appointed the nation's first full-time arts adviser and presidential aide on May 13, 1964. On March 11, 1965, he chaired the new National Council on the Arts. At least a dozen projects, only dreamed of vaguely for years by the arts community, came into being. A roll call would certainly include the National Endowment on the Arts and the National Foundation for the Arts and Humanities. The National Museum Act of 1966 underwrote training, research, surveys, and publications. A new law began the preservation of historic structures. The Corporation for Public Broadcasting, with its cultural programing, was a major innovation. The Kennedy Center for the Performing Arts was a product of Johnson's years, though it was created by many hands, and the same could be said of the acquisition and housing of the Hirshhorn Collection and the realization, finally, of the American Film Institute. Summer arts programs for young people were started in sixteen cities. The old Patent Building became the National Collection of Fine Arts and the National Portrait Gallery, while the old Court of Claims Building became the Renwick Gallery. There were grants-in-aid for regional theaters and for music and dance groups and an awards program for writers, painters, and sculptors.[15] By the 1980s, annual appropriations for the arts and humanities would total well over a hundred million dollars. Here indeed was a legacy of innovation.

The White House, during the Johnson years, was by no means a cultural abyss, as even a casual reading of *A White House Diary*, by Lady Bird, will show. Inside the building itself, an elegant little stage was created, where many of America's great performers entertained their fellow dinner guests. The Festival of the Arts, June 15, 1965, though plagued by problems, was an accomplishment by Lady Bird and Professor Eric Goldman over obstacles. The chef whom she hired for the White House in 1966 was still there in the early 1980s: a sign of good taste indeed.

Accomplishment in civil rights was not without strains. Enactment of the 1964 and 1965 Civil Rights Acts was met in the black community, not by quiet contentment, but by what Johnson much later called "all that crazy rioting which almost ruined everything." One aide who ran totals says that from 1964 through 1968 there were 225 "hostile outbursts" in the nation's cities in which 191 were killed, 7,942 wounded, and 49,607 arrested. So, here the earlier "spirit of questioning" became translated into action. The Detroit riots, July 24–28, 1967, would "remain forever etched in my memory," recalled Johnson. As his representative, he sent Cyrus Vance to work with Gov. George Romney. Finally, as National Guardsmen could not contain the situation, Johnson sent federal troops, but only after 43 died and 324 had been injured. His delay may have been excessive, but—like President Hoover with the Bonus Army—he would not act before being officially requested by local authorities to do so. The mayor later decided that the use of troops had not "bitterly divided" him from Johnson; he also had good remarks to make about Vance and the governor. Maybe the country would now awaken to the needs of the distressed people in the cities, the mayor hoped. Vance's report was workmanlike, and the terrible incident seemed to be closed, but it left scars. Only a year earlier the president had judged that "as the prosperity of the majority becomes more evident, the poverty of the minority becomes more unbearable; they demand a share."[16]

Such awful events required soul-searching and a sure-footed reaction inside the White House. In mid October 1967, on the eve of a civil-rights demonstration in Washington, the attorney general briefed the president and cabinet on the prospects. How many might participate was "undeterminable." There was "risk of unplanned incidents." The media had given "low-key coverage" so far, fortunately. When the Department of Defense took over the briefing, Humphrey asked exactly how the Capitol itself would be protected. Everyone agreed that business as usual would be a good posture.[17]

Desegregation in the armed forces moved forward during these years, for the president was firm in his attitude. To Fortas he wrote that the day was ahead "when every individual who enlists in the service of his country can know that he and his family will not be expected to assume the extra and unfair burden of humiliation, inconvenience, and embarrassment because of their race, color, or creed." Johnson thought that the report of the Gesell Commission on Equal Opportunity in the Armed Forces should be implemented.[18]

Other sore points were addressed as the Johnsons courted distinguished members of the black community. Having earlier persuaded Thurgood Marshall to take the job of solicitor general, Johnson named him on June 14 to the Supreme Court, both a useful and a symbolic act. The Jackie Robinsons enjoyed a fine evening at the White House; the baseball star wrote: "Your inspired leadership more than justifies the confidence we all have in you." Blacks were named to the Federal

Reserve Board and to the cabinet, and Patricia Roberts Harris was made the first female black ambassador (to Luxembourg). Walter E. Washington was named mayor of the nation's capital, as Johnson thought the District had finally moved into "the world of 20th century government." Black leaders, such as Dick Gregory, Malcolm X, James Baldwin, and even Martin Luther King, Jr., were discussed frequently in presidential circles, since there was much planning to minimize the influence of extremists and to build up that of constitutional views. The "American Negro question" was not being internationalized, as Malcolm X wanted it to be; and James Baldwin, feisty author of *The Fire Next Time*, did not succeed in ringing down the curtain of the American dream with total chaos based on risking everything. King and some other black leaders would desert the president on Vietnam, but on little else. Said Marshall, "It has been rewarding to serve under a president who has led the nation to historic gains in the pursuit of equal justice under law."[19]

There were countervailing forces at work in race relations during the 1960s. Edith Efron, a critic of the media, concluded, after making a two-year study, that the TV networks actively slanted their opinion coverage in favor of black militants and against the white middle-class majority, thus "evading" the issue of radical violence. A force that was helping toward intelligent decison making was a study, made by some White House staff members, on the spot, of the worst conditions in Chicago and elsewhere; so, Douglass Cater thought that Johnson was getting "the most accurate profile possible of what is happening to the Negro in our country." Progress was indeed being made in income, education, jobs, and housing, but the black-white employment gap had not yet been solved. Don't believe, Cater told Johnson, that the race was shiftless, uneducated, and deteriorating in family life. A memorandum from aide Sherwin Markman on actual conditions of black life at its worst went into Johnson's pocket, to be kept and read to many visitors.[20]

These years witnessed the dramatic rise and abrupt death of Martin Luther King, Jr., one whose dramatic call for "freedom now" would gain permanent life. The Selma march of 1965, which was part of the drive to register voters, and the five-week Birmingham campaign got major headlines; but a 1966 campaign against slum conditions in Chicago, as well as Operation Breadbasket, which was designed to encourage the hiring of black workers, drew less attention from whites. When King was assassinated on April 5, 1968, the president wrote to King's widow, "Your terrible loss is shared not only by America, but by every country of the world where freedom and dignity are cherished." With the note went an album of messages of condolence sent by world leaders, which was reminiscent of a printed volume assembled in 1966 in memory of Abraham Lincoln. Sadly, King did not live to hear his adversary George Wallace say, in 1978: "Segregation is over. And it's better that it is over . . . because it's never coming back." What the federal government forced on "us" had "turned out for the best."[21]

The Civil Rights Act of 1968 was intended to be a 1966 act, but then the coalition of Republicans and northern Democrats who favored it could not reach agreement. Nicknamed "the open-housing law," it prohibited discrimination in the rental or sale of housing because of race, color, religion, or national origin, except in some owner-occupied or owner-managed units. It made federal crimes out of interference with voting, work, schooling, jury duty, or participation in federally assisted programs. Aimed at real-estate agents was a provision directed at those who were aiding in housing offenses. With an eye to inner-city violence, it increased penalties for rioting. Indian tribal governments were blocked from violating personal rights. Some constitutionalists were by now livid over losses in "property rights."

Black people and all minorities in America profited from the push in legislation and from eager administration. By the end of Johnson's term, the 1954 decision in *Brown* v. *Board of Education* seemed far more than only fifteen years in the past. The courts had done their share, but in his memoirs, former Chief Justice Earl Warren would give Presidents Kennedy and Johnson credit for what they had done. Said Justice Marshall, at an awards evening for black officeholders: "Thank you, Mr. President. You didn't wait. You took the bull by the horns. You didn't wait for the times. You made them!" Johnson had gone so far as to let black leaders Martin Luther King, Roy Wilkins, and Whitney Young consult on and approve of his Howard University speech in advance. Here was a wise step, perhaps, given its drafting by Richard Goodwin and Daniel Patrick Moynihan, two phrase-making intellectuals so different from the one who would deliver it. Appreciaton from Roy Wilkins was fervent, for the prestige of the White House had shaped opinion. Opinion had certainly changed. When people were asked in 1963, "If your party nominated a well qualified Negro man for president, would you vote for him? only 47 percent had said yes; by 1969 it was up to 67. Thousands of black officials were elected during the next decade, so that in 1983 some 334 were in state legislatures, but only three of these were in the party of Lincoln! Bayard Rustin found the South transformed "from a reactionary bastion into a region moderate in racial outlook and more enlightened in social and economic policy."[22]

The measurement and evaluation of racial change has been extensive. At least one author claims that watching the progress in black civil rights was a major stimulus to those who were the founders of the women's movement. In many parts of the country, intermarriage ceased to arouse hostility; at any rate, it increased by 92 percent between 1970 and 1977. An extensive black middle class was born out of the 1960s. By 1976, 30 percent of black families earned more than $15,000, compared with 2 percent a decade earlier. This far exceeded changes in the value of the dollar. The percentage who were living below the poverty line, 42 percent in 1966, had dropped to 31. So the black community itself came to be split—depending on affluence. Yet the unemployment rate for blacks remained obdurate, so that talk of a permanent underclass was common. Moynihan had found in 1965 that all too many urban black marriages ended in divorce and female-headed families; and illegitimate black births were common. A decade and a half later, the rates for all three phenomena had, for whatever reason, tripled.[23] Government, it appeared, could not do it all—a point that Chicago's Jessie Jackson would dwell on years later.

Criticism of the Johnson racial program has been overwhelmed by the praise. Black extremists did flourish, but without the three civil rights acts, would they have commanded a larger revolutionary following? Said Roy Wilkins: "For the sixties, the conception and enactment of the voting rights act was a high point. Despite its competition from grievous assassinations, violent encounters with the police, and spectacular repression of the Negro population, the voting measure may prove to have been the most significant accomplishment of this decade in the area of civil rights." Aging Martin Luther King, Sr., thought that Johnson had sought "vigorously and, I always felt, sincerely, to bring a new atmosphere and new solutions to some of this country's more serious social problems." Said lawyer and political figure Barbara Jordan in 1971 to her mentor, "Mr. President, you make us all feel like first-class Americans." Mayor Charles Evers of Fayette, Mississippi, noted in 1979 that the number of black officials in his state had increased from zero to over three hundred. One of his colleagues observed: "The students today don't remember what the civil rights movement was all about. There has been so much progress in the past fifteen years that people can't believe how things were." One measurement of median family income from 1964 to 1969 showed that per capita income for blacks had risen from 50 to 61 percent of that for whites.[24]

Voting rights made a vast difference. The 29,000 registered blacks in Mississippi in 1964 grew, by 1980, to 330,000; in Alabama, from 110,000 to 350,000; in Louisiana, from 165,000 to 465,000; in South Carolina, from 144,000 to 320,000. Yet, ten years after the Kerner Report, Carnegie researchers found that blacks still needed to be integrated into the mainstream of American society; not enough had changed in regard to jobs, health care, and schooling. Some measurements indicate dramatic progress, however, and this presidency was when this began to happen. One black leader said he had always expected to be stunned when and if a southern accent was heard from the White House. But for him, time had changed circumstances.[25] Black votes helped a contrite George Wallace back into the governor's mansion in the 1980s; the first black councilman in one hundred years took office in Charleston, South Carolina; and black mayors were elected in Atlanta, Chicago, Los Angeles, and elsewhere.

The famous War on Poverty was superimposed on the long-standing social-security, welfare, and veterans-payment programs of government in America. These were liberalized by Kennedy-Johnson appointees, so that total social-welfare expenditures by government at all levels went from nearly $67 to $127 billion during this presidency. While increases in social insurance were relatively modest (from $25.6 to $40.8 billion), public assistance more than doubled (from $5 to $11.9 billion) during prosperous times. It was not just the federal share that grew; state and local expenditures for public aid alone more than doubled. The old program of Aid to Dependent Children (now Aid to Families with Dependent Children) expended $1.5 billion at the outset, but $3.6 billion at the close. Both the number of families and the number of children about doubled. Health expenditures in the entire nation went from $174 to $311 million as the government share rose from $8.5 to a startling $24 million, which was just the beginning, as it would turn out. Some unfortunate figures were up, however. Violent crimes more than doubled (from 2,442,000 to 5,013,000) as the prison population unaccountably decreased from 217,283 to 196,007.[26]

Economic conditions changed during these years. The consumer price index, which had risen by only 9.4 points in an equivalent number of Eisenhower years (from 80.2 in 1955 to 89.6 in 1961), grew by 18.1 points in Johnson's (from 91.7 in 1963 to 109.8 in 1969). And the money supply, which had been nearly stable in the Eisenhower years ($27.6 to $29.1 billion), jumped, in Johnson's, from $31.6 to $44.8 billion. The interest rate on prime commercial paper grew in Johnson's years from 3.55 percent to 7.83 percent.[27] Hidden financial time bombs were buried deep inside the administration. Measuring changes and meanings through time in such areas as these is a challenge.

With the new Medicare payments program for hospitals and physicians and pharmacists came a vast new area of services and costs. Benefit payments to hospitals grew from $2.5 to $4.4 billion as costs of services being rendered by both hospitals and medical personnel accelerated. Payments to physicians climbed from $664 million in 1966 to $1.6 billion in 1969. Congress, both then and later, failed to contain costs at the same time that it facilitated great demand. While the grateful—or critical—public tended to focus on Medicare for aged recipients of social security, a program begun in 1965, the new Medicaid for the needy got less attention. Codifying existing medical services for those on public assistance, it did increase in a single year the amount spent by the federal and state governments from $1.35 to over $2 billion—figures that were destined to climb steadily. Within the War on Poverty, some programs that got heavy praise or outsized criticism were by no means the most expensive. Arranging OEO programs for 1968 in descending order of funding shows, in millions: Community Action, $847; OEO Labor Department programs, $471; Job Corps, $282; Work Experience, $44; VISTA, $29; Migrants, $25; Rural Loans, $17; general, $14; other, $10; unobligated, $7—for a total of $1,746 million. Within Community Action the larger programs were Head Start, $333; Research and Demonstration, $187; Neighborhood Service, $132; Legal Services, $36; Neighborhood Health Centers, $33; Upward Bound, $30; and Employment Services, $22. Such programs as Foster Grandparents and Family Planning received but $10 million each in a year to change a continental nation! Within the Labor Department figure were such major items as three Neighborhood Youth Corps programs, $269 million, and JOBS, only $60 million.[28]

Growing costs brought public criticism and political debate in the Congress. By March 1968 the president had to take official notice of "the soaring cost of medical care," which was due in large part to the new, well-meaning programs. The Aid for Families with Dependent Children program, especially, came in for sharp criticism, which was focused on how to get mothers trained and motivated to seek and hold employment. A vast potential for exciting the public existed in the new bureaucratic eagerness to include family planning (i.e., birth control) as a part of AFDC activities, the object being to contain the numbers of future children on the rolls. The disability retirees and youths who were attending college on social-security payments, once minor matters, were just two areas where the liberalization by law and a generous administration proved burdensome. OEO had to fight every step of the way for appropriations. In these years it succeeded, going from its initial $800 million to over $1.7 billion in fiscal 1968.

A criticized program was the Job Corps, which relocated youths in residential centers in order to give them training. When it was revealed that it would cost the government less to send a youth to Harvard for a year than to keep him in this program, attention riveted on it. The cost fell rapidly from $9,945 to $6,900 per person; but it was too late. Effective control over the Community Action programs was a bitter battle waged within the Democratic party, for city mayors and their political organizations had a stake in these programs. There was suspicion, which was sometimes well founded, that radicals had infiltrated or even had gained control of individual agencies, and the legal program's ability to sue in court to highlight discrimination was not what either political figures or most of the public thought appropriate. Day Care lacked funds, but a program that had relatively smooth sailing was Work Study. Legal Aid was very controversial. None of these concerns and issues had existed, say, in 1960.[29]

By 1968 a federally financed constituency of "the poor" in some cities was showing some of the characteristics of a defined proletariat. A Poor People's Campaign, planned by Dr. King, was carried on after his death, first with lobbying and then with occupation of a shantytown named Resurrection City in the nation's capital. As some three thousand people took up residence in the open air after April 29, the media found the chance for ample spot news, in-depth interviews, and commentary. When the ramshackle "city" was finally closed on June 23, the protesters faded away, but not before a demonstration, in league with middle-class white allies, at the Washington Monument had drawn fifty thousand or so. Uniform public sympathy was never enlisted behind overt demonstrators, but it was in vogue during a period when street marches and noisy campus rallies were the simplistic way to show both unity and the alleged justice of causes, since the media were eager allies. What promised to become a major disputation over a loyalty-oath requirement for workers in various OEO programs withered when a Justice Department ruling exempted the participants in work-study and work-training programs. There were many predictions that students' college loans might never be paid back as legally required; but who could say as to the future?

The Model Cities Program proved to be particularly vulnerable. Fifteen years after it was established, a Princeton University study found that declining population, lower per capita income, and generally aging housing marked the condition of the nation's older cities. It said there was no evidence that conditions in the cities were improving. The 1965 task force was supposed to develop new programs for the projected Department of Housing and Urban Development. The 1966 State of the Union message announced a "demonstration cities program," and a chilly Congress got draft bills for it in late January. Political minds at once realized that appropriating these funds would have an impact on existing urban programs. During the next ten months, it is claimed, "the measure endured as many perils as Pauline, required frequent rescue, and on two occasions was pronounced stone dead, beyond even the resuscitative powers of the President."[30] The proposed $2 billion for two years shrank to $900 million, compromises abounded, and desegregation provisions were watered down as the White House promised benefits for the districts of more than a hundred legislators out of the three hundred who had made requests. The dreams of the task force were shattered. Cities were selected on the basis of congressonal politics. Of the first forty-nine awards, forty-eight went to districts whose congressmen had voted for the bill. Partisans like Robert C. Weaver, the able black secretary of the Housing Department from 1966 to 1968, thought that it was almost enough anyway that President Johnson had "initiated and enacted more housing and urban legislation than any other [president] in our history." Even though the president's rural roots were along the remote Pedernales, he had left his mark on urban America, Weaver thought.[31]

The War on Poverty was permeated with hard work, pressures to achieve results, and worthwhile performance of duties by many who joined the administration, but complaints about high overhead were common. After the first two years, Johnson showed marked reluctance to fill OEO administrative vacancies. His personal perspective was simplistic. To his liking was the motto the secretary of labor sent in a think piece: "Having a chance is most of what life means." Here was a rough paraphrase of HEW's "Hope is the anchor of life." Johnson did not care for the "intellectual types" who gravitated toward his administration for research and experimentation that was heavy in overhead. Hubert Humphrey recalled the suspicions among local officials about what was going on in Washington. To them, the new power centers were unnecessary rivals to their own long-established, but underfunded, administrative units. The war, in any case, had "meager" results in rural America, says a key historian of agriculture.[32]

Congress became restive after the passage of so many bills and the elapse of time; by 1967 it overhauled the OEO act to provide General Accounting Office assessments. The act's outsized authority was whittled away; appropriations were even held up. Legislators came to resent the pressure tactics being used against them. For example, when Senator Dirksen once delivered a speech attacking the War on Poverty, the White House provided its congressional liaison officer with five rebuttal speeches to be placed "in powerful hands." Skeptical legislators sensed that the gap between rhetoric and performance in OEO was very wide. They would not have been surprised to learn that during the late 1970s, a smaller percentage of children were living with both parents than had been the case in 1960. Only 50 percent of black children did. Where were the dramatic results that had been promised—for example, from adding families to ADC, thus making it AFDC? Said one observer, "I think he built the rhetoric far beyond that which had been planned by his advisors."[33] Together, Johnson and his speech writers went far beyond rationality in this respect.

It had been assumed that OEO funding would derive, in the long run, from growth in the economy: increases in employment would increase tax revenues. But, said Sargent Shriver: "Vietnam took it all away, every goddamned dollar. That's what killed the war on poverty. It wasn't public opinion." (By implication, then, it was not Nixon!) In remarks that are missing from official versions of the speech, the irritated president almost said, when accused in 1966 by Robert Kennedy of having short-changed the poor in his budget: "I'm not funding all the programs I got action on last year. More than that, it takes trained personnel . . . ; you just can't mash a button and have a whole working program." The AFL-CIO realistically saw the antipoverty campaign of 1964 as "hardly a first, small step." Bold measures and more money would be needed.[34]

Too many assumed that most individuals would struggle hard in order to better their lot. But in twentieth-century America, motivation was not a universal characteristic: too many had never worked; too many were not wanted. National mobility, an American trait once called the M-factor, meant that many lacked reinforcement from relatives and friends. Disability and mental and physical illness limited the employability of some. Too many menial jobs lacked attractiveness to those who had been educated in the new American way. Adult education, designed to bring employability, was hard work in itself. Money alone could not give the anxious president the results he craved. Almost too late, a training program called JOBS proved to be something of a winner in 1968.

One might think from complaints, then and later, about lack of funding that the War on Poverty had had to get along essentially without funds. On the contrary, from 1965 to 1973 that whole effort cost about $15.5 billion, a sizable figure despite unfavorable comparison with the $120 billion spent on the Vietnam War during the same period. In addition, when Wilbur Cohen handed in his final report on January 16, 1969, he revealed proudly that expenditures for social security had risen from $17 billion in 1963 to $30 billion in 1968. Medicare reached twenty million people aged sixty-five and over (some 95 percent of eligible older people had signed up for the physicians'-fee part). Said the partisan

HEW secretary, who was never one to be cost conscious, "Progress has been notable indeed."[35]

The president clearly believed that a great deal was being accomplished by OEO, social security, the liberalized categorical-benefit welfare programs, and aid to education. But it was hard to bring "the poor" into the mainstream. This would become apparent in the next decade, even though much that he had started was being continued and though appropriations for many programs had climbed. The number of poor would decline, from 1968 to 1976, only from 12.8 to 11.8 percent, measured in terms of cash income. When in-kind benefits (such as services, food stamps, etc.) were included, the decline was from 10.1 to 6.5 percent, a much better showing. One scholar, Barbara Ward (Lady Jackson), wrote him: "I suppose more was done for the really underprivileged during your period of office than in any previous administration and it should, it must, give you immense satisfaction to know that not only this generation but their children and beyond are going to get chances and opportunities which they owe to you . . . ; it will be *your* harvest." Such praise was one thing; statistical measurement was another. There had been results; but the programs did not by any means expunge poverty. In any case, effort of many kinds had been made.[36]

A controversial program from the outset was community action, as we have seen. Little did one Richard W. Boone know, during the drafting of the OEO act, that his phrase "maximum feasible participation" by the poor was destined to get such a play, for it sounded rather simple to have some activities involve poor people in the planning and administration of the program. Apparently neither he nor others who favored community action intended that the poor would control policy. Said the OEO act, a community-action program will be "developed, conducted, and administered with the maximum feasible participation of residents of the areas and members of the groups served." Under ideological stimulation, militants in some places quickly acted as though they had a mandate to ignore governmental authority. OEO finally had to declare, a bit late, that "control" was not intended. Some officials came to see advantages in modest participation but resented it when the federal legal-aid program started to finance politicized lawsuits. Even Black Panthers and agitators were funded into adversary relationships with local governments. One question that can be posed but not answered here is how far freedom marchers, militancy, and demonstrations were responsible for much of Johnson's Great Society effort; that is, was it a *response* to ferment rather than liberal compassion at work? Another side of that coin is the somewhat far-fetched idea that it was Johnson's War on Poverty and/or his Great Society package that somehow *created* the upheavals of the 1960s. To this, Johnson liked to say, "If we've had them with it, you can imagine what we'd have had if we had continued to sit on that dynamite keg."[37]

Administration of OEO proved to be a nightmare. Vice-President Humphrey told Johnson that although the chief might be thinking of his Economic Opportunity Council as analogous to the National Security Council, "it has hardly lived up to this important function" and was not efficient. "Antipoverty programs became political pork-barrel-type programs and were taken over by sophisticated middle-class bureaucrats," says psychologist Kenneth Clark. In some cases, upwardly mobile working-class individuals became subordinated to the more knowledgeable middle-class political controllers of these programs. Antipoverty hustlers emerged. Former secretary Cohen would later admit: "It got out of hand. . . . We extended community action in the poverty program from just about . . . a hundred communities to eleven hundred. And that was just too many; that just could not be done. . . . We tried to do too much in too many places in too short a time." At the very end of his term, the weary president recommended that the incoming administration continue OEO for two more years but admitted there had been considerable experimentation, with "many successes and some failures." He thought Congress would want to transfer some programs out of OEO to other agencies and then reorganize it.[38]

An area to be explored is how far the Johnson bureaucracy's wholesale liberalizations in the enormous categorical-aid programs for mothers and children, the aged, and the blind, as well as the new program for the disabled, moved them near to temporary anarchy. When a few years later Daniel Patrick Moynihan wrote *The Politics of a Guaranteed Income*, he began with devastating 1971 quotes: from *Newsweek*, "WELFARE: There Must Be a Better Way"; from *Time*, "The U.S. welfare system is a living nightmare that has reached the point of the involuntary scream and chill awakening"; from *U.S. News and World Report*, "Welfare Out of Control—Story of Financial Crisis Cities Face." Future presidencies inherited public-assistance programs, modified by the Johnson bureaucracy, that could no longer be restricted by state or local residency requirements, by whether there was an employable man in the house, or by realistic "needs" tests. One must ponder Moynihan's startling discovery: "The number of persons classified as poor in the span 1959 to 1968 decreased by 36 percent. The number of public-assistance recipients rose 41 percent."[39] This occurred during a period of war-induced increased national employment and relative prosperity.

Clearly, there is no limit to the side effects, "good" or "bad," that could somehow be associated with the Johnson presidency (or, indeed, any presidency). One example would be the full effects of Medicare and Medicaid. People on social security and those considered needy, and therefore eligible for the latter, benefited, of course. But vast increases in service from a finite resource drove up costs of care to an extent where many in the middle class developed into a new medically indigent. At the same time, Medicare payments were soon seen to be quite inadequate to pay burgeoning costs, so vast sums came to be expended by the elderly for supplemental insurance in the hope of avoiding economic catastrophe. Weighing of such changes through time, while adding in the later financial difficulties of a greatly liberalized social-security system, would take us far afield and would certainly involve consideration of more than the years 1963 to 1969.

The national economy in those years was often the focus of presidential attention. The early year of 1964 would be a time of many activities, but none, probably, was more important to President Johnson than wooing the American business and industrial community in meetings, dinners, luncheons, and discussions. Members of the Business Council were sought out singly and in groups, listened to, informed in briefings, telephoned, and courted. For them, the early tax cut and the balancing of the budget had been a big boost. Their new president proved to be fully informed on matters that they cared about. Said one at the close of a long evening, "I'll be damned that I have to admit that I believe him, I trust him, and I think for the first time we have a president who isn't out to dismantle the business structure of this country. . . . I think I'll go along with him."[40] Such an attitude greatly aided the Treasury and Commerce departments in their daily work.

The early obsession with a tax cut, which the new president displayed, was a relatively new commitment, for one expert has noted that tax reduction was not the act that the Kennedy administration intended to perform when it took office in 1961. The new determination was born of possible economic deterioration, dangers in a deficit, and the desirability of blaming any deficit, if it came, on tax reduction rather than on the future spending on administration programs. The Department of Labor and the unions anticipated that there would be resulting high employment. Tax revenues would even balance the budget, the Treasury Department hoped. On June 7, 1962, Kennedy had promised a tax reduction; not until February 26, 1964, did Johnson sign it into law. Economies were forced on reluctant departments as a lever to win over Senator Harry Byrd and others who thought as he did. While Johnson fought cleverly and hard, "at no time was its enactment seriously in doubt." In Congress the will to cut was really there, it has been said.[41]

The Revenue Act of 1964 gave substantial tax cuts both to individuals and to corporations as the Treasury Department watched silently. Henceforth a senior citizen could, one time, sell the homestead at a profit without being heavily taxed, or sometimes not taxed at all. Rules governing moving expenses helped some employees. Many small taxpayers went off the federal rolls. Income-averaging provisions helped those, such as certain professionals, whose incomes were irregular from year to year. Such provisions, and technical ones applying to businesses, made the act one to remember. The president tried to do his share in economizing by insisting that lights in the White House be turned off as much as possible—to the amusement of columnists and cartoonists, who failed to notice, for the most part, the mammoth bill for operating the White House aircraft.

A momentous Johnson proclamation on the budget and the economy was contained in his 1967 budget message, delivered in January 1966, when he said that the nation could and would spend for its military and domestic needs alike: "Both of these commitments involve great costs. They are costs we can and will meet. . . . The struggle in Vietnam must be supported. The advance toward a Great Society at home must continue unabated." Soon, he proposed deficit spending, together with a modest tax surcharge, saying: "This program will require a measure of sacrifice as well as continued work and resourcefulness. . . . This budget represents a careful balance of our abundant resources and our awesome responsibilities." In 1968 he had to introduce "priorities" and "choice," as he confessed, "We cannot do everything we would wish to do." Now there were "competing demands"; so one must choose. Here was a sad progression.

There had been the thought, early on, that when the Vietnam War ended, there would be a fiscal "peace dividend" that would somehow make everything all right. This never developed, partly because transfer payments to individuals, which had amounted to 25 percent of the budget in 1964, rose by 1975 to 40 percent—plus another 15 percent for states and localities. Overall, during the brief Johnson years, purchases of goods and services rose from $65.9 to $98.0 billion; transfer payments, from $29.6 to $50.9 billion; and grants to states and localities, from $9.8 to $19.2 billion. The total budget grew from $117.2 to $184.7 billion. Deficit spending became the order of the day, averaging in the 1960s about $5.5 billion annually. It was not true, after all, that rising federal revenues and growth in production would more than take care of rising outlays in federal programs.[42]

Meanwhile, the Vietnam War helped toward full employment, when the men in uniform are included as being on a payroll; and schools and colleges bulged with students, some of whom were evading the draft. Lyndon Johnson's right-hand man in the giving of economic advice, Walter Heller, was saying in his book *New Dimensions of Political Economy*[43] that the possibility of runaway inflation was minimum and that people should be optimistic about the nation's economic future. As to inflation, in 1957, Gallup-poll interviewees estimated that the minimum weekly amount needed for a family of four was $72; by 1964 this had risen to $81; but by 1969 it leapt to $120. With the trend in federal borrowing and inflation well established, it would soar to $296 by 1982. Perceptive and eloquent on the impact of inflation on Americans was a contemporary journalist: "The record of his monetary and fiscal policies is documented as a confused, incompetent, and gigantic failure that threatens the security of savings, the purchasing power of pensions—all the hard-won material rewards of industrious personal achievement."[44]

A key economic event was the January 18, 1966, meeting between Wilbur Mills and Johnson, when the president said there was no need to boost individual income taxes to finance the war and the Great Society. Mills would later claim that Congress didn't understand the extent of the U.S. war commitment. Thus the seeds of 1970s inflation were planted during Johnson's term. A member of the Council of Economic Advisers has said that the failure to enact a tax increase was a "colossal error," a classic case of fiscal mismanagement which led to the era of inflation. In 1965 the deficit was $1.6 billion; a year later it had tripled. In 1968 the deficit was a full $25.2 billion, in dollars of that day. Meanwhile, the Federal Reserve System allowed the money supply to climb. The 10 percent surtax of 1968, which was obtained by the president from a reluctant Congress, came too late and was too little, as he knew full well.

In retrospect, Johnson, though well-meaning, had made a mistake when he ended the embargo on oil imports in 1966 "to combat inflation by encouraging full and free competition in the marketplace." The result was much as expected, but the resulting flood of oil purchases by Americans from the future OPEC countries pushed the United States toward a subservient posture vis-à-vis the oil-exporting nations. One can scarcely blame the president because he did not foresee this distant result of his attempt to help the American consumer maintain his standard of living through cheap prices for energy while conserving domestic stocks, but the country was certainly set on the wrong road.[45]

In his 1966 Economic Report to the Congress, President Johnson described six "main tasks" of federal economic policy as he saw them. These were: full employment without inflation; opening the doors of opportunity by developing human resources; helping to solve social and economic problems that are beyond the capability of state and local governments and private action; international economic action; maintaining healthy economic competition; and finally, enlisting the voluntary cooperation of business, labor, and other groups. There were inevitable contradictions in such a program, especially when the waging of an expensive war would be coupled with the waging of a heavily publicized program to usher in a Great Society. The real damage would come later, with increases in consumer prices, higher interest rates for government and private borrowing, and loss in the purchasing power of the dollar. Yet, during his last years, the former president could have reflected that the war-stimulated period 1961–1969 would be classified permanently by economists as a period of "recovery" sandwiched between the recessions of 1960/61 and 1969/70.[46]

A frequent assessment of this administration's influence is that it vastly expanded the federal bureaucracy. It did, of course; yet, one must see this in perspective. The number of full-time federal employees increased from 970,000 to 1,008,000 in Eisenhower's final two years. By 1963 it had increased to 1,100,000; by 1969 to 1,300,000; and by 1978 it had risen to 1,400,000. Thus, in a growing country, there was a long-term upward trend, and it was not just in total governmental employment. Rather, white-collar employment in the federal government increased in the 1959–1978 period by 44 percent, while blue-collar employment declined by 25.1 percent! Policy-level jobs blossomed. There was centralization: employment in Washington rose by 41 percent; federal jobs elsewhere, by only 11 percent. Agencies involved with "regulating" grew the most rapidly.

The table of organization in the federal government changed in these years. Two new departments, Housing and Urban Development, and Transportation, both especially interesting to city politicians, were places for increases in personnel. But the idea of merging the Department of Commerce and the Department of Labor died a-borning. Passage of sixteen reorganization plans did not result in noticeable contraction in the federal establishment. Indeed, say not unfriendly experts, "The cumulative effect of Great Society legislation was to produce far greater problems of executive structure and coordination than had existed at any other time, except perhaps during the Civil War, the Great Depression, and World War II." The problems were permanent, they assert, "threatening the capacity of the administrative system to fulfill policy objectives."[47]

In summary, the national government did in fact grow during the Johnson years, as well as during those before and after. But because of the huge increase in the use of outside consultants, agencies, and think tanks in the 1960s and later, the true size of growth is masked. Increases in population and inflation account for some of the apparent growth, of course. Yet, economists say that when a state takes on the task of meeting popular needs, it necessarily grows.[48]

An intellectual who was temporarily in the White House came to reflect, late in 1965, on Johnson's economic posture. "It seems to me," recorded Charles Frankel, "that the president genuinely wants economies and a Great Society; he wants to fight a war in Vietnam *and* to build dams and democracy in the Mekong Valley. He hopes all these things are simultaneously possible. Still, down here where I sit, the effect is disconcerting. On Mondays, Wednesdays, and Fridays we receive messages to go full speed ahead; on Tuesdays, Thursdays and Saturdays, we're told that we're going to have to retrench."[49] It is easy to be sympathetic with members of the White House team, who were so anxious to bring political democracy to Southeast Asia and to bring economic and social democracy to America that dollar costs, at the time and later, seemed a nuisance to be pushed to one side. But they mortgaged the future.

This administration's handling of industry was relatively smooth. Gardner Ackley served as chairman of the president's Council of Economic Advisers (CEA) from November 1964 to January 1968. An economist who had seen previous government service, he joined the council during the Kennedy years, strengthening its dedication to Keynesian economics. He would support wage-price guidelines and tax cuts, but nevertheless, he sought to fight inflation, chiefly by jawboning. One episode of 1965 in which Ackley figured was the matter of the administration versus the aluminum industry. When the price of aluminum was raised 25 cents a pound in the fall of 1965, the administration called the move inflationary; shortly, the government threatened to release 200,000 tons of the metal from stockpiles—after which the industry backed down. A few months later, Bethlehem Steel was successfully attacked because of a price rise, as was Molybdenum Corporation in the summer of 1966. When General Motors planned to increase car prices by $61, the government negotiated them down to $23. But many defeats were accepted—in steel, transportation, and elsewhere. (The nation was not in a declared war.)

Some feel that President Johnson's chairman of the CEA grossly underestimated the probable cost of the Vietnam War, suggesting a figure half of that projected by experts in the Congress. Later, Ackley admitted that he had made a major mistake in this crucial matter. Still, Johnson had Ackley behind him when in 1967 the president belatedly sought a tax increase designed to hold back inflation and to avoid a hectic expansion in the GNP.

The vast expenditures of the Johnson era, while a war was being waged in Southeast Asia, had their appropriate impact on the domestic economy. Even a decade later it was common for columnists to refer acidly to the "guns and butter" aberration of that period. Economist Arthur Burns then stated that the current rate of production was illusory, for "what is produced" is also highly relevant: "Bombs or missiles . . . add nothing to the nation's capacity to produce." Not only the foregone civilian goods were lost; so, too, was the large investment in human and business capital.[50] Another loss was the investment in R & D that was diverted to Vietnam projects by corporations and government agencies; but this diversion would be uneven and difficult to quantify.

Johnson's memoirs offer a short chapter entitled "Bite the Bullet," which relates, with many excuses, how the triumph of the 1964 tax cut evolved into the burden of seeking a 1966 tax increase. He says he knew that history's judgment would not rest on his current standing in the Gallup poll, "but on what I did to steer the economy between the shoals of recession and the rocks of runaway inflation." In his Tax Adjustment Act in 1966 he achieved the temporary restoration of excise taxes on automobiles and telephones and the accelerated collection of tax payments. Now he was told by Ackley, "A little inflation won't be fatal." The cabinet was unenthusiastic anyway about raising taxes. A sizable business group and some labor leaders were opposed. Congress, in an off-year election period, was hostile. Told that insisting would "mess up other programs," politician Johnson settled for much less than half a loaf, because he was unwilling to cut expenditures for the Great Society in order to get votes in Congress for a tax raise. The 10 percent surcharge, which was too late, and the $6 billion decrease, which was too little, were, nevertheless, signed on June 28, 1968.[51]

Organized labor profited during Johnson's presidency. The AFL-CIO even called the Eighty-ninth Congress "the most outstanding in national history!" Nevertheless, the hated section 14b of the Taft-Hartley Act, which enabled states to ban the open shop, stayed on the books. As the president left office, there were nineteen states with right-to-work laws or constitutional provisions. The Department of Labor was able to get Congress to increase and extend minimum-wage legislation, however. The minimum went from $1.25 in 1966 to $1.60 in 1968, during an inflationary period; and nearly ten million more workers were covered. A variety of labor legislation that was supported by the president failed to clear one or both houses of Congress, however, and a new immigration law, while it eliminated racial criteria for entry, placed a limit on admissions from this hemisphere.

Agricultural trends during these years were in keeping with directions set after World War II. The classic problems of overproduction and low income among rural residents continued, while the Department of Agriculture agonized over appropriate levels for price supports. As the result of legislative changes in 1965, by the close of Johnson's presidency surpluses in wheat and corn were down—thanks in part to donations of wheat to other countries. Governmental interaction continued to have its critics, who thought that the market might be relied on to bring equity to producers and consumers alike. Farms became larger; the number of farmers declined; and productivity, aided by machinery and fertilizer, increased. Secretary of Agriculture Orville Freeman took pleasure in passage of the Food and Agriculture Act of 1965, with its production controls, governmental payments to producers, and price supports of the kind that had long been popular in his party. Although funds for pesticide research were enlarged and a bill on pesticide labeling could be pointed to, tight controls were avoided. Unemployment among rural farm workers continued to be a problem, according to "The People Left Behind," a 1967 report by a presidential commission.

It was a period of ferment for the Post Office Department. After the Chicago Post Office had suffered a total breakdown for three weeks in 1966 and the postmaster general had predicted "a race with catastrophe," the Commission on Postal Organization, headed by Frederick Kappel of A. T. & T., recommended in 1968, in its report "Towards Postal Excellence," that a government-owned corporation should operate the service henceforth on a self-supporting basis. This event was a change early desired by Larry O'Brien. Although the affected unions were opposed to this idea, the president endorsed it, and the public was enthusiastic; but action was not to be completed during this administration. The venerable Postal Savings System, which had been founded in 1911, died in 1966. A new law in 1968 made it possible for people to have their names removed from mailing lists. This was an outgrowth of increasing liberality in the publication of sexually explicit magazines and books in which much-noticed *Playboy* was the leader.

While the term "Great Society" caught on and would be remembered, certain other trial-balloon terms never made it. One was "Creative Federalism," a term spoken six times in public by the president, which was applied to the creative and cooperative partnership of all private interests and all levels of government. It had "written the story of American success." In Oklahoma, on August 26, 1964, Johnson observed: "We are entering a new day of relations between government and private institutions and individual citizens. This new federalism—this new day [reminiscent of Hoover's New Day of 1928] of cooperation—is not fully understood. But the problems are apparent." In November the key was "cooperation" at all government levels by "partners." The year would see the last public gesture to the subject, although inside the White House, various staff memorandums would continue to use the term. Thus, the director of the Office of Emergency Planning wrote the president, "The New Federalism has created an attitude of teamwork at all levels of government which did not previously exist." To this, Johnson eventually replied: "The Federal-State partnership we envision under the New Federalism is vital to the continued well-being of the American people."[52] The term surfaced again a decade later; but few recalled its earlier use.[53] Another of Johnson's terms, "consensus," was used in seventeen speeches. Johnson's intent was "to heal and to build," as he told a group of broadcasters on April 1, 1968. A critical commentator observed that the word *consensus* meant that Johnson merely blurred issues and watered down legislation in order to get broad support.[54] On this point, it would take much study to uncover the full truth.

The man who made things move and seemed to take such pleasure in his action on the domestic front, the man who outwardly pretended that all the laws were as good as their titles and their initial sentences of good intention, was even then capable of candidly admitting that there were real limitations. At a midstream time for taking stock, on August 20, 1966, he said that the country needed a "strong dose of self-discipline" and a sort of domestic Good Neighbor Policy on every block. People would somehow have to become color-blind. "Building a Great Society is not the job of the president alone." Nor could it be done only in Washington, he told his Maine audience. "It has to be the goal of every man and woman, every boy and girl. Every one of you has to pitch in and improve the corner of the country you live in." Obviously, the passage of a mere two and a half years had brought some disillusionment. These truisms should have been stressed much more heavily.

While the Johnson presidency was one marked by several assassinations that shocked the nation—those of Malcolm X, Martin Luther King, Jr., and Robert Kennedy—other forms of violence also brought crime to the fore and kept the Department of Justice busy. Riots, mass demonstrations, and defiance of the federal government's authority to draft youths for military service combined to make law enforcement difficult. Johnson accepted the burden with marked reluctance, given his public emphasis on positive factors. His attorney generals knew that the laws of the land had to be enforced, but they hoped that, somehow, expenditures on education, money for better food and housing, and a multitude of services would keep crime from growing. Some liberals were enraged by the failure of Congress to do anything about firearms control after Robert Kennedy's assassination, when Edward Kennedy's proposal was defeated 29 to 53 in the Senate.

The year 1963 brought the enactment of laws on juvenile delinquency, drug abuse, and the rehabilitation of prisoners, as well as the Law Enforcement Assistance Act. In July 1965 President Johnson appointed the Commission on Law Enforcement and the Administration of Justice, which reported back in February 1967. Its report, *The Challenge of Crime in a Free Society*, quickly showed up on reading lists in the behavioral sciences and in programs where law-enforcement personnel were being trained or upgraded. Issue was taken with conventional assumptions: namely, that crime is the vice of a handful of people and that most crime is being reported. Americans were increasingly staying off the streets at night and were keeping firearms and watchdogs for protection. Federal authorities should stress crime prevention, find new methods of dealing with offenders, eliminate unfairness in the criminal-justice system, recruit and train better personnel, increase research, and take more responsibility at every level for changing the status quo. "The Commission is sure that the nation can control crime if it will," was its conclusion.[55]

By 1980 the Law Enforcement Assistance Administration (LEAA) had dispensed some $7 billion to state and local governments for anticrime hardware and other purposes and to colleges for training programs, an activity that certainly had some beneficial impact but was widely attacked by state and local leaders as being a federal boondoggle designed to take away local rights and powers. The LEAA saw itself, however, as a body dedicated to professionalizing police work, which certainly included the educating of law-enforcement personnel in the law and judicial interpretations of it. Unfortunately, crime rates continued to climb during the LEAA's first decade; one estimate was that because of red tape and overhead costs, the public was getting only twelve cents in improved law enforcement for every dollar spent by LEAA. From 1960 to 1978 the incidence of robbery, murder, aggravated assault, and rape almost tripled in America.[56] Nevertheless, the many new college degrees in law enforcement were bound to have a future impact.

Johnson delivered a major message on crime on February 7, 1968, which received less attention than it should have because of concern over the war. Hoping "to insure the public safety," he gave the attorney general authority to coordinate criminal law enforcement and crime prevention in the federal establishment. The nation would now face up to its problem, he said; decades of neglect must end. The goal, outsized as usual, was to "drive crime from our midst in these United States," he told his audience. To the Congress he soon spoke more carefully: "This message will not solve our nation's crime problem"; neither would other strong words and good intentions. Eventually the Congress passed the Omnibus Crime Control and Safe Streets Act and the Juvenile Delinquency Prevention and Control Act. Yet the same message could have been delivered more than a decade later, for crime in all its forms turned out to be resistant to both toughness and ingenuity. In response to one of many citizens who expressed apprehension about crime, the White House replied, "The president more than shares your concern over lawlessness in a nation that has and must always draw strength from the decency and dedication of its people."[57]

Were—and are—Americans a violent people? It began, in the 1960s, to become quite the thing to publish essays and books saying, in one way or another, that "violence is as American as apple pie." Those who reluctantly served on presidential commissions on the subject did not find it a terribly happy experience; so, there was absenteeism and uneven sharing of the work load. Milton Eisenhower served somewhat unhappily, especially after he asked for the appointment of two scholars to his group, without result. It seemed that this presidency was obsessed with the rights of individuals who had been accused of crime— one of several civil-liberties obsessions of Attorney General Ramsey Clark—so that generating toughness was uphill. Clark's enthusiasm went toward such causes as the almost total elimination of wiretapping.[58]

Joseph Califano would later assess at length the problems involved in effective performance against poverty and crime. These included overpromising by the president and the failure of Congress to fund legislation. In the Omnibus Act, Congress had made major promises that it failed to honor. "Year after year since 1968, crime has continued its persistent rise. The Safe Streets Act has been funded at 50 percent or less of its programmed level, and the American public has been presented with a series of preposterous assurances that there is a cheap and easy way to eliminate street crime." There must be "an annual reconciliation of the public books of promise and performance," he concluded.[59]

Did the Great Society fail? Two writers in 1977 noted that "the view is widely held that the Great Society failed." The case they were hearing repeatedly was that money had been "thrown at" problems; there was still a welfare mess; the heavy hand of government was still operating; we had gone too far, too fast; inflation had been one consequence—so, too, had alienation and racial tension; there were scandals in administration; the impact was not lasting; there had been economic mismanagement. Here was quite an indictment. But, said Sar A. Levitan and Robert Taggart,[60] there had been realistic goals and movement toward a just and equitable society. There was reasonable efficiency; one must expect some negative spillover. The benefits were more than the sum of their parts. Critics had applied questionable standards and had indulged in negative thinking. Rather than admitting that the work ethic had weakened, they said smoothly that "work disincentives have been a continuing concern." Obviously, "failure" is not easily agreed upon!

Overall, a look at a quarter-century of growth in the federal administration of health, education, and welfare programs brings astonishment. HEW was formed in 1953 with 35,000 employees and a budget of $5.4 billion; by 1980 the dollar figure stood at $200 billion—more than 36 percent of the federal budget—and there were more than 150,000 employees.[61] Such dramatic changes cannot be attributed to a single administration, much less to a single individual. But the Johnson years certainly were central in this growth, one that was matched to some extent out in the HEW-supervised states.

Perhaps every presidential administration has a verbal "last hurrah." For Lyndon Johnson that came on the occasion of a sudden March 4, 1968, speech in Dallas to the Rural Electric Cooperative association. He was reminded of old battles. As in years past, he resorted to the most extravagant assertions about the bright future. The Great Society "is taking root, it is thrusting up, it is reaching out to banish need and to bring new hope into millions upon millions of lives." The American future would be "a future of limitless promise where every citizen, regardless of race or region [sic], can grow to his fullest measure. It will be a shining land where rural poverty and urban slums have gone the way of the kerosene lamp—if we only have the vision, the determination, the stick-to-it-tiveness, and do not allow the dividers among us to succeed. . . . Yes," said the old campaigner, "this land will be a shining and peaceful land, where rural poverty has been conquered." Such talk would have stamped all but evangelists as being hopelessly idealistic, but the president could dream bigger, and he had tried to do so when addressing the National League of Cities on April 4, 1966. In Bangkok, on October 29, 1966, he proclaimed grandly: "A Great Society cannot really exist in one nation and not exist in another nation." The full vision of perfectionism in this presidency was a comprehensive world view.

As the president prepared to leave office, he mused quietly in the Oval Office about his Great Society: "In some fields we have made great progress: education, health, housing, the conservation of our resources that belong to all the people. In some respects we've had many disappointments.'' Important was the fact that ''we have had a chance to impress upon the people of this nation those simple convictions that brought us to this town and that kept me here for almost four decades.'' More education was available to children, from Head Start through college to adult education. While there were too many dropouts, he guessed that a million must have been added to the college population. Millions were being served by Medicare, so sons and daughters would no longer have to worry about providing medical care for their elderly parents. All of this gave him ''a great deal of satisfaction.''[62]

Lyndon Johnson, activist politician, wished he could have done more—and this now reminded him of the choice anecdote he told innumerable times during his lifetime: ''I remember a story that they told about Prime Minister Churchill toward the end of World War II days, when a little lady in a temperance group called and said, 'Mr. Prime Minister, we want to test your drinking habits. We are informed that if all the brandy you have drunk during this war could be poured into this room it would come up to half the room.' The Prime Minister looked at the women; he looked at the ceiling; and he glumly commented, 'My dear little ladies: so little have I done; so much I have yet to do.''' Then the president added, clearly for posterity: ''I guess I feel that way as I leave this office. Forty years of opportunity, and so little have I done. So much do I have yet to do. But we do know that we have taken steps that had to be taken. We have marched down a road that had to be marched.''

11

★ ★ ★ ★ ★

WAGING A NO-WIN WAR
OF ATTRITION: VIETNAM

What did the president and his team think they were doing as they plunged deeper and deeper into a war of attrition in Vietnam in 1965 and later? Lyndon Johnson's later answer was succinct: "We had three principal goals: to insure that aggression did not succeed; to make it possible for the South Vietnamese to build their country and their future in their own way; and to convince Hanoi that working out a peaceful settlement was to the advantage of all concerned." Therefore, "defeating aggression, building a nation, and searching for peace" were the tightly braided good intentions of the administration. Restricted bombing would be tried and halted repeatedly. The number of American troops in battle would escalate. Experiments in strengthening the Saigon government would be tried, modified, and abandoned. Civilian and military Vietnamese casualties mounted. "Inside" media accounts from the battlefront and the rear echelon were blended with propaganda from Hanoi to stir protesters at home into ever more vigorous words and action. The equity of Moscow and Peking in America's failure guaranteed that their propaganda machines would see that every American misstep, miscalculation, or failure received worldwide exposure. A military engagement that had begun by facing semi-indigenous Viet Minh and then Viet Cong guerrilla forces became one involving well-supplied army units from an increasingly viable enemy state, one that showed no intention of suing for peace whatever the degree of gradual escalation. In the fall of 1967 the president said that we would have to "ride out the storm, and then try for peace when Hanoi had learned it could not win by the use of force."[1] Yet escalation to the point of crushing North Vietnam was, by then, out of the question politically, and Hanoi seemed to know it. After all, on "Face the Nation" (CBS) on February 13, 1966, Gen. Maxwell Taylor had defined "victory" in such a way as to guarantee Hanoi no great losses in failure: "Victory is just accomplishing what we set out to do, to allow South Vietnam to choose its own government and have Hanoi cease the aggression. That's victory."

Would one or both of the two large Communist powers suddenly go to war with the United States because of escalation? The administration acted as though it thought so. Strategic thinker Herman Kahn addressed himself to this matter in summer 1965, saying it was extremely unlikely that either the Soviets or China would go to war over Vietnam—no matter what. The nature of both governments and their peoples, their geographic relationship to Vietnam, and their strategic interests—all mitigated against having them intervene.[2] The president, however, remained a man unconvinced and unwilling to gamble as he recalled the Chinese intervention in Korea and possibly the catastrophic Democratic defeat in 1952.

So, one can see, but not necessarily appreciate, why Lyndon Johnson did not take the militarily effective steps that were later resorted to by the next administration—such as the mining of Haiphong; interdiction in Cambodia; and escalated meaningful bombing. That the Democratic leadership was overly fearful of the intervention of superpowers and was too solicitous of critical public opinion as manifested on the campuses, in the party, in liberal magazines, and ultimately in the streets is now a tenable opinion. Yet, Johnson correctly assessed the situation in case China or the USSR should become officially embroiled: "No one would be a winner," he told his top advisers on June 5, 1964.[3]

Vietnam came to dominate the Johnson presidency. It could not be escaped, for it impinged on the economy, on appropriations for the Great Society, and on the gamut of desired legislation. The commander in chief sensed that the war would obsess later historians; and he could not then escape its intrusive presence. In the basement of the West Wing was the 15' by 20' Situation Room, with its communications equipment, its lack of decoration except for an enormous map of the world showing the distribution of United States naval forces, a wall of special communications devices and another of telephones, including a direct line to the prime minister of Great Britain and a direct line to the president, wherever he might be. The so-called hot line to the Soviets was served by a Russian translator around the clock. Here Johnson, as Nixon would later, confronted the possibility of awful truths.

A transcript of conversations held in that grim locale would make fascinating reading and would explain much. On one occasion, Johnson blurted out: "Dammit, we need to exhibit more compassion for these Vietnamese plain people. When their own armies move across the countryside and destroy crops and livestock, the poor farmers get no recompense. . . . Can we move in this civil and agricultural side? . . . We've got to see that the South Vietnamese government wins the battle, not so much of arms, but of crops and heart and caring, so their people can have hope and belief in the word and deed of their government."[4] There was some appropriate action, but military decision making and making war took priority.

President Johnson later admitted—in response to the Pentagon Papers—that two "key mistakes" had been made on Vietnam: "Kennedy should have had more than eighteen thousand [sixteen is the correct figure] military advisers there in the early 1960s. And then I made the situation worse by waiting eighteen months before putting more men in. [Actually, there were 23,000 after twelve months.] By then, the war was about lost." This was an astonishing evaluation—in retrospect! A second error lay in not instituting censorship, "not to cover up mistakes but to prevent the other side from knowing what we were going to do next." To do this, one judges, a declaration of war would have been an absolute prerequisite. In 1964, he had hoped to negotiate a way out. "The Russians shared our hope," he guessed. Next, by a slow and careful buildup, hawks would not be inflamed, and Hanoi would not ask China in. He was "forced to act" over Tonkin Gulf. This is, at the very least, doubtful. "And just about every member of Congress was marching right along with me"—at the president's vehement request.

Did he secretly plan, during the 1964 campaign, to bomb the North? "Absolutely untrue. On at least five occasions I personally vetoed military requests for retaliation bombing raids in the North. Only late in 1965 did I reluctantly agree to it." After the Pleiku attack of February 1965, when American planes were being destroyed and men were being killed, "I was forced to act. I felt I had no choice. All of my civilian advisers, every one of them, agreed with me. Dean Rusk told me, 'Mr. President, this is a momentous decision.' I suppose it was."[5] The man of former power was now saying that his power—and his mistakes—had been shared.

Opposition to the war took many forms: letters to the editor and to officeholders, quiet marches in college towns, flyers destined for bulletin boards, and mass singing of mournful or angry folk music accompanied by the inevitable guitar. As the administration departed, however, there was a different level: bombing of ROTC buildings and computer installations, and hysterical challenge to authority wherever it might be, especially on university campuses. Johnson's freedom of movement was even affected. Columnist Mike Royko later reminisced succinctly from Chicago about the leaders of the protest movement during the 1960s. Some—like Martin Luther King, Jr., Saul Alinsky, and Father John Egan—were great men, he said; while others of little fame were quietly dedicated. "A few were funny while preaching their message, such as Dick Gregory. And zany, such as Abbie Hoffman. And thoughtful, such as Tom Hayden. And abrasive, such as Jane Fonda. And beautiful, such as Joan Baez. And inspirational, such as Studs Terkel and Pete Seeger and Dr. Spock." Royko liked most of them, because "they were decent people who had respect for others and a commitment to justice."[6] They absolutely did not appear in any such guise to those who were seeking to prevail in Southeast Asia—or to many observers with greying hair. Frustrated veterans of World War II and Korea often gritted their teeth in their homes, but reservists naturally hoped they would not be needed.

The threads of dissent that came to be identified as the protest movement were for the most part in the American tradition, although the idea was galling for many. A group of historians found dissent in three earlier wars, quoting Lincoln as having said of the Mexican War that it was "unnecessarily and unconstitutionally commenced."[7] Inside the government the protesters received mixed reactions. A scholar in the bureaucracy said, "I don't recall encountering a single official in the State Department who questioned the right of any citizen to sign petitions or demonstrate against the war," although many, as a conditioned reflex, thought that such people were irresponsible. Dissent that went through proper channels went down better.[8]

Some of the numerous excesses must be recorded. Daniel and Philip Berrigan of Clergy and Laymen Concerned about Vietnam poured blood on selective-service files in Baltimore in October 1967, set fire to draft records in Catonsville, Maryland, and fled in order to escape jail. A minister's book cried out, "O, where will this frenzy of evil end?" as the efforts to defend America, admittedly far from home, were put in the ugly aspect of "a national and noble taste for blood." There would be 221 college riots in 1968 alone. America's youth splintered: a later study found that members of the elite fighting unit the Green Berets, much like the majority of Americans, enjoyed hiking, excitement, adventure, and performing military skills; but the war and draft resisters of similar age tended to place their own conceptions of morality ahead of all other concerns, and they rejected traditional authority in general.[9]

A problem for the presidency during those troubled years was the inability to decide at what point the emotional and abnormally visible antiwar movement might be speaking for a majority in America. The 116 anti-Vietnam demonstrations outside the White House in 1967 were visible enough, especially when many appeared on the evening news. But inside the building, aide Fred Panzer quoted Gallup as having said that 74 percent of the people agreed that Johnson was doing his best in a tough job, 63 percent opposed stopping the bombing, and 64 percent thought Bobby Kennedy would be no better or worse than Johnson.[10] To the president, the protesters were way out in left field.

Arguments against the Vietnam War varied. The war was called "immoral," simply because it was a war and even the best war was said to solve nothing. It was hated, because television showed that Vietnamese noncombatants—old men and women, even infants—were among its tragic victims. The public gained visual familiarity with napalm and defoliant chemicals; therefore, modern technology and giant corporations became targets of the antiwar movement. The destruction of villages, though engaged in by both sides, was singularly unappealing living-room fare, even when many people in a village might have engaged in placing land mines or in assassinating their leaders. The bombing of North Vietnam evoked memories of World War II damage to populations and property; protesters did not believe there had been any meaningful increase in "pinpointed accuracy" by high-level bombers during the intervening years, even though there certainly had been. Saigon's removal of villagers to compounds sounded like "concentration camp" policies, whatever the motive of protecting the helpless against enemy intimidation and torture by putting them in "enclaves." The body-count measure of progress revolted the public's sensibilities.

The administration faced a barrage of abstract arguments from such celebrated persons as political scientist Hans Morgenthau and minister Reinhold Niebuhr, who could not agree that Vietnam was analogous to a European country's struggling for freedom and democracy. Communist Asians did not strike fear as had Fascist Europeans, apparently. Did American security really rest on determining the kind of government that should prevail in southern Indochina? China might have a point in seeing the region as vital to its self-protection. While no case could really be made for Soviet meddling, some radicalized or socialized Americans thought that the wave of the future in underdeveloped countries resided in government ownership of the means of production, the crushing of capitalist merchants, and new farm communes. Didn't the peasants of Asia need full stomachs, rather than "one man, one vote"? American corporations surely would profit from the spread of capitalism; anyway, wasn't the destruction worse than letting communism take over? Some conspirators among opponents of the war hoped that effective antiwar organizations could help to build a permanent radical "movement" in America—with incalculable possibilities! And so it went. Pictures of the ever-present wounded, in living color, created revulsion everywhere in the nation that no amount of idealistic presidential rhetoric could overcome. There was bound to be merit in some points that were repeatedly offered; therefore, many democracy-loving observers who hated communism nevertheless lapsed into confused silence.

There was a full literature of excess, sometimes even approaching treason, but more often of naïveté, which was produced by New Left writers, Communists, and "progressives" who were allied actually or spiritually with the Soviet Union, China, or Trotsky and by some who were just fuzzy of thought—though famous. Author and editor Norman Podhoretz emerged from writing a book in 1982 with telling quotes: "We are fighting on the side of Hitlerism," said the Berkeley Vietnam Day Committee. Novelist Susan Sontag, after visiting North Vietnam, found it to be "a place which, in many respects, *deserves* to be idealized," for here was an "ethical society" with a government that "loves the people" and "genuinely cares about the welfare of the hundreds of captured American pilots." Essayist Mary McCarthy visited Hanoi and found no dissent and no free press there, but she still thought the government "moral" and "ascetic." Writer Frances Fitzgerald's account of assassination tactics of the National Liberation Front (NLF) was forgiving, for Ho's Marxism-Leninism only showed his people "the way back to traditional values." These three non-Communists were able to state the Communist case in a style acceptable to an audience that would have been repelled by old-style Communist prose from party members, says Podhoretz. A new form of ideology—anti-anticommunism—arose to become powerful in the American world of ideas. Said historian Staughton Lynd and activist Tom Hayden, "We refuse to be anti-Communist," for such a position would help to justify "a foreign policy that is often no more sophisticated than rape." Expectorated critic Noam Chomsky: "By any objective standard, the United States has become the most aggressive power in the world, the greatest threat to peace, to national self-determination, and to international cooperation." Johnson's war, to him, was a depravity, an obscenity, an act of moral degeneration.[11]

So, one of the tragedies at home was the extent to which normally lucid people did not distinguish between methods and goals, between the rare and the typical, and between what factual history showed about the record of American democracy versus that of communism on the march. Some elitist writers got away with siding with the enemy in this war; during earlier wars such conduct as displaying the enemy flag or desecrating the stars and stripes would have aroused popular hatred. But then, Johnson had been determined from the outset, rather peculiarly, not to turn hatred loose against the enemy. Instead, it would be turned loose against him! Socialist Norman Thomas was one who said he could not work with those who seemed to love the Viet Cong more than peace; he preferred the *old* Left.[12]

Some generals who had recently been in uniform turned critical. Gen. David M. Shoup, a former commandant in the Marine Corps, said he didn't think that all of Southeast Asia was worth the life of a single American. While a solution reached by Asians might not be one that we would admire, "at least what they will get will be their own and not the American style, which they don't want and above all don't want crammed down their throats." Former Lt. Gen. James Gavin crusaded against the administration, sure that "a free, neutral and independent Vietnam can be established, with guarantees of stability from an international body." Another retired general said that the war was "not a war of self-defense or even of general self-interest." Gen. Matthew B. Ridgway saw nothing "in the present situation or in our code that requires us to bomb a small Asian nation back into the stone age." The president was naturally troubled by the prestige of experienced leaders like these and by their frontal assault against the very foundations of his policy.

As opposition leader Richard Nixon watched the wave of protest while he worked to gain the office that was its major target, he was repelled. He recalled: "The discords of that decade and of its aftermath critically weakened the nation's capacity to meet its responsibilities in the world, not only militarily but also in terms of the ability to lead."[13] But protest, sometimes crudely anti-intellectual, achieved respectability from many alleged intellectuals.

A word about the protesters is in order. There were the usual grounds for opposing the waging of war (such as pacifism). There were good enough reasons for opposing this war as not being in the national interest. There were reasons for believing that this war was not being waged with appropriate regard for the lives of noncombatants. And it could be argued that any bombing in the vicinity of civilians was no longer acceptable, whatever the record of World War II. We now know that the strategy with which this war was waged was not such as to bring it to a quick conclusion, and many at the time sensed this. So, protest was certainly legitimate. But the president was on firm ground in considering that the methods of protest were sometimes extralegal and that many protesters normally showed far less than customary interest in the well-being of those who were fighting under an elected president's orders and with funding and a resolution passed by the elected Congress. Overall, there seems to be a permanent irreconcilable conflict between surviving protesters, who remember their role in those years as being their "finest hour," and other citizens, who continue to believe that the nature and noise of protest made it much too hard to bring the enemy to the point of acceding to a negotiated end to the war.

Domestic events that were portentous for the Johnson administration happened in a hurry after 1965. The National Coordinating Committee to End the War in Vietnam encompassed thirty-five organizations. Students for a Democratic Society (SDS) increasingly organized and agitated. There would even be two fiery immolations—reminiscent of some monks in Saigon—which horrified the public once again. The existing Committee for a Sane Nuclear Policy was joined by Americans for Democratic Action, the National Student Association, the SDS, and a Hebrew and a Methodist body in making a march to Washington. Protests accelerated in 1966 as draft boards ceased to grant automatic college deferments; so that the draft, as well as the war, became a target. Some protests gained strength by incorporating irrelevant campus issues, some of which were of long standing. It became difficult for some faculty to award failing grades to those who faced draft boards; therefore, academic standards, which had already been weakened by a vast influx of poorly motivated or only partially prepared students, dropped. Several organizations to "protect" conservative faculty were founded. Some youths departed for Canada.

It became customary to gather signatures of "groups" on nationwide petition letters addressed to Johnson. Hundreds of college student-body presidents and editors made the front-page news columns of the *New York Times* in a "tie-in" with their concurrent advertisement, for it was thought to be news "fit to print." Many Rhodes scholars in England and many Peace Corps returnees signed protests. Behind the scenes, Allard Lowenstein of SDS, who was not an antisystem radical, devoted full time to secretly organizing most of these nationwide proclamations. Many other liberal Democrats wavered as the politician in the White House watched apprehensively. A spring mobilization on April 15, 1967, in New York and San Francisco, which received gratifying TV coverage, helped to unify liberals and radicals against the "ruinous, no-win war."

Presidential reaction to *hate* had been displayed early. Off the record, to state governors, Johnson said on November 25, 1963, "We have hate abroad in the world, hate internationally, hate domestically. . . . We have to do something about that." Its roots were poverty, disease, and illiteracy; meeting those problems would be meeting hate head-on. A nation that believed "in mankind and in humankind" should do well, he thought. By 1965, as teach-ins sought *pro forma* spokesmen for the government cause, Johnson blurted out in private that aides like McGeorge Bundy should not have been out debating somebody. "I would have disapproved." But lectures were all right. The faculty who protested were considered the "intense" ones with "a little screwball loose."[14] But many faculty of pacifist or idealistic view did not accept the idea of a "just war" (or that this was one), although some might admit grudgingly that a democratic Vietnam was desirable.

There were some protesters whose goal was revolution: destruction of "the system." Recalled Stokely Carmichael, who was for a time the chairman of the Student Nonviolent Coordinating Committee (SNCC), "I wanted revolution." His goal: "tearing this country apart." He conceded: "How stupid and arrogant I was. I actually thought we could change things overnight." Joan Baez, who as early as 1964 was singing "We Shall Overcome" on the Berkeley campus, would in later years lose some of her appeal to radicals when she criticized the excesses of the Democratic Republic of Vietnam during the postwar years. The president seems to have considered some of the war opponents racist when they opposed his crusade for dark-skinned peoples.[15]

Johnson's impatience and irritation over the activist New Left was partly rooted in his faith in the quiet working of the American political and economic system. Still, he took personally much of what was said and done. His inability to accept the sincerity of protesters stemmed partly from the knowledge that he was trying to wage the "other war," one targeted at the hearts and minds of Southeast Asia. When Robert Komer, a member of his staff, was early called in to be put in charge of this "other war," he had to ask what it was! The idea was sort of a Tennessee Valley Authority (TVA) and Rural Electrification Administration (REA) in Southeast Asia, which focused on roads, a green revolution, and law and order under regular police protection. How could Ho Chi Minh possibly pass over such an opportunity for progress? George Meany would have snapped it up, thought Johnson. George Ball, at the State Department, said that Johnson was almost poetic in visualizing a postwar Vietnam with a Mekong River program that would serve four countries. Wrote an aide earnestly to a constituent, "I know you realize that there is no man in this country, indeed on this earth, who is more desirous of obtaining peace in Vietnam than President Johnson."[16]

The president had nothing but trouble in trying to sell his case to the nation, especially to the media, students, and clergy, for his credibility was fading, and criticism of the authoritarian Saigon government was intense. General Westmoreland said that the news media seemed to think that wartime South Vietnam, which had had no experience in democracy or self-government, ought to be able to reach American levels of democracy and self-government and to be free of corruption. That America had had several hundred years of experience, while Vietnam had had only months, was ignored. "The South Vietnamese were presumably expected to demonstrate an advanced form of democracy while fighting for their survival. The enemy leaders were made to appear to be the 'good guys.' "[17] Those who are familiar with World War II censorship will find it easy to grasp his case. Morning, noon, and night, the TV screens of the 1960s, with an eye to ratings, conveyed a "realistic" version of events that were considered "newsworthy" and/or "entertainment," while the White House relied on the written and spoken word to portray what the chief executive favored. Such a struggle was clearly an uphill one.

Always, there was a vast audience of men who had formerly been in uniform and admirers of America's tradition of fighting and winning crusades who were completely unpersuaded by *how this war was waged.* Limited means for limited results, relying on attrition, had no appeal for them. They had never heard of orchestrated gradualism and sending of "signals." Wasn't the nation fighting with one hand tied behind its back? Wearing his aviator's hat, Barry Goldwater later recalled the restrictions that had been placed on United States pilots. Enemy airplanes and SAM bases must fire first. When these restrictions were ignored on one occasion, nine MIGs were destroyed in twenty-four hours. "I told Johnson our no-win policy was directly responsible for the loss of thousands of American lives."[18]

In June 1968 General Westmoreland, who was about to head the Joint Chiefs of Staff, gave a departing soldier's upbeat official report on his difficult tenure in Vietnam. There had been restraints on conducting the war, but "as we gained experience and our troop strength, logistics, and helicopter and fixed wing aircraft inventories built up, our operations became increasingly effective." He had been distressed not to be able to take the ground war into Cambodia or southeastern Laos, "through which ran the enemy's main route of logistic support." Thus the enemy could never be destroyed "in a traditional or classic sense." Maximum enemy casualties remained the goal, along with building viable South Vietnamese armed forces and police.[19]

The tug of war over strategy between the president's civilian advisers and the high-ranking military ebbed and flowed. In retirement,

Westmoreland would continue to fight for some of his basic views in a large memoir and in speeches, articles, and interviews. "Hanoi was able to cultivate the fiction that there were no North Vietnamese troops in the South, that the war was basically a people's revolution and that it was an illegal and immoral war. It is astonishing that great numbers of our citizens, and many representatives of the news media were taken in by Hanoi's propaganda." The media judged that it was not the "in" thing to praise the South Vietnamese units, even though they fought well. "President Nguyen Van Thieu [a general who was elected as South Vietnam's president in 1967] became a favorite target for the media and was unfairly maligned, while the conduct of the autocratic leaders in the North was not given equal attention. They were ignored, [for] there were no TV cameras behind enemy lines." Freedom from censorship gave the media "awesome power," said the general. The award of Pulitzer Prizes in 1964 to David Halberstam and Malcolm Brown worsened things by showing how a journalist might gain recognition, he thought, still smarting from attacks on him. Even in the 1980s, CBS and Walter Cronkite continued to revile him, to the point that a law suit was filed against CBS, Mike Wallace, and others.[20]

At the height of the struggle the United States was deploying two-fifths of its combat-ready divisions, half of its tactical air power, and a third of the navy—so that victory should not have been in doubt. But enemy morale held up while ours was deteriorating. The one-year combat tour, with rotation of officers and men, was the chief culprit, judged one observer. Drug abuse, combat refusals, and even fragging (i.e., shooting) of one's own officers eroded the nation's combat power. Strangers served together for only a few months in the U.S. units; thus the cohesion of small units was lost. RAND interviews with prisoners showed that the PLA's three-man buddy system and tough cadre leaders, who were imbued with party goals, nationalistic spirit, fatalism, and a sense of "face" and concern with one's status, were important factors. The PLA soldier was constantly reminded of his duty to his two buddies, his unit, his country, and his party. The enemy survived "the most continuous and intense firepower ever directed against any army";[21] but he did not face the kind of military effort that was demanded in "The Failure of Gradualism in Vietnam," issued April 18, 1968, by high-ranking retired military men who had been assembled by the Republican party.

Once Johnson had determined to carry on in Vietnam, what could he have done—or avoided doing? A declaration of war would have made many things possible: for example, censorship at the scene of battle and a drawing together of the nation. A flat refusal by Congress to declare war would have clarified the necessity for withdrawal. With a declaration of war, rapid rotation of forces would not have been necessary. There could have been a real crackdown on misconduct and the use of drugs among the combat forces. Stability in war assignments would have permitted cohesiveness at the unit level. A solid moral case for the war might have been made. The public might have been let in on the exact nature of some peace initiatives. "Gradualism" might have been repudiated early on.

Five conceptions (really myths) seem to have dominated the minds of American policy makers. First, it was thought that if Diem only had American advisers and equipment, his regime would be able to resist the NLF insurrection, or even invasion, if it were sent torrents of supplies and if it were to enjoy an intensified advisory effort. Next, perhaps limited applicaton of air and ground support by United States combat forces could persuade the enemy to cease its attacks. It was a myth that this Marxist state would pull away from its Moscow and Peking allies—or, conversely, that somehow they could be persuaded to stop their support of North Vietnam. The most devastating idea, perhaps, was the president's belief that leaders of the public mind, and the people themselves, would continue for years to support a no-win limited war of attrition thousands of miles from home, an undeclared war that was being waged, unaccountably, on behalf of an Asian people who had had no previous emotional ties to the United States.

Between the May 1965 decision to escalate the American military to the 70,000 to 75,000 level, and the close of his term in 1969, President Johnson and his civilian and military advisers gradually lost faith in the carefully studied but naïve guess that the inexorable escalation of American forces in the Vietnam conflict would discourage the nation-seeking oriental and Marxist enemy from North Vietnam and bring him to terms. "The president had staked everything on the casual assumption that the enemy could be quickly brought to bay by the application of American military might," says one historian. It was in May 1965 that lawyer Clark Clifford wrote the president, after viewing some CIA materials, "This could be a quagmire." Ultimate victory might not be a realistic hope. Ground forces should be "kept to a minimum." Korea was not a real precedent. Do probe avenues leading to a settlement.[22] Many, who were not unpatriotic, thought this way. The intensity of growing opposition at home was not anticipated, nor was hostile European opinion. Allies helped far less than was anticipated. Appropriate gestures were made by the South Koreans and Australians; but few others did except for the Republic of China, and theirs were repelled.

Old rationales for combat proved to be threadbare in the age of television. Government propaganda was half-hearted. Those who viewed the December 1965 government film *Why Vietnam?* could find its case tiresome. Here was "the big picture," said the subtitle. Ethiopia, Austria, Hitler, Chamberlain, World War II, and Korean "aggression," defeated because "something was done." Limited aggression, if unchallenged, becomes general aggression victorious. South Vietnam was the victim of guerrilla warfare, assassinations, and atrocities, with rice being the true objective. "This is war," says the president—a "difficult war" in which our allies have suffered *heavy* losses. "We seek no wider war," says McNamara. "Our war aim in South Vietnam is peace," says Rusk! "We will not surrender and we will not retreat," says Johnson, reminding viewers that three presidents for over eleven years had committed themselves and made promises. A more effective pamphlet with the same title contained a foreword by the president.[23] Servicemen, service clubs, reserve units, and students would view these old-fashioned efforts at propagandizing the administration perspective, which were no match for slick TV. From Hollywood the president got no help on the Vietnam crusade except for an almost counterproductive but well-meaning John Wayne patriotic effort, *The Green Berets*.

One effect of both affirmation and criticism was a belated obsession with the war among members of the bureaucracy. A White House aide has said that he found it on people's minds so much that he had trouble getting them even to consider other business. "This government is distracted, divided, sullen, in its obsession with Vietnam." The figure of Lyndon Johnson was seen at excessively late hours, wakeful and worried. At such times Lady Bird might engage him in substantive conversation; on January 11, 1966, the two discussed the prospects for the years ahead. "They are so fraught with danger and with decisions whose outcome we cannot see," she recorded. "I am torn between two feelings. One, the healthy one, that I should enjoy each day in this job and live it to the fullest. The other, that the end of the term is like a light at the end of a tunnel." She urged Lyndon to stay healthy, laugh a little, and remember that he was as tough as presidents who had lived through the same or worse. Soon Johnson would sign one of thousands of heartbreaking letters of condolence: "The war in Vietnam is a thousand contradictions, and the death there of your boy seems even more tragic. But I do not believe, I genuinely do not believe, he died for a senseless or empty cause." He said that those who had died had been defending the same principles of freedom as those on which the United States had been founded. It was the forces of tyranny that were responsible. Aggressors "imperil liberty and freedom around the world." The deaths were not in vain. It was in this spirit, perhaps, that a presidential candidate about to be elected in 1980, Ronald Reagan, would declare this was "a noble cause." And a decade after the Paris agreements, the leader of some picketing South Vietnamese at a Los Angeles conference would say: "Instead of feeling guilty, Americans should feel proud of what they did."[24]

While President Johnson and the public heard the noise of criticism from many directions, he did get reinforcement for his policies from sources that mattered to him. In his briefing papers, aides placed an early quotation from Bobby Kennedy that aggressive and expansionist Communist regimes should be opposed: "We will win in Vietnam, and we shall remain here until we do." When Hubert Humphrey returned from an overseas trip, he related that, except in Pakistan, every Asian leader who was publicly critical was privately encouraging the United States to remain in Vietnam, for America would be a buffer against an irrational China. Souvanna Phouma of Laos twice said that if the United States wished to win, it must bomb the dikes in North Vietnam and thus flood the crops; the vice-president was shocked. "That's the only thing that will be effective," he heard. On his 1966 trip to Asia, Averell Harriman found that American determination was being well received everywhere. "I wish Fulbright and company could understand that if we quit in Vietnam, the props would be pulled out from under most countries in the East. Even in such countries as Japan and India, the Peking appeasers would get the upper hand."[25]

Uncertainty was what Congress was hearing, however. After a spring recess, journalist Arthur Krock was told of "confusion and discontent" in home districts. The growing involvement reflected "a colossal blunder of statesmanship," he now thought. Gross miscalculations, "official evasions and outright misrepresentations of current and prospective conditions of the war" should be replaced by candor, for "the president acts on a body of information which no one else in the government has in its entirety. He may have sound answers he cannot responsibly give." The president must share what he knows. But Johnson still gave overly long disquisitions to visitors on the official line. After one of these on the anguish of decision making, an official of New York's Liberal party wrote to Johnson "with a heavy heart, realizing the anguish you are going through."[26] The real point, however, was the agony, not of the president, but of the country.

A phenomenon of the war on the home front was the division of the electorate into hawks and doves—expressions that were beloved by the media and throughout the executive branch but were seldom used in daily interaction by mere citizens. In early 1966 George Reedy drafted a think piece on the deep divisions that were turning many hawks into vultures and doves into chickens—thus hampering the conduct of foreign policy as shadings were being lost. People were being pushed into camps, so that an honorable way to close out the situation in Vietnam was being sidetracked. The writer deplored the unanimity among the president's advisers. Why not bring General Gavin and scholar George Kennan in for quiet discussions with the president for their good as well as his? Maybe they had a point when they worried that Vietnam ought to be handled as an integral part of an overall United States world strategy. Both were responsible men and had said nothing unforgivable. The president could turn to them for advice ''without demeaning himself.'' Maybe a calmer atmosphere would then emerge in the country. Meanwhile, William S. White was offended by ''the little band of wilful men, of so-called elite thinkers,'' who were trying to impose their will on the majority. Suggestions that the United Nations ought to be used to bring peace brought the official response that if Hanoi requested United Nations observers, the United States would support the idea. ''I get more free and unsolicitated advice,'' mused Johnson, ''than anybody in this country.'' Meanwhile, he claimed that he read a hundred letters a week from soldiers in the field.[27]

On October 25, 1966, came the Manila Declaration, signed by the United States and six other countries, which agreed on fundamentals: freedom from aggression; conquest of hunger, illiteracy, and disease; a region of security, order and progress; and an effort to get reconciliation and peace in Asia. With such lofty goals on his side, Lyndon Johnson had trouble, said Humphrey, accepting criticism of his policies. Johnson did not see himself as an insensitive militant who was trying to bring a small nation to its knees; rather, he knew that he was restraining American power, ''constantly holding back.'' He was keeping his word and his country's, ''even when you have to pay the price.'' If little Israel called for help ''you keep your commitment,'' he hinted, rather too cleverly. A trip to Cam Rahn Bay on October 26, 1966, brought increased dedication, soberness of purpose, and some exultation. Everything went right, Rostow wrote to Lady Bird. The president was deeply moved by ''three of the most memorable hours of his life.''[28]

Enroute, Johnson awarded Westmoreland the Distinguished Service Cross. Never, said the general, had Johnson tried to tell him how to run the war. Tactics and battlefield strategy were left to him, for the president did not even pass judgment on it. (Of course, there were those *restraints!*)[29] Westmoreland could not engage in hot pursuit into Laos or Cambodia; could not invade the enemy's country; could not have the dikes bombed so as to make the civilian population realize the consequences of Ho Chi Minh's aggressive war; could not, until 1968, tap any reserve forces, with their experienced personnel; and could not assume command over all allied forces, and thus put the Republic of Vietnam's army to its best use. The final triumph of generals like Lincoln's Grant, Wilson's Pershing, Roosevelt's Eisenhower and MacArthur, or Truman's Ridgway could never be his. It was hell.

The fury against this presidency, felt by many who fought, would be enduring. Halfway measures seemed to make no sense. Historians of the naval air war point out some handicaps that were endured by American pilots: Operation Rolling Thunder involved no strike that did not have the administration's prior approval; no prestrike photography; and no follow-up second strike. Unexpended ordnance could not be used on a target of opportunity; aircraft could not be attacked without positive identification, which is tough at 1,000 mph; and a flight that was canceled because of weather had to be reauthorized before it could be tried again.[30] All this involved greater risks for men and equipment, and it had an impact on the results. American ground forces reached 542,000; the South Fleet grew to 64,000; 20,000 served in the Thailand air bases; allies furnished 68,000; and perhaps a million south Vietnamese fought. Many individuals were heroic. Most officers were professional enough. But the strategy and tactics were inappropriate to the need. The war was not "fought by the book." Adm. U. S. Grant Sharp, who was in charge of the air war, was frustrated beyond endurance by his shackles; writing in retrospect, he was caustic.

Controversy surrounded the sharply restricted bombing almost from the beginning. There were five official goals: first, to reduce, it was hoped, the movement of supplies and enemy soldiers into the South; then, to make the enemy pay a high cost for its invasion, to break North Vietnamese will, to force concessions at the future peace table, and to strengthen morale in the United States and in Saigon. The first two were stressed in public, but officials in both the Johnson and Nixon administrations were hopeful that the last three would eventually prove valid.

The debate over gradual escalation ("gradualism") versus the use of sudden maximum pressure was often bitter, especially in the National Security Council. The president's reasoning was outlined in an open letter to Senator Henry M. Jackson on March 1, 1967, after the two had discussed the matter. "We are bombing North Vietnam because it is violating two solemn international agreements," said Johnson. Bombing had been begun in order to back our troops, to impose a cost on Hanoi at home, and to hurt the infiltration process—not to end the war. All three goals were said, incorrectly, to have been achieved, although some five hundred airmen had been lost. Johnson said he took "no satisfaction" from any effect the bombing might be having on economic and social development in the North. In peacetime, if the North Vietnamese wished, they would have "the support of the United States in providing for their people an environment of progress."[31] Arthur M. Schlesinger, Jr., would later call this kind of talk "sentimental imperialism."

In 1966, RAND had made a secret five-month study; its report said that the restricted bombing had been of doubtful value. One of the authors published a book in which he said: "We have intensified bombing as I speculated we would, and the general lack of effect is about what I anticipated in the report." While the air attacks had put a severe strain on enemy resources, the report still concluded that there was no evidence of critical or progressive deterioration or disruption of enemy activity. After all, Hanoi still had access to Soviet and Chinese military and economic aid. "U.S. failure to make a maximum effort to deny access to imports by sea and over land thus emerges as the outstanding gap in the logic of U.S. coercive strategy against North Vietnam. A serious question arises as to whether the advantages of continuing or intensifying the attack would outweigh the potential net gains from cessation or drastic and demonstrative de-escalation." A study by the Institute for Defense Analysis in 1966 said that the bombing had had "no measurable effect." After the war, a group of experts was very critical of the chosen bombing program, saying that it had made total mobilization in the North possible, had created the POW issue, had aided USSR-Chinese commonality, and had run out of targets. Said a general, until Nixon authorized bombing in 1972 "over the objection of virtually every adviser" in the government, air power had never been used appropriately.[32] The sixteen suspensions of the bombing, some of which were secretly linked to possible peace negotiations, did not help.

Vietnam was inevitably an issue in the congressional election of 1966. At the National Governors' Conference, a successful effort was made to frame a resolution of support for the government's policies; only one "No" echoed through the meeting—that of Republican governor Mark Hatfield of Oregon, who was then a candidate for the Senate. "I've never felt so alone," he said. But his concerns were those of a growing number of Americans. What *are* our true goals? Is there really a SEATO commitment? Are we drawing a line in the world that Communists must not cross? Our allies are puzzled. The public is confused. Hatfield's posture of favoring a cease-fire or use of the United Nations— but not going so far as to favor immediate withdrawal—won him an easy victory over a popular incumbent congressman. But the president still saw himself as following in the footsteps of Franklin Roosevelt, and Johnson reveled in whatever praise came along.[33]

What he received was a random quilt of commentary. For example, in cabinet meetings, there was never any discussion of strategy or about the details of the American commitment! (Out of discussion, out of mind.) Johnson could be bitter when visitors used their contacts with him in order to make later headlines that advanced their criticisms. Humphrey says that Johnson might have been more open to suggestion if so much of it had not surfaced in this way. Anytime Congress wished, it could stop funding Vietnam, the president said defiantly. To LBJ's liking was when George Jessel, back from the front, said that Lincoln was "so right in the war that was right" whatever the opposition to it. Recalling this, the president said over and over: "My job is never a question of doing what is right. Any president's greatest ambition is to do what is right when he holds that high office. My problem is knowing what is right." McNamara certainly told him, belatedly, in December 1966. He saw "no reasonable way" to end the war soon, not even in two years. Gird, openly, for a longer war, getting into a military posture "that we credibly would maintain indefinitely."[34]

It was early in 1967 that McNamara mysteriously decided to dig out buried information about the rationale for Vietnam; apparently he assumed that some changes might result. Here began the saga of the Pentagon Papers. A task force of thirty-six persons was set up in the office of the secretary of defense and was enjoined to produce an "encyclopedic and objective" history. Researchers were not to reveal their task; outsiders would not be interviewed. Documents would be those available in the Defense Department, plus whatever could be quietly obtained from the State Department, the CIA, and elsewhere. The Johnson White House was excluded, for there was apprehension that an angry president might order that the work be terminated and that all copies of the study be destroyed. The group consisted of "relatively dovish" officials from the Office of International Security Affairs. The work continued for eighteen months under the leadership of a recent employee of ISA, Leslie H. Gelb of Harvard, and a deputy assistant secretary of defense, Morton H. Halperin. The limited contribution of the then-obscure Daniel Ellsberg was to draft part of John F. Kennedy's section and to add comments on the 1965/66 volumes. There was material on the Diem coup, the Tonkin Gulf episode, liaison with South Vietnam and with our civilian and military leaders there, decisions on bombing, and negotiations with North Vietnam.

Halperin and his coauthor have described the effect that they thought some major matters that had been kept secret from Americans had on policy formation in a democracy. They would contend that secrecy about the "real" Ho Chi Minh of 1945 and later had kept the Congress from making educated decisions on aid to France and had furthered the desire to form a permanent South Vietnam. What we knew of the planned coup against Diem could have been used to warn him, thus saving his government and his life. "While President Kennedy's public denial of American complicity may have been literally true, it did not represent a forthright disclosure of the actual American role." Also, "The development of contingency plans for massive intervention went forward in secrecy during the [1964] campaign," even though Johnson was not yet committed to implementing them. Threats to bomb were conveyed through Canadian intermediaries before November, so that, it was said, Johnson "misled the electorate by appearing to support a policy of victory without escalation." Awareness of the provocative secret surveillance of the North Vietnamese coast might have ameliorated the anger that resulted in such a broad mandate after the incident in Tonkin Gulf. The four withheld volumes about the negotiations are said to show that from 1964 to 1966 the administration felt it would have to negotiate from a position of weakness, so it chose to avoid any compromise settlement. This fooled the public. All in all, the famous study is judged by these authors to reveal "a consistent pattern of deception by the administration," which involved the withholding of vital information from both the Congress and the public.[35] The reader of Johnson's *Vantage Point* certainly gets no such impressions as these!

It does seem fair to say of the Johnson presidency, as of those immediately before and after it, that one enormous hole in the Vietnam process was that the Congress, the media, and the public—potential aids to decision making—did not have appropriate information on matters of vast consequence. Certainly, anyone who reads the *Public Papers* set, the *New York Times*, random articles indexed in the *Readers Guide to Periodical Literature*, and Johnson's memoirs finds it easy enough to comprehend the rationale for the Johnson administration's decisions on foreign policy for Southeast Asia during the years 1963 to 1969. Yet, when aided by the Pentagon Papers, some key memoirs, and the increasingly available classified governmental paper work of the day, as well as third-generation monographs, a different perspective becomes possible—even necessary. *The public did not know what it needed to know in order to make decisions at the polls or to reply intelligently to pollsters.* The media became increasingly restive as they walked the path from the Bay of Pigs to Tonkin Gulf to the Pentagon Papers to Agnew's resignation, to Watergate, and to Nixon's resignation. Here is a sequence that afterward gave birth to public disillusionment and to excesses in adversary journalism.

Early in 1968, members of the White House staff took special note of a Harris poll that showed, to their surprise, that the public was taking a tougher line on the war. People, although they wanted the Vietnamese to take over the fighting, also hoped to convince the Communists that they would lose if they continued the war. The survey showed surprising percentages: 49 to 29 favored invading North Vietnam, 47 to 21 favored invading the demilitarized zone (DMZ), and 42 to 33 favored mining Haiphong, even if Soviet ships might be sunk! A hard-core percentage of 25 did not even oppose the bombing of China or the use of atomic weapons if need be. Harris said he was called by an impressed Soviet official at the UN about this. The Japanese often called him, saying that the Chinese paid much attention to his polls as being an indication of public opinion. One aide told Johnson that the forthcoming State of the Union message should be influenced by this poll, and results of the poll should be distributed far and wide.[36] *But the public's desires were soon to be ignored, even actively thwarted.*

As the year opened, there were 492,900 members of the American military in Vietnam, nearly 17,000 had died, and the president's current policies were favored by only 48 percent, though many of the rest favored an even tougher stance. The vice-president says that Johnson now "desperately" wanted peace. "Those who deny him that bit of humanity are wrong."[37] Things were not going to get easier. Intelligence warned the White House that an attack on a considerable scale was coming. When it came, during the traditional Vietnamese Tet holiday, it would cost the lives of 3,895 Americans, 214 allies, and 4,954 Vietnamese military men; 14,300 South Vietnamese civilians; and fully 58,373 dead among Viet Cong and North Vietnamese forces, almost wiping out the cream of the former. The manner of the ferocious attack on just about every populated city and military installation, its drama in reaching even the United States embassy, its high visibility for newsmen on the scene, and the way it forced a multitude of "explanations" from those in authority made Tet the major battle of the Vietnam War.

One newsman who was there and returned for further study, Don Oberdorfer, later wrote a memorable book with no more than *Tet!* for a title. Asking himself "Who won?" he replied, "Nobody." Everybody lost; the enemy lost a battle, and the United States government lost the confidence of its people back home. Yet there could be no doubt that the attackers had "suffered a grievous military setback." Moreover, the South Vietnamese people did not rise up to help them, so they suffered a blow to any claim of being liberation forces. The Saigon government survived and escalated the draft, so that its forces increased from 670,000 to 1,100,000. The Hanoi goal of decisive victory was thwarted.[38]

But burned in the American memory was a picture of a Saigon general shooting a captive who had his hands tied behind his back; and there was the telling wisecrack of hostile newsman Peter Arnett (which originated with an army officer) that, in the case of a place called Ben Tri, "It became necessary to destroy the town to save it."

When, late in World War II, the Germans in desperation had, as Eisenhower put it, "rushed out from his fixed defenses and suffered a grave defeat," the public had accepted the event as victory, despite the loss of thousands of Allied troops. In Vietnam, the reality of the enemy's even considering that such an attack as Tet might succeed against the mighty United States was a terrible shock to the uncertain American public. This became especially true as members of the media tried their best to use the attack to highlight the appropriateness of viewpoints that were critical of the war. Peter Braestrup's blistering two-volume study about this propagandistic aspect, *Big Story*, would later conclude that "rarely has contemporary crisis journalism turned out in retrospect to have veered so far from reality." Reporters had focused on everything sensational and had generalized on single incidents and thus had presented a totally misleading picture of Tet as a *military* defeat, which it certainly was not. This had been a "major distortion of reality."[39]

Tet did involve some setback and losses, of course; but the administration made a crucial error when it failed to use every means at its disposal to convey the full truth about overall military aspects. Even though the commander in chief admitted that he had received an accurate appraisal that "the Communists had suffered a disaster, a debacle, and a serious military loss," he would finally concede, "I don't think that ever got communicated to the American people." Humphrey indicates that civilian advisers now even began to reverse themselves, saying that America's course must be changed and opposing efforts of the military to get more men and munitions. Newsman Arnett and anchorman Walter Cronkite remained unrepentant years later, and a leading newspaper retreated only to the extent of using a phrase like "no matter who really won the big battle."[40] Here was a communications fiasco, with truth being only one of its victims.

So, some people would come to argue, with justification, that the American psychological collapse after Tet had stemmed from a diabolical or inept press and TV. But Johnson's own lackluster performance in giving out public information—for example, at a February 2 press conference—was disastrous. On that occasion he said: "It may be that General Westmoreland makes some serious mistakes or that I make some. We don't know. We are just acting in the light of information we have." The future? "There will be moments of encouragement and discouragement." Here may have been candor, but here also was collapse of leadership in a crisis. But many other leaders of the public mind also failed to do their bit at the time. Leaders of opinion outside the security classification system were handicapped, of course. Cronkite's famous post-Tet reversal on TV against the Vietnam crusade was damaging—almost as though he held a high elective office, such as that of Chief Pundit. He and Westmoreland would still be sparring in the 1980s. Overall, in the undeclared war that was being waged by the media, the executive branch stood isolated when things went sour.[41]

Quite probably, by the winter of 1968, this president's credibility with the media and with national and even world opinion was such that it would not permit him much success in attempting to make a favorable interpretation of Tet. Ever since the early stories on "credibility gap" in the *New York Herald Tribune* of May 23, 1965, and the *Washington Post* of December 5 that year, there had been what the latter publication called "growing doubt and cynicism concerning administration pronouncements." Six televised hearings of the Senate Foreign Relations Committee in the winter of 1966 gave antiadministration ideas a respectable forum. While George Reedy is probably on firm ground in asserting that "most of the so-called lies [LBJ] is alleged to have told about Vietnam actually amounted to nothing but excessive optimism and a refusal to face ugly facts," there was also self-deception. Always, Johnson felt it essential to protect his beloved Democratic party from being saddled with unvarnished bad news, especially anywhere near a national election. As a person, he clearly had delighted in being secretive if not devious. It was a poor posture from which to salvage anything from an apparent disaster with even the most eloquent speech, had such a disaster occurred. As historian Guenter Lewy has observed, "National leaders who habitually practice concealment and evasion will erode the trust of their people."[42]

General Westmoreland later turned highly critical of his commander in chief: "Johnson hoped the war would go away, so he could concentrate his energies on building a 'Great Society' at home, but his key Vietnam decisions were destined to drag out the war indefinitely." The enemy had great latitude for action. The intermittent bombing sent exactly the wrong message: not that Hanoi could not win, but that we were weak and insecure. The guns-and-butter policy made the economy boom, so "no one bore a burden or met a hardship except the men on the battlefield and their loved ones." Johnson should have sought annual reaffirmation of the Gulf of Tonkin resolution, but he and congressional leaders were afraid of an open national debate. Determination to "entice" the enemy to the conference table meant that pressure could not be increased after Tet—as it should have been.[43] Not since General George McClellan, perhaps, had a commanding general turned so totally against his wartime leader as Westmoreland had against Johnson, five years after the latter's death. But Admiral Sharp felt much the same way.

Contemporaries would not know until months into the next presidency about some degradation that lay buried beneath the surface; for on March 16, 1968, there occurred the My Lai massacre—the deliberate killing of up to four hundred civilians, including old men, women, and children and their livestock, by personnel in two companies of Task Force Barker. Fortunately for Johnson, this isolated event would surface only in November 1969 to become an excruciating burden of the Nixon administration. Commander in Chief Johnson and his top team, both military and civilian, seem not to have known anything about it. Lt. Gen. W. R. Peers, who headed the inquiry, concluded that this gruesome tragedy was "a black mark in the annals of American military history, and revealed failures in leadership at all levels in the chain of command." Said Peers: "The full and true story of the My Lai incident has not yet been told—not in the Inquiry report, the House Armed Service Subcommittee Report, this or any other book, or all of them together." What little is known reflects no credit on all who seem to have prevented the awful truth from spreading so that punishment could be administered. The cover-up was so complete that when, five weeks after the event, a colonel and a major gave Westmoreland a routine sector briefing, the My Lai military action was described without mentioning that *any* action had been taken against the inhabitants, let alone that they had been machine-gunned in groups. The full sordid story has still not been told.[44]

The war had been one of atrocities from the beginning; for the Viet Cong relied on assassination, terror, and torture of civilians and soldiers alike. It was not long before some frustrated and angry American soldiers—apparently both black and white, rural and urban, for all that is known—were reduced to engaging in violations of human rights that went well beyond anything authorized by distant superiors. One problem was that civilians were by no means necessarily noncombatants; so that as buddies were lost to innocent-looking peasants and as booby traps seemed to be located almost anywhere, base instincts, born in rage, took over. Such conduct would be fully portrayed in living rooms back home by correspondents who were well aware of the emotional potential in such events. One careful historian offers this appraisal: "Every mistake, failure or wrongdoing was sooner or later exposed to view and was widely reported by generally critical press and television reporters," so that "a situation gradually developed in which the Americans and South Vietnamese could do hardly anything right." Mistakes of judgment were translated into wanton breaches of the laws of war. The atypical wanton murder in My Lai was not "the American way of war," but many Vietnam veterans later felt its crushing psychological burden, even though it is obvious that "the overwhelming majority of American soldiers kept under control and fought heroically." After all, some 2.2 million individuals served in Vietnam with the military, from first to last. Some 11,250,000 wore the nation's uniforms during those years.[45]

The Johnson presidency's final place in history is bound to be affected somewhat by the perception that battlefield excesses could have been prevented by the man in the White House, unfair though that may be. Johnson was duly warned in March 1968—eleven days after My Lai!—by McGeorge Bundy, who was no longer in the government, that there must be a stop to "the current practice of permitting any amount of return fire on friendly villages." The Viet Cong had trapped us into "murderous attacks on our own friends, and on every ground—moral, political, and military—this sort of thing must be stopped." It was no help to know that in Korea, 70 percent of those killed, by both sides, had been civilians, while in Vietnam it was 45 percent—a figure similar to that of World War II.[46]

Controversy has surrounded the choice of weapons, tactics, and intentions of the United States military in Vietnam. The use of helicopter gunships *(Puff the Magic Dragon)*, the expenditure of almost unthinkably massive amounts of ammunition and bombs, and especially the use of herbicides were all controversial. Beginning in 1962, Agent Orange (2,4,5-T) was used, as part of what would be called Mission Ranch Hand, which is not mentioned in *The Vantage Point*, to defoliate the jungles or to kill rice crops that, it was thought, would probably be used to feed the enemy. This was done in South Vietnam but not in North Vietnam! Use of Agent Orange ended in 1970/71 because a 1969 study showed that it caused certain malformations in test animals and because of complaints at home. In all, some 3,733,899 acres were defoliated, some more than once. A word that was commonly used was *ecocide,* for there was justifiable unease about both temporary and long-term destruction of the flora and, indirectly, of some of the fauna of any Third World area, regardless of possible military gains. In any case, a contemporary RAND study called the use of Agent Orange counterproductive; it should be canceled, said the researchers.

Some observations seem safe; others less so. Agent Orange was devastating to mangrove swamps and thus harmed the marine environment; it killed tall trees but did not sterilize the soil. Reports of effects on babies, presumably from the contaminant TCDD, were not confirmed by 1969 and 1974 studies. Interestingly, while some 44 million pounds were being sprayed in Vietnam, 78 million were sprayed by American agriculturalists at home. Veterans, who voiced a wide variety of physical and psychological complaints against Agent Orange, kept it in the public eye in the 1980s. Some 15,867 veterans, half of whom were found to have a disability from some cause, sought compensation. A careful study showed that pilots who had sprayed Agent Orange and were virtually drowned in it were not dying at a higher rate than other servicemen. The position of the Veterans Administration was: "The best available scientific evidence fails to indicate that exposure to Agent Orange or other herbicides used in Vietnam has caused any long-term health problems for veterans or their children."[47] Nevertheless, outcries and research would definitely continue into the 1980s, at the very least, as a by-product of the Southeast Asian war.

The American relationship with the Vietnamese at every level came under fire. Corruption was rife, says a later RAND study based on interviews with former Vietnamese leaders; there was "racketeering in scarce and often vital goods; bribery of officials; buying and selling of jobs and appointments; and the collection of army pay from ghost and roll call soldiers." There was mutual misunderstanding. Efforts to shift the burden to the Vietnamese were called, by some cynical native officials, "the U.S. dollar and Vietnam blood sharing plan."

In spite of everything, withdrawals of United States ground troops had not begun by the close of Johnson's presidency. Said Clifford on September 9, 1968, "the level of combat is such that we are building up our troops, not cutting them down." Specialist Paul Warnke claimed there was literally no way of bringing the conflict to a military conclusion at that time, for "the enemy forces, if they get the hell beat out of them in South Vietnam, can always retreat across the borders into the total sanctuary of Cambodia or North Vietnam, or the partial sanctuary of Laos."[48]

Under such depressing circumstances, President Johnson had to grasp at every straw for comfort. Aging historian Allan Nevins wrote that he appreciated "the discernment, the patience, and the wisdom" that Johnson had displayed in recent months, so "history would do you the same justice that it did to Lincoln and to Woodrow Wilson after their stormy administrations ended." White House advisers routed to their leader such letters of approbation for obvious reasons; of course his emotions were intimately involved with their own. Humphrey believed that "presidential advisers too often simply try to anticipate the president's decision, telling him not what he ought to hear, but what they think he wants to hear." Toward the end, all the tired Johnson really wanted to hear, one guesses, was positive evaluation of what he had done and what good could eventually come of it. He had become like the Lincoln who had observed, "But the tired part of me is *inside* and out of reach."[49]

It is premature to render firm judgment on the integrity with which the president handled the seventy-two alleged opportunities to end the war that were brought to his attention or that he initiated. Whether it was editor Harry Ashmore or Justice William O. Douglas, most persons who brought tidings that the enemy was secretly willing to end the war met with a chilly Johnsonian reception that left them permanently estranged. The president admitted: "I think I did a very poor job of pointing up to the American people that one time, two times, a dozen times we made substantial overtures to Ho Chi Minh—willing to go anywhere, anytime, talk about anything; just please let's talk instead of fight. And in not one single instance, not one, did we get anything but an arrogant, tough, unyielding rebuff." Early on, Bundy had warned that negotiating or displaying the desire to do so would further the deterioration of morale in Saigon. The president appealed to the Pope, the Polish government, the Canadians, the Italians, the British, the United Nations, and elsewhere. He did not, however, offer to submit the dispute to arbitration. He did hate the war—one in which his two upright sons-in-law were serving. Sadly, the need to justify this vehicle for death and destruction meant reiterating reasons for continuing it. Maybe the overall outcome would be a Great Society for Asia![50]

There would seem to be little excuse for gratuitously pointing out, as does one Johnson biographer, that billions of dollars flowed into Texas as the result of the war;[51] yet many Americans did profit, for the govermental deficit in dollars also represented salary figures for companies, employers, and stockholders. The majority of Americans have accepted Roosevelt's assertion, "I hate war." Perhaps they should do no less for Lyndon Johnson, who told his last press conference as president: "If I could have one thing presented to me today that I would rather have than anything else in the world, it would be that I could bring back from Vietnam all the men I sent out there and that we could have peace in the world so that those men could come and enjoy being with their families again and enjoy the benefits of our affluence in this great society that we have." These were not just the words of a politician. Here, he surely spoke the truth.

A memorable judgment was made on his mission as president when Lyndon Johnson claimed privately, but for the ultimate record, that he had "raised the level of our attention" in fields that were most important to the nation: education, health, beauty, and, amazingly, in the light of the long war he waged, *"peace in the world"* (italics mine).[52] His reference must have been to the avoiding of central (i.e., nuclear) war and to general U.S.–USSR relations. The president had certainly waged a *major war;* of that there could be no doubt. The "level of attention" that he raised, by inadvertence, was really in the area of national pacifism: building the longing for peace at virtually any price, even at the sacrifice of democratic gains abroad in years to come. After this presidency it would be difficult to bring Americans to their feet cheering at the thought of using their expensive military might to help a small nation throw off tyranny or to repel Communist invasion or subversion.

The record of the Johnson presidency on Southeast Asia is easy to criticize. Initially, when there was something of an opportunity to try to "neutralize" Vietnam and when there existed the option of withdrawing mere advisers who had been sent by his predecessor, these options were not taken seriously. Then, escalation was not pursued in a manner calculated to persuade the enemy that we were absolutely determined to prevail. In midstream, the president fought a contained and restricted war, in which he deliberately avoided arousing the American people's full emotional commitment. Johnson's chagrined top military leaders preserved public silence, held their commissions, and got promoted. Army morale hit bottom. Left to the next administration was the opprobrium of interdicting the enemy in Cambodia, mining Haiphong, bombing rail lines to China, and other meaningful bombing—all of which finally brought American involvement to a sudden yet uncertain end.

Alternatives presented problems. It appears that *neutralization* would have brought a coalition government in Saigon, with all that this might have entailed. *Withdrawal* was unthinkable, because the 1964, 1966, and 1968 elections could have brought retaliation, and the lifelong politician in the White House was not willing to place his beloved Democratic party in jeopardy. *Real escalation in order to prevail* was rejected because of the record of Chinese intervention in Korea and because of the influence of liberal doves. *Invading North Vietnam* would have split the president's party even more, for invasion would have borne the unacceptable aspect of aggressive warfare, or so it was thought. Why was so uncertain a military policy pursued—one that achieved none of the goals of this presidency in Southeast Asia? Throughout, the key was the simple idea, wryly expressed later by several, including Dean Rusk: "We thought we could win."

How did President Johnson come to feel about his Vietnam decision as the years passed? Not—as has been asserted—that the protesters were right. Possibly the best fully reliable source is an uncirculated statement made on October 25, 1968, in which he said: "We are involved in a struggle in Southeast Asia, where more than half a million of our men are tied down to protect our commitments; to preserve our integrity; to guarantee our security. We want peace so much we are working at it diligently and earnestly; but it is an elusive thing, and we have been unable to find a formula that would give us peace with honor in that area of the world—and stop the killing; although we will continue to search to the very last moment when we leave this office. I think that's the biggest disappointment we've had."[53]

It certainly cannot be said that while Johnson was president he apologized for the involvement of the United States against communism in Vietnam or elsewhere. There had been progress! "We are proud of the fact," he continued, that "through long and persistent and dedicated efforts of diplomats and military people" since 1960 "we have worked out an arrangement that prevented Laos from being taken over by the Communist leadership of Southeast Asia; we have protected the people of South Vietnam from Communist rule; we have not yielded a foot of soil anywhere in the world to Communist domination." There was a visible payoff: the Communists had suffered severe reverses in various parts of the world; India and Pakistan had not had grave problems with China; Communists had not advanced in this hemisphere; they had lost great ground in Indonesia and Malaysia and elsewhere in Southeast Asia; and they no longer confronted America with ultimatums in Berlin. We had not succumbed to Communist "threats and advances" in the Middle East. Still, "We are quite disappointed that we do not have peace in Vietnam itself."[54] When still president of the United States, Lyndon Johnson did not give an inch to opponents of his militant anti-Communist policies.

The status of the Vietnam War at the close of the presidency may be judged from a comprehensive survey that was conducted in January and February of 1969 by the new administration to assess the situation preliminary to new actions. National Security Study Memorandum 1 (NSSM-1), "Situation in Vietnam," was assembled from replies from throughout the government to a six-page list of questions. The memorandum revealed sharp divisions of opinion. Military leaders displayed optimism: the enemy was weak and was meeting in Paris from weakness. Gains in pacification were real. Phrases like "should hold up" and "the tides are favorable" were used. But the CIA, Pentagon civilians, and some persons in the State Department suggested "stalemate" militarily and "inflated and fragile" gains in pacification. Hanoi was not dealing from weakness, its objectives were unchanged, and neither the USSR nor China controlled its decisions. The new national security adviser, Henry Kissinger, found that intelligence experts disagreed on enemy forces and on the importance of the Cambodian supply route: "There was no consensus as to facts, much less as to policy."[55] Here was a mixed, uncertain vote from the incumbent bureaucracy on the trusteeship of the long struggle. Uncertain movement in strategy on the ground—from creating enclaves to using big units engaged in search-and-destroy missions—had made for confusion. Pacification had been nearly incompatible with major combat operations, and the army had become a sick man.[56] Here was a legacy of both military and civilian leadership.

The long Vietnam War would have a complex army of critics. They came from both major parties, had many motives, and chose different targets for their fire. There must be a degree of uncertainty in judging the opinions of some who were hostile, supporting "a" war but not "this" war. Others had once been supporters, in the spirit of Wilson or Truman, only to change sides when the war dragged on. McNamara, McGeorge Bundy, and Moyers, once supporters, would, in opposition, preserve a degree of silence; but Clifford would speak out publicly—although only *after* the Democratic party had lost the presidency. The pro-Kennedy, anti-Johnson Democrats of 1960–1963 found it especially easy to march to the attack as Vietnam turned sour.

The appalling direct and indirect costs of the Vietnam War were unnerving. Says an expert who calculated *all costs* (including loss of lifetime potential wages of deceased soldiers, loss in production of civilian goods by those who volunteered or were drafted, and the probable future extent of medical care and veterans benefits), *Vietnam, from beginning to end, cost $842 billion to $885 billion* (in 1969 dollars).[57] Here was the final total bill for fighting what a caustic Johnson once called "a raggedyass little fourth-rate country" like North Vietnam.[58]

The historian is faced, inescapably, with the question of why the president and his key advisers—meeting, for example, at the Tuesday luncheon sessions—took the nation ever more deeply into the Vietnam commitment. Some have said that this was a "quagmire," with each small decision weighing down the situation into the quicksand. Daniel Ellsberg suggests that the escalation decisions stemmed from apprehension over the idea of "retreat" and/or a possible Communist victory. Thus, time was being bought: *This* is just not the moment to allow the enemy to prevail. Psychologist Irving L. Janis has advanced the conception of "groupthink" among the president's advisers. Here, a small cohesive group maintained a confident esprit de corps by unconsciously sharing illusions and norms at the expense of critical thought and the testing of reality.[59] Each hypothesis has its attractions; each makes a person pause. All seem better than the simplistic "Texas macho" accusation made by some, or the capitalism-on-the-march conception of others. What Johnson's team (once Kennedy's) were doing was simple enough: they had said there should be an independent, self-governing, and democratic South Vietnam; and they were not about to give up—no matter what.

In the last analysis, appraisal of Johnson and Vietnam will have to hinge on whether posterity regards the Southeast Asian military adventure of Kennedy, Johnson, and Nixon as a just war. Books and articles have been written in an attempt to define such a war so that it may be readily recognized. An effort by a professor of Christian ethics suggests five criteria: The war must have been a last resort; this helps its morality. It must be declared explicitly by competent authority; this helps it to be honorable. There must be a reasonable chance of success; thus, something meaningful might ensue. Intentions are important: the correcting of wrongs or the achieving of righteousness and order. In the waging, there should be the principle of proportionality: that is, strategies must not be entirely out of keeping with the amount of havoc to be created. And, finally, noncombatants must be immune, at least in principle.[60]

How far each of these troublesome criteria applied, between 1961 and 1973, to the crusade to establish a democratic and viable state of South Vietnam would be a nice test of scholarly thought. There was little agreement by contemporaries. Strongest of these criteria were the intentions. Especially controversial is the judgment of a die-hard few that the attempt to save South Vietnam from communism was "born of noble ideals and impulses," a view that resurfaced weakly in the early 1980s.[61] Careful examination of each of the above points shows that the president, at least, would have thought himself in the clear on most matters that counted. But many people—then and later—could never agree.

Lyndon Johnson clearly would like to have had associated with himself what he said as he made his final four awards of the Medal of Honor. Each man had "heard the call of duty in an hour of hard challenge, and each man answered that call with a courage beyond demand." The president hoped that "never again would war summon the best that men can give." When such a day should come, he believed, there would be a place of honor for the good and gallant fighting men who had discharged their duty.[62] The commander in chief probably thought that he was one who had gone the distance in such praiseworthy directions.

12

★ ★ ★ ★ ★

"I'VE GONE THE DISTANCE"

In a sense, a presidential election normally begins the day after the close of the previous election. Potential candidates and their supporters spend four full years jockeying for position, seeking actual or potential funds, and creating just the right posture. But in another sense, the intensified activity that the public calls "the election" begins with primaries, continues through the party conventions, and reaches a climax in the autumn. Yet behind the scenes the party organizers, the regulars, are at work, preparing the party machinery to conduct the coming battle.

One must take seriously the belief that Lyndon Johnson was personally responsible for the deterioration of the Democratic National Committee as a viable force—thus weakening the election chances of any Democratic candidate for president in 1968. He treated the committee and its Kennedy-appointed chairman as one would who never expected to need their services again. John Bailey had watched helplessly in 1964 as Johnson cut the committee's budget and killed the voter-registration program. Johnson had his own very viable fund-raising entity—the President's Clubs—and his friend Arthur Krim to work with them. There was rancor in the national committee over the clubs, so Bailey wanted to resign in 1966; but he stayed on, even after the 1966 loss of three Senate seats, forty-seven House seats, and eight governorships. After this the voter-registration drive was reinstated. Bailey was "just a figurehead," says national party leader India Edwards, adding that the committee's vice-chairman, Margaret Price, was never consulted or treated as though she had any intelligence. Edwards says that Johnson never let Bailey do anything and that there was no communication between the White House and the committee. The amenities were observed, however, for the White House Diary shows that both women were present at a number of social occasions and that Bailey, at least, was telephoned by Johnson or that he visited the Oval Office several dozen times during those years. Asked why he became such a do-nothing chairman, Bailey replied that he abdicated his duties because "I either had to do it or I had to get out. And so I decided just to ride along and let things go."[1]

Considering the Democratic National Committee in retrospect, Humphrey said that Johnson trimmed fat from it—but also muscle. It became a haven for people that were not wanted in the White House, in government, or in their own offices. "Political retainers and sycophants accumulated there, smothering able people in an atmosphere of flabby incompetence." While its decisions were being made with slow caution, the president lost track. He thought he had mastered all details, as during his Senate days; but he did not, for in party politics, Johnson "was not good," whatever his other skills, judged the vice-president. Johnson simply did not build a national political structure.[2] Such criticisms, long considered truisms regarding Eisenhower, read strangely when directed at Lyndon Johnson, one whose biographies include such titles as *The Professional* and *The Politician*.

In April 1968 the committee had no staff and no materials to distribute. Failing to reach the treasurer for two weeks, India Edwards got an immediate appointment with a president who was astonished that she was getting no cooperation. Krim, John Criswell (the treasurer), and John Bailey were told that she was "to have whatever she feels she needs." Problems ceased. But Johnson failed to understand the need for a *national* committee. Once he asked Bailey: "What do you need a staff for at the national committee? I could run it with one secretary." Edwards charges that Johnson didn't "understand national politics." During the campaign, as people called from everywhere seeking campaign materials, it was "pathetic" because "they couldn't get anything."

Just before leaving office, the president read with concerned interest a newspaper story about the committee, which said that it was licking its wounds, confessing error, and resolving to repair "its organization, its treasury, and its shattered national constituency." The deficit would be over $7 million. Johnson went over the clipping with the incoming chairman, Senator Fred R. Harris, especially noting, in bright yellow, a sentence that said that majority leader Mansfield and the new whip, Edward Kennedy, "have a national outlook that Mr. Johnson and Mr. Rayburn did not have."[3] It must have been a charming meeting.

Anyone constituted as was Lyndon Johnson would long have been aware that election year 1968 would be a time of special challenges for political leaders like Richard Nixon, Nelson Rockefeller, and Robert Kennedy; even, depending on what Johnson should decide to do, Hubert Humphrey might find this year rich in opportunity. The Republicans could be counted on, this time, to put their most unifying foot forward; Johnson himself seemed to have control over the Democratic nominee, whatever might happen. It would not be a Kennedy if Johnson could help it—the "Bobby problem," the staff called it. All along, says Johnson's totally political brother, the president "wasn't about to let Bobby Kennedy establish an independent power base inside his administration."[4] This was easier said than done, for Jack Valenti would recall how easy it had been, for a time after John Kennedy's death, for "the residue of my own innermost affection" simply to move over to Bobby, as by osmosis.

Vice-President Humphrey, like Kennedy, knew that 1968 could be his year. As early as the spring of 1967 he had written the titular head of his party: "With 1968 approaching, it seems to me it would be useful for the White House to take a direct, sustained interest in local Democratic party leadership throughout the country—to make them feel *involved, in touch, committed.*" For fifty weeks, Johnson should invite them in batches to Washington. "I could serve as the White House Liaison. Meet them, greet them, arrange a one- or two-day routine . . . and stay in touch with them when they go home."[5] Here was a good idea from more than one person's standpoint.

Indeed, as 1968 approached, it did look as though strenuous measures would be required to ensure the viability of the Democratic party. In December 1967 an aide began a long memorandum to a colleague in which he called for candor and said that "the mood of the nation is somber." While national frustration and impatience were being blamed on Johnson's personality, they really came from rising expectations. Inner-city poverty was a reality; "well intentioned government programs have not hit their targets." The president should locate the underlying unity and purpose of the society, as he had done in 1964.[6] This was expecting a great deal. One thing that was dividing Americans was the draft and those who were violating it. In 1967 no less than 952 young men had been convicted of violating the Selective Service laws—up from 272 in 1965 to 536 in 1966. While these are impressive figures, 1918 had brought 8,422 convictions; and 1944, 4,609!

On January 16 it was learned that 51 percent of the student bodies of Harvard and Radcliffe had signed a request to Johnson to avoid further escalation and seriously to try to reach a settlement. Three days later came the announcement that 302,000 young people would be inducted in 1968. An end to graduate-school deferments came on February 16. Now controversy was intensified, even though Robert Kennedy said on March 25, "If I were called up, I would go." It was evident that significant numbers of Americans of draft age disagreed completely.

February was a difficult month to be president. At one point, Johnson called Sam Houston at 2:00 A.M. to play some dominoes, but his mind soon seemed far away, and there seemed to be a look of loneliness and anguish in his eyes and his mouth was tight set. Reminded that it was his move, Lyndon replied: "That's just the trouble, Sam Houston—it's always my move. And, damn it, I sometimes can't tell whether I'm making the right move or not Now take this Vietnam mess. How in the hell can anyone know for sure what's right and what's wrong, Sam? I got some of the finest brains in this country—people like Dean Rusk, Walt Rostow, and Dean Acheson—making some strong convincing arguments for us to stay in there and not pull out. Then I've got some people like George Ball and Fulbright—also intelligent men whose motives I can't rightly distrust—who keep telling me we've got to de-escalate or run the risk of a total war. And, Sam, I've got to listen to both sides. . . . I've just got to choose between my opposing experts. . . . But I sure as hell wish I could *really* know what's right." Off he went to the Situation Room for the 3:00 A.M. report from Saigon.[7] So the statistics from Vietnam on the killed and wounded got to the president, just as similar reports a century earlier had wounded Lincoln. The prairie lawyer and the hill-country teacher had been equally drained.

In winter 1967/68 the nation and certainly most Democratic politicians saw 1968 as a year with special problems. Larry O'Brien, who had ties with the Kennedy family, would be late in learning important truths from the president. He records that because of Vietnam, "none of us had any illusions about repeating 1964." There were uncertainties among members of the White House staff over the emerging McCarthy and possible Kennedy candidacies and how to handle the primaries. Whose cause would gain O'Brien's practiced support? He finally announced in support of the president on March 20. Yet he told Johnson, cold turkey, where he stood: "I think you are going to be badly defeated" in the Wisconsin primary, "sixty-forty . . . , maybe two to one. . . . Frankly, your supporters are very depressed . . . , very depressed."[8] So a major Johnson effort would have been in order—a week after New Hampshire and several days after Kennedy's declaration of candidacy.

There would be posturing: a fiery Johnson speech, couched in basic language and simplified ideas, on March 18 to the National Farmers Union in Minneapolis, where he declared, "You want the justice, the decency, and the opportunity that every American has the right to claim as his native right—and you will have them." Communist aggression was threatening to engulf Southeast Asia "and to affect the safety of every American home" and "every nation allied with us." This was World Wars I and II, Korea, and Berlin all over again. Aggressors' appetites must not be allowed to go uncontrolled. In pithy, one-sentence declarations, President Johnson told heartland listeners that a much wider war, involving perhaps another million men, was one option; but "we do not think that is a wise course."

Here were his policies: "We don't want to conquer you. We don't want to destroy your nation. We don't want to divide you. We just want to say to you that we have an obligation. We have signed forty-two alliances with people of the world. We have said that when an aggressor comes across this line to try to dominate other people, and they call on us to help, we are going to come and help, until you decide to leave your neighbors alone." Then the president added, "I think they will find out in the days ahead that we are reasonable people, that we are fair people, that we are not folks who want to conquer the world. Let's not "tuck our tail and violate our commitments." Here, in plain English, was Johnson's best foot forward.

Four days later came the results of a confidential poll of Democrats, conducted by Penetration Research, Ltd., on March 19 and 20. Interviewed in haste by telephone, 452 adults who would surely vote caused the pollster to conclude that the president was in much weaker condition in Wisconsin than he was in New Hampshire. Don't stress "experience" and "record." More would be voting for Kennedy or McCarthy than for Johnson, a situation that was "extremely unsatisfactory," especially since few were undecided. The odds were very much against Johnson, especially since Republicans would cross over and vote against him. Problems of Wisconsin voters in March 1968 were said to be taxes and spending, the racial situation, and Vietnam. Domestic accomplishments of the president were not gut issues. Hawks were said to outnumber doves 3 to 2! Voting Democrats felt, by 75 to 25 percent, that he hadn't been completely honest with the public on Vietnam. The chances of getting a majority in Wisconsin were "slim." On March 30, however, Johnson was informed that poll taker Louis Harris was finding that three-quarters of the public thought that Bobby Kennedy was an opportunist, while more than that thought the president was doing his best in a tough job. This, commented one aide, is more solid than asking how people will vote. Pollster Harris confided to the White House (improperly?) that it would crystallize the situation if Johnson would declare as soon as possible.[9]

In late March 1968, in the aftermath of Tet, the president discussed at length with high-level advisers the possibility of making a fundamental change in the war policy. Should more men be sent to Vietnam? Had the time come to cut back in some way? Johnson received conflicting advice during this intense period of rethinking—a matter dwelt on by many of the books on Vietnam. Generally a combination of adverse projections by the Office of Systems Analysis and abandonment of escalation by outsiders such as Dean Acheson and the new secretary of defense, Clark Clifford, left the president short of allies for his established policy. Armed with a Westmoreland estimate that in order to seize the initiative by moving into Laos and Cambodia on the ground it would mean adding 206,000 men to the 525,000 in being, the Joint Chiefs of Staff made clear to the president the inability of present levels of effort ever to prevail. (Immediate withdrawal was by no means the issue in these debates among high-ranking military personnel and top advisers in and out of government.) Unwilling to put the nation at this late date on a "real" war footing, President Johnson determined that a first step in a new direction would be to cut back on the bombing.[10] Naturally, he agonized over announcing to the public any decision that would appear to be a major reversal, one that could be seen as an admission that the nation's course had long been in error. In a TV address of March 31, 1968 he finally announced an offer "to stop the bombardment of North Vietnam," if talks with Hanoi should begin promptly, would be serious, and would dwell on "the substance of peace." The level of hostilities would be reduced by no longer attacking North Vietnam except "north of the DMZ" where there was enemy build-up. There would be no attacks henceforth on the principal populated or food-producing areas. Soon, this vagueness would be regarded as new duplicity. As he came to the close of the speech, the president now told an astonished nation that he would not be running for another term in the White House!

Controversy has surrounded the motives for this totally unexpected decision to withdraw. It is widely believed that this represents an instance when the nation's "youth" or "protestors" or "students" or "New Left" or "doves" were able to drive from office an incumbent president because of sharp disagreement over continuing to wage war in Southeast Asia. Years later, Barry Goldwater judged that "the angry, disillusioned American public forced Lyndon Johnson to abandon his hope for a second term." Even one of the most knowledgeable still asserted in the 1980s, "With his party so badly split, Johnson decided not to run."[11] This represents the conventional wisdom, shored up by logic and some facts, but it apparently is incorrect. The decision not to try for renomination had been made much earlier and stemmed from serious personal considerations. These will now be reviewed in detail.

Thirty months after leaving office, Lyndon Johnson asserted, "My March 31 decision had been in my mind since August 26 of 1964." During the next four years he had felt "almost sure" that he would not be a candidate. So, the public announcement was just "giving expression to what I had believed and hoped for and expected to do for a good long time." This is by no means what he had told his fellow countrymen earlier, when he was president! He says in his memoirs that in 1964 he had experienced misgivings about even trying for his *first* four-year elected term. A written pep talk from his wife then had helped to tip the balance.[12] These general recollections have long provided clues that have been ignored, probably because they do not incorporate any additional truths that would make them credible.

Although a *Washington Post* headline on November 24, 1963, was "Johnson Can Seek Two Terms," the truth was that nature had long since seen to it that, in good conscience, he should not try to do so: His physical constitution simply was not up to it. This major theme has escaped both biographies and history books. Outwardly, Lyndon Johnson was an impressive masculine specimen, who wore a shirt with a 17½ collar and 37-inch sleeves and who stood 6 feet, 5¾ inches tall. His handshake was firm. The huge body deceived observers but not its owner. A recital of his ill health—which involved great pain, major surgery, fear, and many hospitalizations—when assembled in one place, will be a surprise. His many ailments were not psychosomatic, as one biographer has charged, and they had no pattern of coming on the eves of elections (thus representing his shrinking from "conflict") except coincidentally.

The state of health of a president has long been of concern to the public. Presidents have died in office, and one—Woodrow Wilson—was incapacitated. The death of Franklin Roosevelt very early in his fourth term alerted the nation to the problem of knowing the truth about the continuing vigor of the chief executive. In the case of President Johnson, some who have focused on Vietnam have made unsubstantiated, really unwarranted, charges about his mental health. Few have expressed skepticism about his physical well-being. As to the latter, his White House physician, Dr. George G. Burkley, said in a private oral-history interview on December 3, 1968, that Johnson's "ability to perform under stress is excellent" and added that his "general health" for his age was better than that of most men. Of course, "he knows and we all know that you do get older." The reply was cagey. The reader should know that the doctor admitted that, aside from his own central role at certain surgical operations and hospitalizations, his contacts with Johnson had been "really almost of minor significance." There are, in fact, good reasons to explore the lifelong Johnson health and his attitude toward it.

Johnson's lack of physical well-being is the key. In 1937 he had his appendix removed—the beginning of innumerable trips to hospitals. While in the navy in 1941/42 he admits having had "chest trouble"; actually, he really had six to eight bouts with pneumonia. He even contracted bronchiectasis, which entitled him to 10 percent veterans disability pay (then $15 a month), for which official ruling he applied successfully in 1955. "We determined that residuals of pneumonia and chronic bronchitis were service connected," reported the Veterans Administration. But having established this point, the senator renounced the compensation.[13] A ureteral kidney stone was removed in 1948 by manipulation through a cystoscope. He had a dangerous operation for a kidney stone at the Mayo Clinic in 1955, followed, for a time, by life in a brace.

The next bout with bad health would involve a life-and-death struggle for this classic example of "Type A Behavior Pattern"—"a particular complex of personality traits, including excessive competitive drive, aggressiveness, impatience, and a harrying sense of time urgency." Two heart specialists in 1974 said that Type A people are prone to have early heart attacks, are filled with deep-seated insecurity, and "seem engaged in a chronic, ceaseless, and often fruitless struggle— with themselves, with others, with circumstances, with time, sometimes with life itself." This description precisely fitted the senator, who later became president.[14] While in Congress, Johnson smoked two to three packs of cigarettes a day. He also spent endless hours closeted with smokers, thought nothing of skipping lunch and postponing dinner for hours, weighed a flabby 225, displayed acute stress, ate as and when he pleased, got little exercise, and walked around with a dangerous, even frightening, inherited time bomb. Johnson's father had died at the age of sixty after having had two heart attacks; two uncles had died at the ages of sixty and fifty-seven. While his brother says that he saw Lyndon drunk only once during his days in Congress (Justice William O. Douglas has confirmed this), George Reedy says that during the later Senate years, there was a huge daily intake of scotch—although, for political reasons, Johnson pretended that he drank bourbon—an American drink! As president, he tapered off to help control his weight; instead, he consumed huge quantities of Fresca, Tab, and tea.

It was on July 2, 1955, that this high-risk specimen had a major myocardial infarction—that is, the death of part of the muscle of the heart. His blood pressure fell drastically. The official statements somehow recorded that the attack had been "moderately severe" but that he was still "critically ill." On July 5 his colleagues heard a prayer for "the stalwart leader in this body who so recently spoke from his place of high responsibility with passion and deep sincerity regarding public questions." Now he conversed fervently with Lady Bird about retirement— otherwise, his life would probably be shortened, it was thought. But the doctors tried to be reassuring. After a month in the hospital, a gaunt Johnson was off to the Ranch to await an agonizingly slow recovery. He kept a clipping from a fellow Texan, the survivor of an attack, who claimed that for a long life, a person should have his attack at an early age so as to be forced to learn to care for himself!

Lyndon Johnson made an excellent recovery after a terrible scare that involved weakness, frightening arrhythmia (missing heartbeats), and, for a time, mental preparation for possible early death. He even put his affairs in order. To his initial Texas audience after five months, Johnson gave thanks to those "who came to my help with their prayers only a few weeks ago when there was little to preserve my life except prayer." Nevertheless, he remained fully aware of his incapacity; it could not be expunged from his mind and spirit. In December 1955 his six-doctor team said that the senator must have relief from work that could be handled by his staff, "carefully regulated hours of work and rest," and frequent short vacations; for "anyone in a responsible position involving mental strain or tension should guard his health very carefully." Impatience and brief rages were a natural concomitant of the realization that one's life might suddenly cease—with his destiny remaining unfulfilled. John P. Roche, later an associate, said, with accidental astuteness, that people often thought that Lyndon was screaming at them, when "in fact he was screaming at the universe, and they were just witnesses to it."

Suddenly becoming president eight and a half years later, and without a vice-president for fourteen months, Johnson was determined to bury the slightest public suspicion about his healthful vigor. This was quickly tested. At the time when he was moving out of the Elms to the White House, he had a very severe cold and chest condition, but this was concealed from the media. One of his doctors later recalled that after the presidential race of 1964, "the heart did not become much of a problem . . . ; it was not discussed much." The use of "much" is highly significant, since no heart irregularities or even discussions were ever admitted publicly after 1955! Once in the White House, Lyndon required naps and swimming as a medical prescription, but he found exercises boring. Something passing for relaxation came to this man-in-a-hurry only on weekends, especially at the Ranch. The president quit smoking, he attempted to rest in the afternoons in his pajamas, he had a carefully controlled and supervised diet, he kept somewhat fit, and he was monitored—humiliatingly and, he sometimes thought, unfairly—by his wife and his physicians. There were massages and enemas, even during working hours, which caused misunderstanding and later snide commentary on what was considered blatant immodesty. He almost feared to close doors, to be alone; would there be another attack, with no one to help? So, at the very outset of his presidency in 1963, the nation had a leader who, in the secret recesses of his mind, was not entirely "well." Moreover, he concentrated on his physical distress, says Reedy. Yet the country got a president who had "a much stronger emotional, sort of gut reaction" to medical legislation as a result, says the distinguished heart specialist Dr. Michael DeBakey; Johnson had been affected in this way by illness even more than Eisenhower had been.[15]

No doubt, when any president leaves the country, his health must be protected. One is a bit overwhelmed, however, on reading of precautions taken in Johnson's case. His food and water were taken along. A White House physician left ahead of time. The secret service located all relevant overseas hospitals and reported on medical coverage. All American military services were alerted, so that their medical facilities would be ready. Blood types were forwarded. For his trips to Latin America, a navy ship, with a complete "team" and with helicopter coverage, was stationed appropriately. This was also done when it was thought that Malaysian medical facilities might not be adequate. A physician always flew with Johnson to Texas. The prestige of his doctors was such that he could hastily promote Dr. Burkley to vice-admiral in 1963, and his staff physicians held joint appointments at the Bethesda facility.

The new president would get well acquainted with doctors and hospitals during the years 1963 to 1969. Three days after inauguration day 1965 he was taken to the hospital by ambulance at 2:26 A.M. with symptoms publicly termed a "cold," although the vice-president called them in his later memoirs "chest pains."[16] In the morning his limited visitors included the chief justice, the secretary of state, and his pastor. Lady Bird moved into a room above his, allegedly with the same cold. Reporters who interviewed Humphrey in Minnesota described him as "solemn" and "grim." He said he had "fears and apprehensions."

There was full testing of LBJ's blood and heart, with the latter coming up "completely within normal limits." The harried press secretary was told little, so that in a letter to me he claims the whole episode was typical Johnson hypochondria or a "sore throat." Press coverage, at first on page one, faded as Winston Churchill's death displaced interest. Once again the old Johnson weakness for pneumonia had been avoided successfully. With all medical records still "not available for research," we can only speculate why Humphrey was so deeply concerned and later referred to chest pains, rather than the term "heavy cough," which was offered to the press at the time. Did Johnson then or at any other time in the presidency have touches of heart arrhythmia? Did he carry or ever use nitroglycerine pills, as he admittedly did soon after leaving office? Back at the White House once again in January 1965, in one night he sweated through three pairs of pajamas, "an old enemy" condition and "a symptom of his illnesses" for all of the years his wife had known him.[17]

There would be further hospitalization. The night before Labor Day 1965 he had a severe onset of stomach pain, which a concerned husband and wife, recalling how the 1955 heart attack had started, did not tell Dr. Burkley about, at Lyndon's insistence, until morning. The diagnosis was a gall-bladder problem, but the media was not informed that there was a problem. An operation would be scheduled for October 5, amidst hope that nobody need know until afterward; but this unthinkable idea was abondoned, allegedly at Eisenhower's urging. Ten doctors, including heart specialists, attended the two-hour operation, which resulted in removal of the gall bladder and a kidney stone. Even in late November the state of recovery was such that "limited activities" were insisted on by physicians until the end of the year.

It would be a combination of abdominal and throat surgery that took Johnson to the hospital again on November 16, 1966, amid great family concern. "Thank the Lord, the growth was benign," wrote Lady Bird at Bethesda (her fourth stay there with him since July 1955). There were other, less serious reminders of human frailty in the presidential years. Lyndon had thirty to forty skin lesions removed off and on, which were precancerous and benign except for one on his ankle. Later it would have to be denied that he had secretly suffered from "skin cancer." He often complained of "foot trouble," but entirely in private. Sties on his eyes were not uncommon. An English newsman placed on the first page of his 1966 biography of Johnson a reference to "recurrent anxieties about his health."[18]

We simply cannot know how often or why President Johnson saw his doctors (or just avoided seeing them) during those years, for the various oral histories from physicians tell little, and the bland and self-serving one by Vice-Adm. George G. Burkley is just annoying. Three days before the dramatic March 31, 1968, speech, he saw a doctor for some unstated reason. In the fall, on December 16, he came down with chills and fever in the middle of the night, but he told the doctor he would not go to the hospital in the night because of the possible effects on the stock market, the day's coming decisions and appointments, and "the rumor machine." Lady Bird was unable to sleep. Soon back in the hospital still another time, Lyndon Johnson just lay there for several days, says Lady Bird, "not talking, not reacting, just lying still—a very untypical posture . . . and the measure of his misery." On December 27 he commented: "I am not sick but I am tired. . . . I do still have this hacking cough. . . . I am getting [tired] and disgusted with it."[19]

Not surprisingly, many noticed but tactfully said little in public about the physical frailty and deteriorating aspect of the previously dynamic Texan. Early in 1966 John Steinbeck said he didn't like the leader's appearance; he was "too drawn and too taut"; so, "I wish he would slow down and get some joy in his eye but I know damned well he won't." Assistant Frankel recorded in 1967, "At the White House reception for the Diplomatic Corps this evening, the president looked grey with exhaustion." Henry Gonzalez, Texas congressman and good friend, recalls, "He told me to my face that the reason he didn't run again was that several doctors had told him he wouldn't last another term." He said he felt it best not to carry on. It was in October 1967 that Dr. Willis Hurst warned Lady Bird of his great concern over the state of her husband's health. She much wanted to tell him of the decision that had already been made not to run again but "did not feel free to do so." Now there would ensue still another discussion between husband and wife on exactly *when* to make the announcement public. One of his pilots told me of Johnson's decline during the summer and fall of 1968 and the winter of 1968/69. A reporter who interviewed Lady Bird years later would write, "More so than most wives, Mrs. Johnson early confronted the unhappy certainty that she was destined to become a widow." Lyndon had said it was "a lead-pipe cinch." The first lady recalled, "He was very conscious of the fact that he was not going to live as long as I was." Preparing late in 1968 for his patient's life in retirement, Dr. Burkley quietly arranged for a heart specialist to be stationed henceforth at Brooke Army Hospital at government expense, a location convenient to Johnson City. Arrangements were made sometime for two government helicopters to be in the Austin area for his use.[20]

Such precautions were welcome, for Johnson was acutely aware that Franklin Roosevelt, whose poor appearance was much noted in private in late 1944, lived after his reelection to a fourth term only the few months until April 12, 1945. In Johnson's case, he overdid in the spring of 1969 at the Ranch and experienced chest pains and shortness of breath—a fact that the retiree, now out of office, casually admitted to a reporter a full year later. Is it completely out of the limits of conjecture to guess that, very privately, during his White House years, this man had occasionally had heart irregularities that frightened him and reinforced his decision to retire? Such is my educated belief. Episodes like these come and go with many who recover from myocardial infarctions, but there is really little to be gained by revealing them to loved ones or doctors, especially since the latter are likely to say reassuringly that such "benign arrhythmias" are common among many who are healthy. We know the Johnsons worried about a heart attack during the years 1963 to 1969. During the night of September 7, 1966, the mysterious stomach pains he was enduring gave rise to a montage of thoughts and emotions. Says Lady Bird: "We didn't actually talk about what was most on my mind, and I assume on his—could this be the beginning of another heart attack?" The first one had begun just that way! "For a long time—months, years—I have been keenly aware how lucky we have been." Declared her husband: "I frankly did not believe in 1968 that I would survive another four years of the long hours and unremitting tensions I had just gone through."

A by-product of the Kennedy assassination and, to a degree, of Johnson's hospitalizations involving anesthesia, was the Twenty-fifth Amendment to the Constitution, on the subject of presidential succession in the case of disability. Approved by the Congress July 6, 1965, and ratified finally by February 10, 1967, it enjoined the president to notify the Congress of his inability to serve. Should he prove unable or unwilling to initiate proceedings, the vice-president and a majority of the cabinet were given the authority to take at least temporary power for the former, subject to congressional approval. Despite careful framing, the amendment was not to be utilized at the time of the attempted assassination of Ronald Reagan and the two subsequent operations. One guesses that Johnson would have dragged his feet rather than transfer power during his operations of October 6, 1965, and November 16, 1966.

That the retired president had angina pains in the chest due to coronary blockage became generally known by March 1970. While he was hospitalized in San Antonio, his rapidly greying hair of 1969 now turned white. In spring 1972 came another heart attack, his third, followed by a pain-wracked ordeal. Now, recourse to nitroglycerine pills was constant, and reliance on oxygen was sometimes necessary. "I'm hurtin' real bad," he would say. The care he had taken of himself as a public duty in Oval Office years had by now been totally abandoned. His weight had risen from 190 to 235; after fifteen years of not smoking, he began to chain-smoke at the level of three packs a day. There was more than ample alcohol. "I don't want to linger the way Eisenhower did," he proclaimed. "When I go, I want to go fast." In April 1972, when he would have had a full nine months more of executive responsibility had he been reelected, and with still more suffering from a recurrent problem—diverticulitis (inflamed pouches on the intestine)—and with two of his coronary arteries useless, Lyndon observed that he was standing there and taking it "just like a jackass in a hailstorm."[21] Used up physically, the former president died on January 22, 1973, just two days after a mostly unendurable second term would have been over, that is, if he had somehow managed to survive that long under presidential strains and burdens.

It should be altogether clear after this revealing recital, which I have pieced together with much difficulty, that the 269 weeks that Lyndon Johnson spent in the presidency were about all that he could have taken physically and that he and his wife were quietly aware of this well ahead of time. Long before the preparation period for the election of 1968, the Johnsons, husband and wife, knew that in the national interest, as well as their own, there should be no further years of arduous labor as chief executive after January 20, 1969. So, Johnson's withdrawal from candidacy for another term could have been—but clearly was not—due to Tet, the war in general, rival challengers in his party, the protesters, the polls, the "system" working, any alleged mental quirks or supposed tendencies toward avoiding conflict, or the fear of losing.

Johnson tells us that back in 1964 his wife did not want him to run in 1968. Daughter Luci soon agreed, for "she insisted she wanted a living father." So, he made his decision as early as summer 1965. He began to let a tiny handful of trusted intimates from Texas know, but only when absolutely necessary. Each one seems to have thought that he was the first and only person to hear this as he was told, in strictest confidence, the block-busting news. Johnson's message was that they should not base any important personal plans on the idea that he would be serving after early 1969. Some—probably most—seem to have disbelieved.

In summer 1965 one close friend was told to accept an indefinite appointment to a federal office, rather than a seven-year term, because Johnson would not be around to renew the appointment. Arthur Krim, who was, along with his wife, a frequent guest at the White House and was chairman of the vital President's Clubs (politician Johnson's financial mechanism), was told as early as fall 1965; he couldn't believe it, remaining one of the most reluctant to accept the idea even when told repeatedly. Jack Valenti was told on September 4, 1966, as the president said that he would resign right then if he could, since the country needed a fresh face. "His voice was heavy, weary, flat. He seemed very tired." At about that time, Eric Goldman says, Johnson's private conversation began to include phrases like "in the time left to me" and "there is so much to do and so little time." Lady Bird told trustworthy Supreme Court Justice Fortas in May 1967 and recorded this in her diary: "Many months ago I set March 1968 in my own mind as the time when Lyndon can make a statement that he will not be a candidate for reelection. For the first time in my life I have felt lately that Lyndon would be a happy man retired." In September 1967 she recorded that she did not want to face another campaign; with four more presidential years for a husband in his sixties, "bad health might overtake him . . . ; a physical or mental incapacitation would be unbearable, painful for him to recognize."[22]

By mid 1967, highly practical matters made it necessary for the president to begin sharing the news of his coming retirement with important associates. In August he told James Webb, director of NASA, for a deputy needed to be broken in to replace Webb later; but only Lady Bird and John Connally were as yet aware of his final decision, Johnson averred. Texas congressman Jake Pickle says that the absolute decision not to run no matter what was made on Labor Day 1967 after he, Governor Connally, and Johnson spent four or five hours in discussion at the Ranch. Connally absolutely needed to know if he must seek another term as governor as a service to the national ticket; if not, he wanted out. Asked conversationally by Lady Bird what the group had decided, Lyndon replied, equally conversationally: "All right, you've been talking about this for a long time, so we'll make this decision right now and make you happy. . . . I've decided that I won't run for reelection." For both of the Johnsons, this was non-news; as we have seen, he already knew it, and so did she. Walt Rostow heard his leader tell senior advisers on October 3, 1967, that he was "inclined" not to run. In the cabinet room a small group was told, "I don't want any of you to plan in terms of my being a candidate next year."[23] Such people disbelieved routinely, because they never heard credible reasons.

Sometime during that year the chief executive launched a secret actuarial study on his life expectancy, saying: "The men in the Johnson family have a history of dying young. . . . I figure with my history of heart trouble I'd never live through another four years. The American people had enough of presidents dying in office." (The study's prediction of death by age 64 proved to be correct.) The time was clearly at hand in the late fall when certain outstanding personalities simply must be told—and told the truth. General Westmoreland says that in November 1967 his commander in chief told him that McNamara was leaving, Clifford was taking over, and Johnson himself would not be running for reelection. Johnson drew the general's attention to his earlier heart attack, saying that he was tired and had carried a terrible burden for a long time. He talked of invalided presidents. A president should be in perfect health; no chances should be taken. Politics was not discussed. Now it was General Eisenhower's turn, as Johnson told the former president the same points. After all, he was reminded, no president who had succeeded a president who had died in office had ever run as an incumbent for more than one full term. Says General Goodpaster, after Ike told him of this conversation, "This I found very revealing."[24]

Would the commander in chief have lied on such a matter to his field general or to a former president (aware that these West Point graduates were steeped in regard for honor)? No. Here, in LBJ's physical health, seems to be the long-ignored truth. For this experienced and pragmatic politician, it would be easier to skew the truth in a nationwide speech and in talks with the media, for this might bring about gains for causes to which he was deeply committed. In summary, the whole business of March 31 on TV—about not running in order to devote more time to his job and to encourage negotiations with the enemy—was engineered to obtain a useful payoff for the nation, while still not revealing the state of his health. To have told the blunt truth about his conception of his limitations, in so many words, would have been to reveal how much various truths had been bent.

Someday, perhaps, candid revelations by physicians, both those who were in attendance and those who visited, the opening of surviving medical records, and bits and pieces of information may shed additional light on the physical health of this president. Until then, it is worth remembering that here was a man who from 1955 to 1969 was hospitalized many times (not less than six); he had endured various preliminary diagnostic procedures and much strong medicaton that just might work; there were X-rays, anesthesia, full tests, ample pre- and postoperative pain, and many of what some patients call "indignities." He lived, as an adult, with a bronchial disability and with a growing intestinal problem that involved discomfort, especially with any change in altitude. That all of this may have had an impact on his desire to continue for four more years is not surprising. Now: Did it have an impact at all on his mind, in the sense that body and mind interact? Or was there sudden pain on some occasions that was misunderstood by visitors? Or, entirely probably, were there from time to time "side effects" from some of the powerful drugs that accompanied his indispositions? Once, a qualified visitor said afterwards, "Clinically, I'm alarmed." Why? There have been stories about Johnson's having said that he had communicated with the Holy Ghost and about a morbid preoccupation with Woodrow Wilson's picture (Wilson being one who had become disabled when in office). Given the unbearable weight of the daily Vietnam casualty reports on the commander in chief, and all of the above considerations, the mind and body could easily have interacted on occasion.

When the White House physician was asked in late 1968 by an oral-history interviewer if he knew any health-related reasons behind the decision to withdraw, he said oddly, "I have no knowledge of any health reason except that he is now sixty years old." The doctor did not consider health "a question in his decision." Given what the Johnsons have said, either the doctor did not know his patient very well or, more likely, he was being professionally silent. Having revealed nothing substantive in his 25-page interview, he observed that he had "probably talked more about the president personally than I have at any time in the past."[25] Here, medical ethics definitely collided with the right of the public to know. After all, Lady Bird says in her diary that the decision to run in 1964 was only made after searching conferences with cardiologists James Cain and Willis Hurst, with the subject being whether Lyndon was up to a full term either psychologically or physically. (They thought he should try.)

Could Johnson have won? He thought so. Aging Democrat Jim Farley, himself once considered for the office, said that LBJ would be a cinch to win, so that "a lot of gutless politicians" who were then panicking would climb on the bandwagon the next year. But columnist Richard Strout of the *New Republic* guessed that, with the war continuing, Johnson would be defeated, for nearly half of the eighty-four senators who were polled by the AP said they did not endorse the war policy; and several polls showed erosion. Inside the White House this was well known, for the most important domestic concerns of the public were, in percentages chosen from a list: race riots and civil rights—79; economic—34; social welfare—20; the draft—3; crime—2; education—3; and farm—1. In foreign affairs the concerns were: Vietnam—76; Middle East—26; other—28; communism and Red China—10; foreign aid—3; foreign trade—2; and U.S. image—2. The Republican dissidents of 1964 were by now back in their own camp. A White House polling effort in October 1967 showed Johnson with a substantial margin over Robert Kennedy among Democrats, and over George Romney of Michigan by

16 points, over Nixon by 17, over Charles Percy of Illinois by 19, and over Ronald Reagan of California by 23; but Nelson Rockefeller of New York led him by a point. Still, the country was polarized both on Vietnam and on Johnson as a leader, so, here was a consideration for one facing possible leadership from 1969 to 1973 to remember.[26]

Twitted by newsman Raymond Sherer on December 18 about lacking the trust of the people, Johnson flatly denied it, while admitting that there had been some erosion: "I think there is some uncertainty and division in the country; but the minority would still be one on election day." About that time he was being assured that "Vietnam is well in hand" in public sentiment; so gears could be shifted to domestic issues. For the first time since July, the percent who approved of Vietnam had passed those who disapproved (46 to 41). A private Quayle poll in New York showed Johnson beating all Republicans, except for running neck and neck with Rockefeller. Nevertheless, at the Ranch during the holidays he said in front of four aides that he might not be running; so don't be talking about "holding things" for some future State of the Union message; get them in this one! Dependable Horace Busby was one who heard this. The nature of the coming full-time life at the Ranch was then discussed. Among the aides, Christian and Busby were for stepping aside, with the former saying there was a time to go, and this was it. Lady Bird by this time began to count "first the years, then the months, then the days" until Texas would again be home.[27]

By now it should be evident that 1967 was a year in which an essentially firm private decision not to serve another term became a decision shared with intimates. His son-in-law John Robb told Johnson on January 4, 1968, that he should run only if he wanted to; this was after Johnson had told Robb about having talked to Westmoreland about his health. Timing the announcement proved to be troublesome. A mild inclination to do it at the end of the State of the Union address faded, perhaps on the spot. Johnson thought it would be "kind of strange" to announce his own retirement after exhorting his former colleagues to do their utmost for the country. So, there would be further delay. Richard Nixon's antenna had long since picked up a change in Johnson's level of effort—really, as early as the second half of 1967: "He seemed to be running away from . . . his policies in public" and so was failing to generate continued support.[28] Not knowing much of what has been revealed here, veteran politician Nixon still easily perceived the first consequences of a decision that he did not even know had been made!

As early as March 11, 1968, Arthur Krim invited heir apparent Humphrey to be the President's Club speaker for April 30; and Humphrey promptly accepted. Johnson mentioned to Humphrey at the time that all of the men in his family had died in their early sixties or before; so, "Even if I should run and be re-elected, I most likely would not live out my term." *Thus did Johnson confirm what he had already told Humphrey on the day after the 1964 election,* at which time, Humphrey later recalled, "I did not believe it." Nor had an early January 1968 hint from Dean Rusk gotten through to this perennial optimist.[29] No wonder Johnson had so painstakingly interviewed Humphrey in 1964: Johnson thought he was selecting a future president!

It is altogether true that in late March 1968 the president consented to see union officials who wanted to discuss politics (and he saw Meany on March 28 and probably told him). Johnson conversed with John Bailey, and he saw Senator Russell for breakfast on March 25 and probably told them. Johnson went through the old routine of asking Krim about getting precincts organized. Meanwhile, he had the most serious of his long Vietnam-related discussions on March 27 with Clifford, Wheeler, Abrams, Humphrey, and Christian. But at the same time, the president's interaction involved many such personal items as talks with Bell Helicopter of Fort Worth, Dale Meeks at the Ranch, and the faithful Moursund on business matters. There was even some kidding at the dinner table with Mary Lasker and Lady Bird about whether the customary but functionless service plates would still be around next year at the Ranch. There were many other meetings, especially on whether a bombing restriction might bring a response from Hanoi.[30]

So when the time finally came, Lyndon Johnson announced dramatically on March 31, 1968, that he would not be a candidate: "Accordingly, I shall not seek, and I will not accept, the nomination of my party for another term as your President." Listeners were incredulous; Eric Sevareid and other TV anchormen were at a loss for interpretations, just as Johnson had hoped they would be. Contrary to what some have alleged, Lady Bird was "radiant"; to her Lyndon she said, "Nobly done, darling." Mary Lasker said, "I know it must be the right thing to do, since the President did it." Recalled Johnson much later, "I felt that it was just giving expression to what I had believed and hoped for and expected to do for a good long time."[31] What Eisenhower, Westmoreland, and others, who had been told that LBJ's retirement would be because of his health and longevity problems now thought about the Johnson *character* as he offered the American people his nation-serving but false explanation about retiring to help end the war is not known. This was by no means what he had told them!

In telegrams of reaction appeared such phrases as "finest hour," "We know him for the first time," "Don't dare leave us," and "You have never stood taller." Quite naturally, the president genuinely hoped that the manner of his action would help lead to peace. He played this entirely worthy theme to the hilt. Completely silent in public on the health question, he told the cabinet that he had acted in the interests of unity and "in our nation's best interest." To O'Brien he said fervently: "I'm doing everything I humanly can do to bring peace. . . . But there'll always be those who will say all I care about is politics. . . . Larry, I've done everything you fellows urged me to do and more: I've cut back the bombing and I'm trying to negotiate and I won't be a candidate again. I still doubt that it'll work, but *I've gone the distance*" (italics added). His physical condition at the moment did not escape attention. Goldman had not seen him in person or on TV for some time; he was shocked, for Johnson looked "old, weary, battered," with "the face deeply lined and sagging; the drawl occasionally cracked and wavered."[32]

Johnson quickly thanked his cabinet for their services and let them know that he hoped they would stay on, although they had every right to pursue their best interests. Arthur Goldberg of the United Nations spoke for the group, saying that the president looked ten feet tall; the administration would go down as one of the greatest in history. Attorney General Nicholas Katzenbach said that Hanoi's reaction had included some hopeful material, but Clark Clifford said cautiously that everything depended on how one translated their statement—and on that there were different opinions. The same day, Robert Kennedy would be briefed for an hour on the international situation, the economy, and other matters. He and his aides had been as surprised as anybody.[33] The cabinet members knew that Humphrey might run; as to that, Johnson said: "I don't want to appoint my successor, but I do have friends and men I love." And, pointedly, "I do think Hubert Humphrey is A-triple plus."

For a few brief days the euphoria stemming from the announcement coup continued. Bess Truman wrote, "If you aren't on that ticket in November, I'm not going to the polls." Typical of letters from the White House was this sentiment: "His decision to place the presidency above partisanship reflects his heartfelt desire for unity in America and peace in Vietnam. He will continue to devote himself to these paramount interests." American public opinion should have been calmed. But soon a newsman would observe ominously: "People seem to be transferring their hatred to Kennedy. It is quite surprising how passionate this distrust is."[34] The public, like the president, had been through too much: so much change, so much reform, so many promises, all those war dead and wounded on TV, and the excesses from protesters.

Johnson's hopes for something like a miracle from his dramatic action were to be dashed soon enough. He later admitted that he had hoped for much more than he had received. He had expected that there would be some realization that America "would rather talk than fight" but would not let aggression triumph; maybe the enemy would meet us halfway; maybe other nations would see his act as a decent and humane thing.[35] There was a little of this in the incoming mail. Some in the media cynically speculated about whether the withdrawal statement was really ironclad.

The trouble was that Johnson, quite understandably, had never discussed in public his weak physical constitution. So, withdrawal seemed to be due only to his announced reasons and the adverse odds—nothing else. Thus, Professor Frankel could record with bite: "Sometimes the noise gets through. Lyndon Johnson, after all, did finally decide that he had had it." It would become trite to say, as did Joseph Kraft a decade later, "Lyndon Johnson gave up his office under fire." But how could this leader have discussed in public his health and his bone-tiredness a full ten months before the end of his term? Wrote Sam Houston Johnson, "I was relieved to know that he wouldn't have to put up with all the abuse he was bound to receive during a long campaign, with thousands of demonstrators insulting him, cursing him, calling him a warmonger and murderer—not to mention the potential danger to his life. He was out of it, free to pursue peace without the nagging pressure of partisan politics." To Lyndon he wrote emotionally very late that fateful night, "I am proud to be your brother."[36]

On April 3 it was learned that the North Vietnamese would confer—whatever that meant. But almost before the nation could grasp this possibly meaningful consequence of the withdrawal speech and the bombing curtailment, an act of violence in Memphis captured the front pages in the nation and the world. It was a terrible event, the shooting of Martin Luther King, Jr.; and it was followed immediately by riots in Washington, D.C., and elsewhere. This was an unexpected blow to the hopes that Lyndon Johnson had cherished—namely, that his highly visible act of self-sacrifice would gradually permeate the national and world consciousness by monopolizing the attention of commentators and columnists for weeks. Still, he could write in his memoirs, "I was never more certain of the rightness of my decision." Afterward, when it was all over, he said, "I felt better." And still later, "All that I could do I had done."[37]

To a press conference at 11:00 P.M. on March 31 he said that Lady Bird had played "the same role she plays in every decision I make—a very important one." His health, said a calculating Lyndon, was "never better." An analogy would be to say that the day's weather was good while reflecting silently that the climate was poor. No, he had no intentions of attending the convention or of being a delegate. As the questioning persisted, he cut off the "high school discussions about it," since he said he was "genuinely sincere." Yes, he had considered that he might lose influence during the rest of his term; but do bear in mind that Truman's similar announcement had been released on March 29, 1952. Would his own announcement take the war out of the campaign? Was his action a plea to do so? "No." On being praised as an "achiever," the president replied: "I have not done near enough. That is one of the reasons for the announcement tonight. I want to do a lot more these next nine months."[38]

Lyndon Johnson later said privately that it did look as though, after forty years of public life, he and his wife would have a chance "to sleep with each other and live with our families and spend our waking moments together instead of with the night reading and with the files and with the crisis decisions." Last year they had thought "that the time had come to have someone else to work at these problems, try to ascertain what challenges face them, and what answers they could provide to those challenges—*new answers*; we have given ours." His successor would have to find "a means of communicating with our young and providing leadership and inspiration for them so that they will realize that they do care; find a way to help for better understanding to come to our races, so that we can live together in peace and harmony and equality—with justice to all; see how we can build an impregnable defense of our freedom without endangering it by getting caught in devastating nuclear war."[39]

By now it should be clear that the public at the time and critical writers then and since have not understood correctly why President Johnson did not try for another term. In summary he and his wife had long been convinced that because of his uncertain physical state and his limited life expectancy, there would be no possibility of serving out nine years and two months in power. The prospect of being limited to only five years did not unnerve them as much as might be thought. Lady Bird was enthusiastic at the twin prospects of leaving Washington and returning to Texas. He was fully aware of historical precedent: Theodore Roosevelt, Calvin Coolidge, and Harry Truman, all inheritors of the presidency, chose not to run for more than one full term immediately afterward. Not one had revealed his plans to the public until he was good and ready. Always concerned with the precedent of what Truman had done, Johnson had especially inquired of Rostow what date Truman had chosen; then he acted accordingly. Truman had chosen March 29, a Saturday; Sunday March 31 seemed like a better prime-time slot to

Johnson. Coupling the necessary retirement statement with an announcement about a bombing modification that might somehow further peace was a natural step for one who was of a pragmatic, practical, and opportunistic turn of mind and who certainly did not shrink from shaving the truth. Why not get *something* from the inevitable?

This interpretation of the Johnson withdrawal from the campaign of 1968 fits the facts. Lyndon Johnson had early decided not to continue. He was not forced from office; he left it voluntarily for retirement. His private reasons—that it was a physical necessity for him and that it would remove the danger of putting the country through still another presidential trauma under emergency conditions—were praiseworthy, and they were nation-serving. His announcement, though disingenuous, was artfully contrived to help the national interest while preserving his medical privacy. Now, after serving over forty months in the Oval Office, he finally had publicly advised his fellow countrymen of their coming responsibility to choose a new president and commander in chief.

13

COMMANDER IN CHIEF
DURING AN ELECTION: 1968

While March 31, 1968, had been a milestone for the Johnson presidency, the man in the Oval Office remained the president, was still the commander in chief, and was a factor of importance in the Democratic party. Some things had changed, but many had not. It would be nearly ten more months before time to depart for Texas. Elements of the Great Society awaited enactment, the war continued, his party needed two national candidates, and party figures at every level wondered about the primaries and the fall election.

Some personal concerns could not wait: for example, plans to transfer presidential papers and museum items to Austin with an eye to history. By May, Johnson was beginning preliminary negotiations regarding publication of a future memoir. Arthur Krim advised him on the task of setting up a foundation to collect funds for the library, which had to be constructed with private donations. As early as 1967 Lady Bird had been writing to friends for material that would be of interest to the archivist of the United States.[1] By the fall of 1968 the presidential interest in all this had been aroused.

A voluminous record of every single accomplishment of his administration, domestic and foreign, would be assembled. For example, the president acted to make certain that his progress with regard to conservation would be highly visible in the record. And he demanded that each department and key independent agency prepare charts and graphs of their accomplishments, comparing their records, if possible, to those of prior administrations. Many an official practically stopped regular work in order to shift over to this memorializing activity. Johnson also anticipated the proprieties of his future conduct, as well as the possibilities in it, when he would be out of office. The presidential seal should not be present when former presidents speak, he learned. He wondered what kind of seal should go on his letterhead henceforth. A youthful subordinate was entrusted with the task of finding out whether or not former presidents had spoken out very much in public after leaving the White House. Her report—"Messrs. Taft and Truman are the only presidents who have done any significant talking after retirement"[2]—was not adequate, for Theodore Roosevelt had continued to be a national figure and force as a speaker, and Herbert Hoover spoke to the extent of over seven volumes of published addresses on public issues after leaving office.

Johnson remained, as before, an overworking and overworrying president, concerned largely about his role as commander in chief and how to appear to be nonpartisan. He was not going to release prematurely the reins that were his and his alone. As to Hubert Humphrey, Johnson told Muriel Humphrey: "He is the greatest vice-president in history. . . . If I could resign today and give the presidency over, I would." Years before, Humphrey had said to a friend: "You'll be surprised; my vice presidency is going to be more than just four years of mothballs and doldrums." But this was not to be, partly because of a stance that he assumed early in the National Security Council against the bombing of North Vietnam.

The vice-president had proved useful to the administration; of that there can be no doubt. He gave leadership on the civil-rights fight; aid on model cities; enthusiasm for the idea of a Great Society; help with NASA and oceanography; and liaison with liberals, blacks, and Democratic political figures from coast to coast. He waged a quiet fight for the nomination, but he was hurt by columns like one in the *New Republic*, which asked: "Has anybody seen Hubert Humphrey lately? Who is he? *What* is he? We used to know him, he used to be a nice man. Now the liberals think he is a liberal and the conservatives a conservative."[3] But the vice-president said wryly that he had only "a constituency of one." The president's men were depressed in 1968 as they watched the three-way contest between Humphrey, Eugene McCarthy, and Kennedy. No longer was the political spotlight on their leader. Much planning had to be shelved.

Back when it had been hoped that the president would run, Harry Truman was sounded out quietly by a mutual friend, who learned that the man from Independence was 100 percent behind Johnson; the fellows running against him in both parties were "a damned bunch of smart-alecks." But Truman did warn, "President Johnson dominates party leaders too much and does not consult them enough." An eye was kept on America's other living former president. When Eisenhower sent a careful statement on Vietnam to the Republican Platform Committee, it was duly noticed. You have given "wise and timely counsel," Johnson wrote Eisenhower; here was indeed "the course we must pursue for peace"; Ike had placed the nation's interest ahead of political pressures. Much later in the campaign, Johnson instructed aides carefully to research the kind of aid that Eisenhower had given to Nixon in 1960, for here was a precedent, and he was getting a lot of gratuitous advice on when and how to help Humphrey.[4]

Unrest on many college and university campuses remained a problem for the president in 1968. The war and the draft; rise of a drug culture, youth cult, and sexual permissiveness; distrust of the older generation: many causes and consequences blended during the 1960s. Can such upheaval in a decade of assassinations be attributed only to the performance in office of any president? A young girl from Portland, Oregon, wrote in a letter to the editor in June 1968: "What sort of world am I being raised in? A world of killing and hatred. This country, as I was always told, is supposed to be full of freedom and love. I do love America and this is not what life should be like."[5]

Traditionally minded adult Americans suffered as the country writhed in 1968. The president of Freedoms Foundation of Valley Forge, Pennsylvania, Kenneth D. Wells, announced in late spring the formation of a movement to display the stars and stripes, for, he said, "Our country faces great trials." A thirty-state trip showed him that "great numbers of our citizens are profoundly troubled. Many are restive. An apprehensive air of divisiveness exists. Insurrection is growing." A constructive and law-abiding American Way of Life needed to be furthered, together with a determination to ensure equality of opportunity together with liberty under law.[6] Many in the World War II adult generation could share in at least the spirit of these remarks. For them, "hippie" was a new six-letter swear word, and Haight-Ashbury (a hippie enclave) was an abomination.

An event on June 5 that shocked the country was the assassination of articulate and energetic Robert Kennedy in Los Angeles, a catastrophe that Johnson said later "seemed to symbolize the irrationality that was besieging our nation and the world." Further, "another voice that spoke for America's poor and dispossessed was stilled forever."[7] The relationship between the two leaders had varied from barely civil to downright bitter, although each, on occasion, had been able to make an accommodating remark or two. Johnson could not but feel that this second Kennedy assassination would, like the first, make any recognition of his own stature more difficult. Now Eugene McCarthy stood against Humphrey as Democratic politics heated up during the summer. Recorded a dismayed and reflective Lady Bird, "It was clear that nothing could be the same, that we were in a state of suspension, waiting for the hand of fate."[8]

The national conventions proved to be showcases for the generation gap, protest against "the system," and new versus old life styles. Richard Nixon accepted his nomination with a call on the silent majority of forgotten Americans to help him. TV-watching America could scarcely believe the turbulent events at the Democratic Convention in Chicago in August 1968. There was long premeditated obstructionism followed by violence. A weird blend of assorted youthful and traditional radicals faced off against a powerful urban boss, and the armed police were attacked by—and in turn attacked—a youthful mob on a beer-and-drug-punctuated holiday that ignored the central point that conventions form a part of the American system of self-government. Police overreaction got outsized attention on TV. Many thought that the resulting nomination would be of little value to Hubert Humphrey. Above the battle at the White House or the Ranch, the Johnson staff could at least reflect that the chief had somehow reached the right conclusion when he had resolved not to accept Mayor Daley's hopeful invitation to go to embattled Chicago. Johnson's sixtieth birthday could be celebrated next to the Pedernales instead.

As it happened, that very week saw the invasion of Czechoslovakia by the Russians, so the president's attention turned out to be sharply divided between the sad events in Europe and those in Chicago. Wrote Lady Bird in a poignant mood: "The world is in convulsions all around us—our party, our country—the whole world. Lyndon is plowing right on, working as hard as he can every day on those things he can control and assaulting those things vigorously that he has even a little hope of controlling. I know that it is a wracking year for Lyndon physically, and it must be mentally and spiritually as well."[9] Johnson recalled those days vividly: "Soviet troops marched brutally into Czechoslovakia on August 12 and stamped the heavy boots of oppression on the first serious shoots of freedom that had appeared in Czech soil in twenty years. When the Russians made this move, they slammed the door on the missile talks we had painstakingly worked out and planned to announce the next day, August 22."

Whatever degree of personal responsibility Johnson later felt for the defeat of his party in November stemmed in part from his guilt feeling that under his leadership "the Democratic Party had pressed too far out in front of the American people." The polls proved it, he thought, and social reform had been an action for which there had come a reaction. Civil rights, health, education, housing, conservation, poverty, hunger, job training, and consumer protection had changed too rapidly; the changes helped to defeat his would-be successor, as many hostile voters went to the polls. Said Johnson: "The blue collar worker felt that the Democratic party had traded his welfare for the welfare of the black man. The middle class suburbanite felt that we were gouging him in order to pay for the antipoverty programs. The black man, having tasted the fruits of equality, began demanding his rightful share of the American promise faster than most of the nation was willing to let him have it." The rising crime rate and a breakdown in local authority, Johnson guessed, looked like a failure of the federal government. "The votes of all these disenchanted Americans were decisive in the 1968 election." People were tired; they wanted to catch their breath; they were sick of being pushed. (Such a view contrasts sharply with the commonly held one that it was Vietnam that defeated Humphrey as torch bearer of liberalism.)

After Chicago, Humphrey would be the candidate—but he would be a Prometheus Bound. Johnson contends that he did not turn over a hopeless cause to his party's nominees. If he could only have made a substantial move toward peace in Vietnam, all other obstacles would have faded. "Achieving such a breakthrough was one of my objectives in stepping out of politics, but for reasons far more profound and far broader in scope than the fate of the Democratic party in an election year."[10]

Many forces were at work to torment both the president and the vice-president during 1968, and these must be examined. Conspicuous was the headline-drawing activity of many campus radicals, who operated at all times from the palpably false assumption that they were representative of a thwarted American majority against the war in Southeast Asia. They were articulate, dedicated, and daring; but they were actually representative of a breakdown in traditional value systems, especially the work ethic. Fortunately, this breakdown did not affect all young Americans.[11]

There was bound to be a nationwide reaction to the formation of the New Left. Already in existence was a large moderate element—built around anti-Communist themes left over from Cold War scares—and the small right-wing John Birch Society. Organizations that were dedicated to the right to bear arms, as guaranteed in the Bill of Rights, were articulate. There were conservatives and reactionaries. But real political power escaped both the Right and the Left. (Lady Bird would say later on several occasions that it was the Far Right that really concerned the president when he ruminated on unpleasant possibilities in America of the future.)

Few were willing and able to take on the explosive, certain-sure New Left in verbal combat. One who did was the distinguished historian George Kennan, former ambassador to the USSR. Speaking in June 1968 at the Hall of Burgesses in Williamsburg, Virginia, he referred to the "intimidation and blackmail" that was jeopardizing American society, with demagoguery and dictatorship in the offing. There had been an "excess of tolerance" toward arson, looting, and sniping; no other country in the world would have stood for it. So, charges of police brutality were "simply ludicrous." The radical student had emerged from "the disintegrated family, the bored, over-affluent parents, the timid secularism of parental and school authority, the television set, the over-crowded schoolroom and the false freedom of the automobile." A survey of sixty thousand faculty members revealed that four-fifths were convinced that "campus demonstrations by militant students are a threat to academic freedom." Three-quarters thought those students should be expelled! The radicals got a hearing that was entirely too free of media criticism, and the illusion was current that the president was, somehow, to blame for the excesses. Writes Vietnam critic David Halberstam: "One reason that Richard Nixon was elected in 1968 . . . was a sense, beyond ideological or partisan politics, that Lyndon Johnson had simply lost control of the country; there was too much disorder; and inevitably, if unconsciously, people connected that chaos to him." Said Republican Senator Mark Hatfield, a political scientist, on July 30: "We observe rage and hate. The land is in a tumult." There was "a poverty of the spirit" in America. Jerry Rubin, founder of Yippies and proud to be one of the Chicago Seven, recalled the 1960s this way: "It was like being totally alive every moment. When all that ended, it was very hard on me. I was living totally in the past, and it was like I was in my deathbed in my mid-30's."[12]

From the administration's standpoint, confrontations "offended the majority of American citizens and pushed them to the right," so that "the violence in Chicago was one of the greatest political assets Nixon had," said Johnson. The later candid assessment by Rubin was that in the ensuing trial of the Chicago Seven, "the prosecution was right all along . . . ; we were guilty as hell." Their demands had been outrageous in order to guarantee their unacceptability. Then the city might well react "as if it was a police state and to focus the attention of the whole world on us."[13]

Older Americans had been formulating and advancing logical

programs for bringing the war to a close, working "within the system," since mid 1965. Full-page ads offered fellow countrymen ideas on how to extricate America from its morass. On July 28, 1968, the National Committee for a Political Settlement in Vietnam offered the plans of such famous individuals of the day as academician Clark Kerr, social thinker Daniel Patrick Moynihan, labor leader Walter Reuther, and social scientist Seymour Martin Lipset.[14] Another plan was the work of four Princeton professors, including Klaus Knorr and Richard A. Falk. Here the goal was still neutralization, essentially—an idea which, possibly not known to them, had been thrust at the president years earlier.

The burdens of Hubert Humphrey as politician and person in 1968 bordered on the unbearable. When, in July, a column by Evans and Novak seemed calculated to upset the delicate balance between Humphrey and his chief, the former called a White House aide with a long message of denial and protestation. Humphrey said that he was "proud of his association with the president and proud of his part in the administration." Any repudiation on Humphrey's part was unthinkable; he could be neither nominated nor elected in such an event. "VP said he feels heartbroken," was the aide's report. Reporters were trying to stir things up. Humphrey just hadn't had a chance to talk with Johnson in a long time; the president should know that Humphrey would rather lose the election than appear to be doublecrossing the man he had been proud to serve.[15] One is appalled by such an episode.

The fight over the Democratic plank on Vietnam proved to be exceptionally bitter and caused a sensation within the inner circles of leadership. Humphrey went to great effort to get one and all—even Rusk and Rostow—to approve it in advance. But at the last moment, Johnson said it still was not acceptable to him, shouting into the phone: "This plank just undercuts our whole policy and, by God, the Democratic party ought not to be doing that to me and you ought not to be doing it; you've been a part of this policy." Said Humphrey, "Well, Mr. President, we'll have to do the best we can." When the platform committee sided with the chief executive, the candidate caved in, saying later that the "Vice President has very few guns in a battle with the presidential artillery."[16] Johnson did endorse the ticket of Humphrey-Muskie on August 19, calling hopefully for party unity.

While the political scene was heating up, the president was having a major constitutional problem of his own making. The beginning came with a request by Chief Justice Warren on June 12 that Johnson receive him. Warren wished to retire. Now came a careful letter that, effective at Johnson's pleasure, Warren would retire from his post. Warren had handed the lame-duck president the opportunity to influence American history toward liberalism for a generation! Ten days later the attorney general discussed with Johnson possible candidates for the vacancy that would develop if a present justice—clearly Abe Fortas—should be elevated. Among those considered were Homer Thornberry, Cyrus Vance, Senator Muskie, Treasury Secretary Fowler, and Albert E. Jenner. Senator James O. Eastland early advised that a fight lay ahead if the nomination of Fortas as chief justice were to be pushed. An odd note was struck by evangelist Billy Graham, who prayerfully urged that a conservative would be named so as to balance the Court! By June 25 Johnson's mind was made up, however, and in quite a different direction. It would be Fortas, his long-time intimate, for chief justice and Thornberry, a good friend from Texas, for the resulting vacancy. By noon a filibuster was being organized. Eastland had talked with ten senators who showed almost unexampled bitterness toward Fortas; it was already evident that southern Democrats were going to vote no. This made the Republican attitude crucial.

The hearings on Fortas, which began on July 11, ultimately filled 1,284 pages. In spite of the fact that of 125 Supreme Court nominations during election years, 104 had been confirmed, and even though a close relationship rather commonly existed between presidents and their nominees to the court, charges of cronyism and politics abounded. On cronyism, Fortas said: "I don't know how anybody can be a person and not discuss with his friends [!] these days questions about the budget and about the Vietnam war. I'm a person too." The remark displayed neither sensitivity nor candor. Soon a question about Fortas's views on obscenity developed, but he refused to testify more than once. Various aspects of civil rights concerned many senators. That Fortas was Jewish was foremost in some minds out in the country, as revealed in hate mail received at the White House. Some cases that had been accepted by Fortas as an attorney were pushed to the forefront; then there was the subtle matter of the quasi-secret advisory relationship of the justice with the president, which had overtones of frontally violating the separation of the executive and the judicial branches.

The president spoke out at his July 31 press conference on the confirmation question, even venturing to say, oddly, that he had not anticipated that there would be any opposition. Meanwhile, Republicans recalled that their former party leader had been thwarted in making some judicial appointments. Many senators wanted Fortas to be questioned further on the legal status of pornographic movies.

Opinions expressed during White House strategy sessions differed sharply on whether, if the nominee were to make another appearance, this would facilitate a new fishing expedition by his opponents. Johnson thought it would be fatal if Fortas did not appear; the attorney general disagreed. New hearings in September revealed interest in just how much Fortas had participated in framing the 1966 State of the Union message—the "cronyism" issue. The Judiciary Committee now voted 11 to 6 for confirmation. Interest came to focus on a $15,000 fee that Fortas had received from American University for participating in a lecture series—a payment to one of the highest paid of federal officials. A two-thirds vote to close debate seemed unlikely, as many senators now said that their mail was hostile to Fortas, whereas public-opinion polls showed the opposite to be true as much as two to one.

The closure vote on October 1 was a narrow 45 to 43, so the nomination of Fortas was a hopeless cause. The handwritten withdrawal letter was checked and edited in draft at the White House. It marked the end of a smooth road to power for the brilliant Washington attorney. The Court was to begin its session in seven days, he said; moreover, continuing attacks on the Court, as well as himself, would be harmful to the Court and to the nation. The justice offered a hopeful peroration: "I pray that we shall see, in all of our nation, renewed dedication to the principles of fairness and justice and moderation, without which our democracy cannot continue."[17]

The proposed appointment of Fortas carried far too many burdens; a fully observant president and sensitive politician should have known this. If Johnson had read old files on the initial Fortas appointment to the Court more closely, he might have sensed that the early private acquiescense from Senator Dirksen might not hold when all possible charges surfaced, as they were bound to. There has been a tendency to attack opposition senators for displaying partisanship and narrowness of viewpoint, but there are ample signs that the public was upset about the controversy over the outside fee and pornography. The figure of Fortas as a fighter for civil liberties was insufficient, in itself. The Fortas contretemps was regrettable from many standpoints; it was also avoidable. When Senator Russell wrote Johnson that at least 99 percent of Russell's incoming letters demanded a vote against Fortas, he was revealing a hidden sentiment so meaningful that Johnson should have been able to sense defeat far in advance. But friendship, ideology, and a determination to prevail one last time blinded this tired leader, who certainly knew better.[18]

The occupants of the White House kept a weather eye on Humphrey's every move throughout the campaign. Clark Clifford believed the candidate was trying to reach out as far as possible to the Vietnam doves without actually breaking with anything the president was saying. Avoid confrontation. Rusk agreed. Why not say we were interested in Hanoi's restoring the demilitarized zone? They would almost certainly say no! Said Rostow, the press should be told that the White House was keeping away from the candidate's comments. Hadn't Johnson on September 10 said that "re-establishing the DMZ, I think, is so critical to peace in Vietnam"?[19]

Many forces pushed Humphrey to make crystal clear where, if anywhere, he differed with his chief on Vietnam. Johnson was nervous at the prospect. For three crucial weeks he persuaded the candidate to postpone the inevitable, saying he hoped to bring the enemy to the peace table. "I've given up the presidency, given up politics, to search for peace. No one worries more about this war than I do. It's broken my heart—in a way, broken my back. But I think I can get these people at the conference table if you will help."[20] The delay was one of many factors that caused Humbert Humphrey to lose the election.

In any case, on September 30 in Salt Lake City, with the vice-presidential seal somehow missing from the rostrum, Humphrey did speak to the subject of bombing North Vietnam. The president was notified of Humphrey's text only after newsmen had been given copies. If elected, Humphrey said, he would "be willing to stop the bombing" as "an acceptable risk for peace." Negotiations and a shorter war might result. But first, he would have to have evidence, "direct or indirect, by word or deed" that the demilitarized zone would be restored. And bad faith by Hanoi would bring renewed bombing. The entourage around the candidate now proceeded to interpret and reinterpret the "true meaning" of these plain words for the press, thus dishonestly making the speech seem more dovish than its language warranted, says Dr. Edgar Berman, Humphrey's biographer. Within a week the bulk of the press was supporting Humphrey, using headlines like "Humphrey for Bombing Pause." Liberals rallied around. "With this new perspective, which Humphrey accomplished by an assertion differing little from previous ones," says Berman, "the reporters reversed their field—and there was momentum."[21]

In Johnson's camp, aides said that Humphrey was ambiguous as to a conditional or unconditional bombing halt; so, why not just tell the press that the candidate was being consistent with the administration's position? This would settle its meaning! McPherson thought the best way to help Humphrey was for the president to continue to give an enlightened and dedicated performance in office. Years later the candidate said that going along with the Johnson position on the war had been "the right thing to do." If elected, he would have ended the war "promptly" anyway. He didn't indicate how he would have accomplished this.[22]

Part of the president's troubles with the Paris talks, he came to think, stemmed from that speech in Salt Lake City, which he later called "a speech that was widely interpreted as a refutation of the administration's Vietnam policy, particularly with respect to bombing." He was alert to the reinterpretations by Humphrey's staff. Even though Humphrey had called in advance to describe the address and to say that it was not intended to be a major departure from current policies ("I believe he meant it," said Johnson), the resulting judgment everywhere was that a major departure in policy had been attempted by the "president's candidate." In Saigon, leaders suspected that the American government had sent up a trial balloon. To the Republican candidate the speech was shrewd, for while it scarcely differed from Johnson's position, Humphrey "made it sound like a major new departure."[23] In a TV spot, Nixon said there would be an honorable end to the war if he were elected. "Never has so much military, economic, and diplomatic power been used so ineffectively as in Vietnam." Though urged by Goldwater to exploit the theme of war mismanagement, Nixon held back. He did say generally, as to Johnsonian credibility, "Hope is fragile, and too easily shattered by the disappointment that follows inevitably on promises unkept and unkeepable."

Shortly after their nomination, Nixon and Spiro Agnew visited the Texas ranch for a full-scale intelligence briefing by Rusk, Vance, and CIA director Helms, which was later given also to Humphrey and Muskie and to Wallace and LeMay. The Nixon visit was marked by cordial hospitality from Lyndon and Lady Bird. "I could see that he was already enjoying his role as a noncandidate," recalls Nixon. Both men were aware of the true situation: Nixon was a Republican partisan, hellbent for a victory that had been denied him in 1960; Johnson was a lifelong Democrat with a capital D, who could be expected to support his party's and his own chosen candidate. But would the president eventually try to tip the balance? The Republican contender thought that politics might well replace statesmanship.

After Salt Lake City, Humphrey had more campaign funds and fewer demonstrators. Yet he continued to be faced with organized heckling, even from bull horns. Chanting youngsters, hippies high on drugs, schoolchildren, pacifists, potential and actual draft dodgers, and poor losers from the McCarthy and Kennedy camps made life for him and Muriel almost completely miserable. At one point, Humphrey was called in by Johnson, who had been angered by a leak that he thought was traceable to his vice-president. If Humphrey didn't mind his p's and q's, Johnson would see to it personally that Humphrey would lose Texas; Johnson would hurt Humphrey in liberal states as well. Mayor Daley still listened to him, Johnson warned; one way or another, Johnson would dry up every Democratic dollar from Maine to Texas. Staggered by this outburst, Humphrey soon confided to a dear friend, his Boswell, "I had trouble holding back, but I wasn't going to come down to that bastard's level." He said he had walked out without uttering a word, instead.[24]

The president had his own sources of strain during those months, for he remained "an activist to the end," relinquishing little power and attacking problems with fervor. Disappointments increased, and the decision-making process became more complicated. He held his power "by sheer will and obstinance." Among presidential concerns were the peace talks; the possibility of a nuclear nonproliferation treaty; somehow freeing the *Pueblo's* crew; peace in the Middle East; the need for steps to stop the spread of arms; the final stages in sending astronauts to the moon; and of course, paving the way for an inevitable successor. The president would profess that he had "deliberately taken myself out of political contention in order to devote all of my energy to the urgent tasks that remained,"[25] and he somehow convinced himself that he would be wholly free of any political motivation when dealing with the enemy in negotiations and in battle.

A test was whether to halt the bombing. A complete halt of the bombing would have to be contingent on obtaining serious talks involving both North and South Vietnam. On October 14 the president and his advisers decided to give serious consideration to a suspension. Interaction on October 28 between Rusk in Washington and the Harriman-Vance team in Paris revealed that America could get "no flat guarantees"; an unconditional halt was demanded. "But they had told us that if we stopped the bombing, they would 'know what to do.' " It is hard for those who are not familiar with the nuances of diplomatic interchange to see such language as warranting a major shift in policy, but it seemed the best that could be gotten. The Soviets said any doubts over Hanoi's position were groundless. This—somehow—gave "added confidence."[26]

At an amazing all-night meeting with Gen. Creighton Abrams, who was secretly fresh in from Saigon, the commander in chief reviewed recent events in detail and summarized the apparent "understanding." Agreement was reached with the general, who assumed that bombing could easily be resumed (he was clearly not a politician). Would President Nguyen Van Thieu agree? Some thought that Republican agents were urging him to drag his feet, or maybe his advisers were recalcitrant. In any case, says Johnson, "Those three days were a blur of meetings and phone calls, of cables and conferences. I seemed to be listening, reading, or talking right around the clock." At one point, Rusk said that since 1961 some $75 billion had been spent and 29,000 men had been lost because of the course set by President Kennedy to save South Vietnam. "We must be careful not to flush all this down the drain." Wait for Saigon's acquiescence. But Clark Clifford, lawyer-adviser of presidents, disagreed. We are incredulous to learn that Johnson actually said, "I would be willing to postpone things a day or two [NB] before I broke up the alliance." He spoke to the National Security Council with a throat that was raw and hoarse and won their agreement. There would be hard bargaining, he said. The secretary of state added, "There will be some hard fighting too, Mr. President." The crucial paragraph in the San Antonio speech of announcement was drafted by Rusk: "prompt and productive talks" were to be the quid pro quo. The president wrote the final paragraphs himself.[27]

Meanwhile, the Republican candidate could envision "traditional Democrats returning to the party of their fathers" as "antiwar liberals decided to bury the hatchet." Eugene McCarthy had finally endorsed Humphrey, and the "spoiler candidacy" of George Wallace, who represented fading southern and conservative orientations, was dwindling. Dramatic presidential action could hurt. Then, on October 31, Nixon's phone rang. In a conference call to the three candidates, the president announced that there had been a breakthrough in Paris; so, he had decided to call a bombing halt that would be announced on TV in two hours. "I'm *not* concerned with an election. You all *are* concerned with an election. I don't think this concerns an election." While Saigon wouldn't go along, he was proceeding anyway. The three politicians naturally agreed to go along with their president. Recalls Nixon, "I thought to myself that whatever this meant to North Vietnam, he had just dropped a pretty good bomb in the middle of my campaign." Johnson had made "the one move that I thought could determine the outcome of the election."[28] When Nixon mentioned the halt to a partisan rally in Madison Square Garden, the audience booed the decision. Humphrey had stayed away from the National Security Council meeting so as to avoid false appearances, wanting to be able to avoid any accusations of serving his own interests.

So, on October 31 the order to stop the bombing went out. Lyndon Johnson concluded his nationwide TV speech that revealed his decision: "I do not know who will be inaugurated as the thirty-seventh president of the United States next January. But I do know that I shall do all that I can in the next few months to try to lighten his burdens, as the contributions of the presidents who preceded me have greatly lightened mine. I shall do everything in my power to move us toward the peace that the new president—as well as this president, and I believe, every other American—so deeply and urgently desires." The restricted bombing, which had begun on February 7, 1965, and had so often been suspended, now came to an end for this presidency. In forty-three months it had used in essentially rural Vietnam more explosives than had been dropped on urban Germany in World War II and had cost over nine hundred American planes and many courageous pilots and crews.

Surely the halt was political in its timing. Considering the lengthy duration of the bombing, this unseemly haste for a president who in the summer had been contemptuous of those who sought a bombing halt is surely to be noted. Pondered Nixon, "Had I done all this work and come all this way only to be undermined by the powers of an incumbent who had decided against seeking reelection?" But he had expected something like this. "Announcing the halt so close to the election was utterly callous if politically calculated, and utterly naïve if sincere." But to oppose the halt would have been political suicide; nor could charges be made against the president's sincerity. Two days before the election, Nixon said, imitating an Eisenhower ploy of 1952, that he would go to Saigon if it would help to bring peace. Meanwhile, at the Houston Astrodome, Johnson gave Humphrey the kind of support that the latter had long needed. "He moved heaven and earth," remembered Humphrey, with typical overstatement. It is alleged that Johnson blurted out about this time, "Nixon is supporting my Vietnam policy stronger than Hubert." So, why should he whistle-stop Texas? The networks turned increasingly favorable to Humphrey, displaying quite open partisanship.[29]

In the final place for decision, the ballot boxes of the nation, the voters barely chose the Republican candidate. Humphrey lost by a mere seven-tenths of one percentage point in the popular vote, even though the electoral vote was 301 to 191, with 46 for Wallace. When Humphrey and Muskie nearly overtook Nixon, it was largely because of the last-minute support of Wallace-LeMay partisans.[30] Johnson thought that the choice of Muskie had been a key weakness. From Saigon, President Thieu cabled Nixon, "The Vietnamese government, the Vietnamese people, and our soldiers fighting in the front lines against Communist aggression will be most happy to receive on Vietnamese soil a staunch defender of freedom, which you have been for many years." His presidential hopes shattered, Humphrey reflected bitterly on Johnson: "I never should have let him do it to me." He added, "My dreams and hopes were smashed in a year when so much more in America was destroyed." On New Year's Eve he flushed the toilet as a gesture.[31]

There seems to be no point in blaming the 1968 defeat of Hubert Humphrey on Lyndon Johnson. David Dubinsky said that Democrats themselves caused the defeat. Moreover, the candidate wrote the national committee in January 1969; "Our party was not defeated. We defeated ourselves." The reader of his memoirs will see that everything went wrong.[32] Wrote Johnson, "You have carried your convictions and the standard of our party with eloquence and magnificent courage." These were called Humphrey's finest hours. Johnson was proud of the brave, enlightened, and vigorous campaign the Minnesotan had waged. Humphrey certainly did not have to be told he had fought "well and hard."[33]

The president wrote Nixon that the latter had shown perseverance and determination that had to be admired by every American. Johnson would do all he could to make the winner's burdens lighter; narrow partisanship should not interfere. The margin of victory was narrow, but aide George Reedy sent his chief a think-piece prediction that there would be no coalition government—just a Republican administration without a mandate. So, Democrats must proceed responsibly, for the next four years were certainly going to be extremely difficult. Congress, of course, was still Democratic in both houses.[34] Meanwhile, the enormous multi-million-dollar debt run up by the Democrats, who lacked the President's Clubs, would not be retired until 1982. In effect, the party had campaigned with a buy now, pay later procedure.

Whatever experts would say,[35] President Johnson was quickly assured by key Democratic confidants that he had done well on the bombing halt. Wrote partisan Clifford: "Your performance on the Vietnam bombing cessation problem has been magnificent. It was handled with courage, rare discretion, and the most admirable states-manship."[36] What the president would get for his trouble, on December 8, was a Saigon delegation in Paris; then, on Jaunary 18, he got Hanoi's agreement on procedures for future meetings, to begin on January 25, 1969. What Nixon felt his candidacy had gotten, only six days before the election, was a bombing halt that had unquestionably resulted in a last-minute surge of support for Humphrey, because the militant liberals had come back into the fold.

The bombing halt failed to bring the war to an early negotiated end. Nor did it keep Johnson's beloved party in control of the executive branch. Here was failure both abroad and at home. The administration knew, says Rostow, that it was placing before Nixon the difficult problem of resuming the bombing if Hanoi failed to comply with "the understandings that underlay the October 31 decision." While the halt "did not yield a serious negotiating process," it had been a "necessary test" of Hanoi's willingness to negotiate. It was, judged the chief executive at the time, "the right thing to do."[37] It was also, beyond any doubt, the political party-serving thing to do. The war continued for years and came to an end only after great escalation, which included renewed and far heavier bombing. "History" would have many factors to take into account.

A week after the election the president-elect and Pat Nixon visited the White House. Nixon was briefed on Vietnam by Rusk, Clifford, Wheeler, Helms, and Rostow. Nixon thought that the travail of the long war was etched on the faces before him. They were all able and intelligent men, he thought, who had wanted desperately to end the war before leaving office. "They seemed very nearly worn out. They had no new approaches to recommend to me. I sensed that, despite the disappointment of defeat [in the election], they were relieved to be able to turn this morass over to someone else." And, continued Nixon in his memoirs, "They all emphasized that the United States must see the war through to a successful conclusion—with negotiations if possible, but with continued fighting if necessary. They agreed that an American bug-out, or a negotiated settlement that could be interpreted as a defeat, would have a devastating effect on our allies and friends in Asia and around the world."[38]

The transition period from election day to January 20 witnessed some maneuvering in foreign policy. The new team was determined not to allow any summit conferences or strategic-arms talks in light of the Soviet invasion of Czechoslovakia. But at Johnson's request, Nixon met with the administration's final state visitor, the amir of Kuwait, who wanted to know what America would do if Iraq were to attack Kuwait. Nixon also had two abortive exchanges with North Vietnam, stressing his readiness for serious negotiations. He said that Johnson should feel free to settle the shape of the controversy over the peace table—that is, whether it should be four-sided or round—before the inauguration; Nixon thereby gave the Johnson team a small but visible last-minute success.

One reason that Johnson gave on TV on March 31 for not campaigning for reelection had been the idea that much of his domestic program awaited passage by Congress. While it is commonly asserted that 1968 was the year in which a has-been president merely killed time while waiting to be eased out of office, the list of new laws that were passed seems almost the equal of those of earlier years, at least in extent. These laws dealt with fair housing, an Indian bill of rights, safe streets, wholesome poultry, Food for Peace, commodity-exchange rules, U.S. grain standards, school breakfasts, bank protection, defense production, corporate takeovers, the export program, Gold Cover Removal, truth-in-lending, abatement of aircraft noise, a study of auto insurance, new narcotics bureaus, gas-pipeline safety, fire safety, sea-grant colleges, the District of Columbia School Board, a tax surcharge, better housing, international monetary reform, the International Grains Treaty, oil revenues for recreation, Virgin Islands elections, the San Rafael Wilderness, the San Gabriel Wilderness, fair federal juries, protection of candidates, juvenile protection, guaranteed student loans, a visitors center for the District of Columbia, an FHA-VA interest-rate program, health manpower, Eisenhower College, gun controls, Aid-to-Handicapped Children, Redwood National Park, Flaming Gorge Recreation Area, Biscayne Park, hazardous-radiation protection, Colorado River reclamation, scenic rivers, scenic trails, the National Water Commission, federal magistrates, vocational education, increases in veterans' pensions, North Cascades Park, the International Coffee Agreement, intergovernmental manpower, control of dangerous drugs, the Military Justice Code, and programs dealing with heart disease, cancer, and strokes.

The transition from Johnson to Nixon was a model of how the American constitutional system is supposed to work. This was no accident, for beneath the campaign rhetoric there was a community of interest on Vietnam; both men thought it proper that an effort had been made to thwart communism in the Southeast Asian region. On September 8 the Republican candidate had secretly used the Reverend Billy Graham as a conduit behind the scenes between himself and the non-candidate president—a fact mentioned briefly in both men's memoirs. But from the minister's original notes we learn that Nixon conveyed his respects to Johnson "as a man and as the president." A postelection working relationship would result, including special assignments "perhaps to foreign countries for LBJ." When Vietnam should get settled, Johnson would be given a "major share of credit." Johnson's advice would be sought "continually." And said the Republican candidate, "[I] will do everything to make you a place in history because you deserve it."[39] This astounding message was duly conveyed to Graham's friend Lyndon a week later; each item was repeated twice, because Johnson could not read Graham's handwriting. "He was not only very appreciative but I sensed he was touched by this gesture." The evangelist thought he had participated in an unprecedented event, as he brought back the president's warm expression of appreciation: "I intend to loyally support Mr. Humphrey, but if Mr. Nixon becomes the president-elect, I will do all in my power to cooperate with him." As early as 1965 it had been arranged for word to reach Johnson that the man who had served two terms as vice-president was opposed to any plans to call the Vietnamese conflict Johnson's War.[40]

Noteworthy are steps the president took that served the well-being of his successors in office. In June 1964 he arranged for former presidents to have military air transportation whenever desired, except for political trips. In September 1968 he acted to provide secret-service protection for widows and the minor children of former presidents. In October he tried to arrange for increases in the pay and allowances of former presidents. A list of laws "to support a president after leaving office" was put together at his direction. In January he recommended doubling the salary of the president henceforth to $200,000 annually, for "a president must be paid, and his compensation must bear some relationship to the changing times in which we live." He told Nixon about the perfectly legal idea of emulating him by taking a tax deduction for donating prepresidential papers to the National Archives. Kennedy aides had used this benefit, he added. Diplomatic passports were obtained for Lady Bird and himself.[41]

As early as September, the outgoing president wrote to tell Nixon that under the presidential Transition Act of 1963, he was preparing for an orderly transition.[42] Although Johnson had reservations about Nixon that went back many years, he was also aware—because aides had soon informed him—that the Gallup poll in mid December revealed that 57 percent of Americans expected Nixon to be a good president (his cabinet appointees were thought to be of high caliber). Nixon appeared to LBJ's aides to be doing all he could do to prepare himself for the problems ahead. Overall, then, even though a sourly partisan note could be struck in a *New York Daily News* headline—"Lame Ducks Slow Nation down to a Waddle"—there is every reason to agree with the later judgment of Johnson's pastor in Washington that "never in our history has a more gracious exchange of power been made than between President Nixon and President Johnson." Johnson and Nixon conferred profitably on November 11 and again on December 12. Kissinger recalls, "We had considerable respect for the leading members of the Administration. . . . We did our utmost to ease their transition into private life." The Nixon team made no critical comments in public during those months. It was a time for learning. For years, former president Johnson would be routinely briefed at the Ranch by senior governmental officials, and favors from the White House would be common.[43]

An avenue of impropriety taken by an astonishingly casual president, beginning in 1967, consisted of four secret trips outside the borders of the United States to remote ranchland he had leased thirty miles from Carmago in rural Mexico. At the Ranch the military pilots in civilian clothes filed fake flight plans and pretended to be practicing touch-and-go landings so that Johnson could slip aboard without the knowledge of reporters. A physician went along; but the destination lacked electricity, so that on the first flight an engine of the Convair propellor aircraft had to be kept running to provide communications capability. (Quickly, a plane was modified at the California factory.) How the commander in chief was supposed to discharge his national responsibilities is unclear, and what regulations and laws of two countries were violated is not known. The motive(s) for these trips to the Chihuahua area, adventures whose existence is verified by two men in an excellent position to know, has not been established—unless Johnson's love of cattle, land, and/or profit, coupled with overwork and letdown, is sufficient. Here is something of a mystery. After the close of the presidency, the military flew in pipe and equipment and performed other services for this and various other personal projects.[44]

Late in his presidency, hard on the heels of a long recital of his views on the office, its responsibilties, and his performance of his duties, Lyndon Johnson tried summing up, for an internal film record, how he felt at the close of five years: "I'm looking forward to the day when I can close this door and go back to my people, to my own home on the banks of the Pedernales instead of the 'people's home' on the banks of the Potomac; when I can sleep in a bed with my wife (and my grandchildren can play around on it), instead of going to bed with my night reading and waking up with my intelligence reports."[45] As he slowly made these remarks, he looked exhausted physically and appeared to be dispirited. The bombing negotiations were in the offing.

Johnson advised his outgoing cabinet members, very tactlessly: "Each of you had better leave this town clean as a hound's tooth. The first thing Democrats do when they take power is to find where the control levers are. But the first thing Republicans do is investigate Democrats. I don't know why they do it—but you can count on it." For their part, says budget director Charles Zwick, "all cabinet members were going to start doing in the last few months the things they hadn't done for eight years." The result was inevitable conflict. Said Johnson, "The cabinet officers are all trying to see how the history books will write their future." The memoirs of the Johnson team tell how some members felt on departing, and so, no doubt, do an array of buried letters to their friends. Wrote former M.I.T. professor Rostow to Fortas: "We do look forward to plunging again into academic life in Austin. I shall be starting on the articulation of some new ideas—and that is always a true adventure." To Mrs. Rusk the president sent, on December 9, a special message: "The man who has served me most intelligently, faithfully, and nobly is Dean Rusk." The transition to a new administration involved designation of office space and many other details. Henceforth a retired general on the White House staff would be assigned to engage in liaison with former presidents and their staffs, handle their housekeeping requirements, and be a channel through which requests could flow.[46] Retirement, though devoid of power and involving a period of physical decline, would be first cabin all the way.

A final responsibility and opportunity was the preparation of the State of the Union and budget messages. From HEW, Wilbur Cohen wanted the theme to be "improving the quality of life"—that is, "a message of hope and aspiration, lifting our visions higher and higher, less materialism and more quality to our lives and our society. More responsibility . . . more participation." Aide Gaither said to "give a strong endorsement to the War on Poverty and the preservation of the existing programs." Johnson himself took special pains and became emotionally involved, insisting at the time of delivery that his infant grandchild be present at the scene for historical and sentimental reasons. A sentence that survived only until the sixth draft still bears quoting: "History, and not the contemporary judgment of a participant, will determine the ultimate value of what was achieved in those years." Perhaps it was removed because this truth hardly needed to be said. More confident was the prediction of professorial Walt Rostow, who earlier had decided, "History will salute us."[47] He had even reminded his leader in March that the Korean effort years earlier "both stabilized security in the northern Pacific area and gave the South Koreans a chance to show what they could do in building a vital, modern, democratic system."[48]

To Dwight Eisenhower, after receiving a copy of the Book *Crusade in Europe*, the chief executive wrote from the heart: "Speaking to another man who knows well the special character of these final days in the White House, I need not tell you how some moments are touched with a swelling sense of pride and nostalgia." Kissinger soon found Johnson in a melancholy mood. The departing executive launched into a soliloquy on the war, urging the use of military pressure plus serious negotiations. Make sure the bueaucracy is loyal, he warned, saying to this outsider that he thought that the systematic use of leaks had played a part in destroying him![49] An hour after leaving office the former president awarded the Medal of Freedom to a personally selected group of individuals, clearly the ones *he* wanted: Eugene Black, Averell Harriman, Clark Clifford, Cyrus Vance, Michael DeBakey, David Dubinsky, Henry Ford II, Ralph Ellison, Bob Hope, Edgar Kaiser, Mary Lasker, Gregory Peck, Laurance Rockefeller, Walt Rostow, Merriman Smith, William S. White, Roy Wilkins, Whitney Young, Jr., McGeorge Bundy, and John W. Macy, Jr. Earlier, an award had gone to James E. Webb of NASA.

At the inaugural ceremony, Henry Kissinger reflected, as Johnson came down the aisle to the strains of "Hail to the Chief": "I wondered what this powerful and tragic figure thought as he ended a term of office that had begun with soaring inspiration and finished in painful division. How had this man of consensus ended up with a torn country? Johnson stood like a caged eagle, dignified, never to be trifled with, his eyes fixed on distant heights that now he would never reach."[50]

The time for leaving the White House was at hand. The president and his team were fully aware that they were leaving behind them a nation still at war, unsettled relations with the Soviet antagonist, and an array of very recently enacted programs that could be vulnerable to future budget cutters. The navy team of photographers was still able to put out its monthly film ("January 1969"), which as usual accentuated the positive. Footage included trips to Camp David and to New York City for a testimonial dinner party, portions of the State of the Union message, awards ceremonies, the last (eightieth) cabinet meeting, Nixon's arrival, and a tall Texan at the airport, who looked thin in the chest, frail, almost wan. Secretly, two appropriate aircraft with crews, two boats, stewards, a masseur, and other logistic support for life in the greater Austin area had been ordered to Texas, thereby lowering balances in White House accounts and establishing obligations for the future. The pilots were officially assigned to Nixon. Twelve communications personnel settled down at the Ranch for the next four years.[51]

As Juanita Roberts packed up the final items from President Johnson's desk on the morning of the twentieth, all of those who had been close to the president were only too aware that it had been five years and two months since they had been given the power to try to change the United States and the world and had decided to do so. Lady Bird discussed inaugurations with Leonard Marks, while her husband, in the bedroom, worked on final papers and got a haircut. Soon the entire family, together with the Humphreys, the Nixons, and the Agnews, assembled in the Red Room amidst "considerable gaiety." The outgoing and incoming presidents went into a corner and conversed privately for ten minutes. There were pictures on the outside steps and waves to the servants, but no last look or show of outward emotion.

Finally it would be off to the Cliffords' house, with Johnson's friends agreeing that the best line in Nixon's speech had been, "We can't learn from each other until we stop shouting at each other." Politician Johnson duly noted the absence of hard data about a domestic program and that there had been no revelation of a specific road to peace. There was a jovial atmosphere and good-natured kidding. The gift of the hastily assembled, uninscribed Medals of Freedom was made to recipients who were on the scene; paperwork and engraving would be completed later. A heartwarming sign said "Well Done, Mr. President." He was "obviously moved." So ended, on January 20, 1969, the presidency of Lyndon Johnson, with the former chief executive already "speaking nostalgically."[52] Five years earlier there had been three living former presidents on whom the Texan could rely; now he would be one of three available to his successor. Possibly this was deep within his mind as he told the crowd greeting him at the airport in Austin, "We love our country."

14

"HISTORY WILL JUDGE"

The presidency of Lyndon Johnson was one that brought changes to the United States. These changes were major: in meaningful laws passed; good that was done; spending and inflation that would long be continued; regulations that would be inflicted; and vain promises that would be recalled as coming from the pulpit of the White House. Much that had been thought enduring in American life would never be the same again. *This presidency made a difference.* The nation was transformed in civil rights; in the financing and administration of every level of education; to an extent in forms of action taken against poverty; in payments for medical care for aging citizens, the disabled, and the poor; and in a new conservation effort that would soon mushroom.

While the tangible results from the antipoverty crusade were neither spectacular nor permanent, the directions set, the goals proclaimed, and the hopes expressed—as well as the compassion visibly displayed from the Oval Office—had some staying power. Higher social-security payments for many constituted tangible evidence of change. The very fervor of presidential concern helped to recruit many citizens to worthwhile causes, some of whom had been standing to one side with too intellectualized a view of family and individual distress. Meanwhile, the civil rights of all Americans under law, and especially members of minorities, took on increased meaning. This was due to the struggles of those who were affected, to dynamic leadership at the top of government, and to changes in opinion in the South and elsewhere as events in the 1960s unfolded. It has seemed appropriate to say, when accentuating the positive, that "for all its defects the aspiration and striving of the domestic policies of the Great Society period represent the best in the human spirit." One could at the same time issue a warning to presidents in general: "When he makes the promises that all political leaders make in moments of euphoria, he arouses expectations that will not be quieted except through fulfillment."[1]

What President Johnson achieved would look better if he had not promised so much more, so frequently, and without reservations. He wanted desperately to be—and to appear to be—a great, not just a good, president. He wanted to tackle the big problems of our time, says former secretary of HEW Wilbur Cohen. Some events, however, entrapped him. "As I left the Presidency," wrote Johnson later, "I was aware that not everything I had done about Vietnam, not every decision I had made, had been correct." How many men should have been sent? When? Should supply lines and sanctuaries have been attacked? Should Haiphong have been mined? Were the major bombing halts a mistake? "Did I do all I could have done to make clear to our people the vital interests that I believed were at stake in our efforts to help protect Southeast Asia?" Well, he said, possibly thinking of the future rather than of historians and biographers: "*History will judge* these questions and will render its verdict long after current passions have subsided and the noise in the street has died away. *History will judge* on the basis of facts we cannot now know, and of events some of which have not yet happened" (my italics). Earlier, he had promised former President Truman that history was "the final and impartial arbiter."[2]

Once, Lyndon Johnson had been shown a flattering Associated Press comparison between his performance and that of John F. Kennedy. James Marlow had written that historians in fifty years would reappraise the two. The rich carpet of martyrdom had produced in JFK a glistening figure; but when historians turned their attention to *achievement*, they would face reality. "Kennedy never worked as hard at the presidency as Johnson, who never stops working." His knowledge of Congress and how to get what he wanted was better than that of Kennedy. "It's doubtful Kennedy could have obtained congressional approval for the mass of major legislation—some his, some Johnson's— which Johnson got through in 1965." The Texan had fought harder for liberal programs with Congress and more successfully. Dying when and how he did, Kennedy had been the beneficiary of an "embroidery of mythology, adulation, sentimentality, and magnified appreciation."[3] Such words, friendly to himself, pierced a soft spot in Lyndon Johnson's armor.

Speaking extemporaneously to a fascinated audience later on, he said he wished he had known "a little more than I did know when I made the decisions. Every decision comes to a president's attention with so many unknowns, and he has limited access to groups." On the eve of leaving office, he had made clear to visiting Senator Goldwater that he knew the Great Society programs were not working but couldn't understand why. In spite of money and effort the programs to help the poor, the needy, and the black had been ineffective. "This job is a killer," Johnson confessed. According to his longtime opponent, "There was an overtone of sadness and a sense of resignation."[4] Perhaps here was simple letdown; more likely he had come to know how big is the job of president, how small the possibility of meeting all of its requirements. For history to judge any president fairly there must be recognition of this key truth.

Says another opponent of those years, Richard Nixon, reappraisal of Johnson would eventually come, but not until the passage of years and easing of "the hatreds which divide the country." The Johnsons had long since known this. Lady Bird told the cabinet at the end: "It was the best of times, it was the worst of times." Soon she jotted down, "The time has come, the role has been filled to the best of our abilities and is finished."[5] As for Lyndon, potential rancher, he hopefully but unrealistically told friends, "I'm going to enjoy the time I have left."

In office, President Johnson was a man with power, in the sense that he could make things happen and that what he desired did make the wheels move. Vested with the authority of a presidential office that he greatly strengthened, at least temporarily, he resolutely used that authority as many of his predecessors had not. By so doing, he gained the prestige that is accorded to the man of decision and action. He also gave the appearance of having power—at least during the early and middle periods of his incumbency. In the final months, as a lame-duck president, he did lose some strength.

The fact that this president did not "manage" Vietnam as a victorious national undertaking was not a sign that he lacked the power to do so. Rather, it indicated that he was unwilling to use much of the power the nation had and that he would not take risks that real escalation of the war seemed to entail. He also held back elsewhere, not committing the nation fully to an all-out fight on poverty, while publicly talking as though he had. Here, there were constraints: the fear of losing the white middle-class electorate, the cost of obligations already assumed toward education and medical care, and the need to gesture toward containing federal spending in order to combat inflation. Although many critics at that time and later did not think so, Johnson cautiously avoided full commitment of his and the nations's resources to any of the expensive causes he espoused, at home or abroad, with the single exception of the moon-landing project.

This president, concluding three decades in public office, took seriously the constitutionally prescribed tasks of the presidency. The overly critical should weigh the sage opinion of Milton Eisenhower on the matter: "It's one thing to sit on the outside when you're not responsible and say that this is the ideal thing that should be done; it's quite another when you're the president and must make that ultimate decision and you have to negotiate with the other guy and find the middle ground that he will accept and that you'll accept. You know, so few people in the United States recognize this." It was a British writer who said that Johnson was "an exceptionally able president," yet some had initially blurted—as did one journalist—" 'After Kennedy, I'm never going to accept this goddam nose-picking Texan as *my* president.' "[6] How could such a person remotely sense the daily duties that went with being *president*?

In political philosophy, President Johnson seems to have pictured this vista: The federal government will legislate comprehensively—really, without limit—for the people's own good, whether they have yet come to recognize the need or not. Then there will be aggressive administration for both the majority and defined minority groups. Nothing that much resembled major communistic redistribution of private property was required. Nor would government move generally in the direction of socialistic competition with the private sector. The biographer T. Harry Williams once observed that Johnson "never questioned the capitalist system, never questioned the bases of capitalism." The man from the frontier assumed that the minorities and poor, who were going to be newly educated and enjoying full civil liberties, would certainly become taxpayers *within the system*, thus strengthening it. So, the evolving Great Society would be composed of a better people, free of fear of communistic threats at home and abroad, a people who would before too long reside in a beautiful land of pure air and water and a protected national estate. Would not recognition as a great president be given to the man who pursued such noble precepts?

When sitting in judgment, so much depends on the position of the one who is judging. Dean Rusk, during those years, was considered an architect of an unwise war; but to his own leader, who lived with the constant danger of central—that is, nuclear—war with the Soviet Union and a possible clash with giant China, the secretary of state was one who had successfully maintained a great measure of peace and order in the world. Thus, to an audience at the Pan American Union, this wartime president could affirm that it had been a "great privilege to work with all of you toward peace and freedom in this world in which we live." On September 1, 1966, when signing a bill to let Vietnam War veterans join the American Legion, he even said that "in our earnest desire for peace, we have chosen the path of firm resolve [i.e., war]." Here was a leader who was trying to guarantee peace by waging war—an idea that had ample precedent. In domestic affairs there were many side effects from presidential action. Said an otherwise friendly novelist, "His most successful measures have produced impatience and released forces and energies which obscure the full extent of his accomplishments." The unexampled pace of change was in itself a problem. Johnson's own view was, "A great many people did say that we went too far and we went too fast." But, unrepentant, "Well, we might have, but the country was long overdue."[7]

Here was a president who could come to care about anything and everything he surveyed as he looked about, even eradication of rats—a brief crusade. Perhaps he was, at least in part, as one who focused closely on his work in education says, "a compassionate samaritan." Yet his 1968 budget director recalled in 1969 how he, Secretary Freeman, Charles Murphy, and Califano and his staff beat on Johnson continuously to enlarge the food program, "the feeding programs." They didn't win, he says, so that this president "went out of office without a big feeding program."[8] Eying the casualties of his expanded war, his outsized regard for the success of the Democratic party, and his constant concern for the fortunes and renown of Lyndon Baines Johnson, such an extravagant label has to be a bit jarring. Those writers who dwell narrowly and with hostility on the growth in the Johnson family's fortune in Texas during the years of his public responsibilities in Washington cling to strong reservations, of course. Many of the nation's taxpayers at the time could not help but reflect that Lyndon Johnson but occasioned the expensive laws; it was *they* who had anted up the money to finance those laws—with or without compassion. Many continue to see it this way.

It was a philosophical President Johnson who ruminated for posterity on October 25, 1968, "As I repeat, no man ever ran for president on a platform of doing what's wrong; and if he does what's wrong it's just because he doesn't know any better, and the president, and the office, and the institution usually have more information and more counsel and more knowledge on the problems of the country than any single office has or any single individual has. And if there's anything to the old saying that a man's judgment is no better than his information, then the president's judgment should be good, because the people of the land have provided him with the best information that is obtainable."⁹ But had he arranged for it to filter down very well?

Considering Vietnam in the light of these postulates, it has to be reiterated that Johnson had more than enough information in November and December 1963 to bring a fully responsible leader to the conviction that it would be next to impossible to create an independent and secure state around Saigon without vast and extraordinary effort, costs, and commitment of American forces. Right at this early point came this presidency's major blunder. Next came concealment of the extent of military involvement. Finally, President Johnson then declined to wage the kind of war that could quickly achieve the goals he had set. The war was waged by both Kennedy and Johnson, as Henry Kissinger has said, with "a commitment large enough to hazard our global position" but was executed "with so much hesitation as to defeat their purpose."¹⁰

It was true enough, as the president so often said, that he struggled to know what was right and "for the best interest of the people of this country." But in the Vietnam adventure that insight and his perspective failed him. That the course chosen tended to represent the opinion of a national majority who *had* to rely on his assurances, promises, and inside information is all too evident. To put it succinctly: this president helped to convince the people that communism must not expand in that particular locale; then he claimed, in exculpation, that he represented majority opinion as he pursued his costly policy of war-making containment. This circular situation will not do, especially since the public, in their ignorance, thought the Vietnam crusade to be readily feasible, while their leader absolutely knew from the very beginning that it would require vast, sustained, and, almost inevitably, bloody effort.

"Historians will assess as they will our efforts and achievements, failures and frustrations," replied the president to the retiring ambassador to Poland in May 1968, when that official promised him that "the mark of greatness" would surely be his.¹¹ Stature in history was not to be left to chance, as even the most casual visit to the presidential library and museum at Austin instantly reveals. Here was a dynamically memorializing activity. "He would conquer history," judged historian Eric Goldman wryly. Johnson did intend, in retirement, to uphold fully the then-existing code of conduct for former presidents: Do nothing in public that will have an adverse impact on the vital decision making of one's successor in office.

The time of a former leader's death is a time for making tactful appraisals. Eulogies were delivered in the rotunda of the Capitol on January 24 and 25, 1973. Thirty-two thousand copies of the resulting document were printed in order to spread across the land the judgment then rendered on "the life, character, and public service of the late President."[12] Senator Edward M. Kennedy caused to be reprinted some civil-rights legislation of those years, for history would record Lyndon Johnson as "one of our finest leaders." Senator Humphrey recalled a "total political man," marked by ambition and immodest, yet "a unique, remarkable individual." Maybe the public would focus on domestic accomplishments rather than Vietnam; in any case, "history will judge" and "history will note." He did wish Vietnam had never happened.

Republicans spoke with courtesy and brevity. Senator John Tower said that Texans could think better of themselves because of Johnson; Congressman Gerald Ford thought Johnson had "longed for peace under honorable conditions." Senator Charles Percy saw the record in domestic legislation as greater than Roosevelt's and there had been devotion to principle; nevertheless, there was Vietnam. Texas Democratic Congresswoman Barbara Jordan spoke out forcefully, and perhaps for her entire race: "He was a great man and a great president of the United States. Historians may regard that judgment as premature. But those of us who felt the power of his compassion and were the beneficiaries of his legislative prowess and effectiveness cannot await the historian's judgment." He had "stripped the federal government of its neutrality and made it the actor on behalf of America's old, poor, and black citizens."

So, in 1973, with peace having just been announced, but before the humiliating debacle in Saigon of 1975, their former colleague was praised most fully for his *goals* and his *efforts*. It was still early to assess *results*, and these were mixed in any case—depending on where one looked and what one valued. In regard to Vietnam, all maintained a cautious optimism that rested on hope for the best. Little or nothing was said about Santo Domingo; or violence in the nation's capital, Watts, and Detroit; or inflation; or climbing taxes following the legislative spree; or the mixed legacy from the social programs; or credibility gaps; or crudeness, pressure tactics, and self-serving. It seemed inappropriate to raise old points about the inevitable losses in the rights of some that had necessarily resulted from the new regulations and the national guarantees of civil rights for others. The emphasis was to "speak well of the departed."

From the White House, President Nixon saw his predecessor as being "devoted to the cause of freedom and equality for his fellow man" and to the land he loved. "History has yet to make its judgment," but Johnson had held the nation on course at the time of the assassination.

Having the courage to do what many of his contemporaries condemned him for, he would get warm praise "in the history books of tomorrow."

The Reverend Billy Graham officiated at the Ranch, as Lyndon had requested. Graham remembered the time when his friend Lyndon had said, "I hope you'll tell people about some of the things I tried to do." The speaker predicted that Johnson would "stand tall in the history books" because of his thirty-eight years of public service. National wealth had been harnessed to assist the plight of the poor. (Here, surely, was a certain literary license.) As for Vietnam: it had been "his destiny"!

Out of the vast array of media comment, one of the most penetrating appeared in the *Christian Science Monitor,* which said the nation had been driven too fast, but in the right direction, by an overly ambitious and oversized human being who had erred from "goodness and bigness of heart." The gargantuan social legislation would place him in history as "one of the truly great presidents." Yet he had "failed big" in Vietnam while "failing to make all Americans love each other and work harmoniously together." "LBJ was something else," exclaimed the *Shawnee* (Okla.) *News-Star.* Many editorialists accepted at face value Johnson's own explanation of March 31, 1968; so that the *Wyoming Eagle* duly found that he had put peace "ahead of his own political ambitions." Columnist Marianne Means zeroed in on *the person:* a towering presence, a ham, a schemer, a "people person," yet one who thrived on adversity and the making of great decisons. Conservative David Lawrence would have pleased Johnson: "The huge sacrifices made in Vietnam will always remain an exhibition of the humanitarianism of the United States." Few of the war's opponents and not enough veterans saw it that way, to say the least. One of the most favorable overall generalizations came from columnist Carl Rowan: "Not in four years nor forty will they erase all that Lyndon Johnson did to change this society." One-time critic Walter Cronkite, before uttering his Olympian "And that's the way it is," conceded that Johnson had been "a zealous public servant with a compelling dream of a better America—who made enormous strides to make that dream come true." David Halberstam had already called him "a politician and a force the like of which I doubt we shall see again in this century."[13]

But to say the least, there would be harsher assessments then and later. A political scientist, a historian, and others have judged that the presidency was a "tragedy" for either the American people or Johnson or both. Behind the idea of tragedy, it sometimes appeared, however, lay the concept that if only the president had not escalated the war in Vietnam, the result would have been still more legislation and higher expenditures, which would somehow have guaranteed a "better" society. All who have accompanied the narrative of these pages through the staggering lists of legislation placed so rapidly on the books—to the astonishment of a public that never quite got around to demanding a great deal of it (e.g., there was no strong public support for a transportation department)—will be inclined to doubt that much more could have been done in law making without general and very articulate popular resistance then or later. Somewhere the line must be drawn on gestation of laws by one branch in a federal system, unless that system is to be changed fundamentally under the Constitution. Contemplating the sheer bulk of what he had done, Johnson said in January 1969, "It's a little like whiskey. It is good. But if you drink too much it comes up on you."[14]

Although much has already been said in judgment of the Vietnam War, much remains. *Efforts to contain communism have great virtue; and some kind of effort in Southeast Asia after 1954 was definitely worth trying, at least for a time and even with some degree of sacrifice.* Vietnam, as a commitment, had roots going back many years; it was not undertaken exclusively by Johnson. But as a *war*, it developed in fact into "Johnson's war"—and at his hand. One radical scholar has called the expression "facile, unfair, and misleading," for there were the holdover advisers, such as Rusk, McNamara, and Rostow, for example, who saw themselves as zealous watchmen on the walls of freedom. Why keep belaboring "Ol' Lyndon"? A simple answer could be that *he* kept all these officials in office, even after his personal triumph and mandate of November 1964. As to naming the war, Nixon wrote Johnson on November 24, 1972, that it would ultimately bear neither Johnson's name nor his—but America's, and "proudly so." Earlier Nixon wrote that attacks upon a man after he has left office "and particularly when he is a former President of the United States [are] completely beyond the pale as far as I am concerned."[15]

The final extent of Vietnam's *direct* costs, though traceable in part to other presidents, came to an absolute minimum of $159,420,000,000 overall (in dollars of that day) spent for *an escalating military stalemate.*[16] A far higher and more realistic figure can be used, as we have seen (see p. 281). The initial withdrawal of sixty thousand troops on September 16, 1969, would be Nixon's, as he said, "The time has come to end this war." Nothing is stranger than the dedication of the Johnson presidency to cost-benefit analysis in routine governmental business and its abandonment of such rational action in the largest expenditure categories of all. There was also an intangible cost: dissension between the nation and its allies, and the terrible division at home.

While the figures on casualties and those missing in action during the Vietnam War are still being contested, it is said that during the Johnson years some 222,351 service personnel were killed or wounded; 122,708 are listed for Nixon's years. Deaths, 1963 to 1974, from hostile action came to 46,498, while another 10,000 died from other causes. (The Vietnam Memorial would ultimately include 57,939 names of those listed as killed or missing in the war, from July 1959 to the spring of 1975). Total deaths among the allied forces approached the 300,000 mark, and South Vietnamese civilian deaths approximate a similar figure. Bombing of the North during the Johnson years perhaps killed 52,000 civilians, many of whom can by no means be divorced from the war effort. If the North had prevailed in the early 1960s, casualties in the South might, of course, have been substantial; and they turned out to be, in one form or another of the word *casualty*, after 1975. The "boat people" would suffer. So would Hmong and Cambodians in huge numbers. More than 600,000 Southeast Asian refugees would find some form of refuge in the United States. Others died enroute to freedom or languished in rudimentary camps in Thailand or elsewhere. "Costs" to the American spirit and morale from the crusade to establish a perma- nent democratic nation in the form of a Republic of Vietnam can scarcely be quantified.

Because of the way in which the war was fought—without a declaration by Congress, as mentioned in Article I, section 8, of the Constitution—the nation got, in 1973, the restrictive War Powers Resolu- tion, which was passed over an able presidential veto. Here was an official reprimand for three presidencies: "The president in every possible instance shall consult with Congress before introducing United States Armed Forces into hostilities or into situations where imminent involvement in hostilities is clearly indicated by the circumstances." During the course of the war, the Court refused to decide on the constitutionality of the Vietnam War, says Justice William O. Douglas, because the Court feared a head-on collision with the executive branch. In any case, one result of the war was a presidency that was somewhat crippled in the field of foreign affairs, and at least a temporarily inward looking nation. In overall foreign relations, however, assesses one who was close to the events, "I don't know that we would have done anything very differently if there had been no Vietnam."[17]

Both the Kennedy and the Johnson years saw the increasing involvement of members of the academic community in the govern- ment. This brought new brains into the governing establishment. It also, unfortunately, could sometimes bring a certain inflexibility and an unwillingness to compromise into a governmental system that is rooted in compromise. Johnson did not appreciate any set of mind that might stress ideologically based, single-minded devotion to one policy, posture, or issue at the price of the pragmatic. He liked the accommodating American system and was impatient with those who could view temporary stays in government as a time for striking blows for fundamental change in the system.

The ideology of Lyndon Johnson is not easy to capsulize. When campaigning, he sometimes talked like a populist of old, focusing on the rank and file of his countrymen. Many of his policies and much in his personal approach to building a private estate won him the regard of many rich and powerful Americans, who recognized a fellow believer in the American dream of success when they saw one. The early effort to describe him in terms of the populists of the 1890s or the demagogue Huey Long was premature and certainly fails to communicate the socioeconomic views and values of the whole man, however accurate it is about his frontier and parental heritage. In the early 1980s, authors Ronnie Dugger and Robert Caro strongly questioned Johnson's populism, while scholar Margaret Canovan's 1981 book *Populism* makes clear how imprecise is that nineteenth-century word when resurrected indiscriminately in the late twentieth century.

In any case, Johnson did not talk like a populist ideologue, for the views he offered to the United States Chamber of Commerce in 1964 were a smash hit, and he blurted out to a National League of Cities meeting on March 31, 1966, in words that were quickly concealed: "You get into bad business when you go to saying that he veered to the right, or he veered to the left, because I really am not conscious which way I'm veering a good many times myself, and how are you going to know what the president is going to do, when the president doesn't know!" An example of this problem of a shifting ideology: in 1964 he insisted that nothing in the 1964 Civil Rights Act "would create preferential treatment." But at Howard University in 1965 he said that just bringing a person to the starting line, where he would then be free to compete, was not being completely fair. So, in one year, he had moved toward endorsing what would be called affirmative action.[18] Some early evaluations of this presidency by historians, made before the unfolding of the Vietnam War inclined even the more partisan toward caution, suggested that Kennedy and Johnson together had brought fulfillment and culmination to both the New Deal and the Fair Deal—whatever this might indicate in ideological terms.

That the federal bureaucracy, especially in the District of Columbia, increased during the Johnson years is altogether evident. This was part of a long-term trend, however. By the mid 1970s Washington, D.C., was the richest metropolitan area per household in the nation; Montgomery County, Maryland, the richest county in median household effective buying income. Overall, one in five among employed persons worked for the federal government a decade after the Johnson presidency.[19] Increases in personnel due to legislation passed during those years were more than noticeable in state and local governments and in all institutions that receive and account for federal funds. For such results this administration's responsibility in the creation of new bureaus and agencies and in the growth of existing machinery seems to be abundantly evident.

One must not try to connect all profound changes during the 1960s and later to this presidency. There was, it is said, a decline during the 1960s and 1970s in the quality of many American goods and services. Yet, the space-technology research effort during this presidency brought with it stress on extreme accuracy and reliability, intricacy, computerization, and miniaturization. Science and technology in the future was profoundly altered by Johnsonian loyalty to Project Apollo.

Values and life styles certainly changed. There was, for example, a definite Vietnam-related rise in pacifist feeling among youth, a much-remarked "generation gap," and a decline in faith in traditional liberalism of the kind that found solutions in a big national government. A drug culture emerged, which was partly linked with GI experience in Southeast Asia; and there was increased street crime and burglary, which was related to financing one's "habit": here, some relationship to the Asian war can be drawn. Returning veterans would have their problems, rooted in experiences of war and of instant reentry. A rise of interest in Oriental religions appeared. Living together without benefit of clergy became commonplace, for now had dawned the age of "the pill." Beginning in 1963 it was, in music, the era of the Beatles and the amplified guitar. Dustin Hoffman, in the movie *The Graduate* (1967), spoke effectively for rebellious youth, accompanied by the music of Simon and Garfunkel. Progress in civil rights for minorities in the 1960s is surely related to later outcries for rights for women, for senior citizens, for the physically and mentally handicapped, and, possibly, for homosexuals. Rural America came to have a new appeal. Here are many changes of those years and later, not necessarily only Johnson-presidency-related, to excite future researchers.

Many have said that, whatever the benefits of this presidency in legislative enactment, there was a severe setback later because of *the way things were done*—such as the pace, change of focus, constant pressure, restlessness, federal domination, and more. Writing in 1969, George Reedy judged, "The great majority of Americans are tired of 'action' and are in a mood to blame their current difficulties upon the hectic spurts of activity during the Johnson administration." Irving Howe said, "Many Americans were frightened by the hullabaloo of the late 1960s. Opportunities for major reform were frittered away in verbal violence, dopey irrationalism, apocalyptic gesture." From the New Left came "a social-political hangover."[20] So, responsibility was shared. While the president was valiantly trying to bring reform through conventional leadership of congressional legislative activity and routine communication with the greater public, many youths in an age bracket that could have helped mightily were allowing almost self-appointed leaders (really, agitators) to divert energies and critical faculties to self-serving resistance to the draft and ultimately, in some cases, to subverting the idea of order in the system itself. Yet, their revulsion to war had long humanitarian roots.

The difficulties in bringing about social change were underestimated by the presidential advisers of the 1960s, thinks scholar and political figure Daniel P. Moynihan. Senate Democratic leader Mike Mansfield was one who told Johnson to his face: "We have come too far too fast during your administration. The people want a little let-up and a little rest." Waterfront philosopher Eric Hoffer thought that the period of the 1960s was a disaster for the majority; it naturally struck back then and later. Change was being *forced*; 90 percent didn't want it. Many had lost interest in work, in the new welfare environment; and many—to state it bluntly—had become cowards. The Reverend Theodore M. Hesburgh, president of the University of Notre Dame, could toll off a list of positive results in those years, but he still had to deplore how the 1960s had led to the loss of creativity and enthusiasm and leadership; the failure to seek solutions; and the unpopularity of earlier worthwhile causes. The voice of liberalism faded, said philosopher Irving Kristol. His opinion was that "in succeeding, its flaws became self-evident." Given the stature of the speakers, such views cannot be ignored.[21] Undoubtedly, faith in governmental solutions for problems, in the sense of 1930s liberalism, suffered greatly.

Certain actions of this presidency stand out. *As to the Vietnam War:* the determination to escalate only gradually in order to send "signals" to the enemy; rejection of winning in any conventional sense; ultimately shifting to "peace" as the really vital goal. Yet a service of the Vietnam effort was the reminder to Americans that even a massive military campaign waged for a decade may not be able to prevail against ideology and nationalism that are deeply rooted in history. *As to the Great Society:* overpromising of utopia in spite of passing laws that got only modest appropriations; quiet administrative changes in the giant conventional payments programs for individuals that later would escalate their costs immeasurably; legislating the financing of much medical care without containing costs; and instituting new programs without prior testing for effectiveness. Yet, a service of the Great Society crusade was the reminder to Americans that government need not stand by indefinitely without at least trying to strike effective blows against injustice, extremes of poverty, and the failure to educate the young.

The addition of federal dollars at every level of the American educational system, followed by regulations, was revolutionary and brought changes in scale, quality, and control of policies. Civil-rights legislation corrected many old abuses. For that day the laws were daring and appreciated, though they were attacked. They proved less definitive than many at the time expected. The posture on conservation, though challenged by certain new environmentalists as being only half a loaf, was one of progress in improving the air, the waterways, beauty, and the national estate. There was innovation in crime prevention, but results were hard to measure—and crime increased. Finally, overreaching in the presidential office then and later, unfortunately, brought attacks on its magnified role in the constitutional system.

Lyndon Johnson and his aides forgot how impatient the American public can be when expecting quick results from highly publicized laws passed at home and undertakings abroad. "I think we overestimated the patience of the American people," said Dean Rusk. "If they could have only been told we can win . . . ; but lacking that, they said, " 'Well, chuck it.' " And in a nuclear age the administration was afraid "to stir up public opinion" in the conventional way. It is said that Johnson had "Persevere" for a motto. As early as 1966, however, thinking of Valley Forge, he had observed that footprints were getting bloodier and folks were falling out.[22] Staff memorandums reminded him hopefully about public impatience in earlier wars.

President Johnson worked very hard and displayed great concern. Senior journalist Arthur Krock judged, that "though the burdens of the age on President Johnson appear superficially to be the heaviest ever borne by a White House incumbent, many of them were even more painfully encountered by Hoover in his Presidency." We see one difference: Hoover had little or nothing to do with creating a depression; Johnson had a great deal to do with creating a war. He had to accept its fallout. Both presidents worked excessively long hours and worried inordinately. But it was Johnson's idea to try to change or add to the laws of the nation in practically every area, thus greatly increasing the strain of his job. This, however, would bring a reward; for aide Joseph Califano suggests, stressing quantity over quality: "Greatness must be measured by productivity. . . . Start with George Washington and study the problems in relation to the solutions. Lyndon Johnson is in a class by himself."[23]

Johnson was the greatest president for the poor and for the Negroes, someone has claimed. Corrective of such ultimate praise is a newspaper judgment: "We set out with firm resolve and the best of intentions to conquer poverty, ignorance and prejudice in our land—and our effort produced frustration, resentment, anger and violence." The underfunded and scattershot War on Poverty did not amount to all that much then or later, unless one includes, perhaps inappropriately, cash increases and expansion of eligibility and services in *existing* giant aid programs, veterans benefits, and social security. If, somehow, turbulence did arise from great expectations, should the attempted solutions bear the blame? Would spending less have had a calming influence? Anyway, said a prominent Republican, "If Johnson fell short of achieving the Great Society, it was not for a lack of good intentions."[24]

What the nation got in the form of new laws, overall, was indeed a series of what were said to be crash programs aimed at using the federal government to try to cure all of the ills of society. Proponents waxed lyrical at the extent of the effort. Opponents deplored the impact on the American federal system; thought many of the programs midguided, granted (sometimes) that there had been good intentions, but really rejoiced when November 1968 promised an end to the legislative orgy. Some said "We Shall Overdo" had been the slogan throughout! Constitutionalists thought that the executive branch, as in Franklin Roosevelt's day, had grown to an improper ascendency. Moralists felt that so great an alleged deterioration in personal values in the 1960s, much remarked on, had stemmed to some extent from the nation's top symbol of leadership. Yet, there can be little disputing that the First Family, as a dynamic four-member family unit always in the public eye, had set an admirable example from beginning to end.

Persons of practical bent deplored what journalist Henry Fairlie called "the politics of expectation." We have seen to what extraordinary lengths President Johnson, as candidate and leader, developed this art— with an extravagance in promising and conceptualizing that lacked basic honesty, except by the strange standards of politics on the stump. The secretary of agriculture sent to Johnson, as descriptive of their situation, a full-page quotation from an early Eric Hoffer book, *The True Believer*: "We inadvertently 'out-promised ourselves.'" People resent it when "the millenium hasn't arrived." A political scientist finds that Johnson had "unwittingly aroused higher needs and values that he could neither comprehend fully nor gratify." *Time* would ruminate at the close, on

January 24, 1969, "Dark forces endure in U.S. life; stubborn problems remain to be resolved."[25]

Nearly all scholarly observers give high marks to this presidency for extending civil rights for minorities. This would have pleased President Johnson, for in his last formal public effort, the 1969 State of the Union address, he sought that accolade: "I hope it may be said, a hundred years from now, that by working together we helped to make our country more just for all of its people, as well as to insure and guarantee the blessings of liberty for all of our posterity. That is what I hope, but I believe at least it will be said that we tried." On that, there could be no doubt.

Unrewarding is the concept that President Lyndon Johnson was not loved—or even liked very much! A critic said that Johnson just could not get "that respect, affection and rapport which alone permit an American President genuinely to lead." Uneasily, too many dwelt almost voyeuristically on a figure, as Theodore H. White put it, "of boundless power appetite and reckless historical ambition." But among black and Mexican-American activists there was an evaluation with a far more positive stress, in line with the 1969 judgment of Lyndon's own pastor: "More poor are being helped, more students of all races are in college, more sick and disabled are being helped, more members of minority groups have been given opportunity, now, than when he took office, *by far.*"[26] Maybe, as Dale Carnegie, once the household word on making friends, confidently asserted, doing things for people does not bring love.

To read the president's incoming mail from plain people about what specific innovations meant to them personally is to sense that vast numbers were quietly grateful, whether their views prevailed among many of the intelligensia or not. For them this presidency could not even remotely be considered a "tragedy." They gave ample approbation. Friends reported in. "You are entitled to a good feeling about yourself," enthusiastically wrote Abe Fortas in a 1967 letter. Johnson had served others unselfishly, using "the extraordinary talents of mind and heart that God has given you." He had opened a new chapter, comparable to Lincoln's, and so had fulfilled democracy. Communism henceforth would be less of a threat and a destroyer of man's aspirations. The president should feel good, happy, and content about himself, for here had been "a job well done and a life well lived." Yet, at about that very moment, liberal philosopher Charles Frankel, inside the White House, was putting into his book manuscript this dreadful evaluation: "At the end of 1967, education was in crisis, the cities were in turmoil, and funds were being cut back for most of the programs which the Administration had initiated. During the course of two and a half years I had watched from the inside while an American Administration, rich in promise and enjoying extraordinary support from the people, had stubbornly, obsessively, destroyed its promise and dissolved its power."[27] But in signing the Open Housing Act of 1968, a thrilled president said that such a proud moment meant that he was signing into law "the promises of a century." Such dichotomies seem irreconcilable.

All presidents can be expected to struggle to realize their dreams. Yet all are overwhelmed at the final bell, having failed to achieve what they set for themselves, chiefly because the problems of the nation and the world are enormous and intractable. The means that presidents can use to bring basic change are so limited; and the general population turns out to be of so little help—and seems to care so little—even when advised that a degree of success, for their day, lies just over the horizon. In Johnson's case, Democratic party regular India Edwards said she could just weep when she thought of him: "This man had everything. He had the experience, he had everything to make him, really, maybe our greatest president, everything . . . ," yet he could not get the people to have confidence in him.[28] Here was a common world problem late in a century that became increasingly permeated by media-sculpted imagery. But it really has to be said that in Johnson's case there had indeed been a time when, in the words of Cassius in *Julius Caesar*, he did "bestride the narrow world like a Colossus" and seemed to be the master of his fate. Yet, in the last analysis, the fault—the gradual decline—lay not in his stars but in himself. The master of the parliamentary art had proven not to be a master of the executive art.

When the hopes, dreams, work, and sacrifices of President Johnson are laid adjacent to the finite extent of his actual achievement in Southeast Asia, can it not be said that he ended up as a self-chosen martyr? His countrymen then and later have to share in the martyrdom. The casualties in Vietnam, the loved ones at home, and those who suffered because of conscience were involved to varying degrees in Lyndon Johnson's martyrdom. (*Martyr*: "one who . . . endures great suffering on behalf of any belief, principle, or cause.")[29] Not just the president, but vast numbers of people in and out of Washington and Southeast Asia were identifiable casualties of the war. That no-win war of attrition for democracy and honor, which had no end in sight and was the result of utopian leadership overextended, a continent away, is at the very top of the list of what so many contemporaries could not forgive this well-meaning president. They considered him to be on this matter, at least, not a famous leader but a notorious one. This widespread opinion is not likely to change soon.[30]

When Americans can force themselves to think about the war at all, which is hard, they go with the final decree of President Johnson's earthy brother, who said that Lyndon had gotten caught "in this nowhere position" on Vietnam. Instead, "He should have gone with the hawks for an outright victory or he should have pulled out."[31] There is of course a classic saying: "He who has never made mistakes in war has never made war." But the constraints that this presidency placed on the nation's men in uniform went far beyond "mistakes." The Johnson team's civilian management of the military was a disservice to all who fought and, finally, was a guarantee that a militarily powerful North Vietnam would live on to fight competently and triumphantly in the 1970s. Protesters once claimed that the war was being fought without a decent respect for the opinions of mankind. This hostile view is even yet debatable. Not really arguable, however, is the idea that Vietnam was fought under this commander in chief without a decent respect for the rights of the uniformed American servicemen who fought it. It was immoral to require the fighting of an open-ended war which did not have as its ultimate goal the defeat of the enemy as rapidly as possible so as to minimize casualties and achieve stated goals. Those who *really fought* in Vietnam would not readily forget.

The president knew he had greatly upset the country. How could he avoid knowing, with the "Hey, hey" chants about how many American boys he had "killed today," and the protests and riots related to or responsive to his actions? An aide in December 1967 had decided: "The mood of the nation is somber. There is bitterness, unhappiness, tension, and impatience. Laughter is stilled or stilted. Our men are dying in war. . . . I believe the nation faces an internal, moral crisis of confidence fully as pervasive as that engendered by the 1929 crash and ensuing events." Soon, in early 1968, a sober journalist said that Johnson's leadership had plunged the presidency into a "boiling slough."[32] On the other hand, a traditional American of great stature from earlier years, James Farley, could then say in public that the nation's leader was "a patriot, a man of courage, leading this nation to greatness"![33] Aware of such unbridgeable chasms in judgment of his performance, the troubled chief executive told an elite audience on April 1, 1968: "I learned somewhere that no leader can pursue public tranquility as his first and only goal. For a president to buy public popularity at the sacrifice of his better judgment is too dear a price to pay. This nation cannot afford such a price, and this nation cannot long afford such a leader."

This complex individual naturally felt great satisfaction as he contemplated achievement in regard to the space effort, conservation, civil rights, education, and medical care. May we not agree that he had the right? Warns Kennedy family devotee Theodore Sorensen, "It will be unfortunate if Johnson's massive accomplishments . . . in domestic areas remain obscured by the bitter controversies over his Vietnam policy." Those who then carped too much were dismissed bluntly by Hoffer as he reassured LBJ: "Your detractors and tormenters will end up in the dustbin of history." And a citizen of distant Wenatchee, Washington, confided to the former president twenty-one months after he left office: "Vietnam blinded us, your critics, to the accomplishments you made. You were a doing, acting president. . . . History will give you your credits. It will show how short-sighted we were."[34]

Unfortunately, in spite of this lavish praise, there were portentous economic legacies. *The groundwork was laid for vast inflation of the currency.* Butter plus guns, neither properly funded, brought a devalued dollar and an escalating national debt. In 1968, economic adviser Walter Heller reassured us that the president's contention that the country could have both guns and butter was "dead right." Was the president well served? With a burgeoning money supply, a doubled interest rate on commercial paper, and a consumer price index that had risen eighteen points since 1963, the nation's future was being mortgaged. Said *Newsweek* on January 20, 1969, "Last week, inflationary psychology was spreading like the Hong Kong flu." And why not? Observed one specialist: "During the Johnson administration the number of expenditure programs increased dramatically. Every public problem was thought to be a *federal* problem, and for each of these the administration designed, pushed through Congress, and implemented a specific program to solve or ameliorate it." Thus, by 1967 at least six major programs dispensed money to help communities construct water and sewer facilities; four were new with this administration. For some time in the 1970s a complacent public clung to the 1960s idea that any and all federal programs could be afforded, although eliminating poverty became no more than "an ultimate goal."[35] By the 1980s, in any case, national solvency itself had come into question.

Many thought then and many more thought later that a serious loss by Americans during these years was in the area of freedom from the heavy hand of government. Meddling in and control over personal lives increased. There developed "a bureaucratic glacier, cold and creeping and distant from those it was designed to serve."[36] Both businesses and educational institutions soon felt the heavy hand of eager Washington bureaucrats, who, with some justification, were following federal dollars to the places where they were being spent, but who often were just seeking to exercise the power to control. In a decade this matter would assume major proportions, but in 1968, at the time, the Republican Party's platform only cursorily condemned excessive government controls and called mildly for "a partnership of government at *all* levels." It said mildly that decision making should be broadly based—a mixture of private with public. Many of the agencies that were born or enlarged in power during this presidency would blossom into full flower in the 1970s, still staffed by many in the civil service and appointive positions who saw themselves as "big brother" to a rather remote public. For a time, raw compulsion was thought to be an acceptable governing technique.

In full perspective—that is, viewed from afar—you still have to give it to Lyndon Baines Johnson: his presidency was from first to last a brilliant tour de force. He etched his innovative mark on the century. This leader evidently took seriously the thrust of the scholarly Woodrow Wilson, when he once wrote: "The president is at liberty, both in law and in conscience, to be as big a man as he can." On the other hand, activist President Johnson completely failed to heed the much older counsel of Solon, as translated by classics student Thomas Jefferson: "No more good must be attempted than the nation can bear." For example, because many people during the 1960s had not sought and were not sold on the ultimate value of the man-on-the-moon effort, the giant strides in space technology—which were really analogous to the earlier Manhattan project or the Marshall Plan in ultimate payoff—were not evaluated by masses of contemporaries as a genuine revolution in human history. Here, payoff in the history books and biographies for Johnson has been nonexistent.

The end of this presidency saw the nation in turmoil, with loss of faith in the system itself among many young people and very serious divisions between many adults and their offspring. The social fabric of the United States had not proven equal to the strains placed upon it. Says an astute commentator, "The more the United States did to preserve an independent identity for South Vietnam, the more America's own identity changed."[37] Lyndon Johnson had loved to say, "Let us reason together," and "I want to be president of all the people," and "Consensus" was his middle name. But consensus and mutual rapport were casualties at the hands of the very figure who sought them. Five years of this president's leadership, whatever may have been the degree of his effort, the extent of his hopes, and the magnitude of his achievements, made millions more than satsified that he was going to depart early from the national scene. There were "widespread sighs of relief," judged one news magazine. Even harsher was a senior journalist's view: Johnson had been "presiding over a society sickened by quack cure-alls."[38]

The embattled Johnson presidency would not achieve consensus no matter how hard it tried. It did not bring into being a long-lived democratic South Vietnam in spite of giving the effort more than it warranted, yet less than was needed in order to achieve stated goals. But the nation was unquestionably moved a measurable distance toward the Great Society of the president's dreams. Choosing his words very carefully, one Republican figure of presidential stature has said that this leader "showed us what could be accomplished through government action—and what could never be accomplished through government action." While Johnson had demonstrated what "government could do for people," he had also shown "what people and nations must do for themselves."[39]

Failure and achievement had indeed blended. *Time* told its readers, as the president headed for home, "All too often, big federal spending has produced not social miracles but merely a swollen bureaucracy and the anger of those who feel cheated by the gap between promise and performance."[40] In 1966, the budget director had warned Johnson that "states, cities, depressed areas, and individuals have been led to expect immediate delivery of benefits from Great Society programs to a degree that is not realistic," so that frustration and loss of credibility would result. Here, today's observer may say, was about what should have been expected from utopian prose read to the nation on TV by this president. In any case, his overall abuse of the truth was well outside of the permissive boundaries of political license and was unthinkable in a president. It was simply not this executive's style to keep before him at all times such restraint as that embraced by George Washington, a man of unexampled character in the presidency: "There is scarcely any part of my conduct which may not hereafter be drawn into precedent."[41] Still, as much as any, and far more than most who have occupied the nation's highest office, Lyndon Johnson the man—strong and intelligent—made himself the catalyst that was essential to change in some areas of national life that remain central to the well-being of millions.

The use of government, especially the national government, to seek to accomplish great ends was an overly optimistic reliance on a single repository of power and strength in the American pluralistic system. Both the legislative branch and the vast private sector were partially displaced as responsible partners, while Washington pushed state capitals and county and city jurisdictions toward subordinate positions. The people—especially the employed and the middle class—proved to be unprepared to move so far and so expensively in so short a time. The secretary of HEW surmised as much in 1966: "Many people think the Great Society programs are mainly designed to help the very poor," he told the president, "and they don't believe that this Administration has much interest in the middle-class, middle income family." Then, plaintively, John Gardner had continued: "There must be a way to make these people see that *every* American has an enormous stake in what we're doing."[42] But people are what they are; they could neither accept nor endorse this quasi revolution that alleged it would bring utopia in their own generation. Nor were their leader and his dedicated team, it turned out, able to plan, direct, and administer so much change without serious inadequacies, flaws, and mistakes—especially in the waging of their "wars" at home and abroad. Perhaps no leadership group the nation had produced could have carved out a new America in such a manner—even had it been given nine years instead of five.

This president was not the greatest presidential leader either in waging war or in managing affairs at home. Judged one expert administrator, NASA's James E. Webb, Johnson didn't "understand" administration. Yet, at attaining legislation from Congress he was unsurpassed. Unparalleled was his ability to absorb ideas for change from everywhere and somehow work with his staff to incorporate them into proposed bills. As a person he was not, regrettably, one who would win lasting renown for central elements in his character or personality; many leaders in the nation who could boast far less achievements have been more highly regarded for themselves alone. It would be a nice test of wisdom to say how far some of the less admirable traits were essential to the extent of achievement.

Surveying the entire landscape, the evidence clearly shows that this presidency was *a force for change*: in the efforts to prevail in space, to guarantee civil rights, to wage war on poverty, to provide medical care for the aged and poor, to educate the nation's youth, to improve the environment, to help finance the performing arts and public broadcasting, to support consumerism, and to thwart communism overseas. It obtained its verve and purpose in these crusades from its central figure—Lyndon Johnson—a product of frontier and rural southwestern America. Equipped with an attitude capsulized by a slogan he later expressed—"Man can"—he dared, cared, and shared of himself, and thereby often carried the day.

An unremitting ardor to improve the nation and the world remains the most praiseworthy single thing about the Johnson team and its famous leader. John F. Kennedy once had said of Lyndon B. Johnson, "He really cares about this nation as I want a president to care." The tall Texan aimed high; he sought change on a Texas scale. The fallout was commensurate: institutionalized inflation of the currency; higher taxes; increased regulation and control of individuals, organizations, and businesses—that is, loss of freedom; perhaps some fading of collective self-discipline across the land; and changes in the future conduct of foreign policy as the legislative branch would seek to regain lost stature. These by-products were serious enough to dilute measurably the successes achieved from some of the vast array of new laws.

In final assessment, during the years 1963 to 1969 the executive branch of the United States government developed, in the hands of this leader and his associates, into a dynamic administrative unit never likely to be equaled. It prodded history into new directions. The presidency of Lyndon B. Johnson will inevitably be remembered—and ought to be— for the characteristics of its central figure; for the unintentional but substantial damage that it did with some catastrophic policies abroad and erroneous policies at home; and, especially, for the many worthwhile changes it embedded deeply in legislation, in the lives of millions, and in American society.

NOTES

CHAPTER 1
INTO THE OVAL OFFICE: 1963

1. In Doris Kearns, *Lyndon Johnson and the American Dream* (New York: Harper & Row, 1976), p. 164.

2. W. K. Hopkins to Roy Miller, Nov. 25, 1931; text in *Among Friends of LBJ* (Austin, Tex.: Friends of the Library), July 15, 1978.

3. Ronnie Dugger, *The Politician: The Life and Times of Lyndon Johnson* (New York: Norton, 1982), pt. 11; Merle Miller, *Lyndon: An Oral Biography* (New York: Putnam's, 1980), pp. 118–137; George Reedy, *Lyndon B. Johnson: A Memoir* (New York: Andrews & McMeel, 1982).

4. For 1963 polling see *Public Opinion Quarterly* 28 (Spring to Fall 1963).

5. Data for 1963 is from the author's clipping files; *Encyclopaedia Britannica Yearbook 1964; Facts on File; Historical Statistics of the United States* (Washington, D.C.: Government Printing Office, 1975); Arnold B. Barach, *USA: Its Economic Future* (Washington, D.C.: Twentieth Century Fund, 1964); many tables; and personal memory.

6. John D. Williams, "The Small World," *Saturday Evening Post*, Aug. 6, 1960, p. 68. The World Future Society was founded in 1966; the Institute for the Future, in 1968; Futures Information Network, in 1971. Chapter 1 to this point is rooted in a 35-page footnoted essay on the rise of Johnson, which was deleted because of requirements of space.

7. Press conference, Parkland Hospital, Nov. 24, 1963; White House Diary (microfilm edition); *Public Papers*, 1963–1964, 2:1477. Very brief unattributed quotations of Johnson's language are in this set, if dated, or in his memoir.

8. Paul B. Sheatsley and Jacob J. Feldman, in *The Kennedy Assassination and*

the American Public, ed. Bradley S. Greenberg and Edwin B. Parker (Stanford, Calif.: Stanford University Press, 1965), pp. 156, 176.

9. Jenkins memorandum, "Various Conversations Today," Nov. 25, 1963, in Fortas name file, Johnson Library, Austin, Texas.

10. On McNamara: Horace Busby, in *The Presidency and Congress* (Austin, Tex.: LBJ School of Public Affairs, 1979), p. 285; Jack Valenti, *A Very Human President* (New York: Norton, 1975), pp. 4–11. On Rusk: Warren I. Cohen, *Dean Rusk* (Totowa, N.J.: Cooper Square Publishers, 1980), p. 329.

11. Freeman to Jenkins, in Jenkins to president, Nov. 23, 1963, EX/FG1, White House Central Files. All citations in this format are to this massive file in the Johnson Library.

12. Letters of Nov. 22 and Dec. 13, 1963, and Walter Heller to president, Nov. 25, 1963, EG2/Eisenhower.

13. David Halberstam, *The Powers That Be* (New York: Knopf, 1979), pp. 362–363.

14. James A. Farley to president, Nov. 29, 1963, EX/FO5; Horace Busby to president, Dec. 3, 1963, FG2/Truman.

15. Roy Wilkins to president, Nov. 27, 1963, Wilkins file; also White House Diary, n.d. (Dec. 1963).

16. Elmer W. Lower, in *Kennedy Assassination,* p. 72; Fred I. Greenstein, ibid., pp. 235–236; Moyers to president, Dec. 2, 1963, White House Diary.

17. David O. Sears, in *Kennedy Assassination,* p. 313; James D. Barber, ibid., pp. 128–129; Theodore H. White, *The Making of the President 1964* (New York: Atheneum, 1965), p. 45.

18. Bill Gulley, *Breaking Cover* (New York: Simon & Schuster, 1980), pp. 224–228.

19. Cabinet minutes, Apr. 3, 1968.

20. Valenti, *Very Human President,* p. 152; William H. Lawrence, in Miller, *Lyndon,* p. 331; Cronkite interview, May 2, 1970.

21. In William J. Hopkins to staff, Nov. 29, 1963, EX/FG2/Kennedy; Robert F. Kennedy to recipients, Jan. 22, 1964, and Hopkins's reply, Feb. 5, 1964, EX/FG2/Hopkins; Kennedy to McGeorge Bundy, Feb. 25, 1964, and Bundy's reply, Feb. 28, 1964, EX/FG2/Kennedy.

22. Robert F. Wagner to president, Nov. 29, 1963, Democratic National Committee papers, box 126; memorandum, Nov. 29, 1963, EX/FG2/JFK.

23. Movie film sound track of LBJ narrating in the Oval Office on Oct. 25, 1968, transcribed by the author.

24. White House Diary, Nov. 25, 1963.

25. Frankfurter to president, Nov. 29, 1963, Frankfurter file.

26. Quoted by the Reverend Billy Graham, Jan. 25, 1973, in *Lyndon Baines Johnson: Memorial Tributes Delivered in Congress* (Washington, D.C.: Government Printing Office, 1973), p. 267; Jim Bishop, *A Day in the Life of President Johnson* (New York: Random House, 1967), p. 88; in Henry A. Zeiger, *Lyndon B. Johnson: Man and President* (New York: Popular Library, Dec. 1963), p. 117.

27. Earl Warren, *The Memoirs of Earl Warren* (Garden City, N.Y.: Doubleday, 1977), p. 358.

28. William Colby and Peter Forbath, *Honorable Men: My Life in the CIA* (New York: Simon & Schuster, 1978), p. 221.

29. Jean Daniel of *L'Express*; *Washington Post*, Nov. 29, 1963.

30. To Leo Janos, "The Last Days of the President," *Atlantic*, July 1973, p. 39, and to Harry Middleton, *Among Friends of LBJ*, Jan. 1, 1983, p. 5; to Richard Helms, Helms reminiscence, Sept. 16, 1981, p. 18.

31. *New York Times*, July 18, 1979.

32. President to Mrs. Kennedy, Dec. 15, 1964, EX/FG2/Mrs. JFK; Cronkite interview, May 2, 1970; Lady Bird Johnson, *A White House Diary* (New York: Holt, Rinehart & Winston, 1970), p. 725.

33. Notation on Pauline Moore to president, May 22, 1964, PL6-3/Rep. Party.

34. Salinger to addressees, Feb. 10, 1964, EX/FG2/Kennedy.

35. Bruce Catton, *Four Days* (New York: UPI and American Heritage, 1964), pp. 3–5.

36. In Cliff Carter to president, Jan. 9, 1964, EX/FG1.

37. A secretary, Estelle Harbin, in Robert A. Caro, *The Years of Lyndon Johnson: The Path to Power* (New York: Knopf, 1982), p. 229; Tom Wicker, "Requiem for the Great Society," *Saturday Evening Post*, Dec. 28, 1968–Jan. 11, 1969, p. 30; Richard Strout, *Christian Science Monitor*, Dec. 3, 1982.

CHAPTER 2
A JOHNSON TEAM IN ACTION

1. Walter Heller, "Economic Policy Advisers," in *The Presidential Advisory System* (Boston: Little, Brown, 1979), p. 37; Henry Kissinger, *White House Years* (Boston: Little, Brown, 1979), p. 47. The word *subpresidency* is from Emmette S. Redford and Marlan Blissett, *Organizing the Executive Branch: The Johnson Presidency* (Chicago: University of Chicago Press, 1981), pp. 9, 231.

2. Johnson reminiscence (to Elspeth D. Rostow), Sept. 28, 1970, 2:6. All reminiscences are in the Johnson Library.

3. Walter Lippmann, "The Deepest Issue of Our Time," *Vital Speeches* 22 (July 1, 1936): 603; Philip C. Bom, "Academocracy: American Scholarship in the Sixties" (Ph.D. diss., Free University, Amsterdam, 1975), p. 156; Jack Valenti, *A Very Human President* (New York: Norton, 1975), pp. 61–65; memorandum (name withheld), Jan. 1964, EX/FG1.

4. *Saturday Review*, Nov. 6, 1971, p. 41; *New York Times*, Oct. 31, 1971; *Oregonian*, Nov. 13, 1980.

5. Lady Bird Johnson, *A White House Diary* (New York: Holt, Rinehart & Winston, 1970), pp. 694–695.

6. Paul Southwick to Bill Moyers, Nov. 27, 1963, EX/FG1.

7. Freeman telephone message, in Jenkins to president, Nov. 23, 1963, EX/ FG1.

8. Theodore C. Sorensen, *The Kennedy Legacy* (New York: Macmillan, 1969), p. 94; Kenneth P. O'Donnell and David F. Powers, *"Johnny, We Hardly Knew Ye"* (Boston: Little, Brown, 1970), p. 403; Johnson, *White House Diary,* p. 734; Valenti to Moyers, Dec. 11, 1964, EX/FG2/Kennedy.

9. Kissinger, *White House Years,* p. 296; Paul C. Warnke reminiscence, Jan. 17, 1969, p. 9; quoted in Fred Panzer to president, Feb. 14, 1968, Goldberg file.

10. Paul Nitze reminiscence, Dec. 16, 1968, pp. 9–10.

11. Kissinger, *White House Years,* p. 231, and other inputs, including P. M. Kamath, *Executive Privilege versus Democratic Accountability* (Atlantic Highlands, N.J.: Humanities Press, 1982).

12. Valenti to president, Jan. 6, 1964, EX/FG1.

13. Texts in Valenti, *Very Human President,* pp. 96–97.

14. Newspaper accounts; Eric Goldman, *The Tragedy of Lyndon Johnson* (New York: Knopf, 1969), p. 297; *Los Angeles Times,* Jan. 17, 1983.

15. George Reedy, *Lyndon B. Johnson: A Memoir* (New York: Andrews & McMeel, 1982), p. 159; Bill Moyers, interviewing President Jimmy Carter on PBS, Nov. 13, 1978.

16. Interview in Donald R. Burkholder, "The Caretakers of the Presidential Image" (Ph.D. diss., Wayne State University, 1973), pp. 97–99.

17. Charles Frankel, *High on Foggy Bottom* (New York: Harper & Row, 1968), pp. 195, 198, 135; Alan Otten, "The Men around LBJ," *Wall Street Journal,* Aug. 18, 1965; Joseph Kraft, "The Post-Imperial Presidency," *New York Times Magazine,* Nov. 2, 1980, p. 94.

18. Valenti to president, Dec. 18, 1963, EX/PE2.

19. Valenti, *Very Human President,* p. 39; *Among Friends of LBJ,* Jan. 1, 1983, pp. 8–9.

20. John W. Macy, *Public Service* (New York: Harper & Row, 1971), pp. 85–87; *Public Papers,* 1965, 1:392–394; Patricia G. Zelman, *Women, Work and National Policy: The Kennedy-Johnson Years* (Ann Arbor, Mich.: UMI Research Press, 1982), pp. 70–71, 114, 116, app. A.

21. Zelman, *Women,* pp. 1–5, 23, 38; Martin Binkin and Shirley J. Bach, *Women and the Military* (Washington, D.C.: Brookings Institution, 1977), p. 12.

22. President to Peck, Jan. 14, 1964, and Peck file.

23. President to Mike Monroney, May 15, 1964, EX/FG2/Kennedy.

24. Bill Gulley, *Breaking Cover* (New York: Simon & Schuster, 1980), chaps. 1 and 2.

25. Unedited interview by Robert E. MacKay of NEA, May 21, 1965, p. 12; Califano reminiscence, June 11, 1973, p. 29.

26. Valenti, *Very Human President,* pp. 67–68.

27. Moyers to Bromley Smith, Apr. 1, 1964, Krim file.

28. Califano to Krim, Apr. 6, 1966, EX/SO2.

29. In Jim Bishop, *A Day in the Life of President Johnson* (New York: Random House, 1967), p. 114.

30. See correspondence, 1964–1968, in Krim file.

31. In *Equal Opportunity in the United States* (Austin: University of Texas Press, 1973), p. 175; Jacqueline Kennedy Onassis reminiscence, Jan. 11, 1974, pp. 6–7; Johnson, *White House Diary*, p. ix.

32. Joseph Kraft, "The Washington Lawyers," in *Presidential Advisory System*, p. 155.

CHAPTER 3
FIRST MANDATE: THE LEGACY TO CONTINUE

1. Busby memorandum, Nov. 25, 1963, White House Diary.

2. File "Remarks," Joint Session of Congress, Nov. 27, 1963.

3. Bundy to president, Dec. 2, 1963, White House Diary.

4. Partial transcript in White House Diary, Dec. 3, 1963; Neil MacNeil, *Dirksen: Portrait of a Public Man* (New York: World, 1970), p. 227; Dick Nelson memorandum, Dec. 4, 1963, and Rusk to president, Dec. 4, 1963, White House Diary.

5. Bundy to president, Dec. 6, 1963, White House Diary.

6. Bundy to president, Dec. 12, 1963, White House Diary.

7. Jenkins to Edwin L. Weisl, Dec. 18, 1963; Democratic National Committee papers, box 126; Valenti to addressees, Dec. 9, 1963; State of the Union 1964 file.

8. G. King to Juanita Roberts, Dec. 20, 1963, White House Diary; President to Speaker, Dec. 23, 1963, EX/FG1.

9. J. Frank Dobie to president, Dec. 29, 1963, EX/FG1; William A. Mindak and Gerald D. Hursh, in *The Kennedy Assassination*, ed. Bradley S. Greenberg and Edwin B. Parker (Stanford, Calif.: Stanford University Press, 1965), pp. 137, 141.

10. Sidney Verba, in *Kennedy Assassination*, pp. 350–351.

11. R. A. Dungan to president, Dec. 13, 1963, FG2/Eisenhower.

12. "The 1964 Johnson Legislative Program," 34 pages, n.d. (filed Jan. 20, 1964), EX/FG1.

13. Lyndon Baines Johnson, *The Vantage Point: Perspectives of the Presidency, 1963–1969* (New York: Holt, Rinehart & Winston, 1971), pp. 39–41.

14. Busby backgrounder, Dec. 30, 1963, EX/FG1.

15. Special Studies Project, Rockefeller Brothers Fund, *The Challenge to America: Its Economic and Social Aspects* (Garden City, N.Y.: Doubleday, 1958).

16. In Carl M. Brauer, "Kennedy, Johnson, and the War on Poverty," *Journal of American History* 69 (June 1982): 115.

17. John C. Donovan, "A President's War on Poverty," in *The Presidential Advisory System* (Boston: Little, Brown, 1978), p. 209.

18. Hubert H. Humphrey, *The Education of a Public Man: My Life and Politics* (Garden City, N.Y.: Doubleday, 1976), pp. 410–411.

19. William E. Leuchtenburg, "The Legacy of FDR," *Wilson Quarterly,* Spring 1982; Fred Panzer to Jake Jacobsen, Nov. 26, 1966, EX/WE9.

20. John Bibby and Roger Davidson, *On Capitol Hill* (New York: Holt, Rinehart & Winston, 1967), pp. 225–230; Arthur M. Schlesinger, Jr., *A Thousand Days* (Boston: Houghton Mifflin, 1965), p. 1012.

21. In "The Office of Economic Opportunity during the Administration of Lyndon B. Johnson, November 1963–January 1969," manuscript, Johnson Papers; TRB, *New Republic,* Mar. 14, 1964, p. 2.

22. Fortas to Jenkins, quoting Mary Lasker, Mar. 28, 1964, EX/FG165; Vaughn Davis Bornet, *California Social Welfare* (Englewood Cliffs, N.J.: Prentice-Hall, 1956).

23. Harrell R. Rogers, Jr., *Poverty amid Plenty* (Reading, Mass.: Addison-Wesley, 1979), p. 19; John C. Donovan, *The Politics of Poverty* (Indianapolis: Bobbs-Merrill, 1973).

24. Daniel P. Moynihan, "What Is Community Action?" *Public Interest* 5 (Fall 1966): 3–8.

25. Donovan, "President's War," p. 217; Daniel P. Moynihan, *Maximum Feasible Misunderstanding* (New York: Free Press, 1970), p. 94.

26. Lawrence M. Friedman, *Government and Slum Housing: A Century of Frustration* (Chicago: Rand McNally, 1968), p. 180.

27. Sar Levitan, "The Myth and the Pendulum," in *The Presidency and Congress* (Austin, Tex.: LBJ School of Public Affairs, 1979), p. 190.

28. Johnson, *Vantage Point,* p. 81.

29. Interview by Kathleen Patterson, *Kansas City Star,* Jan. 4, 1976.

CHAPTER 4
ENLARGING ON AN INHERITANCE IN SOUTHEAST ASIA

1. Speech in Bangkok, Oct. 19, 1966; text of letter is in Lyndon Baines Johnson, *The Vantage Point* (New York: Holt, Rinehart & Winston, 1971), app. A.I., p. 573.

2. George C. Herring, "The War In Vietnam," in *Exploring the Johnson Years,* ed. Robert A. Divine (Austin: University of Texas Press, 1981), pp. 27–82, gives titles; also Norman Podhoretz, *Why We Were in Vietnam* (New York: Simon & Schuster, 1982).

3. Text of May 23, 1961, is in William S. White, *The Professional: Lyndon B. Johnson* (Boston: Houghton Mifflin, 1964), p. 240.

4. Lady Bird Johnson to Madame Nhu, Feb. 4, 1964, National Security Files, Head of State, Johnson Library.

5. Harvey DeWeerd, "The Triumph of the Limiters: Korea," RAND P-3949, Oct. 1968, p. 2; Republican Committee on Programs and Progress, *Decisions for a Better America* (Garden City, N.Y.: Doubleday, 1960), p. 185; Milton Eisenhower reminiscence, Nov. 1969, p. 29; Arthur Larson, *Eisenhower as Ex-President* (New York: Scribners', 1968), pp. 185–191; Rusk and McNamara to

president, Nov. 11, 1961; New York Times, *The Pentagon Papers* (New York: Bantam Books, 1971), p. 151.

6. Johnson, *Vantage Point*, p. 116; Hubert H. Humphrey, *The Education of a Public Man: My Life and Politics* (Garden City, N.Y.: Doubleday, 1976), p. 340.

7. Ronald Steel, *Walter Lippmann and the American Century* (Boston: Little, Brown, 1980), pp. 550, 556; Anthony Howard, "Lippmann v. Johnson," *Observer*, May 21, 1967, p. 11.

8. Lodge to Rusk, Dec. 13, 1963; Thomas L. Hughes, State, Jan. 20, 1964; and Hilsman to Rusk, n.d. (Mar. 14, 1964)—all in Vietnam Country File, National Security Files, Johnson Library (hereafter cited as Vietnam).

9. Mansfield address at Michigan State University, June 10, 1962, "Observations on Vietnam," Aug. 19, 1963, carbons to Johnson, Vietnam.

10. Mansfield to president, Jan 6, 1964, and Rusk and McNamara to president, Jan. 7 or 8, 1964, Vietnam.

11. Mansfield to president, Feb. 1, 1964, Vietnam; James Reston, "The Tragedy of Skepticism," *New York Times*, Oct. 2, 1966.

12. William Colby and Peter Forbath, *Honorable Men* (New York: Simon & Schuster, 1978), pp. 222, 226; Cronkite interview, Feb. 6, 1970.

13. Interviews cited in Merle Miller, *Lyndon* (New York: Putnam's, 1980), pp. 380–381; William P. Bundy reminiscence, May 26, 1969, p. 14; Theodore Sorensen, *Kennedy* (New York: Harper & Row, 1965), p. 654; *Public Papers, Kennedy*, 1963, p. 893; Reston, *New York Times*, June 10, 1979; Kennedy press conference, Mar. 6, 1963; Wallace J. Thies, *When Governments Collide: Coercion and Diplomacy in the Vietnam Conflict, 1964–1968* (Berkeley: University of California Press, 1980), p. 21.

14. Hilsman to Rusk, Mar. 14, 1964, with Bundy to president, Mar. 18, 1964, Vietnam. For NSC 263 of Oct. 11, 1963, and 273 of Nov. 26, 1963, both declassified in 1976, see Documents of the NSC, 1947–1977, microfilm (Washington, D.C.: University Publications of America, Inc., 1980); Roger Hilsman letter, *Atlantic*, May 1982, p. 4.

15. NSC 280, declassified in 1977, is in *Documents . . . NSC*; James Todd Hayes, "Lyndon Baines Johnson's Public Defense of the Vietnam War, 1964–1969: The Evolution of a Rhetorical Position" (Ph.D. diss., University of Wisconsin, 1975), pp. 204–220.

16. Edgar Eugene Robinson, "America and the World," *Commonwealth*, Dec. 8, 1967.

17. Milton Eisenhower to author, July 7, 1982.

18. William P. Bundy reminiscence, May 26, 1969, pp. 11–12.

19. Rusk to Lodge, Dec. 6, 1963, CIA Situation Appraisals, Nov./Dec. 1963, Vietnam; Warren I. Cohen, *Dean Rusk* (Totowa, N.J.: Cooper Square Publishers, 1980), p. 191.

20. Forrestal to president, Dec. 11, 1963, Vietnam.

21. CIA Situation Appraisal 8–14, Dec. 1963, Vietnam.

22. Ball to Lodge, Dec. 16, 1963, Vietnam.

23. In Gareth Porter, ed., *Vietnam: The Definitive Documentation of Human Decisions* (Stanfordville, N.Y.: Coleman, 1979), pp. 221-223.

24. McNamara report of Dec. 21, 1963, in Porter, *Vietnam;* McCone to president, Dec. 21, 1963, Vietnam.

25. President to Symington, Feb. 19, 1964, EX/CO312/FG2/JFK; president to Minh, Feb. 12, 1964, National Security Files, Head of State; Thies, *When Governments Collide*, p. 23.

26. In James Pinckney Harrison, *The Endless War* (New York: Free Press, 1982), p. 247.

27. McNamara to president, Mar. 16, 1964, Vietnam; most open documents in these files were declassified in 1975.

28. Gen. Maxwell Taylor to McNamara, Jan. 22, 1964; *Pentagon Papers* (New York: Quadrangle Books, 1971), pp. 282-285; president to Vietnam students, Mar. 25, 1964, National Security Files, Head of State.

29. Outline filed June 2, 1964, EX/CO312/PR15-7.

30. Herbert Y. Schandler, *The Unmaking of a President: Lyndon Johnson and Vietnam* (Princeton, N.J.: Princeton University Press, 1977), p. 5; Mark A. Stoler, "Aiken, Mansfield and the Tonkin Gulf Crisis," *Vermont History,* Spring 1982, pp. 80-94.

31. George C. Herring, *America's Longest War: The United States and Vietnam, 1950-1975* (New York: Wiley, 1979), pp. 121-122.

32. Guenter Lewy, *America in Vietnam* (New York: Oxford University Press, 1978), p. 36; *Pentagon Papers*, p. 303n.

33. William Bundy memorandum for discussion, June 10, 1964, in Porter, *Vietnam*, pp. 281-283.

34. Sharp to JCS, Aug. 17, 1964, in Porter, *Vietnam*, pp. 315-318.

35. Moyers to president, July 3, 1964, PL6/Republican Party; McNamara to president, Aug. 4, 1964, EX/CO312; Johnson, *Vantage Point*, p. 117; Carl Rowan to president, Aug. 6 and 7, 1964, EX/CO312.

36. Herring, *America's Longest War*, p. 130.

37. Ibid., p. 134.

38. NSC memorandum 328, Apr. 6, 1965, signed by McGeorge Bundy, in Documents of the National Security Council, 1947-1977.

39. Letters in EX/ND19/CO312.

40. Speech to Commonwealth Club of California, May 7, 1965, *Commonwealth*, May 17, 1965.

41. Thies, *When Governments Collide*, chaps. 1 and 8.

42. AP from Peking, *Oregonian*, July 31, 1979.

43. TRB, *New Republic*, Dec. 11, 1965, p. 2.

44. Thomas E. Dewey to president, Nov. 18, 1965, Dewey file; Ezra Taft Benson to president, Dec. 22, 1965, Benson file; Oliver Quale & Co. study 288, Sept. 1965, and Harris to White House, June 17, 1965, PR16; George Ball to president, July 1, 1965; *Pentagon Papers*, pp. 449-454.

45. TRB, *New Republic*, Aug. 7, 1965, p. 2.

46. Farley to president, Dec. 29, 1965, EX/HO7.

47. See *National Observer*'s series in spring 1965.

48. Based on confidential sources and reading at RAND, 1959–1963 and 1969.

49. Thies, *When Governments Collide*, Introduction; also Schelling file, Johnson Library, and Thomas C. Schelling, *Arms and Influence* (New Haven, Conn.: Yale University Press, 1966).

50. Text in Humphrey, *Education of a Public Man*, pp. 320–324.

51. Cohen, *Dean Rusk*, pp. 254–257; Truman quote from Harriman to president, Apr. 26, 1965, EX/FG2/Krim.

52. Larry Berman, *Planning a Tragedy: The Americanization of the War in Vietnam* (New York: Norton, 1982).

53. See civilian and military casualty tables in Lewy, *America in Vietnam*, app. I.

CHAPTER 5
WINNING BIG: 1964

1. White House Diary, Nov. and Dec. 1963.

2. UCRL to president, Nov. 26, 1963, White House Diary.

3. Milton Eisenhower reminiscence, Nov. 1969, p. 8.

4. Harris Wofford, *Of Kennedys and Kings: Making Sense of the Sixties* (New York: Farrar, Straus, Giroux, 1980), and Milton Viorst, *Fire in the Streets: America in the 1960s* (New York: Simon & Schuster, 1979), for example.

5. Closing remarks in *Equal Opportunity in the United States* (Austin: University of Texas Press, 1973), p. 163.

6. Transcription of taping, Johnson with Sorensen, June 3, 1963, Ac 66-1, G. Reedy Papers, Johnson Library.

7. Steven F. Lawson, "Civil Rights," in *Exploring the Johnson Years*, ed. Robert A. Divine (Austin: University of Texas Press, 1981), pp. 93–95; Joseph Califano, *A Presidential Nation* (New York: Norton, 1975), p. 215.

8. Barbara Jordan and Shelby Hearon, *Barbara Jordan: A Self-Portrait* (Garden City, N.Y.: Doubleday, 1979), p. 128.

9. Daniel Berman, *A Bill Becomes a Law* (New York: Macmillan, 1966).

10. Edgar Berman, M.D., *Hubert* (New York: Putnam's, 1979), p. 51; O'Brien to Dirksen, Aug. 17, 1964, Dirksen file; president to Eisenhower, Mar. 16, 1965, FG2/Eisenhower; *Memorial Services . . . Everett McKinley Dirksen* (Washington, D.C.: Government Printing Office, 1970).

11. President to Justin G. Turner, July 23, 1964, EX/FG2/Kennedy; Rowland Evans and Robert Novak, *Lyndon B. Johnson: The Exercise of Power* (New York: New American Library, 1966), p. 378.

12. T. V. Smith, "What It Takes to Be a Great President," *New York Times Magazine*, July 20, 1952, p. 7.

13. Evans and Novak, *Lyndon B. Johnson*, pp. 424–426.

14. Jack Valenti, *A Very Human President* (New York: Norton, 1975), p. 85n.

15. William S. White, *The Professional: Lyndon B. Johnson* (Boston: Houghton Mifflin, 1964), chap. 4, "What Manner of Man?"

16. Sam Houston Johnson, *My Brother Lyndon* (New York: Cowles, 1969), p. 162.

17. Outline, n.d. (filed June 2, 1964), EX/CO312.

18. Valenti, *Very Human President*, pp. 153–154; Lady Bird Johnson, *A White House Diary* (New York: Holt, Rinehart & Winston, 1970), p. 192.

19. Harriman to president, July 13, 1964, EX/FG2/Kennedy; paraphrase by Lt. Gen. M. S. Carter to president, July 29, 1964, EX/FG2/Truman.

20. Barry Goldwater, *With No Apologies* (New York: Morrow, 1979), pp. 156, 160.

21. Milton Eisenhower reminiscence, Nov. 1969, p. 5.

22. Hubert H. Humphrey, *The Education of a Public Man: My Life and Politics* (Garden City, N.Y.: Doubleday, 1976), pp. 289–308; Goldwater, *With No Apologies*, pp. 191–192.

23. Goldwater, *With No Apologies*, pp. 192–193.

24. File Republicans for Johnson, EX/PL; Valenti, *Very Human President*, pp. 146–147; TRB, *New Republic*, Sept. 26, 1964, p. 2.

25. John H. Kessel, *Presidential Campaign Politics: Coalition Strategies and Citizen Response* (Hammond, Ill.: Dorsey Press, 1980), p. 134.

26. Dick Scanmon to Cliff Carter, Sept. 10, 1964, EX/FG2/Kennedy.

27. Harriman to president, Sept. 25, 1964, Harriman file.

28. Jon Louis Ericson, "The Reporting by the Prestige Press of Goldwater" (Ph.D. diss., University of Wisconsin, 1966), p. 175.

29. Robert Spero, *The Duping of the American Voter: Dishonesty and Deception in Presidential Television Advertising* (New York: Lippincott & Crowell, 1980), pp. 74–75.

30. Valenti, *Very Human President*, p. 204.

31. The Rev. Martin Luther King, Sr., *Daddy King: An Autobiography* (New York: Morrow, 1980), p. 138.

32. Valenti to John Steinbeck, Nov. 10, 1964, Steinbeck file; Wilkins to president, Nov. 5, 1964, PP2-2/ST32; Cater to president, Dec. 30, 1966, EX/FG2/Eisenhower.

33. *U.S. News and World Report*, June 7, 1965, p. 51.

34. Clifford to president, Nov. 5, 1964, EX/PP2/2/FG216; Truman to president, Aug. 27 and Sept. 4, 1964, EX/FG2/Truman.

CHAPTER 6
SECOND MANDATE: ENDORSED WITH VOTES

1. Manuscript. n.d., "Policy Formulation during the Johnson Administration," Gaither Papers, box 17, Johnson Library.

2. Quoted in Norman C. Thomas and Harold L. Wolman, "Policy For-

mulation in the Institutionalized Presidency," in *The Presidential Advisory System* (Boston: Little, Brown, 1979), pp. 135 ff.

3. Ibid., p. 142; "Task Force Reports," a finding aid, Johnson Library.

4. Elizabeth B. Drew, "On Giving Oneself a Hotfoot: Government by Commission," *Atlantic*, May 1968, pp. 45–49.

5. Valenti to president, Dec. 26, 1965, EX/SP204; Willard Wirtz to Moyers, Jan. 4, 1965, State of the Union 1965; Harry McPherson, *A Political Education* (Boston: Little, Brown, 1972), pp. 296–297, 300.

6. DNC Editors' News Service, Jan. 5, 1965, Territo files.

7. Lyndon Johnson, *The Vantage Point* (New York: Holt, Rinehart & Winston, 1971), p. 219n.

8. Ibid.

9. Quoted in Merle Miller, *Lyndon* (New York: Putnam's, 1980), p. 27; unedited interview by Robert MacKay, May 21, 1965, pp. 13–14; Thomas E. Cronin, "The Presidency and Education," *Phi Delta Kappan* 49 (Feb. 1968): 295; Humphrey, quoted in Miller, *Lyndon*, p. 407.

10. President to Truman, May 13, 1965, FG2/Truman.

11. Congressional Quarterly, *Congress and the Nation, 1965–1968* (Washington, D.C.: Congressional Quarterly Service, 1969), 2:710.

12. *Chronicle of Higher Education*, Jan. 19, 1973, p. 3.

13. Dr. Michael DeBakey reminiscence, June 29, 1969, pp. 13–14.

14. University of Chicago Center for Health Administration Study, *Oregonian*, Jan. 12, 1978.

15. *New York Times*, Feb. 11, 1979.

16. *Barron's*, Jan. 25, 1982, p. 7.

17. Califano reminiscence, June 11, 1973, pp. 1–3.

18. Califano to Prof. T. C. Schelling, June 7, 1966, EX/WE9.

19. Jack Valenti, *A Very Human President* (New York: Norton, 1975), p. 178.

20. Everett McKinley Dirksen reminiscence, May 8, 1968, p. 12, and July 30, 1969, p. 3.

21. Califano reminiscence, June 11, 1973, pp. 10–14.

22. Johnson reminiscence, Sept. 28, 1970, pp. 3–4.

23. Cabinet memorandum, Oct. 16, 1967.

24. "GER" memorandum, Apr. 1, 1964, FG2/Eisenhower; also file EX/FG400/MC.

25. Barry Goldwater, *With No Apologies* (New York: Morrow, 1979), p. 200; *Saturday Review*, Nov. 6, 1971, p. 41.

26. Robert A. Divine, "The Struggle over Foreign Policy," in *The Presidency and the Congress* (Austin: LBJ School of Public Affairs, 1979), pp. 174–176, 209–215.

27. Robert Hardesty and Carl Albert, in *The Presidency and the Congress*, pp. 383, 404; the *Congressional Record* for Oct. 22, 1966, contains penetrating assessments.

28. Johnson reminiscence, Sept. 28, 1970, p. 10.

29. Graham memorandum, HC/106/G674; and Richard Tanner Johnson,

Managing the White House (New York: Harper & Row, 1974), chap. 6; Kermit Gordon, "The Budget Director," in *Presidential Advisory System*, p. 58.

30. Quoted in Miller, *Lyndon*, p. 443.

31. Messages, Mar. 11, 1967, and Jan. 29, 1968.

32. See David Novick, *Efficiency and Economy in Government through New Budgeting Procedures*, RAND R-154, Feb. 1, 1954; Charles Hitch and Roland McKean, *The Economics of Defense in the Nuclear Age*, RAND R-246, Mar. 1960.

33. Liz Carpenter column, *New York Times*, Jan. 22, 1974; film dialogue, reported in *Austin American-Statesman*, Jan. 16, 1983.

34. India Edwards reminiscence, Feb. 4, 1969, p. 5.

35. Udall to Moyers, Jan. 2, 1965, State of the Union 1965.

36. *Public Papers*, 1965, pp. 155–165.

37. Lady Bird Johnson, *A White House Diary* (New York: Holt, Rinehart & Winston, 1970), p. 241.

38. *Beauty for America*, Proceedings, White House Conference on Natural Beauty (Washington, D.C.: Government Printing Office), May 24–25, 1965, pp. 17–22.

39. Johnson, *Vantage Point*, pp. 336–337.

40. *New York Times*, May 27, 1979.

41. Dr. Michael DeBakey reminiscence, June 29, 1969, p. 34.

42. Confirmed by telephone call to Mrs. Lasker, Sept. 5, 1982.

43. John L. Sweeney, in Miller, *Lyndon*, p. 353; Rockefeller to president, Jan. 19, 1967, and reply, Jan. 26, 1967, EX/FG738.

44. Beatrice Hort Holmes, *History of Federal Water Resources Programs and Policies, 1961–70* (Washington, D.C.: Government Printing Office, 1979).

45. Senate Committee on Interior and Insular Affairs, et al., *Congressional White Paper on a National Policy for the Environment*, 90th Cong., 2d sess., Oct. 1968; Fred Bohen to Califano, Dec. 1, 1967, Statements container 52.

46. John P. Crevelli, "The Final Act of the Greatest Conservation President," *Prologue* 12 (Winter 1980): 173–191; Johnson, *Vantage Point*, pp. 562–563; William O. Douglas, *The Autobiography of William O. Douglas: The Court Years* (New York: Random House, 1980), p. 318; Emmette S. Redford and Marlan Blissett, *Organizing the Executive Branch: The Johnson Presidency* (Chicago: University of Chicago Press, 1981), p. 217.

CHAPTER 7
IN THIS CORNER: THE MEDIA

1. Steinbeck to Moyers, Sept. 3, 1966; and Christian to president, Aug. 10, 1967, Steinbeck file.

2. Phil G. Goulding, *Confirm or Deny* (New York: Harper & Row, 1970), p. xii.

3. Rowland Evans and Robert Novak, *Lyndon B. Johnson: The Exercise of Power* (New York: New American Library, 1966), p. 412; Eric F. Goldman, *The*

Tragedy of Lyndon Johnson (New York: Knopf, 1968), pp. 191–192; David Halberstam, *The Powers That Be* (New York: Knopf, 1979), p. 6.

4. Wallace Carroll et al., "Press Conferences," *New York Times Magazine,* Feb. 21, 1960, pp. 16–17; "The President's Press Conference," manuscript, Brookings Institution, Nov. 16, 1960, and Rowe to Salinger, Feb. 24, 1964, FG2/Former Presidents; Salinger to president, with biographies and pictures, Dec. 12, 1963, White House Diary.

5. Watson to president, Apr. 2, 1966, EX/FG2/Eisenhower; Donald R. Burkholder, "The Caretakers of the Presidential Image" (Ph.D. diss., Wayne State University, 1973), pp. 3, 92–95.

6. Sam Houston Johnson, *My Brother Lyndon* (New York: Cowles, 1969), p. 194; Goulding, *Confirm or Deny,* p. 52.

7. James Deakin, *Lyndon Johnson's Credibility Gap* (Washington, D.C.: Public Affairs Press, 1968), pp. 1–26; Richard Strout, *Christian Science Monitor,* Dec. 3, 1982; Wilbur Cohen reminiscence, Mar. 2, 1969, p. 5. For some examples of excesses in language and conduct see Bill Gulley, *Breaking Cover* (New York: Simon & Schuster, 1980), pp. 86, 76, 57, 75, 111, 114, 121 126; Reedy, *Lyndon B. Johnson;* Ronnie Dugger, *The Politician* (New York: Norton, 1981), p. 21; and Merle Miller, *Lyndon* (New York: Putnam's, 1980), p. 534; on "style" see Arthur Krock, *Memoirs* (New York: Funk & Wagnalls, 1968), p. 392.

8. O'Brien to president, June 15, 1964, PL6/Republican Party.

9. Panzer to president, Jan. 23, 1967, EX/FG1.

10. Kintner to president, May 9, 1967, EX/PR18; TRB, *New Republic,* Sept. 9, 1967, p. 4.

11. *Parade,* May 2, 1982, p. 6; Charles Frankel, *High on Foggy Bottom* (New York: Harper & Row, 1968), p. 231.

12. Deakin, *Credibility Gap,* pp. 13, 61; Edith Efron, *The News Twisters* (New York: Manor Books, 1972), p. 47; James Reston, *New York Times,* Apr. 12, 1978.

13. David S. Broder, reviewing Stephen Hess, *The Washington Reporters* (Washington, D.C.: Brookings Institution, 1981), in *Oregonian,* Mar. 25, 1981; Rowe to president, Apr. 9, 1964, EX/PR18; Johnson, *My Brother Lyndon,* p. 231.

14. George E. Reedy, *The Twilight of the Presidency* (New York: World, 1970), p. 100; Ronald Steel, *Walter Lippmann and the American Century* (New York: Atlantic, Little, Brown, 1980), chaps. 43 and 44; Bundy to Lippmann, Apr. 28, 1965, and Bundy to Rev. Don Falkenberg, May 5, 1965, Name file, EX/ND19/CO312.

15. Kintner to president, Aug. 12, 1966, EX/PR18; Lyndon Baines Johnson, *The Vantage Point* (New York: Holt, Rinehart & Winston, 1971), p. 96.

16. Cater to president, Dec. 5, 1967, Lippmann file; uncut, complete film in Johnson Library.

17. Reedy, *Twilight;* Burkholder, "Caretakers," pp. 77–92; George Reedy, *Lyndon B. Johnson: A Memoir* (New York: Andrews & McMeel, 1982), pp. 51, 67.

18. Joe Laitin to president, May 25, 1966, and memorandum, Dec. 12, 1966, and Kintner to president, May 5, 1967, EX/FG2/Eisenhower; Stephen Cooper,

"A Rhetorical Assessment of Lyndon Johnson's Presidential Press Conferences" (Ph.D. diss., Louisiana State University, 1972), pp. 4, 89.

19. Undated memorandum (c. Sept. 1968), Fortas-Thornberry chronological file.

20. Cooper, "Press Conferences," pp. 6, 89, v, vi.

21. TRB, *New Republic*, Mar. 11, 1967, p. 4.

22. Fortas to Jenkins, Mar. 26, 1964, and Robert Spivak memorandum, Apr. 3, 1964, EX/FG1.

23. Quoted in Halberstam, *Powers That Be*, p. 596; Patrick O'Donovan of the *London Observer*; William L. Rivers, "The Press: The Other Government," *Stanford Magazine*, Summer 1982, p. 19.

24. Moyers to Graff, July 9, 1965, Graff file; Stewart Alsop, *The Center: People and Power in Political Washington* (New York: Harper & Row, 1968), pp. 60–61; cabinet minutes, Apr. 3, 1968; Deakin, *Credibility Gap*, p. 63.

25. Robert M. Entman, in *Politics and the Oval Office*, ed. Arnold J. Meltser (San Francisco: Institute for Contemporary Studies, 1981); Doris Kearns Goodwin, ed., *The Johnson Press Conferences* (New York: Earl M. Coleman, 1978), 1:ix, viii.

26. Gulley, *Breaking Cover*, p. 70; Johnson, *My Brother Lyndon*, p. 251; president to Eisenhower, Dec. 5, 1966, EX/FG2/Eisenhower; George Christian, quoted in Richard Nixon, *Memoirs* (New York: Grosset & Dunlap, 1978), p. 412.

27. Johnson reminiscence, Sept. 28, 1970, 1:11, 2:1–4.

28. Jack Valenti, *A Very Human President* (New York: Norton, 1975), p. 103; Tom Johnson to president, Aug. 30, 1967, PR16/Confidential; Bob Fleming to president, Jan. 25, 1968, EX/PR18; Watson to president, Mar. 3, 1965, FG2/Truman; Leo Janos, "The Last Days of the President," *Atlantic*, July 1973, p. 36; Reedy, *Lyndon B. Johnson*, p. x.

29. *Time*, Dec. 6, 1982, p. 91; Hubert H. Humphrey, *The Education of a Public Man: My Life and Politics* (Garden City, N.Y.: Doubleday, 1976), p. 427.

30. Quoted in Miller, *Lyndon*, p. 343; Frank Cormier, *LBJ: The Way He Was* (Garden City, N.Y.: Doubleday, 1977); William C. Spragens, "The Myth of the Johnson 'Credibility Gap,' " *Presidential Studies Quarterly*, Fall 1980.

CHAPTER 8
AMERICA: CUSTODIAN OF THE WORLD

1. Briefing memorandum, Dec. 12, 1963, White House Diary.

2. Walt Whitman Rostow, *Diffusion of Power* (New York: Macmillan, 1972), p. 423.

3. Rutherford M. Poats reminiscence, Nov. 18, 1968, pp. 1–6.

4. Rostow, *Diffusion of Power*, table 31-1, p. 421.

5. George C. McGhee reminiscence, Mar. 24, 1975, p. 3.

6. List of July 2, 1964, PL6-2, Democratic Party Files, Johnson Library; Angier Biddle Duke to president, June 25, 1964, EX/FG2/Kennedy; briefing card,

Nov. 26, 1963, White House Diary; Budapest MTI International Service (in French), Dec. 23, 1963, EX/FG1.

7. Jackie Kennedy to N. Khrushchev, Dec. 1, 1963, Museum file.

8. *New York Times*, Nov. 24, 1963; Robert H. Estabrook, in *Washington Post*, Nov. 28, 1963.

9. "Worldwide Reaction to the First Month, Johnson Administration," USIA, Dec. 24, 1963, EX/FG1.

10. Bundy to president, confidential, Jan. 3, 1965, State of the Union 1965; memorandum from Paris, n.d., passed to president on Nov. 15, 1965, EX/FO5.

11. Busby backgrounder, late Dec. 1963, EX/FG1.

12. Lyndon Baines Johnson, *The Vantage Point* (New York: Holt, Rinehart & Winston, 1971), p. 23; David Bruce reminiscence, Dec. 9, 1971, p. 7.

13. Valenti to president, with CIA estimates, Mar. 5, 1966, EX/CO50-2.

14. Milton Eisenhower reminiscence, Nov. 1969, pp. 8–10.

15. Jerome Levinson and Juan de Onis, *The Alliance That Lost Its Way* (Chicago: University of Chicago Press, 1970); Walter LeFeber, "Latin American Policy," in *Exploring the Johnson Years*, ed. Robert A. Divine (Austin: University of Texas Press, 1981), p. 85.

16. See John Johnson, *The Role of the Military in Underdeveloped Countries* (Princeton, N.J.: Princeton University Press, 1962).

17. Meanwhile see Phyllis Parker, *Brazil and the Quiet Revolution* (Austin: University of Texas Press, 1964).

18. Johnson, *Vantage Point*, pp. 349–351; Rostow, *Diffusion of Power*, p. 425.

19. Fortas to president, Apr. 14, 1967, Fortas file.

20. Farley to president, Nov. 29, 1963, EX/FOS/CO1-8.

21. Angel Milan and Juan Caanovas to president, Apr. 29, 1965, EX/ND19/CO62.

22. Editorial, *New York Daily News*, May 12, 1965; Carl Rowan survey, to president, May 2, 1965, EX/ND19/CO62.

23. Moyers to Goodwin, n.d., ND19/CO62.

24. John C. Wiley to *Washington Post*, May 11, 1965.

25. Valenti to president, May 7 and 19, 1965, with May 24, 1965, *Newsweek*, Goldberg file and EX/ND19/CO62; Valenti and Cater to president, May 12, 1965, and Valenti to president, Friday, May 14, 1965, ND19/CO62.

26. Valenti to president, May 18, 1965, EX/ND19/CO62; Valenti to president, May 27, 1965, Fortas file.

27. Rostow, *Diffusion of Power*, pp. 411–415.

28. Nitze reminiscence, Dec. 26, 1968, pp. 5–6; Gen. Andrew J. Goodpaster reminiscence, June 21, 1971, p. 28; Milton Eisenhower reminiscence, pp. 18–19.

29. Bundy to Norman Thomas, July 1, 1965, PE 15-7; Jerome Slater, *Intervention and Negotiation* (New York: Harper & Row, 1970); LaFeber, "Latin American Policy," p. 75.

30. *A New China Policy: Some Quaker Proposals*, a report prepared for the American Friends Service Committee (New Haven, Conn.: Yale University Press, 1965); *New York Times*, Apr. 22, 1964.

31. Paul Nitze reminiscence, Dec. 10, 1968, pp. 11–12.

32. Draft in Territo files, box 1407.

33. James C. Thomson, Jr., "How Could Vietnam Happen?" *Atlantic,* Apr. 1968, p. 53.

34. G. Mennen Williams to Moyers, Dec. 4, 1963, Secret, White House Diary.

35. Atlanta journalist Ralph McGill to president, Apr. 4, 1967, EX/FO5.

36. Lucius D. Battle reminiscence, Dec. 5, 1968, pp. 3, 14; William Colby and Peter Forbath, *Honorable Men* (New York: Simon & Schuster, 1978), p. 138; Harriman to president, Nov. 14, 1966, Harriman file.

37. In Felix Frankfurter to president, June 24, 1964, Frankfurter file.

38. Rostow, *Diffusion of Power,* p. 415.

39. Fortas to president, July 6, 1967, Fortas-Thornberry file.

40. Johnson, *Vantage Point,* chap. 13; Rostow, *Diffusion of Power,* pp. 415–421.

41. *Weekly Compilation of Presidential Documents,* June 12, 1967, pp. 832–833.

42. Phil G. Goulding, *Confirm or Deny* (New York: Harper & Row, 1970), chap. 4.

43. James M. Ennes, Jr., *Assault on the "Liberty": The True Story of the Israeli Attack on an American Intelligence Ship* (New York: Random House, 1979); *Christian Science Monitor,* June 4, 1982, Frank Maria letter to *Monitor,* Oct. 2, 1980; Richard K. Smith, "The Violation of the *Liberty," U.S. Naval Institute Proceedings,* June 1978, pp. 62–73. Also, cleared portions of National Security Files: Israel, Middle East Crisis; NSC history of that crisis; and special committee file "Liberty," Johnson Library. Much is still classified.

44. Chaim Herzog, *The Arab-Israeli Wars* (New York: Random House, 1982), p. 166; Smith, "Violation of the *Liberty,"* p. 69.

45. Rostow, *Diffusion of Power,* pp. 418–419.

46. Quoted in James L. Payne, *The American Threat: The Fear of War as an Instrument of Foreign Policy* (Chicago: Markham, 1970), pp. 128–129.

47. Seyom Brown, "The Great Foreign Policy Debate," RAND P-3815, Apr. 1968, pp. 4–5.

48. Rostow to president, Sept. 22, 1966, Goldberg file.

49. President to C. Stanley Wood of Oakland, Calif., Mar. 24, 1966, Goldberg file.

50. *Oregonian,* Nov. 20, 1980. For reasons see Juliana G. Pilon, "Through the Looking Glass: The Political Culture of the U.N.," *Heritage Foundation Backgrounder,* 206 (Aug. 30, 1982).

51. In J. R. Jones to president, Dec. 12, 1968, EX/CO.

52. Rostow to president, Jan. 13, 1968, FO/PR15-7.

53. President to Robert Hardesty, in Miller, *Lyndon,* p. 427.

54. *New York Times,* Dec. 13, 1970; a contemporary survey is Edgar Eugene Robinson, "Lyndon B. Johnson: Extensions of Power," in *Powers of the President in Foreign Affairs,* ed. Edgar Eugene Robinson (San Francisco: Commonwealth Club, 1966), pp. 199–244.

55. Eugene V. Rostow, "President Johnson's Foreign Policy," in *To Heal and to Build: The Programs of Lyndon B. Johnson*, ed. James McGregor Burns (New York: McGraw-Hill, 1968), p. 122.

56. See Paul M. Kattenburg, *The Vietnam Trauma in American Foreign Policy, 1945–1980* (New York: Transaction Books, 1980).

CHAPTER 9

BUILDING POWER ON EARTH AND IN SPACE

1. Mortin H. Halperin, "The Gaither Committee and the Policy Process," in *The Presidential Advisory System* (Boston: Little, Brown, 1979), pp. 185–208; Panel II, Special Studies Project, *International Security and Military Aspect* (Garden City, N.Y.: Doubleday, 1958).

2. *New York Times*, Jan. 24, 1958; House Republican Committee, "American Strategy and Strength," *Congressional Record*, 86th Cong., 2d sess. (June 20, 1960), pp. 1–86.

3. Edgar M. Bottome, *The Missile Gap* (Cranbury, N.J.: Associated University Presses, 1971), chap. 6.

4. Paul Nitze reminiscence, Dec. 26, 1968, p. 11.

5. Reliably related to the author in the early 1960s.

6. Herman Kahn, *On Thermonuclear War* (Princeton, N.J.: Princeton University Press, 1960); Leonard C. Lewin, *Report from Iron Mountain on the Possibility and Desirability of Peace* (New York: Dial, 1967), Introduction; see also Bernard Brodie, *Strategy in the Missile Age* (Princeton, N.J.: Princeton University Press, 1959), and Albert Wohlstetter, "The Delicate Balance of Power," *Foreign Affairs*, Jan. 1959, pp. 211–234.

7. See RAND open indexes and E. S. Quade and W. I. Boucher, *System Analysis and Policy Planning: Applications in Defense* (New York: American Elsivier, 1968).

8. Transcription, Johnson with Sorensen, June 3, 1963, Ac 66-1, G. Reedy Papers, Johnson Library.

9. Nitze reminiscence, Nov. 20, 1968, pp. 7–9.

10. McNamara to American Association of Newspaper Editors, Apr. 20, 1963, in his *The Essence of Security* (New York: Harper & Row, 1968), p. 88.

11. Memorandum of Nov. 29, 1963, White House Diary.

12. *Public Papers*, 1963–64, 2:1078–1081.

13. On the neutron bomb see Sam Cohen, *The Truth about the Neutron Bomb* (New York: Morrow, 1983); the present author's RAND oral-history interview of Cohen on the bomb in 1961 remains classified secret; Reinhold Niebuhr, in *New York Times*, Dec. 4, 1970, sketches the history; Yvonne Larsen for National Commission for Excellence in Education, Apr. 10, 1983.

14. *Public Papers*, 1965, 1:62–71.

15. Desmond Ball, *Politics and Force Levels* (Berkeley: University of California Press, 1980), p. 251; Alain C. Enthoven and K. Wayne Smith, *How Much Is*

Enough? (New York: Harper & Row, 1971); Phyllis Schlafly review of Caro's biography of Johnson, Copeley News Service, about Jan. 10, 1983.

16. Facts from "Department of Defense Achievements, 1967," in Rostow to president, State of the Union files.

17. Lyndon Baines Johnson, *The Vantage Point* (New York: Holt, Rinehart & Winston, 1971), p. 475.

18. Walt Whitman Rostow, *The Diffusion of Power* (New York: Macmillan, 1972), table 34-1; Ted Sell of *Washington Post*, in *Oregonian,* Nov. 23, 1969; also *Oregonian,* June 7, 1964.

19. Rostow, *Diffusion of Power*, p. 380; text in *Documents on Disarmament, 1968,* p. 440.

20. Leon Gouré, *Civil Defense in the Soviet Union* (Berkeley: University of California Press, 1962).

21. Nitze reminiscence, Dec. 26, 1968, pp. 12–13; Clark Clifford on CBS's "Face the Nation," Dec. 15, 1968.

22. Henry Kissinger, *White House Years* (Boston: Little, Brown, 1979), p. 197.

23. Ibid., pp. 198, 394.

24. Kintner to president, "Personal," Feb. 18, 1967, FG2/Truman; Richard Nixon, *Memoirs* (New York: Grosset & Dunlap, 1978), p. 489; drafts in CIA Awards Ceremony file, Sept. 18, 1967, Territo files, box 1407, Johnson Library.

25. *New York Times*, Jan. 28, 1977.

26. Ibid., Dec. 25, 1977; *Los Angeles Times*, Feb. 8, 1983.

27. E. Howard Hunt, *Undercover: Memoirs of an American Secret Agent* (New York: Berkeley, 1974), p. 133.

28. Robert S. Boyd, in *San Francisco Examiner*, Apr. 29, 1976.

29. David Culbert, in *Exploring the Johnson Years* (Austin: University of Texas Press, 1981), pp. 235, 246; Bill Gulley, *Breaking Cover* (New York: Simon & Schuster, 1980), pp. 95–103; Johnson Library to Bornet, May 19, 1977, and June 14, 1982.

30. Phil G. Goulding, *Confirm or Deny* (New York: Harper & Row, 1970), p. 33.

31. Draft speeches, Jan. 31 and Feb. 5, 1968, Territo files, box 1407.

32. Johnson, *Vantage Point*, p. 532; Goulding, *Confirm or Deny*, p. 299.

33. Nitze reminiscence, pp. 18–19; Paul Warnke reminiscence, Jan. 15, 1969, p. 26; quoted in Sam Houston Johnson, *My Brother Lyndon* (New York: Cowles, 1969), p. 241.

34. James M. Ennes, Jr., *Assault on the "Liberty": The True Story of the Israeli Attack on an American Intelligence Ship* (New York: Random House, 1979), p. 191; *New York Times*, Jan. 24, 1968; *Washington Post*, June 9, 1982; Ennes to *Oregonian*, June 22, 1982.

35. *Oregonian*, Feb. 13, 1982.

36. Nitze reminiscence, p. 14.

37. Johnson, *Vantage Point*, chap. 12; R. W. Buchheim and associates at RAND, *Space Handbook: Astronautics and Its Applications* (Washington, D.C.: Select Committee on Astronautics and Space Exploration, 1959), sec. 3, "Ap-

plications," especially footnoted 1956–1958 studies by Buchheim, H. A. Lieske, C. Gazley, Jr., Steve Dole, and others; James E. Webb to Bornet, Feb. 8, 1983.

38. *Space Handbook*, p. 283.

39. Joseph M. Goldsen, chairman, *International Political Implications in Outer Space*, RAND R-362-RC, Oct. 22–23, 1959.

40. Goldberg to president, Dec. 20, 1966, Goldberg file.

41. *Weekly Compilation of Presidential Documents*, Dec. 30, 1968, pp. 1749–1750.

42. Project RAND report SM-11827; James M. Beggs, "NASA Today and Tomorrow," *Commonwealth*, Nov. 29, 1982, p. 327.

43. Nixon, *Memoirs*, p. 429; H. Castelo Branco to president, June 18, 1966, Museum file, Johnson Library.

CHAPTER 10
THE GREAT SOCIETY IN LAW AND IN PRACTICE

1. Paul Berman, "Federal Spending on Social Reform," RAND P-6283, Jan. 1979.

2. Califano to president, Dec. 16, 1967, EX/LE.

3. Arthur Krock reminiscence, Nov. 21, 1968, p. 28; *Congress and the Nation* (Washington, D.C.: Congressional Quarterly Service, 1970), p. 625.

4. *Christian Science Monitor*, Aug. 3, 1981.

5. President to Krim, Oct. 13, 1965, Krim file.

6. Carl Albert, in *The Presidency and the Congress* (Austin, Tex.: LBJ School of Public Affairs, 1979), p. 418.

7. Mary A. Golladay, *The Condition of Education* (Washington, D.C.: National Center for Educational Statistics, 1977), vol. 3, pt. 1, pp. 30, 33, 54, 131.

8. *Congress and the Nation, 1965–1968* (Washington, D.C.: Congressional Quarterly Service, 1969), 2:729.

9. Drafts in file Statements: Remarks, Cotulla, Johnson Library.

10. Logan Wilson reminiscence, Nov. 8, 1968, p. 33; "Lasting Effects after Preschool" (Washington, D.C.: Department of Health, Education, and Welfare, 1979); Irving Lazar, "Invest Early for Later Dividends," *Interstate Compact* (Fall 1979); Hugh Davis Graham, "The Transformation of Federal Education Policy," in *Exploring the Johnson Years*, ed. Robert A. Divine (Austin: University of Texas Press, 1981), pp. 170–176; Philip Rulon speech, "The Other Side of LBJ," at meeting of Organization of American Historians, Mar. 26, 1982.

11. Califano reminiscence, June 11, 1973, p. 40; Thomas E. Cronin, "The Presidency and Education," in *The Presidential Advisory System* (Boston: Little, Brown, 1979), p. 228.

12. Daniel Patrick Moynihan, "State vs. Academe," *Harpers*, Dec. 1980, p. 40 (including editorial note).

13. B. F. Brown et al., *The Reform of Secondary Education* (New York: McGraw-Hill, 1973), pp. 2–4; *The Condition of Education* (Washington, D.C.:

Department of Health, Education, and Welfare, National Center for Educational Statistics, 1975).

14. *Oregonian*, Jan. 20, 1983; Professor Diane Ravitch, "'60's Education, '70's Benefits," *New York Times*, June 19, 1978; also issue of Jan. 4, 1981.

15. Hilton Kramer, "A Critic's Final Look Back," *New York Times*, Apr. 11, 1982; Richard L. Coe, "LBJ and Art," *Washington Post*, Jan. 18, 1973; Elise K. Kirk, "Presidents and the Performing Arts," *Dallas Civic Opera Magazine*, Oct. 31–Nov. 5, 1980, p. 72.

16. Bryan T. Downes, "Social and Political Characteristics of Riot Cities," *Social Science Quarterly* 49 (Dec. 1968): 509; Jerome P. Cavanagh to president, July 25, 1967, EX/HU2/ST22; see PR15-7, box 80.

17. Cabinet minutes, Oct. 18, 1967.

18. President to Fortas, Jan. 26, 1965, Fortas file.

19. Robinson to president, Feb. 4, 1965, EX/FG216; Wilkins to president, Jan. 17, 1969, EX/ME1; Marshall to president, Sept. 1, 1967, EX/FG135-3; Clarence Mitchell, Washington director of NAACP, to president, Aug. 12, 1966, EX/HU.

20. Edith Efron, *The News Twisters* (New York: Manor Books, 1972), p. 47; Cater to president, with enclosure, Oct. 11, 1967; cabinet memorandum.

21. President to Mrs. M. L. King, Jr., Apr. 30, 1968, King file; *Oregonian*, Dec. 8, 1978.

22. Earl Warren, *The Memoirs of Earl Warren* (Garden City, N.Y.: Doubleday, 1977), p. 301; Lady Bird Johnson, *A White House Diary* (New York: Holt, Rinehart & Winston, 1970), p. 758; Wilkins to president, Jan. 17, 1969, and reply, Jan. 23, 1969, EX/ME1; David Zarefsky, "Lyndon Johnson Redefines 'Equal Opportunity': The Beginning of Affirmative Action," *Central States Speech Journal*, Summer 1980, pp. 87–88; Donald J. Devine, *The Political Culture of the United States* (Boston: Little, Brown, 1973), p. 335; Bayard Rustin, "Blacks and Electoral Politics," *New York Times*, Jan. 3, 1978.

23. Sava Evans, *The Roots of Women's Liberation in the Civil Rights Movement and the New Left* (New York: Knopf, 1979); *Oregonian*, Jan. 30, 1979; *New York Times*, Feb. 28, 1978; Labor Department figures, *New York Times*, July 6, 1980; *Wilson Quarterly* 4 (Summer 1980): 122.

24. Roy Wilkins, Dec. 11, 1972, in *Equal Opportunity in the United States* (Austin: University of Texas Press, 1973), p. 92; Martin Luther King, Sr., *Daddy King: An Autobiography* (New York: Morrow, 1980), p. 210; Barbara Jordan, *Barbara Jordan: A Self-Portrait* (Garden City, N.Y.: Doubleday, 1971), p. 159; *New York Times*, Nov. 4, 1979.

25. Hodding Carter III, *Medford* (Oregon) *Mail Tribune*, July 9, 1981; Commission on Civil Rights, *The Voting Rights Act: Unfulfilled Goals* (Washington, D.C.: Government Printing Office, 1981), pp. 89–91; *New York Times*, Jan. 20, 1978; *Oregonian*, Mar. 5, 1978; *Equal Opportunity*, Dec. 12, 1972, p. 163.

26. *Historical Statistics of the United States* (Washington, D.C.: Government Printing Office, 1975), tables H1–47, H346–367, H952–961, H1135–1143.

27. Ibid., tables E135–166, X410–419, and X444–455; see also Robert Warren

Stevens, *Vain Hopes, Grim Realities: The Economic Consequences of the Vietnam War* (New York: New Viewpoints, 1976).

28. On Medicaid see Robert Stevens and Rosemary Stevens, *Welfare Medicine in America: A Case Study of Medicaid* (New York: Free Press, 1974), and a review essay by David Zarefsky, *Texas Law Review*, Mar. 1975, pp. 636–652.

29. A survey is Vaughn Davis Bornet, *Welfare in America* (Norman: University of Oklahoma Press, 1960).

30. Richard Nathan, for Urban and Regional Research Center, *Oregonian*, July 8, 1980; Robert B. Semple, "Signing of the Model Cities Bill," *New York Times*, Nov. 4, 1966.

31. R. Douglas Arnold, *Congress and the Bureaucracy* (New Haven, Conn.: Yale University Press, 1979), chap. 8; Charles M. Haar, *Between the Idea and the Reality . . . Model Cities* (Boston: Little, Brown, 1975), p. 350n; Robert C. Weaver, in *The American City* (Austin, Tex.: LBJ School of Public Affairs, 1974), p. 14.

32. Willard Wirtz, "A Program for Full Opportunity," n.d., State of the Union 1965; Gilbert Fite, *American Farmers* (Bloomington: Indiana University Press, 1981), p. 173.

33. Cater to Manatos, Oct. 20, 1966, rebuttal speeches, Territo files; Golladay, *Condition of Education*, pp. 5, 16.

34. *Philadelphia Bulletin*, May 15, 1966; "Waging War on Poverty," *American Federationist*, Apr. 1964, p. 1.

35. John C. Donovan, *The Politics of Poverty*, 2d ed. (Indianapolis: Pegasus, 1973), p. 178; "Protecting the Unprotected—Under Social Security, 1963–1968," White House Diary, Jan. 16, 1969.

36. Weekly letter, Federal Reserve Board, San Francisco, in *Christian Science Monitor*, Dec. 28, 1979; Barbara Ward (Lady Jackson) to president, Jan. 18, 1969, EX/ME1; critical is Lawrence M. Friedman, *Government and Slum Housing* (Chicago: Rand McNally, 1968).

37. Adam Yarmolinsky and Richard W. Boone, *New York Times*, Oct. 29, 1967, and Dec. 28, 1980; Cronkite interview, Feb. 1, 1973.

38. In Emmette S. Redford and Marlan Blisset, *Organizing the Executive Branch: The Johnson Presidency* (Chicago: University of Chicago Press, 1981), p. 94; reminiscences quoted in Merle Miller, *Lyndon* (New York: Putnam's, 1980), pp. 364–365; State of the Union and Budget Messages for 1969, *Public Papers*, 2:1266, 1300–1301.

39. Daniel Patrick Moynihan, *The Politics of a Guaranteed Income* (New York: Random House, 1973), pp. 5–6, 34, 39.

40. Jack Valenti, *A Very Human President* (New York: Norton, 1975), p. 200.

41. Herbert Stein, *The Fiscal Revolution in America* (Chicago: University of Chicago Press, 1969), pp. 385, 442.

42. Allen Schick, *Congress and Money: Budgeting, Spending, and Taxing* (Washington, D.C.: Urban Institute, 1980), pp. 24–26.

43. Walter Heller, *New Dimensions of Political Economy* (New York: Norton, 1967).

44. Gallup poll, *Oregonian*, Mar. 21, 1982; Arthur Krock, *Memoirs* (New York: Funk & Wagnalls, 1968), p. 402.

45. Leonard Curry and James Hildreth, Newhouse News Service, *Oregonian*, Mar. 23, 1980.

46. Leonard Lempert of Statistical Indicator Association, in *Christian Science Monitor*, Oct. 26, 1981.

47. James T. Bennett and Manuel H. Johnson, *The Political Economy of Federal Government Growth, 1959–1978* (College Station: Texas A & M University Press, 1980), pp. 29–33; Redford and Blissett, *Organizing the Executive Branch*, p. 11.

48. Bennett and Johnson, *Political Economy*, chap. 4.

49. Charles Frankel, *High on Foggy Bottom* (New York: Harper & Row, 1968), p. 68.

50. Speech of Nov. 30, 1969; *Oregonian*, Feb. 4, 1980.

51. Lyndon Baines Johnson, *The Vantage Point* (New York: Holt, Rinehart & Winston, 1971), chap. 19.

52. Farris Bryant to president, Aug. 26, 1967, and reply of Oct. 10, 1967, EX/FG11-6/A.

53. Richard Ralph Warner, "The Concept of Creative Federalism in the Johnson Administration" (Ph.D. diss., American University, 1970), pp. 402–403; William Safire, "New Federalism," *Oregonian*, Jan. 29, 1982; Max Ways, "Creative Federalism and the Great Society," *Fortune*, Jan. 1966, pp. 120–123.

54. Fred Panzer to Moyers, Jan. 15, 1969, Gen/SP2-4/1969; Howard K. Smith, in *To Heal and to Build*, ed. James McGregor Burns (New York: McGraw-Hill, 1968), pp. 465, 13; TRB, *New Republic*, Mar. 20, 1965, p. 2, and Mar. 11, 1967, p. 4.

55. *The Challenge of Crime in a Free Society* (Washington, D.C.: Government Printing Office, 1967).

56. Ottaway News Service, *Medford* (Oregon) *Mail Tribune*, Sept. 4, 1980; Charles Silberman, *Criminal Violence, Criminal Justice* (New York: Random House, 1978), p. 3.

57. Whitney Shoemaker to a citizen, June 25, 1968, JL3/R/Kennedy.

58. Clark to Califano, Jan. 6, 1966, Statements: State of the Union 1967.

59. Joseph A. Califano, Jr., *A Presidential Nation* (New York: Norton, 1975), pp. 288–289.

60. Sar A. Levitan, "The Great Society Did Succeed," *Political Science Quarterly* 91 (Winter 1976/77): 601–618.

61. Joseph Califano, Jr., *Governing America* (New York: Simon & Schuster, 1981), pp. 24, 21.

62. Oval Office, unedited movie film, Oct. 25, 1968.

CHAPTER 11
WAGING A NO-WIN WAR OF ATTRITION: VIETNAM

1. Lyndon Baines Johnson, *The Vantage Point* (New York: Holt, Rinehart & Winston, 1971), p. 232, 269.

2. Interview, *U.S. News and World Report*, June 7, 1965, pp. 42–44.

3. Jack Valenti, *A Very Human President* (New York: Norton, 1975), p. 134.

4. Ibid., pp. 133–134.

5. Remarks at Johnson Library luncheon, quoted in Leo Janos, "The Last Days of the President," *Atlantic*, July 1973, p. 39. My corrections are from McGeorge Bundy to president, July 24, 1965, text in Leslie H. Gelb with Richard K. Betts, *The Irony of Vietnam: The System Worked* (Washington, D.C.: Brookings Institution, 1979), app.

6. Column, *Oregonian*, Dec. 3, 1980.

7. Samuel Eliot Morison et al., *Dissent in Three American Wars* (Cambridge: Harvard University Press, 1970).

8. Charles Frankel, *High on Foggy Bottom* (New York: Harper & Row, 1968), pp. 111, 112.

9. Tristam Coffin, *The Passion of the Hawks* (New York: Macmillan, 1964); David Mark Mantell, *True Americanism: Green Berets and War Resisters* (New York: Teachers College Press, 1974), p. 254.

10. Panzer to president, Mar. 13, 1967, EX/PR16.

11. Quoted in Norman Podhoretz, *Why We Were in Vietnam* (New York: Simon & Schuster, 1982), pp. 87–106.

12. Ibid., pp. 85, 80, 88, 106.

13. Richard Nixon, *Memoirs* (New York: Grosset & Dunlap, 1978), p. 5.

14. Text of speech in White House Diary; Johnson interview, unedited, with R. E. MacKay of the National Education Association, May 21, 1965, p. 25.

15. *Oregonian*, Dec. 27, 1978; Frankel, *High on Foggy Bottom*, p. 201.

16. Merle Miller, *Lyndon* (New York: Putnam's, 1980), p. 465; Califano to Frank Altschul, Dec. 17, 1965, Altschul file.

17. Address to Accuracy in Media convention, *AIM Report*, May 1978.

18. Barry M. Goldwater, *With No Apologies* (New York: Morrow, 1979), chap. 23.

19. Gen. William Westmoreland, "Report on the War in Vietnam," June 30, 1968, in *Report on the War in Vietnam*, app. M.

20. Westmoreland remarks, *AIM Report*, May 1978; essay in *Oregonian*, Apr. 8, 1978.

21. Col. William Darryl Henderson, *Why the Vietcong Fought* (Westport, Conn.: Greenwood Press, 1980).

22. George C. Herring, *America's Longest War: The United States and Vietnam, 1950–1975* (New York: Wiley, 1979), p. 145; text of Clifford to president, May 17, 1965, in Gelb and Betts, *Irony of Vietnam*, app.

23. "Why Vietnam?" movie, Audiovisual Department, Johnson Library; pamphlet "Why Vietnam?" (Washington, D.C.: Government Printing Office, Aug. 23, 1965).

24. Frankel, *High on Foggy Bottom*, p. 196; Lady Bird Johnson, *A White House Diary* (New York: Holt, Rinehart & Winston, 1970), p. 349; president to Merriman Smith, Feb. 18, 1966, EX/ND9-2-2; president to addressees, Mar. 2,

1966, EX/ND9/B; Tram Minh Cong, picket leader, outside University of Southern California Vietnam War conference, *Oregonian*, Feb. 10, 1983.

25. Letters exchanged Mar. 5 and 11, 1966, National Security File, Head of State; remark, Aug. 6, 1964, in Robert Kennedy, *Just Friends and Brave Enemies*, quoted in briefing memo, Feb. 22, 1966, EX/FG2,JFK; Hubert H. Humphrey, *The Education of a Public Man: My Life and Politics* (Garden City, N.Y.: Doubleday, 1976), pp. 326, 328; Harriman to president, Mar. 11, 1966, EX/MC/CO.

26. Arthur Krock, "When Will LBJ Give Us the Facts?" *New York Times*, Apr. 20, 1966; Alex Rose to president, May 16, 1966, EX/ND19/CO312.

27. Reedy to president, Feb. 17, 1966, EX/CO312; NET press release, May 23, 1966; Rostow to Richard Fulton, May 28, 1966, Goldberg file.

28. Humphrey, *Education of a Public Man*, p. 344; *Public Papers*, 1966, 2:855; Rostow to Lady Bird, Oct. 26, 1966, Territo files, box 1636.

29. William Westmoreland reminiscence, Feb. 8, 1969, p. 13.

30. Peter B. Mersky and Norman Polmar, *The Naval Air War in Vietnam* (Annapolis, Md.: Nautical and Air Publishing Co., 1981), pp. 27–28; see also Adm. U. S. Grant Sharp, *Strategy for Defeat: Vietnam in Retrospect* (San Rafael, Calif.: Presidio Press, 1978).

31. Text in *Weekly Compilation of Presidential Documents*, Mar. 6, 1967, pp. 358–359.

32. Oleg Hoeffding, *Bombing North Vietnam: An Appraisal of Economic and Political Effects*, RAND RM-5213, Dec. 1966; W. Scott Thompson and Donaldson D. Frizzell, *The Lessons of Vietnam* (New York: Crane, Russak, 1977), chap. 8; Gelb and Betts, *Irony of Vietnam*, p. 147.

33. Hatfield interview, *Eugene* (Oregon) *Register-Guard*, July 31, 1966; address at Campobello, *Public Papers*, 1966, pp. 875–876; Steinbeck letter, *New York Times*, July 11, 1966.

34. Humphrey, *Education of a Public Man*, pp. 339, 333; *Public Papers*, 1966, 2:856; McNamara, quoted in Gelb and Betts, *Irony of Vietnam*, p. 147.

35. Mortin H. Halperin and Daniel N. Hoffman, *Top Secret* (Washington, D.C.: New Republic Books, 1977), pp. 5–6.

36. Harris poll, *Washington Post*, Jan. 4, 1968; Panzer to president, Jan. 4, 1968, Confidential file PR16.

37. Humphrey, *Education of a Public Man*, p. 354.

38. Don Oberdorfer, *Tet!* (Garden City, N.Y.: Doubleday, 1971).

39. Peter Braestrup, *Big Story: How the American Press and Television Reported and Interpreted the Crisis of Tet 1968 in Vietnam and Washington*, 2 vols. (Boulder, Colo.: Westview Press, 1977).

40. Cronkite interview, Feb. 6, 1970; Humphrey, *Education of a Public Man*, p. 357; *New York Times*, Jan. 31 and Feb. 19, 1978.

41. Paul Nitze reminiscence, Dec. 10, 1968, p. 29.

42. George Reedy, *Lyndon B. Johnson: A Memoir* (New York: Andrews & McMeel, 1982), p. 150; Eric F. Goldman, *The Tragedy of Lyndon Johnson* (New York: Knopf, 1969), p. 484; Lewy, *America in Vietnam*, p. 430.

43. Gen. William Westmoreland, "Where Did the U.S. Go Wrong in the Vietnam War?" *Oregonian*, Apr. 9, 1978.

44. Lt. Gen. William R. Peers, *The My Lai Inquiry* (New York: Norton, 1979), pp. 256, 207.

45. Lewy, *America in Vietnam*, chap. 7; Robert Muller, director, Vietnam Veterans of America, *USA Today*, Nov. 10, 1982.

46. Mantell, *True Americanism*, p. 157; Bundy to president, Mar. 27, 1968 (on Ford Foundation letterhead), Fortas file; Podhoretz, *Why We Were in Vietnam*, p. 187.

47. Rodney W. Bovey, *The Science of 2,4,5,-T and Associated Phenoxy Herbicides* (New York: Wiley, 1980), chap. 11; *San Francisco Chronicle*, Dec. 1, 1982; Associated Press, *Oregonian*, Jan. 7, 1983; Lewy, *America in Vietnam*, pp. 257–266, cites Russell Betts and Frank Denton, *An Evaluation of Chemical Crop Destruction in Vietnam*, RAND RM-5446, of 1967.

48. Paul Warnke reminiscence, Jan. 16, 1969, p. 10.

49. Allan Nevins to president, Oct. 16, 1968, Nevins file.

50. For major initiatives see Johnson, *Vantage Point*, app. VI; on arbitration see John A. Perkins, *The Prudent Peace: Law as Foreign Policy* (Chicago: University of Chicago Press, 1981), pp. 40–46; Cronkite interview, Feb. 6, 1970; Bundy to president, Feb. 19, 1965, EX/CO312/PR18; Humphrey, *Education of a Public Man*, pp. 336—340.

51. Miller, *Lyndon*, p. 461.

52. Oval Office, unedited movie, Oct. 25, 1968.

53. Ibid.

54. Ibid.

55. In *Washington Post*, Apr. 22, 1972; Henry Kissinger, *White House Years* (Boston: Little, Brown, 1979), p. 239.

56. "Cincinnatus," *Self-Destruction* (New York: Norton, 1981), pp. 10 ff.

57. Robert Warren Stevens, *Vain Hopes, Grim Realities: The Economic Consequences of the Vietnam War* (New York: New Viewpoints, 1976), pp. ii, 187, and tables 14-1 to 14-13.

58. David Halberstam, *The Best and the Brightest* (New York: Random House, 1972), p. 512.

59. Irving L. Janis, *Groupthink*, rev. ed. (New York: Houghton Mifflin, 1982), p. 35.

60. Edward LeRoy Long, Jr., "What Makes a War Just?" lecture at West Point, *Christian Science Monitor*, Feb. 10, 1981.

61. Podhoretz, *Why We Were in Vietnam*, p. 172.

62. White House Diary, Jan. 16, 1969.

CHAPTER 12
"I'VE GONE THE DISTANCE"

1. James L. Baughman, "John Bailey," *Political Profiles: The Johnson Years*, ed. Nelson Lichtenstein (New York: Facts on File, 1976), p. 27; Marvin Watson

to president, Dec. 17, 1965, Krim file; India Edwards reminiscence, Feb. 4, 1969, pp. 25, 39.

2. Hubert H. Humphrey, *The Education of a Public Man: My Life and Politics* (Garden City, N.Y.: Doubleday, 1976), p. 365.

3. *New York Times,* Jan. 15, 1969; White House Diary, Jan. 18, 1969.

4. Sam Houston Johnson, *My Brother Lyndon* (New York: Cowles, 1969), p. 161.

5. Humphrey to president, May 18, 1967, EX/PL.

6. Fred Bohen to Califano, Dec. 1, 1967, Statements, container 52.

7. Johnson, *My Brother Lyndon,* p. 4.

8. Lawrence F. O'Brien, *No Final Victories: A Life in Politics—from John F. Kennedy to Watergate* (Garden City, N.Y.: Doubleday, 1974), chap. 11.

9. Penetration Research, Ltd., "A Survey of the Political Climate in Wisconsin," study 654, Confidential file, PR16; Panzer to president, Mar. 30, 1968.

10. Leslie H. Gelb with Richard K. Betts, *The Irony of Vietnam: The System Worked* (Washington, D.C.: Brookings Institution, 1979), pp. 170–178, is a summary.

11. Barry M. Goldwater, *With No Apologies* (New York: Morrow, 1979), p. 203; Norman Podhoretz, *Why We Were in Vietnam* (New York: Simon & Schuster, 1982), p. 132.

12. Johnson reminiscence, Sept. 28, 1970, 2:11, Johnson Library; Lady Bird Johnson, *A White House Diary* (New York: Holt, Rinehart & Winston, 1970), p. 192.

13. Max R. Woodall, Veterans Administration, to Bornet, Nov. 3, 1982.

14. Meyer Friedman, M.D., and Ray H. Rosenman, M.D., *Type A Behavior and Your Heart* (New York: Knopf and Fawcett Books, 1974), pp. 14, 100–101.

15. *New York Times,* Jan. 24, 1965, p. 46:8; Dr. James C. Cain reminiscence, Feb. 22, 1970, pp. 1–34; Reedy to Bornet, Jan. 7, 1983; Dr. Michael DeBakey reminiscence, June 29, 1969, pp. 34, 26.

16. Dr. George G. Burkley reminiscence, Dec. 3, 1968, pp. 16, 14, 22; Humphrey, *Education of a Public Man,* p. 314.

17. On medical records, Johnson Library to Bornet, June 14, 1982 (the first failure was in 1977); Reedy to Bornet, Jan. 7, 1983; Johnson, *White House Diary,* p. 232. Such records should be open and in the Library of Congress.

18. *Public Papers,* 1965, 2:1043; Comdr. Tom Coldwell, USN press release, June 28, 1977, PN/2D; Michael Davie, *L.B.J.: A Foreign Observer's Viewpoint* (New York: Duell, Sloan & Pearce, 1966), p. 3.

19. White House Diary, Mar. 28, 1968; Johnson, *White House Diary,* p. 757; press conference, Dec. 27, 1968.

20. Steinbeck to Valenti, Feb. 12, 1966; Charles Frankel, *High on Foggy Bottom* (New York: Harper & Row, 1968), p. 194; Johnson, *White House Diary,* p. 574; Rhoda Amon, *Newsday,* Oct. 11, 1981; Bill Gulley, *Breaking Cover* (New York: Simon & Schuster, 1980), p. 90.

21. Quoted in Leo Janos, "The Last Days of the President," *Atlantic*, July 1973, p. 41.

22. Lyndon Baines Johnson, *The Vantage Point* (New York: Holt, Rinehart & Winston, 1971), p. 427; Jack Valenti, *A Very Human President* (New York: Norton, 1973), p. 155; Eric F. Goldman, *The Tragedy of Lyndon Johnson* (New York: Knopf, 1968), p. 511; Johnson, *White House Diary*, p. 518.

23. Johnson, *Vantage Point*, p. 427; quoted in Merle Miller, *Lyndon* (New York: Putnam's, 1980), p. 497; Walt Whitman Rostow, *Diffusion of Power* (New York: Macmillan, 1972), p. 521.

24. Janos, "Last Days," p. 36; William Westmoreland reminiscence, Feb. 8, 1969, pp. 8–10; Johnson, *Vantage Point*, pp. 428–429; Gen. Andrew J. Goodpaster reminiscence, June 21, 1971, pp. 37–38.

25. "Alarmed" is in Harris Wofford, *Of Kennedys and Kings* (New York: Farrar, Straus, Giroux, 1980), p. 318; "Wilson," in Doris Kearns, *Lyndon Johnson and the American Dream* (New York: Harper & Row, 1976), p. 358, also chap. 11; Johnson, *White House Diary*, p. 584; "Holy Ghost," Ronnie Dugger, *The Politician* (New York: Norton, 1982), pp. 153–154; Dr. George G. Burkley reminiscence, Dec. 3, 1968, p. 22.

26. Ben Wattenberg to president, Sept. 12, 1967, EX/PL2; *New Republic*, Sept. 9, 1967, p. 4; Panzer to president, Sept. 18, 1967, Confidential file PR16; Watson to president, with Krim data, Oct. 30, 1967, Krim file; Valenti call to Bornet, Apr. 1, 1983, on polarization.

27. Panzer to president, Dec. 28, 1967, and Panzer to president, Dec. 19, 1968, Confidential file PR16; James Gaither, quoted in Miller, *Lyndon*, p. 497; interview, *Oregonian*, Nov. 1, 1981.

28. Richard Nixon, *Memoirs* (New York: Grosset & Dunlap, 1978), p. 754.

29. Humphrey to Krim, Mar. 11, 1968, Krim file; Humphrey, *Education of a Public Man*, pp. 358–361.

30. White House Diary, Mar. 26, 1968; Herbert Y. Schandler, *The Unmaking of a President* (Princeton, N.J.: Princeton University Press, 1977), chaps. 14 and 15.

31. Johnson interview, Sept. 28, 1970, p. 5.

32. Telegrams of reaction, Apr. 1, 1968; cabinet minutes, Apr. 3, 1968; O'Brien, *No Final Victories*, pp. 233–234; Goldman, *Tragedy*, p. 512.

33. Theodore Sorensen, *The Kennedy Legacy* (New York: Macmillan, 1969), p. 145.

34. Bess Truman to president, n.d. (received on Apr. 9, 1968), FG2/Truman; Juanita Roberts to addressees, July 17, 1968, sample in FG2/Eisenhower; *New Republic*, Apr. 20, 1968, p. 6.

35. Cronkite interview, Feb. 6, 1972.

36. Frankel, *High on Foggy Bottom*, p. 234; Joseph Kraft, "The Post-Imperial Presidency," *New York Times Magazine*, Nov. 2, 1980, p. 31; Johnson, *My Brother Lyndon*, pp. 248–49.

37. Johnson, *Vantage Point*, pp. 432, 437; Stephen B. Oates, *Let the Trumpet Sound: The Life of Martin Luther King* (New York: Harper & Row, 1982).

38. Press conference, 11:00 P.M., Mar. 31, 1980.

39. Oval Office, unedited movie film, Oct. 25, 1968.

CHAPTER 13
COMMANDER IN CHIEF DURING AN ELECTION: 1968

1. Wattenberg via Krim to president, May 10, 1968, Krim to president, June 3, 1968, and Lady Bird Johnson to Krim, July 20, 1967, Krim file.

2. De Vier Pierson to president, Oct. 18, 1968, Charles Maguire confirming memorandum to president, Nov. 26, 1968, N. Yates memorandum, Dec. 5, 1968, P. Benchley to Bill Hopkins, Nov. 25, 1968, and Doris Kearns to president, Dec. 10, 1968—all in FG2/Eisenhower.

3. TRB, *New Republic*, June 15, 1968, p. 2.

4. Sam Houston Johnson, *My Brother Lyndon* (New York: Cowles, 1969), p. 242; president to Eisenhower, July 31, 1968, also folder "8/1/68," EX/FG2/Eisenhower.

5. Letter in *Oregonian*, June 1968.

6. Kenneth Wells to many addressees, n.d., in *The Retired Officer*, June–July 1968, p. 8.

7. Lyndon Baines Johnson, *The Vantage Point* (New York: Holt, Rinehart & Winston, 1971), pp. 538–539, 543.

8. Lady Bird Johnson, *A White House Diary* (New York: Holt, Rinehart & Winston, 1970), p. 680.

9. Ibid., p. 549.

10. Johnson, *Vantage Point*, pp. 543, 549, 550.

11. Benjamin Zablock, *Alienation and Charisma: A Study of American Communes* (New York: Free Press, 1980).

12. *New York Times*, June 2, 1968; David Halberstam, *The Powers That Be* (New York: Knopf, 1979), p. 559; Daniel Walter et al., *Rights in Conflict* (New York: New American Library, 1968), is a Chicago report; Edgar Berman, M.D., *Hubert* (New York: Putnam's, 1979), pp. 187, 184; TRB, *New Republic*, Sept. 14, 1968, p. 6; *New York Times*, Nov. 11, 1978.

13. Quoted in Hubert H. Humphrey, *The Education of a Public Man: My Life and Politics* (Garden City, N.Y.: Doubleday, 1976), p. 385.

14. *New York Times*, July 28 and Aug. 15, 1968.

15. Jim Jones to president, July 18, 1968, EX/FG440.

16. Humphrey, *Education*, pp. 389, 390.

17. Based on file pertaining to Fortas and Thornberry, Fortas name file, miscellaneous manuscripts; also Warren Christopher to Larry Temple, Dec. 20, 1968, Johnson Library.

18. Russell to president, Sept. 16, 1968, Fortas/Thornberry file.

19. Rostow to president, Sept. 20, 1968, EX/PL8.

20. In Humphrey obituary, *New York Times*, Jan. 15, 1978.

21. Berman, *Hubert*, pp. 220–222.

22. Murphy to president, Oct. 1, 1968, EX/PL7; McPherson to president, Oct. 4, 1968, EX/PL/Humphrey; *Parade Magazine*, Oct. 10, 1977, p. 11.

23. Richard Nixon, *Memoirs* (New York: Grosset & Dunlap, 1978), p. 318.

24. Berman, *Hubert*, p. 211.

25. George Christian, *The President Steps Down* (New York: Macmillan, 1970), pp. 1–3.

26. Johnson, *Vantage Point*, p. 518.

27. Ibid., pp. 519–520, 522, 524, 527; Paul Nitze reminiscence, Dec. 10, 1968.

28. Johnson, *Vantage Point*, p. 526; Nixon, *Memoirs*, p. 322.

29. Berman, *Hubert*, p. 218; Edith Efron, *The News Twisters* (New York: Manor Books, 1972), p. 47.

30. Louis H. Bean, in *Christian Science Monitor*, June 17, 1980.

31. Berman, *Hubert*, pp. 231–232; Humphrey, *Education*, pp. 492n, 406, 429.

32. See also Robert Spero, *Duping the American Voter* (New York: Lippincott & Crowell, 1980), chap. 6.

33. President to Humphrey, Nov. 5, 1968, EX/FL2.

34. President to Nixon, Nov. 5, 1968, and Reedy to president, Nov. 11, 1968, EX/PL2.

35. For examples see Nitze reminiscence, Dec. 10, 1968, pp. 25–26; Paul Warnke reminiscence, Jan. 15, 1969, pp. 19–20.

36. Clifford to president, Nov. 1, 1968, Clifford file.

37. Walt Whitman Rostow, *Diffusion of Power* (New York: Macmillan, 1972).

38. Nixon, *Memoirs*, pp. 336–337.

39. Billy Graham notes, Sept. 8 and 15, 1968, Museum file, Johnson Library.

40. Valenti to president, June 15, 1965, after talking with Henry Cabot Lodge, EX/ND19/CO312.

41. President to McNamara, June 22, 1964; Charles Murphy to president, Sept. 3, 1968; unsigned memorandum, Oct. 25, 1968; H. Smith to Tom Johnson, Dec. 4, 1969, EX/PE11-4; Nixon, *Memoirs*, p. 958.

42. President to Nixon, Sept. 7, 1968, EX/FG11-8.

43. Panzer telegram to president, Dec. 13, 1968, Confidential file PR16; Rev. George Davis, *National City Christian Church Bulletin*, Jan. 25, 1973; Henry Kissinger, *White House Years* (Boston: Little, Brown, 1979), p. 48; Bill Gulley, *Breaking Cover* (New York: Simon & Schuster, 1980), pp. 126–130.

44. Many details in Gulley, *Breaking Cover*, pp. 93–94; my confidential interview with the Air Force pilot, Jan. 1983.

45. Oval Office, unedited movie film, Oct. 25, 1968.

46. Janos, "Last Days," p. 38; Rostow to Fortas, Dec. 19, 1968, Fortas file; Rusk message in Warren I. Cohen, *Dean Rusk* (Totowa, N.J.: Cooper Square Press, 1980), p. 316; James R. Jones to Christian, Oct. 29, 1968, EX/RA2; Jones memorandum for the record, Dec. 30, 1968, FG2/Eisenhower.

47. Califano to president, Nov. 19, 1968, EX/FG2/Eisenhower; Cohen to McPherson, Dec. 12, 1968, Statements: State of the Union 1969; Gaither to McPherson, Dec. 31, 1968, EX/SP2-4/1969. Rostow is quoted in Irving L. Janis, *Groupthink*, rev. ed. (New York: Houghton Mifflin, 1982), p. 120.

48. Rostow to president, Mar. 15, 1968, FG2/Truman.

49. President to Eisenhower, Jan. 4, 1969, EX/FG2/Eisenhower; Kissinger, *White House Years*, p. 18.

50. Kissinger, *White House Years*, p. 3.

51. Gulley, *Breaking Cover*, pp. 108–112.

52. Many details from a long memorandum for the record, "confidential," by Leonard H. Marks, Jan. 21, 1969, White House Diary, Jan. 21, 1969.

CHAPTER 14
"HISTORY WILL JUDGE"

1. Charles M. Haar, *Between the Idea and the Reality: A Study in the Origin, Fate and Legacy of the Model Cities Program* (Boston: Little, Brown, 1975), p. x; George Reedy, *The Twilight of the Presidency* (New York: World, 1970), p. 106.

2. Wilbur Cohen reminiscence, Mar. 2, 1967, p. 15; Lyndon Baines Johnson, *The Vantage Point* (New York: Holt, Rinehart & Winston, 1971), p. 531, italics added; president to Truman, May 5, 1965, FG2/Truman; on "History Meant the Future," its subtitle, see Macel D. Ezell, "Lyndon B. Johnson's Sense of the American Past," *Intellect*, May/June 1976, pp. 600–601.

3. Copy of AP dispatch, Nov. 22, 1966, in James Marlow to Mary Jo Cook, Dec. 21, 1966, EX/FG2/Kennedy.

4. To symposium *Equal Opportunity in the United States* (Austin, Tex.: LBJ School of Public Affairs, Dec. 12, 1972), p. 171; Barry M. Goldwater, *With No Apologies* (New York: Morrow, 1979), pp. 209–210.

5. Richard Nixon, *Memoirs* (New York: Grosset & Dunlap, 1978), p. 754; Lady Bird Johnson, *A White House Diary* (New York: Holt, Rinehart & Winston, 1970), pp. 762, 764.

6. Milton Eisenhower reminiscence, Nov. 1967, p. 26; from Brian Walden, "The Breaking of the President," *New Statesman*, Dec. 1970, pp. 759–760.

7. Press release, Jan. 15, 1969; on war for peace see John Fiske, *American Political Ideas* (Boston: Houghton Mifflin, 1911), pp. 100–101, and historian Harry Elmer Barnes's slogan "Perpetual War for Perpetual Peace"; Ralph Ellison, "The Myth of the Flawed Southerner," in *To Heal and to Build*, ed. James McGregor Burns (New York: McGraw-Hill, 1968), p. 216; Cronkite interview, Feb. 1, 1973.

8. Philip Rulon, *The Compassionate Samaritan: Lyndon Baines Johnson* (Chicago: Nelson-Hall, 1982); Charles Zwick reminiscence, Aug. 1, 1969, 2:14.

9. Oval Office, unedited movie film, Oct. 25, 1968.

10. See Henry Kissinger, *Years of Upheaval* (Boston: Little, Brown, 1982), p. 82; see also his *White House Years* (Boston: Little, Brown, 1979), pp. 226, 232.

11. John A. Gronouski to president, May 20, 1968, and reply, EX/FO2/CO236/A.

12. *Memorial Services in the Congress of the United States and Tributes in Eulogy*

of Lyndon Baines Johnson. . . . (Washington, D.C.: Government Printing Office, 1963).

13. *Christian Science Monitor,* Jan. 24, 1973; *Wyoming Eagle,* Jan. 23, 1973; on CBS, Jan. 25, 1973; David Halberstam, review of *The Vantage Point,* in *New York Times,* Oct. 31, 1971.

14. On the Transportation Department: Emmette S. Redford and Marlan Blissett, *Organizing the Executive Branch: The Johnson Presidency* (Chicago: University of Chicago Press, 1981), p. 218; quoted by Sidey, "The Presidency," *Life,* Jan. 10, 1969, p. 4.

15. William A. Williams, review of *The Vantage Point,* in *New York Review of Books,* Dec. 16, 1971; Nixon to Johnson, Nov. 24, 1972, and Aug. 10, 1970, Post-presidential Papers, Johnson Library.

16. Data from James Pinckney Harrison, *The Endless War* (New York: Free Press, 1982), p. 3.

17. Editorial, An Inward-Looking Nation," *New York Times,* Feb. 25, 1978; Lucius D. Battle reminiscence, Dec. 5, 1968, p. 17.

18. Edited page proof of National League of Cities address, Mar. 31, 1966, is in Territo Public Papers files, Johnson Library; David Zarefsky, "Lyndon Johnson Redefines 'Equal Opportunity': The Beginning of Affirmative Action," *Central States Speech Journal,* Summer 1980.

19. Tom Bethell, "The Wealth of Washington," *Harper's Magazine,* June 1978, pp. 41–60.

20. George E. Reedy, *The Twilight of the Presidency* (New York: World, 1970), pp. 189–190; *New York Times,* Dec. 28, 1980.

21. Daniel P. Moynihan, *The Politics of a Guaranteed Income* (New York: Vintage, 1973), p. 185; Eric Hoffer interview, PBS, Jan. 1978; *New York Times,* Mar. 17, 1973, and Dec. 28, 1980.

22. Interview by Jack W. Germond and Jules Witcover, *Oregonian,* June 28, 1978; George Christian, *The President Steps Down* (New York: Macmillan, 1970), p. 120.

23. Arthur Krock, *Memoirs* (New York: Funk & Wagnalls, 1968), p. 130; on Hoover see Vaughn Davis Bornet, "An Uncommon President," *Herbert Hoover Reassessed* (Washington, D.C.: Government Printing Office, 1981), pp. 71–89; Jim Bishop, *A Day in the Life of President Johnson* (New York: Random House, 1967), p. 146; Redford and Blissett, *Organizing the Executive Branch,* p. 217.

24. Ralph Ellison, in *To Heal and to Build,* p. 216; editorial, *New York Daily News,* Jan. 21, 1977; Senator Howard Baker, *Memorials,* p. 232.

25. Freeman to president, Mar. 21, 1967, Freeman file; *Time,* Jan. 24, 1969, p. 17; James McGregor Burns, *Leadership* (New York: Harper & Row, 1978), pp. 422–424.

26. Eric Goldman, *The Tragedy of Lyndon Johnson* (New York: Knopf, 1978), p. 531; Theodore H. White, *In Search of History* (New York: Harper & Row, 1978), pp. 531–532; Rev. George Davis, *Bulletin,* National City Christian Church, Jan. 1, 1969; Louis Lupas to Bornet, Jan. 28, 1983.

27. Fortas to president, Aug. 28, 1967, Fortas/Thornberry file; Charles Frankel, *High on Foggy Bottom* (New York: Harper & Row, 1968), p. 232.

28. India Edwards reminiscence, Jan. 16, 1969, p. 102, Truman Library.

29. "Martyr," *Random House Unabridged Dictionary.*

30. Based on comments to the writer, 1975–1983.

31. Sam Houston Johnson, *My Brother Lyndon* (New York: Cowles, 1969), p. 209; an identical point of view is in Arthur Krock reminiscence, Nov. 21, 1968, p. 20.

32. Bohen to Califano, Dec. 1, 1967, Statements, State of the Union 1967; Krock, *Memoirs*, p. 382.

33. Farley is quoted in Democratic National Committee to J. Jones, Jan. 11, 1968, EX/PL3.

34. Theodore Sorensen, *The Kennedy Legacy* (New York: Macmillan, 1969), p. 120; Hoffer to president, May 1, 1968, Hoffer file; Wenatchee letter is in the Museum file, Johnson Library.

35. Heller, in *To Heal and to Build*, p. 164; R. Douglas Arnold, *Congress and the Bureaucracy: A Theory of Influence* (New Haven, Conn.: Yale University Press, 1979), p. 129; Tom Wicker, "Requiem for the Great Society," *Saturday Evening Post*, Jan. 25, 1969, p. 70; Sar Levitan, *Programs in Aid of the Poor for the 1970's*, rev. ed. (Baltimore, Md.: Johns Hopkins University Press, 1969), pp. 14, 106.

36. Wicker, "Requiem," p. 70.

37. Leslie H. Gelb with Richard K. Betts, *The Irony of Vietnam: The System Worked* (Washington, D.C.: Brookings Institution, 1979), p. 348.

38. *Newsweek*, Jan. 20, 1969, p. 18; Krock, *Memoirs*, p. 373.

39. Republican Senator Howard Baker, in *Memorials* (1973), p. 232.

40. *Time*, Jan. 24, 1969, p. 28.

41. Quoted by Hugh Sidey, *Time*, Feb. 21, 1983, p. 25.

42. Charles L. Schultze to president, Nov. 7, 1966, EX/WE9, quoted by David Zarefsky, in *Texas Law Review*, Mar. 1975, p. 646.

BIBLIOGRAPHICAL ESSAY

This presidency and its chief figure remain the subjects of controversial historical and biographical writing, for articles and books treat developments during the years 1963 to 1969 in politics, economics, sociology and social work, war and peace, and world affairs. Avoiding a listing of titles, attention will be given here to memoirs of those close to the scene, to leading works on this man and president, and to some basic sources of information. I hope the essay will interest those who have read the book and be of help to some who plan to undertake their own investigations of the presidency of Lyndon Johnson.

Many books on recent presidencies now rest heavily on resources in presidential libraries. The presidential-library system has been described in Donald R. McCoy, *The National Archives: America's Ministry of Documents, 1934–1968* (Chapel Hill: University of North Carolina Press, 1978). The University of Texas made land available for the Lyndon B. Johnson Library and Museum in 1965; by 1967 the site was being leveled and prepared; the dedication came in 1971. Built of pale beige travertine, the eight-story building rises beside reflecting pools and a fountain that can spout water forty feet into the air. The first and only library director (as of 1983), Harry Middleton, was a devoted former Johnson aide from the White House years. Walt Rostow, now a University of Texas professor, occupies an office very convenient to the archival holdings. Lady Bird Johnson has access to a pleasant suite with a kitchen, which also serves such organizations as Friends of L.B.J. and the Johnson Library Foundation. The annual budget in the early 1980s was about $2 million.

The annual rendering of a figure on archival holdings, which stood at over 34 million pages in 1983, constantly grows, but much is not open for use: for example, still classified files, postpresidential materials, and Lady Bird Johnson's records. Exhibits in the interesting museum are in charge of director Gary

Yarington. These rotate or are updated or are borrowed from other presidential museums. They are viewed by hundreds of thousands annually (388,240 in 1981), including groups of schoolchildren. The competent research and archival staff has prepared a variety of helpful mimeographed bibliographies. Lists of books are in Nelson Lichtenstein, ed., *Political Profiles: The Johnson Years* (New York: Facts on File, 1976), and several Johnson biographies. Evaluations of manuscripts, books, and audio-visual aids appear serviceably in Robert A. Divine, ed., *Exploring the Johnson Years* (Austin: University of Texas Press, 1981), a readable and informative bibliographical essay by eight authors. Here is a reference book for the serious researcher to purchase, mark up, and study at length. See also Professor Divine's "Assessing Lyndon Johnson," *Wilson Quarterly*, Summer 1982, pp. 142–150.

The Johnson archives hold many categories of files for the presidential period. The massive White House Central Files were those used here almost entirely. There are also speech folders and the partially complete, and gradually opening, files of some aides and friends of the president. Speaking at the dedication on May 22, 1971, Johnson said, "There is no record of a mistake, nothing critical, ugly, or unpleasant that is not included in the files here." The library would "show the facts" of joy, triumphs, sorrow, and failures, "what man can do and cannot do in one life." Quite out of keeping with this boast is the painstaking screening of every item before it can be used by outsiders, the locking up of the tapings that have survived, and the power to decide what will be opened and in what order. As of October 1982 no Walt Rostow materials (including fourteen linear feet of memos to the president) had been opened or were scheduled for opening, and he still retains some papers from these years. Six-sevenths of McGeorge Bundy's papers as an aide and all of his notes of meetings were not slated to be "processed." Notes by aide Tom Johnson, taken during two hundred meetings, will be processed only in the mid 1980s. So, Vietnam's decision making is buried; yet, vast files on civil rights and legislative matters have been opened. In such a way can an archive decide, deliberately or incidentally, whether the public is to read for a decade on a presidency's triumphs or frustrations, although an intention to direct history cannot be assumed. And State Department records have long been closed, customarily, for at least a quarter of a century; so, there is ample, though not satisfying, precedent. Xeroxing charges in National Archives facilities (twenty-five cents for a single page as of 1982) greatly deter thorough work by absentee graduate students and the unfunded. Is this in the public interest?

Sixty-four administrative "histories" are formidable packages of rav᾽ material and creative opinion that stress accomplishments—for this was their purpose as assigned by the president. The first volume of a Lyndon Baines Johnson School of Public Affairs series, based in part on these, is Emmette S. Redford and Marlan Blissett, *Organizing the Executive Branch: The Johnson Presidency* (Chicago: University of Chicago Press, 1981). Though exceedingly sober and narrowly focused—despite its title—on reorganization plans, transportation, OEO, and urban problems, this well-researched contribution for professionals in public administration (and few others) is a worthy successor to the classic work of Leonard D. White on the nineteenth-century history of hierarchical problems in the executive branch.

The overwhelming bulk of the trove of Johnson paper work will not be noticeably sampled by even the most aggressive and well-funded researcher, for there are, among other things, five years' worth of incoming letters from the general public. But the experienced archival historian soon gets a feel for this kind of exploration: things "ought" to be in a certain place—and usually they are! A massive set in the library consists of 135 task-force reports, back-up data, letters on policy, and analyses by the Bureau of the Budget, but any who hope to determine the impact of the reports on final laws will be greatly challenged.

Masses of unclassified letters and memorandums will be denied to the seeker at this taxpayer-financed, but privately constructed, depository (a not uncommon situation in recently opened archives). Classified items may be opened on appeal, of course, but only after months of waiting. Yet, any unclassified sheet of paper is subject to being ruled "private" for reasons that need not be—and will not be—explained. This is because Johnson followed the lead of the Kennedys, who in 1965 donated papers to the future Kennedy Library, to be available for use only "for such time or times from time to time or at any time [———] specify." Like them, Johnson listed numerous reservations on viewing anything, reserving the right "to restrict the use and availability of any materials . . . for such time as I, in my sole discretion, may from time to time specify, and such restrictions shall be adhered to and observed in all respects for as long a period of time as may be specified or until such restrictions are revoked or terminated by me or persons authorized to act on my behalf with respect thereto, or as otherwise provided in this agreement." The broadest operative words are "may in any manner be used to injure, embarrass, or harass any person." Surely the courts or the Congress can at least eliminate the word "embarrass" if we are ever to learn what went wrong and why in the Kennedy-Johnson years! Obviously, someone must examine *every item* in the light of the enumerated restrictions *before* each and every sheet is released for the first time. Only from, to, and date are displayed when items are withheld. Appeals can be made after two years if one is still interested.

The White House Diary with attachments contains the daily record of visitors, the president's hourly movements, most phone calls in and out, and historic documents, saved somewhat at random. A card index of names shows the frequency of contact with the president. Thus, the name of Dean Rusk fills a 3" by 5" card drawer, and Hubert Humphrey—surprisingly to some, perhaps—half a drawer. Some "histories" of National Security Council "crises" are open.

Press conferences may be found in the *Public Papers* set and in two volumes called *The Johnson Presidential Press Conferences* (New York: Coleman, 1978), edited, with an index, by Doris Kearns Goodwin. Some may hope for illumination on Johnson's thinking from the forewords to the *Public Papers* volumes, which he signed, but these were written for him by aides Richard Goodwin, Harry Middleton, Harry McPherson, Will Sparks, and others. The 1966 essay by

Sparks was OK'd by Robert Kintner and Bill Moyers without even being routed to the busy president. Planned reference to "an America in which the ancient scourges of poverty and ignorance and prejudice have at last been vanquished" fortunately did not make it into print. Texts in the set of official papers lack some integrity after 1966, as Johnson's asides, slurring remarks, misstatements of fact, anecdotes, and even substantive remarks are missing. Lack of integrity in making transcripts was first reported by Anthony Day in the *Philadelphia Evening Bulletin* on May 15, 1966. After that, the practice of making allegedly verbatim transcripts ceased, even though the custom dated back to Franklin Roosevelt. An assurance that it would start again was not honored. A professor compared the texts of the 1966 State of the Union message in two newspapers and the official press release with the text as it was actually delivered and found the startling information that the governmental version has sixty-seven errors and the *New York Times*, thirty-one errors (Professor Robert W. Smith, Alma College, to president, Feb. 25, 1966, EX/SP2-4/State of Union 1966).

There is room for research on such matters. A speech of March 31, 1968, exists as transcribed from a tape with corrections and additions. Hopkins wanted to use the taped version, but Christian prevailed on using the sanitized version, even though Hopkins had earlier supported "historical accuracy as far as the *Public Papers* set is concerned." Much was cut. That volume's preface over Wayne Grover's signature was supposed to say, "Original source materials, where available, including tape recordings, have been used to protect against errors in transcription." The words about tapes were deleted. Said one memorandum, "As you know, it was always selective when we used tapes," to which Johnson acquiesced (Territo to Reedy, Apr. 23, 1965, Territo files, box 269; Watson to Krim and to Ed. Weisl, Dec. 9, 1965, name files). The reminiscences of hundreds of people are in the Johnson Library.

Lyndon Johnson wanted to be a published author, along the lines of Kennedy, so he loaned his name as author of forewords to a number of books and to short pieces for magazines. Apparently much, perhaps all, of this was ghosted. For example, "A New Year Message from the President," in *This Week* for January 2, 1966, may have made people feel closer to their national leader, but it was written in entirety for him by aide Fred Panzer (Panzer to Hayes, Nov. 22, 1965, EX/FG2/Kennedy). In 1964, two paperback books bearing his name were rushed into production by major distributors. *A Time for Action* (New York: Bantam, Feb. 1964; Atheneum in hardcover) presented speeches without any new material, even in preface or conclusion. *My Hope for America* (New York: Random House, 1964) admits nowhere that the entire contents consist of extracts from speeches. *The Choices We Face* (New York: Bantam, Mar. 1969) reprints a very long article that had just appeared in the 1969 *Encyclopaedia Britannica Book of the Year*, a volume devoted entirely to 1968. No clear picture emerges of the busy president, unaided, making the fall 1968 deadline for this yearbook that was published in February 1969. Drafts for such efforts are not available.

Of the very first importance is Lyndon Johnson's volume of memoirs, *The*

Vantage Point: Perspectives of the Presidency, 1963–1969 (New York: Holt, Rinehart & Winston, 1971), distribution of which gave the indicated author enormous pleasure, even though he honestly admitted that it was a manufactured team effort. It undoubtedly received his careful review, emendations, and additions, however. Critics should not dismiss it out of hand, as do some textbook bibliographies. For helping to give "perspectives of the presidency," Johnson thanked Robert Hardesty, William Jorden, Harry Middleton, Walt Rostow, Tom Johnson, and Doris Kearns; they were representative of "dozens of people" who had helped in the "preparation, research, writing, and editing" of the book. Some material containing the first person pronoun "I" derives from an eight-hour period at the Ranch in July 1969, when Harry Middleton says he took down in shorthand every word uttered by the former president. Some verbatim extracts finally appeared in the semi-private magazine *Among Friends of L.B.J.*, January 1983, as a way of humanizing the battered image of the chief. Johnson repeated himself habitually; so, his spoken words are not always new to the heavy reader; often, there can be overlap. The memoirs cannot be ignored. Dorothy Territo lovingly saved the record of those years; hers was an indispensable role. Some who read the memoirs have missed the "inside story." Reviews varied but were better in many cases than might have been expected, given Johnson's sturdy defense of his Vietnam policy.

Useful to own is the handsome volume edited by James McGregor Burns, *To Heal and to Build: The Programs of Lyndon B. Johnson* (New York: McGraw-Hill, 1968), essays and Johnson speeches in a beautiful and heavily subsidized format. By September 1968 some thirty thousand copies had been distributed, including one to every presidential appointee (Cater to president, May 17 and Sept. 6, 1968, Krim file). It remains a best buy as heavily discounted at the Johnson Library bookstore. Surely, here is the most elaborate campaign book of all time. Johnson's White House always wanted to commission or help along favorable books and was acutely aware of unfavorable ones (Valenti to president, Mar. 5, 1966, EX/PU2-6). The president's friend Booth Mooney got early cooperation. Jim Bishop received extraordinary help—nearly two weeks in the White House and at the Ranch—so that he could synthesize his book, which allegedly covered "one day." Henry Graff did well with appropriate help. The staff either could go "all out"—or could "freeze out."

Second only to the president's memoirs in importance is Lady Bird Johnson's *A White House Diary* (New York: Holt, Rinehart & Winston, 1970), which offers one-seventh of her written musings at day's end. As a reviewer noted, it is quotable, kind, shrewd, loyal, and defensive. One cannot account for the opinion of *Harper's* that it is "little more than an expanded guest list." It displays the spirtual and physical stamina that typified her life with her extraordinary husband. Jack Valenti, sensitive author of *A Very Human President* (New York: Norton, 1975), says "I think I knew him as well as anyone beyond his wife and family." This book seems to be an honest account of conversations and events where he was present (he took shorthand). Not to be sneered at is Sam Houston Johnson's effort, *My Brother Lyndon* (New York: Cowles, 1969), an easygoing account that features a penetrating vision of humankind. It derives from his "long association with Lyndon in every critical situation he'd ever confronted." Bill Gulley, a marine sergeant who was on the staff from 1966, supervised communications, aircraft and cars, multimillion-dollar secret funds, and private schemes for four presidents. He was aided by interviewer-editor Mary Ellen Reese, who added the common "wisdom" (often questionable) of other books. The resulting memoir, *Breaking Cover* (New York: Simon & Schuster, 1980; also issued as a best-selling paperback by Warner), makes unpleasant reading, because it focuses on the alleged misuse of funds by four presidents and on the high-handed characteristics displayed toward the end of his life by a tired and worried Johnson who demanded that his life be made bearable by lowly subordinates. Valueless on programs and policies, and containing some errors, it offers certain poorly based, hostile guesses on Johnson's very personal life. But on the ever-present black case, which was related to "the button" that presidents can press, on temptations that were not resisted, and on some odd and clandestine events, it is a sad revelation.

A key citation in my notes is "Oval Office, unedited movie film, Oct. 25, 1968." Here we see Johnson, sans speech writers, telling us on in-house film about his experience in office. This item was discovered because of my curiosity about the public-address-system first-person narration by Johnson, which is broadcast on continuous audio tape in the replica of the Oval Office at the Johnson Library. The undated and hard-to-identify original turned out to be part of an abortive project by Harry Middleton and two technicians, which was made "for filing" under the working title "The President's House." The time is 11:38 A.M.; the chief executive is sitting in the leather chair at his desk, obviously exhausted. Light editing later made a portion of the sound track usable for the museum part of the library, especially after the deletion of such an untoward comment as "most of the people think most of the things we did are wrong." I made my own transcription of the sound track.

Books by several presidential aides and associates generally do credit to their authors. Walt Rostow's *The Diffusion of Power* (New York: Macmillan, 1972) was an early attempt to derive meaning from his firsthand experience with world affairs during the years 1957 through 1972; pages 309–537 treat the period 1963 to 1969. Rostow told me in his Johnson Library office in 1976 that in his value system, he respected liberty and order, welfare and growth, and security. The vice-president's memoirs, *The Education of a Public Man: My Life and Politics* (Garden City, N.Y.: Doubleday, 1976), though very moving, lack candor compared with the volatile book of his Boswell, Dr. Edgar Berman, *Hubert* (New York: Putnam's, 1979), which is nasty toward most persons who crossed Berman's hero. Harry McPherson's *A Political Education* (Boston: Little, Brown, 1972), George Christian's *The President Steps Down* (New York: Macmillan, 1970), and Joseph A. Califano, Jr.'s *A Presidential Nation* (New York: Norton, 1975) and *Governing America* (New York: Simon & Schuster, 1981) seem not to have surmounted the disadvantage of not having "Johnson" in their titles, and therefore have not become routine reading on this presidency. They are vastly superior to nearly all oral-history reminiscences, not surprisingly.

Two university professors on loan to the White House wrote memoirs. For me, *High on Foggy Bottom: An Outsider's Inside View of the Government* (New York: Harper & Row, 1968), by Charles Frankel, a Columbia University philosopher who served from 1965 to 1967, was especially revealing, for it tries to give an "outsider's inside view" of the federal government for academicians on campuses. *The Tragedy of Lyndon Johnson* (New York: Knopf, 1968), by Eric Goldman, a liberal historian from Princeton University, had a vogue as hostile dissection that bruised former colleagues. Its major contribution is on cultural affairs. Some judgments on the decline and fall of Johnson and his team seem debatable in the perspective of time. Goldman had little personal contact with the president, who said sarcastically that Goldman "just knows everything. Everything." *Ruffles and Flourishes* (Garden City, N.Y.: Doubleday, 1970), by Liz Carpenter, Lady Bird's public-relations aide, is breezy and cheerful. Lawrence F. O'Brien's *No Final Victories* (Garden City, N.Y.: Doubleday, 1974) is sounder on Kennedy than it is on Johnson. Jim Bishop's *A Day in the Life of President Johnson* (New York: Random House, 1967) is based on personal observation and made its author Johnson's "fair-minded friend." Inducing humility is his opinion, after having had such an opportunity, that this leader was "not easy to approach or to know."

A variety of books by contemporaries offer insights mixed with information. Rowland Evans and Robert Novak did a remarkable job in *Lyndon B. Johnson: The Exercise of Power* (New York: New American Library, 1966), relying on contemporary conversations; their effort to be fair succeeds, although the White House was then very apprehensive. Michael Amrine, in *This Awesome Challenge: The Hundred Days of Lyndon Johnson* (New York: Putnam's, 1964), sketches the first hundred days very succinctly. George E. Reedy's *The Twilight of the Presidency* (New York: World, 1970) is a circumspect and worthwhile think piece; his *Lyndon B Johnson: A Memoir* (New York: Andrews & McMeel, 1982) is a hostile polemic against the senator and the man, which casts doubt on the integrity of his first book. Reedy thus squared accounts with the leader, who said to him before newsmen in 1964: "Why don't you ever have good ideas like Pierre [Salinger]?" Henry Kissinger's *White House Years* (Boston: Little, Brown, 1979) and Richard Nixon's *The Memoirs of Richard Nixon* (New York: Grosset & Dunlap, 1978) contain personalized anecdotes and sage judgments on the transition, foreign affairs, and the president as a person. Arthur Krock, in *Memoirs: Sixty Years on the Firing Line* (New York: Funk & Wagnalls, 1968), which is intimate on six presidents, envisions the demise of the nation as the world's leader because of LBJ's programs. Frank Cormier's *LBJ: The Way He Was* (Garden City, N.Y.: Doubleday, 1977) is a small gem from a member of the White House pressroom. Charles Roberts, a reporter for *Newsweek*, wrote *LBJ's Inner Circle* (New York: Delacorte Press, 1965), an early appraisal of "the team." Washington in the 1960s is the astute focus of Stewart Alsops' *The Center: People and Power in Political Washington* (New York: Harper & Row, 1968). Contemporary perspectives appear in Hugh Sidey, *A Very Personal Presidency: Lyndon Johnson in the White House* (New York: Atheneum, 1968), while Henry F. Graff has described *The Tuesday Cabinet: Deliberation and Decision on Peace and War under Lyndon B. Johnson* (Englewood Cliffs, N.J.: Prentice-Hall, 1970) in a sound small book.

All volumes in English about Lyndon Johnson were read en route. The "hate" books, which are still appearing at this writing, go too far in character assassination to have credibility. Thus, James Evetts Haley's *A Texan Looks at Lyndon* (Canyon, Tex.: Palo Duro Press, 1964) is a reactionary paperback that has permanently warped the minds of many Texas citizens against a fellow Texan. He says that "nothing in Johnson's public record or statements emphasized any abiding spiritual and moral creed, nor dedication to any firm political and philosophical principle." It was all "betrayal and dishonor" (p. 254). Here, says Texas history professor Joe B. Frantz in a review, is a vendetta, "neither definitive nor balanced." Generally speaking, the Johnson literature divides up into such muckraking, which focuses on attention-getting personality flaws and allegedly fraudulent actions in regard to elections and personal finances; the books on poverty, education and civil-rights, which accentuate the powerful senatorial and presidential role in creating and passing legislation; and the almost entirely hostile books on Vietnam, which wipe out the memory of the domestic record in a forest of fairly well based if lopsided recrimination. The figure of this president will long attract a spectrum of writers, for as a symbol he remains an asset or detriment to a political party's fortunes. Not including books for juveniles, a simple count seems to show the number of books on Johnson, by year, to be: 1964—35; 1965—13; 1966—9; 1967—5; and 1968—18. The ensuing years brought 8, 6, 7, 14, 4, and 2, during which time the titles began to switch to single themes like Vietnam, the War on Poverty, civil rights, education, and aspects of the presidency.

Worth examining are: William S. White's *The Professional: Lyndon B. Johnson* (Boston: Houghton Mifflin, 1964), for its strange evaluations geared to the 1964 election; Frank L. Kluckhohn's *Lyndon's Legacy: A Candid Look at the President's Policy-makers* (New York: Devin-Adair, 1964), a slashing attack on Kennedy holdovers; Leonard Baker's *The Johnson Eclipse: A President's Vice Presidency* (New York: Macmillan, 1966); Oxford graduate Michael Davie's *LBJ: A Foreign Observer's Viewpoint* (New York: Duell, Sloan, & Pearce, 1966), which astutely and correctly assesses Lyndon's frontier, rather than "southern," origins; Philip Geyelin's *Lyndon B. Johnson and the World* (New York: Praeger, 1966); Hobart Rowan's *The Free Enterprisers: Kennedy, Johnson, and the Business Establishment* (New York: Putnam's, 1964); and Alfred Steinberg's *Sam Johnson's Boy: A Close-up of the President from Texas* (New York: Macmillan, 1968), which is said to rest on many "direct talks" with people but which unduly treasures its monolithic thesis that this allegedly benighted man could not rise beyond his "limited heritage and outlook"—an appealing theme for many snobbish dilettantes in urban America.

Doris Kearns, in *Lyndon Johnson and the American Dream* (New York: Harper

& Row, 1976), seems to have overreacted to the Steinberg book title by affiliating Lyndon psychoanalytically with his mother. She relies on undated late-night monologues of the 1970s, delivered by a seriously ailing, though still decidedly clever, man, which were neither taped nor taken in standard shorthand but do appear in quotation marks. The Johnson legislative record is handled professionally. In connection with this book's theme, one can read Dorothy Ross, "Woodrow Wilson and the Case for Psychohistory," *Journal of American History*, Dec. 1982, pp. 659–668; and Roger A. Johnson, ed., *Psychohistory and Religion* (Philadelphia: Fortress Press, 1977), in which Lewis W. Spitz judges, "There are 'grave difficulties' to psychoanalyzing the dead" (p. 69). In connection with the Kearns analysis see the chapter "JFK and the American Dream" in the somewhat earlier book by Nancy Gager Clinch, *The Kennedy Neurosis* (New York: Grosset & Dunlap, 1973), a volume that also chose to associate "great tragedy" and "neurosis"—but when focusing on a different male target.

Merle Miller, *Lyndon* (New York: Putnam's, 1980), subtitled *An Oral Biography*, naturally leans heavily on taped reminiscences, the Johnson Library's and his own. One cannot tell which enterprise the quotes come from, even though a decade separates the two as a rule. Footnoting is perfunctory, and the presidency begins finally on page 309; nevertheless, the book represents a mountain of work. Miller raises few major questions and seems to be little concerned with many major subjects in the presidency. On Miller and Kearns see a penetrating review essay in *American Spectator*, Feb. 1981, by historian Alonzo L. Hamby. There was an earlier *Lyndon* (New York: Praeger, 1973), by the *Washington Post*'s Richard Harwood and Haynes Johnson. Richard Tanner Johnson, in *Managing the White House: An Intimate Study of the Presidency* (New York: Harper & Row, 1974), offers the odd judgment that this rural and small-town Texan, who later interacted with thousands in Washington, D.C., did not talk the language of "the people." Philip Reed Rulon's pleasantly eulogistic, even ardent, biography, *The Compassionate Samaritan: The Life of Lyndon Baines Johnson* (Chicago: Nelson-Hall, 1981) contains innumerable apt quotations from speeches. Focusing on the contribution to education in America, Professor Rulon is convinced that the masses have not appreciated this patriot. For mature insights on the presidency in Johnson's time, a brief buried classic is John Steinbeck's "A President—Not a Candidate," in the *Democratic Convention Program Book*, 1964, pp. 94–101.

Two large books of research that do not treat the presidency are Ronnie Dugger's *The Politician: The Life and Times of Lyndon Johnson: The Drive for Power, from the Frontier to Master of the Senate* (New York: Norton, 1982), which concentrates on "the drive for power," and Robert A. Caro's *The Years of Lyndon Johnson* (New York: Knopf, 1982), which dwells on "the path to power." Dugger's comprehensive knowledge of Texas serves the reader well throughout. Each seems to regard power, and its pursuit, as evil per se. Both, but especially Caro, would have profited by following the motto of the late medieval historian George Lincoln Burr of Cornell University, who said, "It is always through sympathy, never through hatred, that we can understand an age or a people." Serious historiographical problems appear to afflict the Caro tome—a book that Lady Bird suggested, on PBS on December 20, 1982, might make a good "doorstop." For example, despite a listing of half a dozen "sources" for his tale, the alleged sexual aspects of LBJ's possible infatuation during his Senate years have to rest entirely on the woman's later assertions, which she alone could have scattered about. Hundreds of admittedly very interesting pages are virtually irrelevant to the book's title, and some, like those on the Hoover presidency (which are rooted in antique secondary accounts), approach mythology. As innumerable reviewers have acidly noted, judgments throughout are by no means limited to ones that have been arrived at from the mass of prosecutorial evidence. Heredity and environment are strangely, even unscientifically, stressed, in dogmatic assertions on formation of the child, youth, and adult, but it makes a racy and overly consistent story. Judicious readers will want to search their memories for envious reactions when young to any bull-shooting classmate who dominated politics in their secondary school or who tried to be big man on campus. Was that future politician, lawyer, or salesman (perhaps) really *hated*? Caro's abominable Johnson, if he existed in the form conceptualized, could never have led the United States Senate, been selected as his running mate by Kennedy, saved the South for that ticket, or become the president who was overwhelmingly elected in 1964. Surely, what we know as human beings we must not forget as judges. Many reviewers of this massive book did their duty; others seem to have assumed Caro's reliability because of earlier prizes won by the author or of his dogged pursuit of fading memories. It must be admitted that Caro's book will be enormously influential—until his footsteps are someday retraced by someone with blood in his eye. Caro plans two more volumes.

Major attitudes, approaches, and findings in the Johnson literature vary widely, for much depends on one's experience of life, of success and failure, of good and bad health, of administering substantive organizations, and of the meaning of American sectionalism. Thus, Evans and Novak found Johnson "unique among American statesmen and political leaders." Goldman believed him to be "the wrong man from the wrong place at the wrong time under the wrong circumstances" and one who "entered the White House unhailed, and functioned in it unloved." Professor Kearns saw Johnson as the end of the line for a rather quaint "American Dream." Caro's chosen villain "had a seemingly bottomless capacity for deceit, deception, and betrayal" (p. xx). Could such a man ever have risen to the heights with the sustained help of scores who knew him intimately? Nevertheless, George Reedy saw him as "a miserable person—a bully, sadist, lout, and egotist [who] . . . enjoyed tormenting" and delighted "in humiliating," yet "was capable of inspiring strong attachments" (*Lyndon B. Johnson*, p. 157). A dose of Valenti's memoirs is prescribed for those who read Caro, Dugger, and/ or Reedy; for Harry Middleton, the director of the Johnson Library, observes: "And when every unpleasant thing that can be said about Lyndon Johnson has finally been said, there will still remain the memories of those of us who knew him and respected him and liked him, even loved him" ("Lyndon Johnson's Image for History," in *Among Friends of LBJ*, Jan. 1983).

Some will want to try viewing all thirty-two hours of the 16-mm. color motion pictures that were produced monthly by a navy photographic team for White House viewing, at a cost of one-third of a million dollars annually. Resolve fades rapidly after looking at a few. Prepared from June 1966 to January 1969 for "posterity," this series, entitled "The President," is raw material, in the public domain, for TV and classroom reenactments. The half million photographs in the Johnson Library are another resource. The president was grossly overphotographed at taxpayer expense, in any case, by a resident photographer.

The Vietnam research problem is one for books dealing exclusively with that war. There is an outstanding description of the various Pentagon Papers in *American Political Science Review*, June 1975, pp. 675–696. Typical college and university libraries received the basic governmental texts. Beware of facile generalizations added hastily by the compilers of the paperback edition, for White House paper work was not open to the Pentagon team. The Johnson Library has 254 boxes of National Security Files—Vietnam, a small declassified part of which was used carefully by me; most is still closed at this writing. I read many other boxes of general correspondence on Vietnam. For books on Vietnam the reader is referred to third-generation volumes on the subject and urged to be cautious in adopting the first generation's really staggering biases and motivations. *New York Times* military writer Hanson W. Baldwin, in "The Best and Brightest?" *Intercollegiate Review* 9 (Winter 1973/74): 43–50, attempts to demonstrate his conclusion that David Halberstam's influential book *The Best and the Brightest* (New York: Random House, 1972) "almost completely fails in both substance and objectivity" and is "a specious book—a dishonest book"; yet the character sketches admittedly sparkled.

A trend-setting volume that could help to encourage a new literature is Norman Podhoretz's *Why We Were in Vietnam* (New York: Simon & Schuster, 1982), which I read toward the close of my work, along with hostile reviews by persons who were attacked in the text or who are associated with contrary views. An outstanding but little known memoir is by Adm. Ulysses S. Grant Sharp, *Strategy for Defeat: Vietnam in Retrospect* (San Rafael, Calif.: Presidio Press, 1978). Sharp, who was in charge of the air war as commander in chief in the Pacific for four years, says that the war "was lost in Washington, D.C." The bibliography and notes to the hard-hitting exposé by "Cincinnatus" (Cecil B. Currey), *Self-Destruction: The Disintegration and Decay of the United States Army during the Vietnam Era* (New York: Norton, 1981), provide an indispensable guide to the vast military literature on the war. Many book titles that were helpful to me appear in the notes to the present book's chapters 3 and 10. Especially recommended for introductory reading are the documented surveys by Guenter Lewy, *America in Vietnam* (New York: Oxford University Press, 1978), which is readily available in paperback, and by George C. Herring, *America's Longest War: The United States and Vietnam, 1950–1975* (New York:

Wiley, 1979). Lewy is sharply revisionist. Sophisticated and challenging is the volume by the editor of the Pentagon Papers project and his associate, Leslie H. Gelb with Richard K. Betts, *The Irony of Vietnam: The System Worked* (Washington, D.C.: Brookings Institution, 1979). This book urges that doctrines be eschewed in favor of an adjustable foreign policy. It is basic for those who are anxious to "avoid another Vietnam" or "to win" should one develop.

Oral histories (i.e., typed reminiscences that are obtained by formal interviews) at the Johnson Library date from 1968 onward, and many researchers have also conducted interviews of their own, which they seldom share by depositing them at that institution. I am much indebted to several dozen famous leaders of the Johnson years who, without knowing me personally, not only allowed me to read their totally closed interviews but later gave me written permission to quote, often sight unseen, from them. Some added helpful remarks in personal letters. The value of the interviews conducted by a group long led by Professor Joe B. Frantz, conducted when memories were fresh, was considerable in orienting my mind back into those years. Unfortunately, Dean Rusk replied that his 322-page interview is closed to everyone until 1990; Walt Rostow and other insiders also refused, while some 1981 tapes, which could have meant much, had not yet been transcribed and edited—an expensive and time-consuming process, of course.

Few biographies of key figures in this era have been published at this writing, but Warren I. Cohen's *Dean Rusk* (Totowa, N.J.: Cooper Square Publishers, 1980) has merit. An impressive collection of doctoral dissertations on programs and issues exists in the Johnson Library's research room. These can give introductions to difficult specialized areas in government and national life and can offer helpful bibliographical suggestions, together with freshness in viewpoint. Few of these dig deeply into documentary materials, for such research takes much time. Additional grants from foundations and research committees to young scholars-in-training would greatly help to pave the way to a better understanding and dispassionate appraisal of this presidency.

INDEX

397

class to, in 1963, 12; and JFK "tragedy," 33; as JFK's "successor," 47; given credit for War on Poverty, 60–61; receives National Consumers League award, 94; lacks administrative system, 129; compared with Roosevelt, 134; standing in polls, 157; stewardship of thermonuclear responsibility, 217; his racial program praised, 232; by Barbara Ward, 238; side effects of his presidency, 240; hopes vs. effects of actions, 244; by Westmoreland, 274–75; by Allan Nevins, 277; as war casualty, 282; has team document accomplishments, 307–8; and judgment of history, 329–51; by author, 329–51; compared with JFK, 330; as man of power, 331; Nixon on, 331, 335–36, 337; as taking tasks seriously, 332; insulting remark about, 332; as man of "compassion," 333; as seeking to "conquer history," 334; at time of his death—by John Tower, 335, Edward Kennedy, 335, Hubert Humphrey, 335, Charles Percy, 335, Billy Graham, 336, Barbara Jordan, 336, 355, *Christian Science Monitor*, 336, Marianne Means, 336, David Lawrence, 336, Carl Rowan, 336, Walter Cronkite, 336, David Halberstam, 336, *Shawnee* (Okla.) *News-Star*, 336, *Wyoming Eagle*, 336; praised in 1973 for goals and efforts, 335; harsh assessments of, 336–37; presidency called "tragedy," 336; why keep "belaboring"? 337; and the "way" things were done, 340–41; and American mind, 340–41; and social side effects, 340–41; on basis of quality and quantity of laws, 342; as president for the poor and Negroes, 343; gets high marks for civil rights, 344; by Abe Fortas, 344; by his pastor, 344; by Charles Frankel, 344; as a "Colossus," 345; cause of his decline, 345; as self-chosen martyr, 345; as utopian leader, 345; as notorious leader, 345; by a citizen, 347; by Theodore Sorensen, 347; charged with quack cure-alls, 349; by Howard Baker, 349; as blend of failure and achievement, 349; fails to reach goals but, 349; he and team unable to administer so much change, 350; by James Webb, 350; "a force for change," 350; by JFK, 350; prods history into new directions, 351; books about, by contemporaries, 391–93; judgments on major books about, 394; dissertations on, 396
—Domestic Policies and Problems under LBJ: overregulation, xiii; distorts inter-governmental balance, xiii; invasions of privacy by, xiii; and intelligence agencies, xiii; and inflation, xiii; and space effort, 1, 214–17; and Wall Street, 3; plans for early actions (1963), 9; continues JFK's policies, 13; and two mandates, 45; and legacy to continue, 45; his first speech to Congress, 46; and State of the Union (1965), 49, 122; responsibilities in 1964, 93–94; early achievements of, in 1964, 94; and civil rights in 1964, 94–95; his civil-rights speech in 1965, 98; "Great Society" speeches, 101–2, 103; and campaign strategy in 1964, 111; and mandates, 117; Inaugural Address (1965), 122–23; education legislation discussed, 123–27; and relations with Dirksen, 130–31; and Morse, 131; LBJ meets with Republican policy group, 132–33; LBJ interacts with Congress, 133; and legislative victories, 134; and PPB system, 135; and New Conservation, 136–46; sets aside only limited acreage in 1969, 145; and space race, 213–18; and Great Society programs, 219–51; legislative success of, 222; greatly aided by new 21-day House rule, 222; and education laws, 222–23; services to arts and humanities, 223–24; LBJ seeks Great Society overseas, 224; and politicization of legislative gains, 226; and contributions to culture, 227–28; and industry, 244; and the economy, 243–46; and crime, 248–49; legislation on, in 1968, 322; his effort against poverty deemed modest, 331; big domestic food program eschewed, 333; and moves toward affirmative action, 339; and efforts to change numberless laws, 342; and proliferation of public programs, 347; and overregulation, 347; fallout of, summarized, 351
—Foreign, Military, and Space Affairs under LBJ: his previous visits overseas, 1; and foreign-policy "themes," 77; and foreign newsmen, 149; and foreign policy, 163–92; and foreign cultures, 165; his practical vs. academic education, 165; his preconceptions based on "history," 165; and bipartisan meetings, 166; and chiefs of state, 166; overseas reaction to, 168; on Europe, 168–69; receives Erhard, 169–70; major foreign-policy address in 1964, 170–71; and Alliance for Progress, 173; at Puenta del Este, 173–74; and Dominican Republic, 174–78; and China question, 178–81; doesn't deliver prepared

Murphy, Charles S., 33, 46, 333
Murphy, Robert, 42
Music: grants for, 228
Muskie, Edmund S., 33
My Lai, 275

Narcotics: and rehabilitation, 220
Narcotics Treaty, 221
National Academy of Sciences, 31
National Aeronautical and Space Adminis-
tration, 124, 193. See also Webb, James E.
National Association for the Advancement
of Colored People. See Wilkins, Roy
National Capital Planning Commission,
139
National Capitol Garden Club League, 140
National Collection of Fine Arts, 228
National Committee for a Political Settle-
ment in Vietnam, 313
National Coordinating Committee to End
the War in Vietnam, 260
National Council on the Arts, 228
National Crime Commission, 41, 135
National Defense Education Act, 124, 126,
223
National Endowment on the Arts, 223, 228
National Foreign Policy Conference, 188
National Foundation for the Arts and Hu-
manities, 223, 228
National Governors' Conference, 269
Nationalism, 167
National Museum Act, 228
National Organization for Women (NOW):
on Johnson, 36
National Organization of Home Builders,
140
National Park Service, 142
National Portrait Gallery, 228
National Science Foundation, 126, 223
National Security Council, 19, 47, 72, 193,
205
National Student Association, 205, 260
National Teacher of the Year Award, 36
National Urban League, 94
National Water Commission, 323
National Youth Administration, 54
National Youth Conference on Natural
Beauty, 137
Negroes, 5; in government, 36; seek equal-
ity, 53; nature of, 230; increasing accept-
ance of, 231; middle-class, 232; income
figures for, 232; voting figures for, 232.
See also Civil rights
Neighborhood Health Centers, 234
Neighborhood Service, 234

Neighborhood Youth Corps, 234
Nelson, Gaylord, 79
Nelson, Richard, 49
Neutralization. See Lippmann, Walter;
Mansfield, Mike; Vietnam War
Neutron bomb, 198
Nevins, Allan, 277
New Conservation, xiii, 342; Rachel Car-
son's role in, 6; discussed, 136–46;
evolves into environmentalism, 146. See
also Pollution
New Deal, 57, 61, 111, 221, 339; and LBJ's
program, 56
New Frontier, 111
New Haven, Conn.: and War on Poverty,
58; polled on Vietnam War, 86
New Left, 87–88, 258, 311, 341
New Republic, 117. See also Strout, Richard
(TRB)
News management, 156
Newspapers. See Media
Newsweek, 158, 239, 347; on press con-
ferences, 156
Newton, Huey, 59
New York City newspapers and column-
ists, 152
New York Daily News, 175
New York Times, 41, 150. See also Frankel,
Max; Krock, Arthur; Reston, James;
Wicker, Tom
Next 200 Years, The, 145
Ngo Dinh Diem, 48, 64
Nguyen Van Thieu, 263, 318, 320
Niebuhr, Reinhold, 257
Nimitz, Matthew, 220
"1960s, The": as a troublesome unit, 96
Nitze, Paul, 32, 177, 180
Nixon, Richard, 161, 216, 222, 259, 317, 319,
322, 336; makes promises to LBJ in 1968,
323; judges Vietnam War, 337; refrains
from attacking former presidents, 337;
withdraws first troops from Vietnam, 337
Noise: abatement of aircraft, 323
"None Dare Call It Reason," 113
None Dare Call It Treason, 113
North Atlantic Treaty Organization, 168
North Cascade Park, 323
Novak, Robert, 22, 391
Novick, David, 88, 135
Nth Country Problem, 212
Nuclear Nonproliferation Talks, 202
Nuclear Policy, Committee for a Sane, 260
Nuclear umbrella, 202
Nuclear weapons, 213; freeze on, 195;
spread of, 198; treaty on, 212
Nurses: training of, 52